SAP Quick Reference Sheet

Material Master		TransCode
	Create (general)	MM01
	Change	MM02
	Display	MM03
	Create (special)	
	Raw Material	MMR1
	Semi-finished	MMB1
	Finished	MMF1
	Operating Supplies	MMI1
	Trading Goods	MMH1
	Packaging	MMV1
	Configurable Material	MMK1
	Services	MMS1
Customer Master		
	Sold-to Create	V-03
	Sold-to Create Centrally	V-09
	Ship-to Create	V-06
	Payer Create	V-05
	Payer Create Centrally	V-08
	Bill-to Create	V-04
	One-time Create	V-07
	Change	VD02
	Change Centrally	XD02
	Display	VD03
	Display Centrally	XD03
Vendor Master		
	Create	MK01
	Create Centrally	XK01
	Change	MK02
	Change Centrally	XK02
	Display	MK03
	Display Centrally	XK03
HR Master Data		
	Personnel Events	PA40
	Maintain	PA30
	Display	PA20
General Ledger Account		
	Create	FS01
	Change	FS02
	Display	FS03
General Ledger Account in Chart of Accounts		
	Create	FSP1
	Change	FSP2
	Display	FSP3

Cost Element		TransCode
	Create primary	KA01
	Create secondary	KA06
	Change	KA02
	Display	KA03
Cost Center		
	Create	KS01
	Change	KS02
	Display	KS03
Bill-of-Material		
	Create	CS01
	Change	CS02
	Display	CS03
Work Center		
	Create	CR01
	Change	CR02
	Display	CR03
Routing		
	Create	CA01
	Change	CA02
	Display	CA03
Stock Requirements List		
	Individual	MD04
	Collective	MD07
Stock Overview List		
	By Material	MMBE
Implementation Guide		
	IMG Main screen	SPRO

Buttons		
	Enter	<ENTER>
	Save	F11
	Back	F3
	Exit	Shift - F3
	Cancel	F12
	Help	F1
	Execute	F8

Note: *Use /n or /o with TransCodes if not at the main SAP R/3 screen.*

SAP Modules

FI	Financials
CO	Controlling
MM	Materials Management
PP	Production Planning
PP-PI	Production Planning-Process Industry
SD	Sales and Distribution
PM	Plant Maintenance
QM	Quality Management
WM	Warehouse Management
TR	Treasury
WF	Workflow
HR	Human Resources
AM	Asset Management
SM	Service Management
IM	Investment Management

SAP™ R/3 Implementation Guide: A Manager's Guide to Understanding SAP

MACMILLAN
TECHNICAL
PUBLISHING
U·S·A

SAP™ R/3 Implementation Guide: A Manager's Guide to Understanding SAP

MACMILLAN
TECHNICAL
PUBLISHING
U·S·A

Bradley D. Hiquet
A. F. Kelly
Conley, Canitano, and
Associates, Inc.

SAP™ R/3 Implementation Guide: A Manager's Guide to Understanding SAP

Library of Congress Catalog Number: 97-81206
ISBN: 1-57870-063-9

Copyright © 1998 Macmillan Technical Publishing

Printed in the United States of America   4 5 6 7 8 9 0

Warning and Disclaimer

Trademark Acknowledgments

Contents at a Glance

VI | SAP Advantages

Table of Contents

Credits

PUBLISHER
Joseph B. Wikert

ASSOCIATE PUBLISHER
Jim LeValley

EXECUTIVE EDITOR
Bryan Gambrel

MANAGING EDITOR
Patrick Kanouse

ACQUISITIONS EDITOR
Angela Kozlowski

DEVELOPMENT EDITOR
Nancy Warner

TECHNICAL EDITOR
Nam Huynh

PROJECT EDITOR
Dayna Isley

COPY EDITOR
Pat Kinyon

TEAM COORDINATOR
Michelle Newcomb

COVER DESIGNER
Dan Armstrong

BOOK DESIGNER
Ruth Harvey

PRODUCTION TEAM
Carol Bowers
Mona Brown
Julie Geeting
Ayanna Lacey
Gene Redding
Elizabeth San Miguel

INDEXER
Bruce Clingaman

About the Authors

Bradley D. Hiquet

Brad Hiquet is a senior consultant with CCAi, Inc. His responsibilities as a front-line consultant include the implementation of SAP R/3's QM and PP/PP-PI modules. Brad also served as the project leader for this book.

Before joining CCAi, Brad worked in the food and pharmaceuticals industries for 12 years. His primary discipline was in the area of quality management, gaining crucial industrial experience. Brad's experiences include production supervision, quality engineering, and quality control lab management.

Brad is a graduate of Indiana State University with a BS in chemistry.

Anthony F. Kelly

Tony was the founder of KLA Consulting, focusing on business process reengineering, operations support, and enterprise application software implementation. KLA grew to $11 million in revenue within 2 1/2 years prior being sold to CCAi. Anthony is currently Chairman & CEO of A. F. Kelly & Associates which focuses on management consulting, training, sales force automation, and lean manufacturing.

Prior to founding KLA in 1995, Tony was a senior manager for Anderson Consulting. He also worked as a business planner for Marion Merrel Dow, Inc. for three years and as a senior financial analyst/customer service manager for Marion for four years. Tony graduated from Xavier University's College of Business Administration with an undergraduate degree in business management and an MBA in finance and marketing.

Conley, Canitano, and Associates, Inc. (CCAi) Corporate Overview

Conley, Canitano, and Associates, Inc. was founded in 1983 to provide companies with the highest quality service and technical expertise in today's information technologies, delivered by experienced professionals. Today, CCAi has grown to over 400 people doing business in 30 states and five countries. The firm has four major practice areas: SAP Enterprise Systems, Open Systems Development, Oracle Enterprise Systems, and a Customer Support Center. The SAP practice has been recognized as an SAP National Implementation Partner since 1994, certified in the Accelerated SAP methodology, providing experienced and committed SAP professionals. The Customer Support Center provides SAP clients with ongoing post-implementation support and outsourcing services.

The CCAi SAP practice is a team of skilled professionals who have an average of over four years' experience in direct, hands-on SAP implementation. This group also has an average of 15 years of business experience, with backgrounds as logistics managers, accountants, plant supervisors, production engineers, and chemists. Technical expertise includes consultants who are skilled in IS management, programming, systems analysis, software engineering, and application development.

Contributing authors include

Gary Levey	Janice Geary	Robin Mason	Rick Pollock
Ron Crumpler	Howard R. Goldfine	Jennifer McCubbin	Ted Renneker
Lisa Balenciaga	John P. Gravitt	Laura McDonel	Michelle Roenbaugh
Bruce Ballehr	Claudia Franzwa Kendler	Scott Meckert	Jeff Rottinghaus
Michael Belcher	David Kirby	Mazlin Mohammad	Linda S. Schulz
Bryan D. Booze, P.E.	Donald G. Kirby II	Trevor Montgomery	Edward Sensel
Rob Clifton	Howard Knorr	Charles Nadeau	Matt Wischer
Donald M. Dickinson	Kevin M. Luthy	Robert Petersen	Brad Wolfe

Conley, Canitano, and Associates, Inc.
CCAi Renaissance Centre
5800 Landerbrook Drive
Mayfield Heights, OH 44124

Phone: 888–CCAi–1st
      888–222–4178
Internet: **www.CCAi.net**

Dedications and Acknowledgments

From Bradley D. Hiquet

Contributing to this book has been fun, challenging, and a longtime wish come true. It has also been demanding and time consuming. For their understanding, patience, and love, I wish to thank my wife, Tracy, and sons, Jason and Kent. I love you all very much and feel truly blessed to have you in my life. Thank you for the understanding of the long hours worked on this book.

I would also like to give a special thanks to my sister-in-law, Stacy Hiquet. The opportunities and support you have given me through the years are appreciated more than you know. I respect your accomplishments and honor your opinion. Thank you for your support.

Finally, I would like to thank everyone at KLA who contributed to this book. This book could not have been realized without the contributions of many. I am lucky to be associated with such a fine group of people.

Introduction

Understanding the capabilities that SAP R/3 provides to a business requires time to work with the system. It also requires a serious examination of a company's current business practices. SAP is built on best business practices. Often, an SAP implementation involves spending as much time re-engineering business practices to agree with those suggested by the SAP structure as it does configuring the software. This is not to suggest that SAP can't be configured to meet a variety of business methods.

In fact, it is the impressive flexibility that SAP R/3 provides that makes it so desirable to so many different industry segments. This flexibility, or more accurately the flexible configuration SAP allows, makes writing a teaching book about SAP R/3 difficult. Depending on the industry, business practices differ. For example, the process industry differs from the discrete part industry. Within the discrete part industry there are companies that are lot-size-based, repetitive manufacturers, or practice Kanban manufacturing techniques. Each of these techniques may require a different configuration within SAP R/3. To help understand SAP's approach to differing market demands, you will take a look at its industry solutions in the early chapters of this book.

Understanding the Book's Approach

Looking at what SAP has done for a wide variety of market segments can create an appreciation for its flexibility and capability, but it does not demonstrate the tight integration of the system. To help provide an understanding of what SAP can do for a company, this book will take a *day-in-the-life* approach.

You will be introduced to a fictional company, Electro Tech, Inc. Electro Tech is a well established, profitable company struggling to maintain its competitive edge in the ever growing global market. Like many businesses today, Electro Tech suffers from information gridlock. Old mainframe computers don't talk to other mainframe computer systems in other parts of the company. The program code was written in the late 1970s and early 1980s and does not allow for adequate information collection and analysis needed in the 1990s global market. For this reason, Electro Tech is purchasing SAP R/3.

To help provide further understanding, you will look at Electro Tech's daily business activities prior to SAP R/3. Then, once a baseline is established, you will learn how SAP R/3 helps solve many of the everyday business issues encountered. These are not simple issues, however. Determining how SAP R/3 can overcome them requires a thorough understanding of the issues. To accomplish this, you will examine the Business Process Simulation (BPS) process used at Electro Tech.

Through the BSW process, Electro Tech's daily operations are mapped, analyzed, re-engineered if necessary, and empowered by SAP R/3. This process allows for the proper configuration decisions to be made and the transactional steps involved in running a business with SAP R/3 to be scripted. Through this overview, the integration and advantages of the R/3 system will become clear.

To help provide even further clarity, you will look at Electro Tech in the following four steps:

1. You will examine how R/3 helps provide improved customer service through use of available-to-promise philosophies and integration to other modules.

2. You will study how the production planning and execution processes are controlled by R/3, including influencing factors such as plant maintenance, quality control, and inventory management.

3. You will examine the management of purchasing and other material controls.

4. You will examine the financial impacts and other key metrics that are available through SAP.

Many computer books are used as reference material. The reader picks the book up to look up the answer to a very specific question. This book tells a story with the purpose of creating a complete understanding of the application of SAP R/3. It is believed, however, that by breaking the day-in-the-life story into functional parts, this book can still be used in a reference manner.

How the Information Is Presented

This book has been divided into six parts that follow the steps listed in the previous section. These parts are as follows:

Part I—SAP Overview: This section contains a high-level view of SAP AG as a company, the essential basics of the R/3 software, and introduces you to the fictional company used in your case study, Electro Tech.

Parts II through V—Each of these sections covers a day-in-the-life of individuals working in specific areas of the company Electro Tech. You will look at their trials and tribulations prior to implementing SAP. Within these chapters, a case study is presented in the following format:

- The Players—These are the people who are involved in the case study.
- The Situation—This is the background of each case study.
- The Problem—This is the focus of the case study with which The Players must deal.
- The Solution—This is the conclusion to the problem that the case study presented.
- The Assessment—This is evaluation of the work processes and system tools involved in the case study.

These sections continue with a chapter that shows you how to make the move from the past to SAP R/3. Another chapter will follow that will walk you through the how-tos in SAP R/3. And finally, a chapter will cover a day-in-the-life after implementing SAP R/3.

Part VI—SAP Advantages: This section contains a final analysis of the success and failures Electro Tech realizes through the implementation of SAP R/3.

What You Will Get Out of This Book

It is recommended that you read the whole book to gain a thorough understanding of the capabilities of SAP R/3, but the need to use this book as a reference tool is understood. As you read each case study, from the customer service desk through production planning and materials management to metrics, you will see specific SAP R/3 transactions spelled out. Also, during each story, the points of integration will be discussed so the effects of transactions are understood. Using this technique, the following is provided:

- A broad view of the capabilities of the SAP R/3 software application
- An understanding of the integration built into SAP R/3
- "How-to" reference material on the transactional steps of using SAP R/3
- A down-to-earth look at the effects implementing SAP R/3 has on a company
- A fun and reader-friendly approach to a potentially dry reading subject

It is hoped that this approach will provide a higher understanding of SAP R/3 while providing a tool for future use for everyone who reads this book. ●

SAP Overview

The World Before SAP

In this chapter

The early years of SAP

How economic and business influences of the last three decades have helped to mold SAP R/3

The European roots and its growth in America

What it really means to utilize the tools available in SAP R/3

To understand how SAP has become the number one enterprisewide software package in the world, you first need to understand its evolution. To do this, you must understand how the business environment of the 70s, 80s, and 90s has fostered the need for integrated systems. In this chapter, we examine the growth process of SAP and the role that businesses worldwide played.

In the Beginning...

From the time of the industrial revolution to today, many companies have been managed the same way. Company management created individual departments working relatively independently to achieve a predefined piece of the entire corporate objective. As time passed and the charter members of the company retired or passed on, independence grew and corporate objectives became blurred.

As the mainframe computer age dawned, the leading organizations of the day developed computer-based tools to help the workers. Some of these were measurement tools—like general ledger systems. Other tools were control systems for production and quality. Still other systems helped organizations take better care of their customers and vendors—Sales and Distribution and Purchasing systems.

Each of these systems enhanced a piece of the enterprise, often never affecting another organization. As the success of these systems allowed businesses to perform more work with fewer people, word of the success traveled. The messengers for the word were often consultants (generating business after quitting the company that they successfully enhanced operations for and selling these same enhancements to other companies).

Trade magazines sprang up with success stories written by consultants. Parent companies insisted that their subsidiaries adopt these successes in their operations. By the mid-1970s, entire companies were founded on their capability to sell and deliver computer-based departmental support to an enterprise. Typical of these companies were many that sold financial suites like general ledger, accounts payable, and accounts receivable systems.

These software companies' functionality was usually based on the requirements of the first companies that developed or purchased the software. The purchaser would evaluate and select software based on how closely it fit their current operations. Often, an enterprise would select the software package based on a few excellent features. The purchaser would then try to adapt his or her department's operations to be able to use that feature.

Companies, particularly in the United States, felt that they had some competitive advantage by developing computer applications internally. In areas like financial—somewhat generic in functionality—it was determined that there was no competitive disadvantage to selecting outside packages.

Most companies felt that their internal operations were too unique to fit into a commercially sold package. Also, some of the internal operations were proprietary and therefore requirements were not able to be communicated to commercial packages.

By the 1980s, enterprises were made up of a loose confederation of departments all paid by the same entity. Information management organizations began to look into using information from the various departments to enhance operations in other departments. This marked the birth of behind-the-scenes integration. A financial department's general ledger account was used in the Accounts Payable department's system. A material number in the Purchasing department's system was used in the inventory management system in the warehouse.

Finding a Better Way

The department scenario was played over and over again throughout America into the 1980s. There were exceptions, however. Improvement of individual department performance using the computer was a primary purpose of Management Information Systems (MIS) through this time. In Germany, a better idea was developing.

A fledgling company implementing financial systems similar to what was being done in the U.S., SAP began adding a data structure to its packages that eliminated the normal redundancy that typical departmental support systems had until then. Instead of interfacing the data between systems, SAP developed a repository whereby the transaction data from one system could be automatically used by another system in another department.

What this meant was that now, in order to develop a company's financial requirements in the general ledger, you had to consider how the Accounts Payable System, the Accounts Receivable System, or the Inventory System would interact. Instead of passing information from one department to another as required, all departments could retrieve their information from one pool of data.

The concept caught on in Germany. As more companies purchased the system, more money could be spent developing the concept. While American companies were claiming that one system could not work for them and that each department had to have its own requirements met, Europe was developing a model for integration. This was a clear victory for feudalism over Yankee rugged individualism.

America Discovers SAP

European companies seem to have an easier time understanding the implications of cooperative organization and the capability that SAP has to support this. As SAP's integrated package release R/2 was implemented by thousands of companies on mainframes around the world, only a relatively few American companies implemented SAP and the business concepts facilitated by its integration.

During the corporate takeover period in the 1980s, more American companies saw the capability of SAP to deliver a solution to many business situations. Over the years, SAP wisely fed a high percentage of its profits back into research and development in order to develop more functionality required by more departments of an enterprise. Each time SAP added functionality, it meticulously integrated that functionality with all previous functionality. Development of SAP's client/server (PC-friendly) version of software coincided with the expansion of Microsoft

Windows applications. Mainframes were being strategically eliminated, and server applications were appearing in more and more American businesses.

In order to implement what had become a very extensive, full-functioned, enterprise business supporting package, SAP hitched its star to the large consulting houses. These consulting houses sold SAP's capability to even more enterprises until SAP dominated the market.

What It Means to Have SAP

Enterprise packages like SAP have come a long way. Today, it is possible to keep track, in real-time, of the following types of transactions in one system across an enterprise:

Develop and deliver a project (including cost control) for a piece of manufacturing equipment, bring the equipment into operation, schedule it for production to satisfy customer orders, plan predictive and preventative maintenance on the equipment while considering the effect of such maintenance on customer orders, depreciate the equipment in the financial system, scrap and remove it from the system.

Schedule a production run of material across a manufacturing facility and develop capacity limits on the equipment and the people skills required to make the material. Produce the material and make it available for assignment to appropriate customers while keeping track of the raw material usage, manufacturing variances, specifications of the produced product, and where it is to be stored in inventory.

The power of the functionality of SAP can set a new paradigm for business. Currently, companies are adapting to the integrated capabilities of SAP by adapting the work scope of their existing organizations. One of the purposes of this book—one of the reasons why the book is divided as it is—is because to get the best performance out of a business, more change is required.

Essentially, SAP has developed a concept for enterprises to manage and support their assets (resources). These assets consist of the following:

- Employees
- Customers
- Vendors
- Shareholders
- Production Processes
- Material and Services

Departments in business have a similar purpose to trenches in World War I. They protect and defend turf in a limited-mobility environment. The world of the twenty-first century is significantly more mobile than the one for which business is currently organized. The goals of this book are twofold: First, to demystify—by simplifying—the apparent complexity of the SAP functionality in the business world, and secondly, to recognize the real change that businesses need to effect in order to utilize SAP effectively to manage the resources of an enterprise that will allow that enterprise to remain profitable through the even more dynamic twenty-first century. ●

Implementing SAP

SAP R/3 is a highly configurable software package that has been built on the best business practices. The idea is to streamline data collection and processing based on the informational needs of the industry segment. Better information leads to better business decisions, which leads to improved business performance.

This may be simple to say but hard to enact. Change within an organization is often difficult. People become comfortable with "the way things have always been done." To effect the necessary change, a well laid-out plan must be executed. This chapter examines the problems and approaches often encountered when implementing SAP R/3.

Understanding Typical Implementation Problems

Any system implementation project poses unique challenges from financial, functional, and technical perspectives. Many books and articles are devoted to the subject of how to successfully implement systems. Unfortunately, there is no simple solution.

Enterprise Resource Planning (ERP) systems represent the most complicated business systems that a company will implement. This complexity is measured in terms of the number of system users, database size, transaction volumes, and other system metrics. SAP R/3 represents the most complex system available in the ERP market today. While this complexity gives SAP a competitive advantage in the marketplace, it also makes the system challenging to implement.

Problems can arise during implementation at all levels of the project. Technical problems, business problems, software functionality problems, financial problems, and project member conflicts all combine to make project management and coordination nightmarish. However, the differentiating factor that makes one project successful and others failures is not the number of problems that arise but how quickly and well you deal with problems to make sure you do not revisit them unnecessarily.

Resolve problems quickly and do not revisit problems later—a powerful statement that is much easier said than done. In practice, this can only be carried out in a thoughtfully constructed project environment. The environment must facilitate the resolution of problems that arise at any level in a timely manner. It must involve the right decision-makers, empowered by their management, at the right time.

This section addresses some of the common problems that are experienced in SAP implementations. Examples of these problems are provided, as well as insights into how to solve them.

The Typical Implementation

Anyone who has participated in more than one system implementation knows that the concept of the typical implementation is a myth. Every implementation is different. From a mathematical perspective, every implementation has its own set of variables, and few constants can be identified. Even elements that seem like constants are really variables. For example, consider the SAP software itself. It would appear to be a constant across all SAP implementations. However, the SAP software is constantly being upgraded with new functionality and software fixes. SAP averages a new release of the software every two to three months, and software fixes can be applied at any time.

Even so, the variables in an implementation can be categorized into scope, resources, methodology, and management, each of which affect the cost of an implementation. This section will address problems that can arise in an implementation due to different variables in these categories.

Scope Problems

Project scope is a definition of the boundaries of a project to be implemented. It is used to keep the entire project focused on delivering the functionality of the agreed upon implementation. Project scope can be defined in different ways. Some projects define scope in terms of business functionality. Other projects define scope in terms of system functionality.

Part

I

Ch

2

Scope based on business functionality describes the business functions that will be implemented in the software. For example, the project scope definition for the purchasing area may define that the vendor scheduling process is in scope, but vendor analysis process is out of scope.

Most projects start with a scope definition based on business functionality. This is because most companies create a *requirements document* for the software selection process, which is defined in terms of business functionality. Unfortunately, this requirements document is often used verbatim as the project scope document. It may not be defined concisely enough to place a firm boundary around what functionality is in scope for the project and what is out of scope.

One problem with scope based on business functionality is that the business terms used internally to describe business processes do not match up with the terms used to describe functionality in SAP. For example, a company may include in scope its purchasing function referred to as vendor scheduling. However, in SAP terms, vendor scheduling may translate to SAP scheduling agreement functionality. Or it may translate to anything from purchase requisition management, to purchase order management, to vendor analysis.

For an SAP project, it is better to define scope by SAP functionality. (This is the method supported by the ASAP methodology as well.) This helps to avoid ambiguity within the project team as to what SAP functionality is in scope and what functionality is out of scope. Here is an example of why scope definition in terms of SAP functionality is recommended.

In the previous example, the project scope definition for purchasing states that vendor scheduling is in scope. Because vendor scheduling is not an SAP function, exactly what SAP functions are in scope is open for interpretation. Team members unnecessarily waste time discussing whether scheduling agreements, contracts, and vendor evaluation are part of the project scope. Worse yet, some team members assume vendor evaluation is part of project scope, while others assume it is out of scope. If the project scope definition specifically states what SAP functionality is in scope for the project, these problems can be eliminated.

Scope is difficult to manage. Often, even if the scope is defined in terms of SAP functionality, it needs to be periodically changed or refined as the project team understands the intricacies of SAP.

An additional complexity in the definition of scope is the introduction of multiphased implementations. For most mid- to large-sized companies, it is too overwhelming to implement all modules of SAP in a single, big bang implementation. Therefore, most implementations use a multiphase project approach to phase in functionality over time. This approach has the added benefit of realizing benefits in phases as well, instead of waiting for the entire system to be implemented before realizing any benefit.

When implementing SAP in phases, it becomes increasingly important to manage project scope. Each phase of the implementation must have a clear scope definition, and effort must be taken to not allow scope creep between phases.

Scope creep is a phrase generally used in vain by consultants. Scope creep means that more functionality is expected in the implementation than was originally "assumed" in the scope definition. "Assumed" is used because scope creep is generally the result of a misunderstanding due to ambiguity in the project scope definition. However, scope creep should be of concern to both parties, both the company implementing SAP as well as the consulting partner. Scope creep is a major reason for projects resulting in late, over budget implementations.

In large, multiphased projects, it is easy to fall into the trap of expanding scope. For example, a project team decides to implement SAP shop floor control functionality in a subsequent project phase. Some team members argue that it would be easier to just implement the SAP shop floor control functionality rather than interface the existing MES package into SAP. However, project management already weighed the cost of the interface against the time it would take to implement the SAP shop floor control functionality and train the operators. It was decided that a phased approach would be more cost effective in the long run. Many rash judgments about scope are made without considering all aspects of implementation.

To be effective, the project scope should be clearly documented as early as possible in the project. It should be communicated clearly to every member of the project team and should be understood and accepted by upper management or project sponsors. If the scope needs to be further refined during the project, those changes should also be clearly documented, communicated, and accepted.

Resource Problems

One of the keys to a successful SAP implementation is the efficient use of project resources. Project resources are in limited supply because projects must operate within a limited budget. Often project management struggles to determine and maintain the optimal mix of project and financial resources needed to successfully implement.

Project resources can be divided into several categories:

- Infrastructure resources encompass hardware and software components needed to run the SAP system.
- Project resources also encompass the internal and external employees who are participating in the implementation process.
- Support resources are the employees needed to support the SAP system during and after the SAP implementation.

Of these resource categories, the least subjective is the infrastructure resource. SAP provides guidelines for hardware sizing based on numerous implementation factors, including number of users, processing requirements, and so on. If there is any doubt about hardware requirements to support your implementation, SAP Basis consultants can provide hardware sizing assistance. Also, major hardware suppliers have dedicated SAP consultants who can provide hardware sizing assistance specific to their line of hardware.

Internal Resources   Internal resources are the employees of the company installing SAP who participate in the SAP implementation project. The internal resources are responsible for providing first-hand expertise about the company's business. They also have to learn the SAP functionality and understand SAP configuration as it applies to their functional area of expertise.

The selection and management of internal resources is an important part of an SAP project. These people play a crucial role in the implementation process and should be smart, motivated individuals who are capable of making decisions. They should also have a firm grasp of the business requirements in their area. Unfortunately, instead of choosing employees who meet these criteria, some projects assign resources from a department based on other criteria such as seniority or departmental need. Remember that these internal resources are responsible for determining the future of how your company transacts business, and staffing the project accordingly.

A common problem encountered with internal resources is the use of part-time project members. Employees considered indispensable in their current roles are often assigned to the project as part-time members. They are expected to perform their current jobs for some percentage of the time and participate in the SAP implementation for the rest of the time.

Experience has shown that the use of part-time internal resources can hurt a project for several reasons. First, part-time project members are comfortable in their current jobs, tending to spend more time performing them and neglecting the SAP project. Second, for each SAP skilled resource on the implementation, there needs to be at least one full-time internal resource. The internal resource must learn the functionality and configuration in enough detail to be able to make intelligent implementation decisions, to help train SAP users, and to help support the system after implementation. Last, some of the best internal resources who appear to be able to balance the responsibilities of a part-time role do so by working excessive hours, and essentially burning themselves out.

Many companies feel that they cannot possibly give up full-time internal resources for a system implementation. In companies that are already lean due to downsizing, rightsizing, or business reengineering, there just are not enough employees left in the department to offer someone up for a system implementation. This is where companies have to become creative. Options include retraining existing staff to replace someone or resizing. Consider using the project budget to hire temporary employees to help replace project resources in their current jobs. Use more interns. Again, consider using the project budget in creative ways to solve internal staffing problems.

Retention of internal project resources is another common problem encountered with internal resources that must be discussed. Because of the recent market demand for SAP-skilled resources, the internal project resources of today are often the high-priced consultants of tomorrow. It is not uncommon to see a large percentage of the internal project resources leave a company with six to nine months of SAP experience under their belts.

Many techniques have been used to help retain internal resources. Some companies offer incentive programs tied to extended commitments. Other companies create new job positions with higher pay scales for SAP-skilled employees. Do the cost analysis. It may be less expensive in the long run to offer an SAP skill-based incentive program, than be forced to fill the gap for an departed internal resource with a full-time SAP consultant.

SAP Skilled Resources   SAP skills currently come at a premium price. If you are reading this book, that is probably no surprise. Proper management of SAP resources is essential to get the most bang for your buck.

Most skilled SAP resources either belong to consulting firms or are independent. Getting the right resources at the right time can be very difficult. The following items should be considered:

- The number of SAP resources
- Implementation experience
- Industry experience
- Timing (right resources at the right time)

The following support resources should be considered:

- Super users
- Trainers
- Help desk

Methodology Problems

Later in this chapter, both the Accelerated SAP methodology and the Business Process Simulation methodology are discussed. The choice of one of these or other implementation methodologies can greatly affect the success of the implementation.

In ERP system implementations, the current emphasis is on quicker, more efficient implementations. Many of the first implementations in the U.S. got bogged down by trying to implement too much of SAP in a single phase. The ASAP methodology provides a framework for implementing SAP quickly, by implementing the most crucial functionality first.

Many companies are realizing that it is more important to get the core-integrated SAP functionality up and running quickly and then phase in further functionality. The core functionality can begin paying back benefits that can even fund subsequent project phases.

Additionally, studies have shown that large organizations cannot react quickly to change. Change management experts suggest that organizations change more effectively through multiple *cycles of learning*. This concept recognizes that when the average user is confronted with a myriad of new functionality, she will only be able utilize a handful of new functions. It is better to implement the new functionality in phases (or cycles), allowing the users to appreciate and become comfortable with the new functionality before introducing more.

Management Problems

The most detrimental problem any SAP implementation can face is lack of management support. This is not uncommon for any major change within an organization, however. Understanding completely what management support means is the key to avoiding this problem.

Part

I

Ch

2

The following elements define true management support:

- Team empowerment—Select informed, experienced team members who understand the company metrics and vision. Team membership should include representation from all appropriate parties. After the team(s) have been established, allow them to make decisions that guide the business without being second guessed by management. If this requires the inclusion of an upper management representative on each team, then do so, but allow the team to guide the process.

- Decision-makers—This is simply an extension of the above item. If your team members are not willing or able to make decisions, the implementation will stall if not fail. Remember that the reason many team members are unwilling to make decisions is due to fear of management's reaction.

- Issue resolution—If for any reason an issue does present itself that the team cannot come to agreement on, upper management must be prepared to step in and assist in making the decision quickly. To make the right decision quickly, management must be informed of the decisions that have been made that feed the issue and the options available.

- Management involvement—Saying that management must be involved seems contradictory to the first two steps listed here, but it is true. Involvement can be defined in different ways, however. For success to be realized, management must understand, support, and eventually direct the new business processes under SAP. A formal method of obtaining management sign-off on team activities should be considered. This often involves the creation of a steering committee that guides the implementation process at the highest level.

Understanding the ASAP Approach

Over the years, SAP has gained a reputation it is trying to change. The perception is that SAP projects are long, require many consultants, and, hence, are expensive. In order for SAP to be successful in the mid- to small-size market, it must change this perception. Middle and small market companies simply cannot afford to invest in multi-yearlong projects. SAP's answer to this is ASAP—AcceleratedSAP. Commonly referred to as ASAP, AcceleratedSAP is a methodology developed by SAP that provides a roadmap to more efficient, shorter SAP implementation.

An ASAP implementation should last approximately six months or less. Again, ASAP was designed for use on mid-sized companies, which makes this timeframe possible. One key change in the ASAP methodology compared to the traditional SAP implementations is the absence of Business Process Reengineering (BPR). ASAP suggests that the enterprise implement SAP using the existing business processes, also known as the "as-is" environment. Once SAP has been implemented, only then should the enterprise re-engineer the business processes. However, in reality, the enterprise will be forced to do some level of BPR regardless, due mainly to the fact that SAP strongly discourages modifying SAP.

ASAP is comprised of many types of files, all used to guide a project from start to finish with quality checks at predefined points that ensure completeness before continuing the project. Example project plans, white papers, help files, and presentations are all used as a roadmap. ASAP divides a project into six phases:

- Project Preparation
- Business Blueprint
- Simulation
- Validation
- Final Preparation
- Go Live & Support

Phase 1: Project Preparation

The purpose of this phase is to allow the SAP project manager to transition the customer cycle from sales to starting a project. There are certain preconditions that need to be checked before the project begins. As part of the work that must be completed in preparing for the project, ASAP requires that the SAP project manager obtain answers to the five most important fundamental questions related to the project:

- Why install an R/3 System?
- What objectives are we trying to accomplish?
- What will be installed (clarify the scope of the project)?
- How will the R/3 System be implemented (define your implementation strategy)?
- When will the R/3 System be implemented (scheduling: sequence)?
- Who will have what responsibilities (project organization: committees, clearly defined roles and responsibilities)?

The results of this effort form the basis for generating the project charter in Phase 2 (Business Blueprint).

Initializing the Project   Project preparation and organization must be oriented to the business drivers, resources, and potential benefits within the enterprise. This means that knowledge of any previous activities (for example, functional specifications, preliminary studies, or perhaps a BPR effort) and the results of these activities are required. Also, decide how much outside consulting the project will need.

Formulating the Company's Objectives for Implementing the R/3 System   The organization has decided to invest a lot of money into an ERP package. It's critical to know what expectations that organization has in implementing SAP. Formulate these as objectives. A description of the project's objectives is required because the project team, committees, and all affected areas in the company will be orienting themselves to this description during implementation. Project objectives also influence the implementation strategy and scope of your R/3 implementation. Also, determine how much business process re-engineering the organization wants to do, if any.

The more precise the formulated objectives, the easier it will be to define the scope of the project and to evaluate success of the project after implementation. A project management team or steering committee is often formed to help formulate, guide, and measure results of the implementation. It is often beneficial to have not only upper management members on this team but representatives of your consulting team as well.

Determining Your Implementation Strategy   Implementation strategy is based on long-term, potential benefits and includes everything your enterprise plans to do with regard to implementing your R/3 System. It is an essential part of your preparation work and will have a profound influence on your subsequent project(s). The implementation strategy reflects your objectives and requirements.

An example of an implementation strategy might be that the implementation is broken into phases. That is, Phase 1 may be the implementation of the so-called main modules of SAP. Phase 2 could be the implementation of the "fringe" modules, such as workflow, plant maintenance, or asset management. Another example of an implementation strategy could be a plant-by-plant rollout. There are many advantages to implementing a small plant within the enterprise first as a pilot, then rolling out the SAP R/3 System to the other plants systematically gaining valuable implementation knowledge each time a plant goes live.

Determining Hardware Requirements and System Landscape   These requirements are needed for your future R/3 installations. Consult your hardware supplier as appropriate and refer to SAP's recommendations on system landscapes.

SAP can run on a number of different hardware platforms. When determining what hardware to use and sizing it, consider your current computer platform and where your company wants to go in the future. Hardware sizing should consider the SAP modules being implemented, the amount of master data utilized by your company, and the daily transactional load the hardware must support.

Defining the Organizational Structure of Your Project   Use the organizational structure of the project to define areas of responsibility. This organizational framework ensures that everyone involved can interact smoothly and that the project can progress without difficulty.

Unfortunately, this is easier said than done. As with any project, it is imperative that not only a sound organizational structure be put in place, but that it is used properly. Issue resolution is an example of this. A large majority of project time is spent resolving issues. An inefficient issue resolution process can delay or even kill a project. Defining the proper organizational structure, while keeping in mind some key project activities such as issue resolution, is essential for efficient, effective project leadership. Agreeing on how the project will be organized is a major and essential requirement for your project.

Remember that the makeup of the project team, and the way in which committees are formed, must reflect the project objectives.

Creating a Preliminary Project Plan   To facilitate approval of your implementation strategy and projects, prepare a preliminary resource and cost plan.

Present the results of your project preparation work to the steering committee for approval.

Before the outcome of your preparatory work is formulated into a project charter and presented in the implementation project "kick-off" meeting, it should first be approved by the steering committee. In this way, the decision to implement the R/3 System is affirmed, and the essential aspects of the implementation are described to the key players. It is essential to have the affirmation of these key players. Management buy-in is one of the key factors for a successful R/3 implementation.

The kick-off meeting is an event where the start of the project is announced to all employees and managers participating directly or indirectly in the project. The meeting should be structured in a manner to creatively motivate the participants to start the project.

Phase 2: Business Blueprint

The purpose of Phase 2 is to

- Create the project charter and documentation standards
- Gather and gain approval of the requirements
- Install the hardware

The results of this work form the basis for generating the project charter.

Obtain an overview of the structural organization, the individual business areas, and any existing application systems (and how they are related) in your company.

It is critical at this point to begin understanding the processes/functions of the R/3 business applications by working through the individual processes of the SAP R/3 Reference Model, using R/3 documentation where necessary. The project team must have a basic understanding of R/3 functionality to be able to define business processes and estimate the level of functional coverage achieved by the R/3 System. It is during this phase that the project team must attend SAP training in order to accomplish this.

It is now time to perform a *gap analysis*.

> Compare your functional requirements with what is provided by R/3 to determine the degree of coverage.

Develop a strategy dealing with any gaps. Compare the functional requirements of the business processes in the enterprise with the functionality of the R/3 System, information about the scope of your R/3 implementation, the sequence in which it is carried out, and the time and effort required to implement the business processes.

Defining Your Project Standards and Procedures   It is in this phase in which project standards are determined. These are vital for working effectively and ensuring the best possible understanding and communication between project staff members.

Defining the System Landscape   Determining an appropriate system infrastructure (what systems, what clients) helps to define activities. For example, determine the system and R/3 clients, where R/3 configuration takes place, training clients, quality check of configuration, and so on.

Part

I

Ch

2

Phase 3: Simulation

In large part, the Simulation Phase of ASAP takes the business process requirements gathered from Phase 2 and simulates those requirements in R/3. The goal of this phase is to rapidly configure SAP R/3 to these requirements to create a working prototype or representation of the final system that can be continuously improved to meet the final requirements outlined in Phase 4 (Validation).

In addition to the rapid configuration of R/3, the project team also attends level 3 SAP training during this phase. This level of detail training will help the team understand configuration issues and provide better feedback during the playback of scenarios during the next phase.

Finally, the data conversion and interface-detailed specifications are developed during this phase.

Phase 4: Validation

The Validation Phase is an interactive process that transforms the customer's business requirements into a future SAP solution. This interactive process provides continuous feedback mechanisms that initially identify gaps and configuration requirements and then evolve to filling the gaps and finalizing the system configuration.

The Validation Phase is a transformation process that evolves the initial prototype, defined during the Business Blueprint and Simulation Phases, through business cycles until a production-ready solution is achieved.

Technical developments also take place during this phase. Interfaces, conversion programs, enhancements, reports, and forms are all designed, developed, and tested during this phase. In addition, security and document archiving strategies are constructed. One easily overlooked, but critical deliverable for this phase is end-user documentation and procedures. In general, this is the phase where it all comes together. The final deliverable for this phase is an integrated R/3 solution that meets the customer's requirements and is ready for final preparation to go live.

Phase 5: Final Preparation

Phase 5 takes you through the steps of preparing the project to "flip the switch." Production support preparation takes place in this phase, including a go-live/cutover plan, creation of a help desk, and a go-live support team to fight fires and "hand-hold" end-users. Final verification tests are also conducted at this point, some of which are final conversion tests, stress/volume tests, and integration tests. End-user documentation is also finalized, packaged, and delivered as end-user training.

One easily overlooked but critical task that is key to a successful implementation is the management of exceptions for the organizational change, a.k.a. change management. Implementing an enterprisewide application can be a shock to the organization. Throughout the ASAP methodology, ASAP continuously revisits change management plans. Communicating the changes that the organization will see as a result of implementing SAP, such as assessing organizational impact, change of job descriptions, review of transfers, new-hires, and eliminations, can have a traumatic affect on an organization. Change management cannot be ignored or become an afterthought during an implementation. It must be planned in Phase 1 and monitored and managed throughout the project.

Phase 6: Go Live and Support

The purpose of this phase is, in general, to ensure the success of the first few weeks of operation and the ongoing operation of the system. More precisely, it means to verify activities such as the first day, first month-end, first quarter-end, and first year-end processes work correctly. The SAP System must also be monitored for possible optimizations. In addition, once the SAP System is stable, the organization can be proactive in noting those processes that may be enhanced to further improve the overall efficiency of the organization.

From a project management role, auditing the ROI (Return on Investment) and formal close of the project can take place.

Taking the Business Process Simulation Approach

Many consulting firms have a methodology similar to the ASAP approach. A common technique is to analyze the business by using cross-functional teams. From this analysis, a simulation of the business processes is constructed and tested. This methodology is referred to as *Business Process Simulation* or BPS. The process may or may not involve re-engineering activities, but it certainly causes a careful examination of a company's business activities.

BPS is an effective way of implementing SAP R/3 because it structures all the necessary elements for change. This method provides a structured approach to a complex problem. It uses real-life examples to test assumptions. Possibly most important, it documents decisions made and agreement of those decisions. When managed properly, BPS yields all the necessary elements to effect any change.

The keys to running a successful BPS while implementing SAP R/3 are no different than those needed for any major change within a company. It must start with upper management support and *involvement*. This is institutionalized in the BPS process by requiring upper management to review and sign-off on agreed upon business practices as the BPS process hits milestones.

Defining the Project Scope

A *discovery* phase begins the BPS process. Before starting any team simulation activities within SAP, several items must be established. As with any change, a clearly defined project scope is paramount. That's a statement worth repeating: A CLEARLY DEFINED SCOPE IS PARAMOUNT! The first step of any successful implementation is agreement of what will be implemented and when it will be implemented.

Scope drift occurs for a number of reasons.

- Lack of up-front understanding of the systems capabilities or demands
- Conflict between functional business areas or consultant opinions
- Overestimating what can be done in a given time period

Whatever the cause, eliminating scope drift is the responsibility of not just the project managers; it is also upper management's responsibility.

Scope drift is not unique to SAP R/3 implementations. If you are trying to put in any new system, not just computer systems either, scope drift must be avoided. Implementing a new quality system, a new manufacturing method, or a new accounting practice all require a clearly defined, maintained scope. The only way to do this is to educate and involve upper management with the team members early and often during the process. Management has to empower the BPS teams, so it is their responsibility to make certain that the teams know and agree with the vision of the change.

Defining the Business Levels

Next there must be a clear definition of business levels within the company. The definition of these levels and of a consistent scope will guide the process to a division of activities and an order of implementation. The separation of business practices into natural levels helps guide an implementation. Figure 2.1 demonstrates a graphical breakdown of these levels.

After the business activities have been acknowledged, teams can be assigned to begin flow charting the business processes. If re-engineering is involved with the implementation, both "Current" business practices and "To-be" business practices are flowcharted.

The first level examines how a business is to be run. If you think about the entire life cycle of a business, it starts with a demand in the market place. The sales organization takes that demand and converts it into a sales order. The sales order places requirements on the manufacturing facility to convert raw materials into saleable goods. Distribution of the goods is a service and often requires follow-up services. All of these functions require the management of capital. To effectively run a business, each of these activities must be understood and managed. These activities constitute the highest level of BPS.

FIG. 2.1

The Business Process Pyramid depicts the breakdown of business levels.

Once these very high-level processes are recognized, BPS requires that each one is broken down into smaller pieces. For example, if you look at the production process, a company must first define if it is a discrete manufacturer or a process industry. If it is discrete, it must determine if it uses a lot-based system, if it is repetitive, or if it wants to use Kanban techniques. At this second level, areas of the business like demand management, sales order processing, production scheduling and execution, purchasing, distribution, quality management, general ledger, payroll, and plant maintenance are a few things to considered.

The third step examines specific business functions within each process. Looking again at the production phase, planning techniques such as demand management, long-term planning, Master Production Scheduling (MPS), and Materials Requirement Planning (MRP) must be considered. Other items like production order release and status management, production confirmation, and in-process inspection also play a part. One or more BPS teams will be needed to define all of these business functions. These teams break down the existing functions, map them to the to-be environment, test their proposals, note gaps and issues, and adjust as necessary. This is best handled through documenting the flow of the process both as-is and to-be. This step and the fourth level of the pyramid work hand-in-hand to deliver a complete, usable business environment.

The forth step of the pyramid is defining specific business activities that must occur in each area. This is the level of the business for which procedures or scripts of activity are typically written. Completing the breakdown of the production environment, how planned orders are firmed, how they are converted to a production order, or how they are released to the shop floor would be a few of the planning-related activities. Entry of time ticket confirmation or the recording of quality results on the shop floor would be examples of shop floor business activities.

By moving down through the pyramid, a methodical approach to examining a business's practices is provided. Each step of the way, documentation of issues and gaps must be logged and resolved. Training should be occurring throughout, so that when a go live date is reached success is inevitable. Many different ways have been used to manage this process. Often a central documentation point for each BPS team is maintained so scope, decisions, scripts, issues, gaps and resolutions, and integration points from team-to-team can be logged.

In an SAP R/3 implementation, all these things feed the configuration and master data set-ups in the system. They can also document and effect interfaces to legacy systems that survive the implementation. If you review the process described here, however, you will see that this process fits the implementation of any business change, not just an SAP R/3 implementation.

Testing and Sign-off

The final step of the BPS process is integrated testing and sign-off. The management team, to ensure the vision of the change was met, should review the collective documentation. No surprises should occur here, however. Remember that one of the crucial elements of BPS is management involvement. If one surprise occurs at this step of BPS, more are likely to follow. Minor adjustments may occur during management review, but it is important that the scope of the implementation is maintained.

Once upper management has agreed to the layout of the business functions, complete integrated testing should occur. This will help point out any final gaps, issues, or script deficiencies. Again, only minor changes should be necessary to complete the vision of the implementation.

The complete deliverables of this BPS process for an SAP R/3 implementation are

- Complete as-is and to-be process flows
- A configured SAP R/3 System
- SAP R/3 business activity scripts
- User training versus scripts and business process definitions
- Modified company procedures
- Definition of job functions
- System security requirements
- Hardware sizing
- Document archiving procedures

When you are introduced to the fictional company Electro Tech later in the book (see Chapter 7, "Meet Electro Tech, Inc."), you will examine their implementation of SAP R/3 using BPS-type activities. The activities of sales order processing, production scheduling and execution, procurement, financials, and other metrics will be examined. In this manner, the BPS process should become clearer. ●

SAP Target Markets

SAP has recognized that different industrial segments operate in different ways. The requirements of the pharmaceutical industry are dramatically different than the requirements of a utilities organization. These differences contribute to the problems people often have in understanding SAP. The statement, "Show me what SAP does for…" doesn't fit. The software can be configured to different industry segments' needs. There is often more than one way to define a business transaction in SAP R/3.

To address this problem, SAP has created Industry Business Units (IBU). These units take the best business practices of SAP and marry them with industry-specific problems.

Understanding Industry Solutions

The simplest way to understand the approach SAP has chosen for dealing with industry-specific issues is to examine each industry separately. Once each industry segment has been examined, a company wanting to implement R/3 should contact SAP and begin detailed discussions about what SAP R/3 can do to meet its specific needs. In this way, advantages are gained through SAP's knowledge of the system's capabilities and industry-specific studies. The industry solutions are developed between SAP and current customers within that industry.

The Automotive Industry

The automotive industry is in a unique position, with its high visibility in the consumer marketplace, as well as the ever-increasing demands from customers for a high-quality, low-cost product, utilizing the latest technologies. In order to support the automotive industry, SAP provides a customer-pulled supply chain and a worldwide infrastructure for the networked value chain, which links tier 1 system suppliers, tier 2 component suppliers, order entry management and after-market parts suppliers, as well as wholesalers. Additional functionality includes flow manufacturing, KANBAN calculation, sequence planning, line planning, backflushing, enhanced evaluated receipt settlement, supplier shipping scheduling, Material Information Systems (MAIS)-Pickup Sheet, and Global Available-to-Promise capability.

The Insurance Industry

The SAP insurance solution enables the integration necessary to make consistent data available across the organization, from general accounting, claims processors, and agents, to corporate managers. The Management Accounting component allows insurance companies to perform sales and profitability analyses, as well as product costing and calculation of cost variances. The Treasury component integrates processing of all business transactions, from their origins at the trading stage, through back-office processing, to their representation in Financial Accounting. The Cash Management component provides the data required to make short- and long-term cash management and long-term financial budgeting decisions. Up-to-the-minute liquidity and currency and risk-position data ensure optimal responsiveness to conditions in the money and capital markets.

The Public Sector Industry

Like the private sector, public organizations must optimally manage resources, workers, vendors, and customers. These organizations are now looking to improve efficiency and return on assets and are consequently turning to the private sector for ideas. They are now trying to utilize the same technology to get the same benefits as the private sector, which is exactly where SAP's public sector industry solution comes in. Budgeting and real-time analysis of the budget-to-actuals is the first tool SAP offers. SAP procurement helps attain substantial savings by utilizing automatic day-to-day purchasing decisions for request-for-quotation (RFQ) announcements, supplier selection (using predetermined selection criteria), purchase orders, and EDI transactions. Online financial information, including treasury and controlling information, integrates to the Purchasing and Materials Management modules. However, the greatest strides can be found in the HR module. The government has thousands of employees, while many other non-profit organizations have lots of volunteers. The HR module offers employee self-service (ESS) solutions, outsourcing ability, compensation management, benefits administration, human resources reporting, training, and event management.

The Telecommunications Industry

The telecommunications industry is rapidly changing as companies are regularly combining and splitting apart. In addition, there are many markets, such as regular phone service, wireless service, cable service, and Internet service. With deregulation looming, each of these players may enter into one or more of these additional markets. Therefore, these firms need tools that will help them understand profitability of both customers and products in an increasingly competitive marketplace. The SAP telecommunication industry solution provides several tools to enable these firms to better change and compete in the evolving environment. When companies begin forging into new industries, SAP will allow the planning, tracking, and analyzing of new network programs. Pricing and costing of new products and determining profitability of customers are also components of the industry solution. Some of these solutions may come via Activity Based Costing. Optimization of human resources, inventory management, warehouse management, procurement, and cash management will further support these changes.

The Aerospace and Defense Industry

The A&D industry template offers solutions mainly to A&D manufacturers, government contractors, and MRO firms. At a high level, the primary intent of the module is to cut down on cycle times and project costs in the industry while providing better tools to help plan, monitor, and report on these projects. Often these firms provide a combination of traditional manufacturing and government-oriented engineering projects, and need systems that support both. Gone are the days of the multi-year "never-ending" government project. Firms today must give the best product at the lowest price. These firms must plan well and operate efficiently. In order to achieve these goals, SAP's A&D module offers a number of specific functional solutions. The first are the integrated program management tools, which help manage a host of contracts and delivery schedules throughout the life cycle of a program. The second piece of the solution is integrated product and process support, which offers integrated product data management (PDM), multistage bill-of-materials (BOM) reporting (as-designed, as-planned, as-built, and as-maintained), component-supplier management integration, and customization capabilities for engineering change orders (ECOs) and complex manufacturing.

The Banking Industry

The SAP banking solution supports management accounting needs with single transaction/ single position costing, including interest terms contribution, trading contribution, opportunity contribution, commissions and fees, overhead and operating costs, and imputed costs. Additionally, the SAP solution supports profitability analysis through market results, own-account trading results, productivity results, risk results, bank profit center accounting, transformation results, and net interest income. SAP Banking includes a Risk Management component for management of market risk. The Market Risk component includes concepts for quantifying these risks, including value at risk (VAR) and net present value (NPV), instruments to control interest rates, currency and other price risks, and value-at-risk/money-at-risk. SAP Banking Treasury and Cash Management components support banks with integrated processing of all business transactions from their origins, through processing, to financial reporting.

The Chemicals Industry

Most large chemical companies are global, have customers that are also vendors, and produce large amounts of co-product or derivative materials. Environmental concerns, including the production of by-products, also greatly affect the industry. All of these concerns are addressed in the SAP chemical industry solution. The Business Engineer allows companies to configure based on current best practices in the chemical industry. Most chemicals are transported in bulk on barges, ships, trucks, or by rail. The chemical industry solutions allow for the transport of these materials in ways needed by the chemical industry. Often, during the production process of a batch of material, certain actions must be taken at specific points in the process. Process Instruction (PI) sheets facilitate this activity. Another hot topic in the industry is the plant-centric view of a company, which SAP also includes in the Chemical Release. Finally, SAP includes a number of forms that assist on the environmental side of the house. They include "right to know" forms as well as Material Safety Data Sheets (MSDSs).

The Consumer Products Industry

The consumer products industry is one of the most highly impacted areas when it comes to changing business trends. It must be able to stay flexible in order to meet the demands of emerging and changing markets, while retaining/growing market share. Dynamic market conditions demand that businesses be able to quickly improve existing products and introduce new ones. Costs must be minimized and profits maximized right along the supply chain, from procurement to sales. The supply chain becomes the focal point in the quest to stay competitive in the long run. Functionality provided by SAP R/3 Release 4.0 to support the consumer products industry includes promotion planning, free goods management, freight calculation and settlement, letter of credit, payment and credit card handling, distribution resource planning, consumer products industry process modeling, and integration into supply chain management.

SAP has the capability to leverage an industry-specific, preconfigured system that incorporates only the R/3 functionality specific to the consumer products industry, thereby streamlining implementation.

The Healthcare Industry

SAP has formed an Industry Center of Expertise (ICOE) for its customers in the healthcare industry. The ICOE is made up of industry experts, business partners, and customers. Responsibilities of the ICOE include incorporating best business practices into the standard SAP R/3 software, investing in research and development of healthcare industry issues, and communicating ideas with industry associations and others. SAP offers healthcare companies the Industry Solution for Hospitals (IS-H) module in its standard SAP system. The IS-H module addresses inpatient and outpatient management processes. SAP has identified various software partners that integrate with SAP to provide functionality in areas such as scheduling for radiology, surgery, and laboratory procedures.

The High-Technology and Electronics Industry

Time-to-market is key to success in the high-technology industry. As is consistent with the high-technology industry, new products with higher performance levels and lower prices are constantly being introduced to the market. By having information available across the manufacturing enterprise, the company will create faster time-to-market, more knowledgeable decision-making, improved customer service, and optimization and extension of the supply chain. Integrated product development tools help product-design teams in the areas of product configuration management, configure-to-order quoting and estimating, product data management (PDM) functionality, bill-of-material (BOM), and routing development. For semiconductor manufacturers, automated recipe management and routings are included. For manufacturers of electromechanical devices (such as computers and peripherals), extended PDM capabilities include product structure (BOM) data, materials classification systems, and engineering-change-order capability. SAP High-Tech provides a knowledge and rule-based product configuration engine to forecast and monitor dynamic pricing and supply scenarios: supporting varying levels of available-to-promise (ATP) order management including warehouse management, foreign trade, and transportation planning modules.

The Oil and Gas Industry

SAP wanted to be the leader in offering companies in the oil and gas industry software that provides a fully integrated ERP solution, as well as a competitive advantage over companies not running SAP. SAP has added two modules to the standard SAP software to make up the oil and gas industry solution. The two modules are IS Oil-Upstream and IS Oil-Downstream. The IS-Oil Upstream module was developed primarily for joint venture accounting and accommodates specific accounting requirements such as cost allocation between various joint venture partners. The IS-Oil Downstream gives oil companies functionality specific to their industry such as track exchange transactions, hydrocarbon inventory management, bulk products processing, returnable containers, exchange rates, and international taxation.

The Pharmaceutical Industry

There are many challenges that the pharmaceutical industry must face. These include product consistency and quality, government regulation including Good Manufacturing Practices, customer requirements, and timeliness to market. SAP provides the pharmaceutical industry the tools to handle activities such as process manufacturing, quality management, process costing, batch/lot management, and process documentation. The process industry capabilities of SAP allow for the collection of manufacturing data through automated Process Instruction (PI) sheets that can be tied to electronic batch sheets.

The Retail Industry

The retail industry faces the challenge of many different distribution possibilities. Some companies distribute via catalogs, others have customers coming to them, and some are influenced by the latest trend of customers shopping on the Internet. Often these retailers face small margins that force a tightly integrated supply chain to carefully manage inventory and monitor customers' wants. SAP supplies Merchandise Logistics Tools to help managers better understand customer needs and therefore keep better levels of inventory. The SAP Retail module includes software for goods receipt, labeling, store supply, inventory management, and promotions management. SAP takes advantage of tools such as EDI transactions, interfaces with current POS systems, and Internet and intranet capabilities that will help retail firms technologically compete in the future.

The Utilities Industry

SAP serves the utilities industry with two modules. The Industry Specific-Utilities/Federal Energy Regulatory Commission (IS-U/FERC) module provides the regulatory reporting system component to help companies ensure compliance with any government regulations, as well as specific utilities industry reports. It also provides archiving and report regeneration for auditing purposes. The second is the Industry Specific-Utilities/Customer Care and Service (IS-U/CCS) component, which provides specialized customer care functionality required in the utilities industry. Customer information and billing enhancements provide comprehensive customer information and also allow for consolidated billing, mass billing, and metering capability that allows meters to be read remotely and the information automatically transferred to SAP.

The Public Sector

Development of SAP R/3 for the public sector is a bit different than the other IBUs. The Public Sector has been set up as a separate business unit of SAP A/G. This unit supports software development for federal, state, and local governments, as well as higher education and non-profit organizations. Although SAP is behind the competition in the development of software for this business sector, resource and dollar commitment to the development will allow them to make up ground rapidly.

Understanding Mid-Market Solutions

The SAP small market encompasses those accounts with less than $200 million in revenue. This market will be supported by the CBS (Certified Business Solutions) organization established by SAP. The mid-market is defined as accounts with revenue between $200 million and $1 billion in revenue. This market segment is populated with thousands of companies, and should provide a solid market for EAP sells for many years. The accounts in these markets are viewed to be very dynamic, fast growing, and very agile in the marketplace. These may well be the future Fortune 1000 companies.

This market is large, the opportunity is great, and there are many differences from the large market approach to system implementations. Accounts in this market will not be able to support the re-engineering efforts that have caused large account projects to soar in cost and time overruns. These accounts need to realize the benefits of the integrated software very quickly, with minimal loss of resources to support the implementation. These companies will need to be frugal in the assignment of resources to implement the product. They typically will not be able to free resources on a full-time basis to support the project. Employees will be assigned as needed and still required to perform their day-to-day jobs. SAP has developed tools such as ASAP to assist in these efforts.

Part
I
Ch
3

Although these companies have smaller revenues, the functional requirements are still the same as larger organizations. Technology can still provide a competitive advantage for these companies. Enterprise applications can allow these accounts to reduce IT cost and focus on core competencies. At the same time, these companies can become more competitive from a business perspective by allowing themselves the ability to view their business as an enterprise rather than as functional silos. This will allow organizations to plan more precisely for future growth opportunities and also allow them to react and adjust more easily to market demands. Even in smaller organizations, there will be an opportunity to improve processes and utilize resources more effectively by streamlining efforts.

With the utilization of the ASAP tool set and an enhanced set of skills required by consultants, the small- to mid-market will be able to effectively utilize SAP. The ASAP methodology will provide a standard roadmap for implementations. This will allow projects to begin faster with minimal start-up time involved. This also will allow SAP to monitor the progress of these projects and provide needed triage support if projects are stalled. The typical time frame for implementation is 6–9 months. However, it is possible to reduce this time frame if scope and interfaces are reduced.

Given the needs of small markets, SAP has established a program to deliver solutions to these enterprises. CBS organizations have been established in each geographic region of the U.S. that focus on selling to accounts with less than $200 million in revenue. These are value-added resellers of the SAP software and are not owned by the SAP organization. CBS organizations will work with local consulting firms to provide project implementations. In some cases the CBS may be staffed to support the project with their own consultants.

The skills required by the consultants are much different than those required on larger projects. The large projects can support team members who are specialized in one specific area of the software, business functionality, or re-engineering. These projects will support 50–100, or more, project members. The small- and mid-markets will require the consultants to work from a business process focus and understand the integration of their specialized area of SAP to all the other modules. Along with the software knowledge, they also will need to design the business processes as they configure the system—basically re-engineer as they implement. Oftentimes there may only be two or three employees in a given functional area, making it extremely difficult for the organization to assign full-time resources to the project team. This means that consultants for the small- and mid-markets will not only need to be deeply skilled in SAP, they will also need to be able to quickly understand the company's business, make sound configuration decisions, and document and communicate these decisions effectively, with less guidance from the customer than they are accustomed to receiving on large implementations.

With the utilization of the ASAP tool set and a more skilled group of consultants, the time and cost of implementations will be reduced significantly. ●

CHAPTER 4

Description of the SAP R/3 Software

In this chapter

What is the role of Basis in the R/3 structure?

The role of Basis in interfacing with the various modules

The portability of SAP R/3 due to Basis

What is ABAP/4?

What a BDC is and how it is used

ABAP/4's role in reporting, including the screen painter

The integration of SAP R/3's modules

To begin to understand the usefulness of the R/3 software, this chapter starts by describing its foundation. In this chapter, you will examine the building blocks of SAP R/3, starting with its adaptability to multiple hardware platforms. Next you take a brief look at the proprietary programming language that SAP R/3 is written in, ABAP/4. Finally, you will look at the modular structure of SAP R/3.

This will be a short overview—a whole book could be (and has been) written on ABAP alone. However, the subject matter in this chapter is also the most technically demanding. If it doesn't all make sense, don't worry. The intent of this chapter is to build a primary understanding of how SAP R/3 is structured. The intent of the book is to explain how it is utilized to improve basic company activities.

Understanding the R/3 Basis System

The R/3 Basis software, also called *middleware*, is the architecture that provides the environment for the R/3 system. The environment created by Basis allows the system to be extremely flexible and portable. The flexibility of the Basis system is designed to run on client/server architecture. The integration of the R/3 applications (FI, MM, PP, and so on) to the system is provided by Basis. It also allows the applications to run on different platforms.

At a high level, Basis provides several other features for the R/3 system. It houses the administration tools for the R/3 system: the data dictionary and the function library. The interfaces to SAP applications, as well as other systems, are provided by the Basis system.

Basis breaks the different interfaces into three separate areas:

- User interface
- Programming interface
- Communications interface

The *user interface* is simply the graphic user interface (GUI) that makes SAP easily adaptable by the user and a powerful interactive development tool. The GUI interface is not only useful in navigating through the different applications of SAP, but also in developing tables, programs, functions, and many other program structures. For example, the data dictionary allows the user to create a table by simply pointing and clicking rather than creating the table by means of SQL directly at the database level.

The *programming interface* contains the screen interpreter, ABAP/4 interpreter, and the ABAP/4 data dictionary mentioned previously. The screen interpreter is used to control dialog box processing or the flow of screens within applications, as well as the data that passes between them. The ABAP/4 interpreter deciphers the language, ABAP/4, which is used to program the entire SAP system. The two of these interpreters combined is the software of the R/3 system; both interact with the data dictionary.

Keeping the *communications interface* separated from the other interfaces—as well as other areas of the system—is what makes the system so flexible and Basis so important. This interface provides the communication between internal programs, as well as internal-external programs and the exchange of data by electronic data interchange (EDI).

N O T E Electronic Data Interchange, or EDI as it is more commonly known, is the process of doing business with your partners electronically. More specifically, it is a way of exchanging structured data such as sales orders, invoicing, and contracts by an electronic means. This allows for the elimination of paper and paperwork errors. ▪

Portability is another feature that is provided by Basis. Basis allows the R/3 system to run on many different hardware platforms. For example, R/3 can run on all UNIX platforms including SUN, HP, and IBM. Different database systems can be used also. Some of these include Oracle7, Informix, and DB2. The SAPGUI, or graphical user interface, can run on different desktop systems. Some examples of these are Windows 95, 3.1, and NT.

To insure portability, Basis provides three central interfaces to the R/3 system. These are the presentation interface, database interface, and operating system interface. The primary purpose of the presentation interface is to manage the graphical user interface and to manage the windows or sessions that are opened by the user.

The relational database management system is used to store data in related tables. The data itself is stored in a typical database structure, whereas the relationships between tables and the table structures are stored in the data dictionary. The tables and data are manipulated by what SAP calls *Open SQL*. This is an SAP-specific query language that is very similar to SQL. The database interface converts the Open SQL instructions to database instructions. Non-SAP applications can access the R/3 database through the presentation, application, and database servers.

Part

I

Ch

4

Understanding the ABAP/4 Development Workbench

The SAP R/3 system is delivered with the ABAP/4 Development Workbench, which allows you to utilize all of the functionality of its proprietary programming language, ABAP/4. ABAP stands for Advanced Business Application Programming, with the 4 indicating that it is a fourth-generation programming language. SAP is developed exclusively in ABAP/4 to provide a consistent development environment to developers and customers. Therefore, while the programmers at implementation sites may have extensive knowledge of other programming languages, the investment to train the development team members in the use and application of the ABAP/4 Development Workbench is a worthwhile investment.

One of the largest challenges that an ABAP developer must overcome is to understand how SAP data is stored. SAP uses standard relational database concepts to store all master, transactional, and configuration data. The ABAP/4 Dictionary is actively integrated in the Development Workbench and is the tool by which all fields, tables, and structures are defined within SAP. The integration of the Dictionary with the Workbench ensures that changes made to the structure of tables are active in all programs that utilize them. The logical database tool provides the capability to define relationships across tables.

As part of the Development Workbench, the function library provides customer access to all SAP-developed function modules and the option to create custom function modules for use within a specific organization. The use of function modules, when available, reduces development and testing time and, in some cases, eliminates the need to understand the complicated processes behind standard SAP code.

The use of the ABAP BDC session concept to convert data and design interfaces is a safe, effective way to convert external data to SAP in batch. If online processing is desired, the *call transaction* option is used. By using the syntax provided in ABAP/4, programs mimic the manual entry of data through standard SAP transactions. This provides automatic validation and logging of errors (with BDC only), thus decreasing development time and increasing the accuracy of the conversion. While newer SAP tools such as CATT (computer-aided testing tool) and the availability of standard SAP application program interfaces are threatening to replace custom BDC session development, the application of these alternatives are limited in terms of performance and availability, respectively.

N O T E   Some examples of CATT and SAP application program interface limitations are they are not particularly good at testing menu path sequences and they do not work well with list displays because lists deal with a varying number of items. Also, CATT cannot run in Batch Input mode. ▪

ABAP/4 is also used to develop custom reports. While SAP provides many standard reports, some custom development of reports is often required. Because many standard reports exist, the logic of these reports can often be copied and modified to accommodate custom requirements. However, if a similar standard report cannot be found, development is still most easily accomplished via ABAP, as portions of standard logic from multiple programs can be readily included in the new program, and standard function modules can be called to perform complicated processing. Additionally, ABAP supports interactive reporting, including drill-down functionality to accommodate multiple requirements within one report.

Room for Improvement

While the implementation of SAP encourages the re-engineering of business processes, invariably some gaps in base functionality will exist. The development of gap solutions is the area in which understanding ABAP becomes crucial. Most gap solutions that cannot be accommodated with manual workarounds are comprised of enhancements to SAP code, extensions to the SAP software, or a combination of both. Because these solutions must be closely integrated with standard SAP processing, a detailed understanding of the ABAP development behind the related SAP transaction is required. For the purposes of this discussion, an *extension* is defined as the development of a distinct transaction that reads and updates the contents of SAP tables. An *enhancement* is defined as custom development that resides within an approved area of a standard SAP program.

In the development of an extension, the Screen Painter and Menu Painter are used to provide a graphical user interface that is consistent with that of a standard SAP transaction to execute non-standard processing. Because directly updating standard SAP tables is not recommended, extensions often combine customer-specific data that is manually entered on a custom screen, with data from standard SAP transactions, to create a BDC session or call transaction to manipulate data as standard SAP processing cannot. While the Screen Painter tool is used as a means to provide consistent screens to the end-user, the Menu Painter tool is the key to including the transaction in the standard menu paths. SAP provides areas within the standard menus, called *menu-exits*, to which customer developed transactions can be added. In this manner, the addition of the option is seamless and will be preserved during upgrades of the software.

Developing Enhancements

The development of enhancements is an endeavor that requires a deeper understanding of standard SAP transaction processing. While SAP does not support the modification of standard code, it does provide areas in which customers can insert code to adjust the standard transaction processing. These areas are commonly referred to as *user-exits*. This term is used as a general reference. There are many types of user-exits including form user-exits, function exits, field exits, menu exits, and screen exits.

N O T E The different types of user-exits are all integrated into standard SAP code when activated and cannot exist independent of their respective environments. Because they are dependent upon their environments, the logic within user-exits must reference the work areas within the parent SAP program. ▨

Each of these user-exits is described as follows:

- Form user-exits are the oldest type of user-exit. They are empty forms provided within an SAP program in which custom code can be inserted.

- Function exits are a more modular way to enhance SAP code that became available with the release of version 3.0. When a function exit is activated, a call to the function that contains the custom logic is added to the code of the pre-determined SAP program.

- Field exits are provided for custom conversion routines or authorization checks at the field level.

- Menu exits are used to add custom options to standard menu paths, as discussed in the previous paragraph.

- Screen exits are used to add new fields to a screen or to add greater functionality, such as a radio button.

While finding an appropriate user-exit to meet the requirement is a time-consuming task, the use of such exits is the most effective way to ensure that the enhancement does not interfere with standard SAP processing and will be preserved during a software upgrade.

While ABAP/4 may lack the power of other fourth-generation languages, its use during the SAP R/3 implementation process is an invaluable tool to decreasing implementation time and the delivery of a maintainable system.

Part

I

Ch

4

Integration of the Modules

The overall intention of the SAP R/3 system is to empower all normal business processes while simplifying the tasks involved. Looking at a typical company, the work functions are divided by organizational areas. SAP R/3 is also divided this way, with Sales and Distribution, Production Planning, Accounting, Human Resources, and Materials Management being the principle functions. The spectacular thing about this familiar division of functions is it is done with precisely directed integration.

The processes that are normally linked within a business based on similar or orderly activities are systematically linked in SAP R/3. This provides real-time updating of information from one business area to the next. Better information leads to better decisions, which leads to better businesses.

The integration of the modules within SAP R/3 are broken down into four high-level work areas:

- ■ Logistics
- ■ Accounting
- ■ Human Resources
- ■ Business tools

The first three are recognizable from their business functionality. Business tools represents the system management of SAP R/3. This includes configuration of the R/3 system, the ABAP/4 Workbench, and communication and administrative issues. The modular structure is often best represented through a graphical presentation. Figure 4.1 represents the modular structure of SAP R/3.

FIG. 4.1

A graphic representation of the integration of SAP R/3's modules.

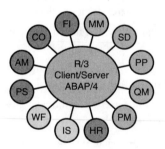

It's easy to see that the modular structure of R/3 allows for complete, yet integrated, management of a wide range of business activities. ●

CHAPTER 5

Getting Started in SAP R/3

If you have never used the R/3 software before, this chapter is especially important to you. In this chapter, you will examine the most fundamental navigation steps of using R/3. Fundamental as they may be, these steps are key to getting the most out of the system. If you are not comfortable with basic navigation in the system, advanced tasks can be troublesome or impossible. Many of the techniques discussed in this chapter are second nature to the advanced user, but helpful and necessary nonetheless. Every user, whether a consultant with 10 years of SAP experience or a novice using R/3 for the first time, must have a basic understanding of these techniques.

Logging On

To begin working with SAP R/3 in a Windows 95 environment, you must first be attached to a LAN/WAN that provides access to the R/3 software, and you must have access to the SAP GUI. This is the client or front-end part of the software that provides the necessary functionality to access SAP R/3 on the network. Often the GUI is loaded on the hard drive of each client PC rather than being run from a LAN drive. If you do not have the proper connectivity or GUI setup, contact your company's system administrator.

To start SAP R/3 from a typical Windows 95 installation, complete the following steps:

1. Select the Start button.
2. From the pop-up menu, select Programs.
3. From the Programs menu, select the SAP menu option represented as SAP Frontend in Figure 5.1.
4. Select the SAP R3 icon.

FIG. 5.1

A typical program listing from the Windows 95 Start button to the icon for the SAP R/3 software.

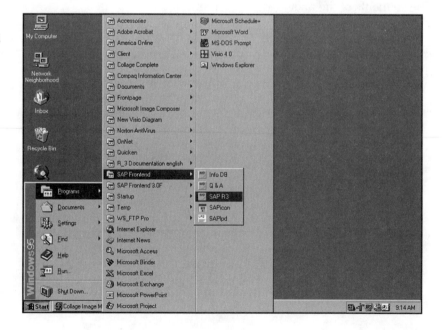

It's possible that an icon may be available on the Windows 95 desktop to start the software. The SAP R/3 software will start, and the logon screen will appear (see Figure 5.2).

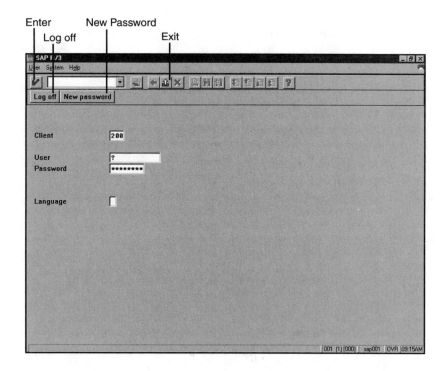

FIG. 5.2

The SAP R/3 logon screen.

The logon screen contains four fields:

- Client: In the SAP R/3 structure, a client is a self-contained operating unit with separate tables and master data.
- User: An ID assigned to a specific person that has security tied to it.
- Password: A personal ID that provides safeguards from unauthorized use of a user ID.
- Language: SAP R/3 is used worldwide and therefore supports multiple languages. This entry determines what language is used for menu paths, field names, and so on. To select English, enter **e** in this field.

N O T E During the development phase of an SAP implementation, there are normally multiple clients set up within a company. There is often a *playground* or *sandbox* area for testing ideas and a configuration client where setup is done in a controlled environment prior to going live. Eventually, there are usually one or more production clients on which live transactions are carried out. ■

Four buttons are active on the SAP logon screen. The Log off button and the yellow arrow button (properly known as the Exit button) allow you to back out of the SAP software without logging on to the system.

The New Password button allows the user to change his or her password. To change your password, complete the following steps.

1. Enter Client, User, and current Password.
2. Click the New Password button.
3. A pop-up box asks for New Password and Repeat Password.
4. Enter your new password in both fields using the tab key to move from one field to the next and click the Confirm button to change your password. Click the Cancel button to abort the password change.

The final button available on the SAP logon screen is the green check button. This button is equivalent to pressing the Enter key from the keyboard. After entering the appropriate data to log on, the user can click this button to log on.

Once the task of logging in has been completed, an SAP copyright box appears. Press Enter or click the Confirm button to clear the box and reach the SAP R/3 main screen.

Navigating the Main SAP Screen

The first time a user sees the main screen of the R/3 software it can seem both ambiguous and intimidating. However, once the user becomes familiar with the screen elements, he or she generally finds SAP R/3 to be well organized with a businesslike approach. Much of what appears on the initial screen is typical of a Windows 95 environment. At the top of the screen is the title bar. This is a Windows element that provides the user with basic information about where he or she is in the software application. At the main SAP screen, the title bar simply reads SAP R/3 (see Figure 5.3).

Directly below the title bar is the menu bar. Here lies the power of the SAP R/3 system. Each menu listing is carefully laid out based on its business purpose. By clicking any one of the eight menu options, the user sees a pull-down menu listing the related business options. These menu selections are only the first layer of, in some cases, many layers of menus the user must become accustomed to in SAP R/3.

Looking at the menu options as seen in Figure 5.3, from left to right they are

- Office
- Logistics
- Accounting
- Human resources
- Information systems
- Tools
- System
- Help

FIG. 5.3

The main SAP R/3 screen.

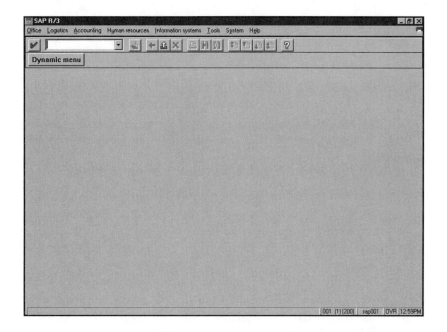

Taking a quick look at each item, the user will see pull-down menus that represent specific actions of the menu option. For example, under the Office menu selection, menu options such as Inbox and Outbox are available. As these items imply, the Office menu selection is the path to SAP's email system known as R-mail.

N O T E In this book, you will concentrate on the menu options of Logistics, Accounting, Human resources, Tools, and System. ■

Looking at the pull-down menus of these selections, you will see menu items that fit into the appropriate business-related categories. Under Logistics, the following menu selections are available:

- Materials management
- Sales/distribution
- Production
- Production - process
- Plant maintenance
- Service management
- Quality management
- Logist. controlling
- Project management
- Central functions

Part

I

Ch

5

Under Accounting, the following menu selections are available:

- Financial accounting
- Treasury
- Controlling
- Enterprise control.
- Capital Invstmt Mgt
- Project management

Human resources has the following menu selections available:

- Personnel admin.
- Time management
- Incentive wages
- Payroll
- Benefits
- Planning
- Recruitment
- Travel expenses
- Information system

Under Tools, the following menu selections are available:

- ABAP/4 Workbench
- Business engineering
- Administration
- Communication
- Word processing
- Hypertext
- Find

And finally, the System menu option has the following pull-down selections:

- Create session
- End session
- User profile
- Services
- Utilities
- List
- Job status
- Short message
- Status
- Log off

Several selections are followed by a right-pointing arrowhead (➤). This arrowhead tells the user that further pull-down menus are available for the selection. As an alternate method of selection, any menu item may be selected by pressing the Alt key and the underlined letter of the corresponding menu option.

Users should feel free to explore all the possible menu paths available from the main screen. This will help you develop a feel for the layout of menus and security based on your user ID, which should stop you from performing unauthorized transactions. The Help option specifically provides paths to further information. Keep in mind that these menu listings are based on SAP R/3 version 3.0F and could change in future releases.

Using Transaction Codes

Due to the numerous menu options that must be navigated to accomplish some SAP transactions, some users prefer to use transaction codes to navigate the system. Transaction codes are alphanumeric codes assigned to specific SAP R/3 transactions. Every transaction within SAP has a four-character transaction code assigned to it. For example, to enter a confirmation of production work performed, the transaction code is CO11. By entering this code in the command field at the top of the SAP R/3 screen and pressing Enter, the user is taken to the Production Confirmation screen.

The corresponding menu path for this transaction consists of the following: Logistics, Production, Production Control, Confirmation, Enter, For Operation, and Time Ticket.

As you can see, the transaction code speeds the process of moving around in SAP, assuming the appropriate transaction code is known.

To find the transaction code for a given transaction, first navigate to the transaction via its menu path. From the desired transaction screen, select Status from the System menu. The pop-up box in Figure 5.4 will appear listing key information about the current system status. The four-character Transaction code can be found in the SAP data section under Repository data. This transaction code allows quick navigation to the current screen.

From the main SAP R/3 screen, the four-letter transaction code can be entered directly into the Command field. However, from most SAP screens, various prefix strings are needed to affect how the transaction codes perform. For example:

/n*XXXX* (where *XXXX* represents any valid transaction code) opens the desired R/3 screen in the current session window. Be careful, however, because any data currently being processed in the current window will be lost.

/o*XXXX* opens a new session window and calls the screen in the new session.

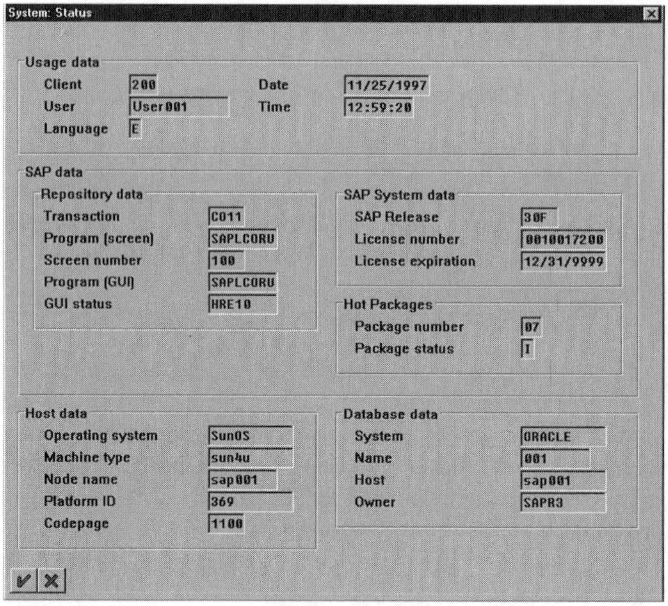

FIG. 5.4

This pop-up box provides current screen status information, including the transaction code.

Using the Options Palette

The Options Palette in Figure 5.5 represents the basic appearance options of the SAP system. If you click the palette, another pull-down menu appears providing control of items such as screen color, font size, screen size, and whether the time of day or response time is displayed on the status bar.

The actual menu options are

- Options
- Clipboard
- Generate Graphic
- Response time
- Default Size
- About

It is the Options selection that allows for control of items such as font size and screen color.

CAUTION

Don't overdo changes to the screen colors used by SAP. Changes to the background and font color often result in screens that are difficult or even impossible to read. Many users have found themselves trapped by accidentally setting the font and screen color to the same setting.

FIG. 5.5
This Options Palette will allow you to alter the basic appearance of your SAP system.

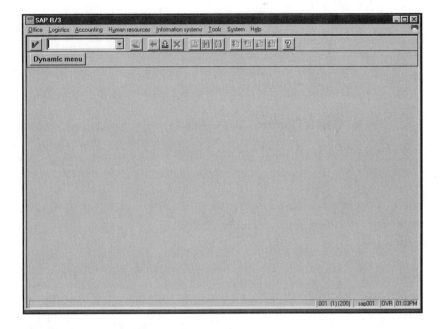

Using the Button Bar

At the top of the SAP R/3 main screen, directly under the main menu bar, is the button bar. The button bar concept is not uncommon in Windows-based applications. The SAP button bar is not a typical-looking Windows button bar, however. The typical cut and paste, print, print preview, and undo buttons are not found on the SAP button bar. That should not imply that the SAP button bar is not useful, though. In fact, the typical user will find these buttons very helpful.

At the main SAP R/3 screen only six buttons are active. They are the Back, Enter, Exit Session, Help, Exit, and Dynamic Menu buttons. Each of these buttons performs a specific task when clicked.

The Back Button The Back button moves the user one screen backward through the path he or she entered. In other words, if you have drilled down through a long SAP menu path, you can reverse that path, step-by-step, by clicking the Back button. The Back button also can be executed by pressing the F3 key.

The Enter Button The Enter button generally performs the same thing as pressing the Enter key on the keyboard. For example, if a four-letter transaction code is entered into the Command Box, you can either press the Enter key to enact the transaction code or you can press the Enter button.

Part
I

Ch
5

> **CAUTION**
>
> Clicking the Enter button does not always perform exactly the same function as pressing the Enter key on the keyboard. Only experience on the system will allow you to become familiar with the situations in which these actions differ.

The Exit Session Button   The Exit Session button performs differently from the main SAP R/3 screen than it does after navigating down through a menu path. From the main screen, clicking the Exit Session will act as if the user wants to close down the current session. If only one SAP session is open, the system assumes the user wants to log off.

N O T E   Running and managing multiple SAP sessions will be discussed in the "Running Multiple Sessions" section later in this chapter. ■

The Exit Button   If the user has navigated down through an SAP menu path, the Exit button moves backward through the menu navigation, one menu layer at a time. This differs from the Back button depending on the state of the transaction to which the user has navigated. To execute the Exit Session button from the keyboard, press Shift+F3.

The Help Button   Clicking the Help button starts the SAP R/3 Online Help. This help library is an extensive listing of topics broken down by business functions that generally match the modules of R/3. The help library is a good starting point for the new user and a useful tool to the experienced user.

The Dynamic Menu Button   The remaining active button on the main screen is the Dynamic Menu button. This button somewhat represents a link of the menu bar and the transaction codes. When you click the Dynamic Menu button, a listing of the menu bar options appears in a tree structure. As you click down through the tree elements, you will see that it follows the menu paths available through normal navigation. When a truncating operation is reached, the transaction code for that task is listed. Clicking that option takes the user to the selected task. Any time the Dynamic Menu button is available, the four-letter transaction codes can be entered into the Command field directly. If the Dynamic Menu button is not seen, you must use the added prefixes.

Understanding the Status Bar

The last element of the main SAP R/3 screen to explore is located at the bottom and is known as the Status Bar. The Status Bar provides the user with basic information about the environment he or she is working in. As seen in the main SAP R/3 screen, the Status Bar is made up of five rectangular sections (see Figure 5.6). The first long rectangle is open space available for use as the information to the right requires more room to be displayed.

FIG. 5.6
The Status Bar.

`| 001 (1) (200) | sap001 | OVR | 12:59PM |`

The first box that contains information lists important system usage information. The first listing is the system number. The system number identifies the host computer system. The next item, displayed in parentheses, is the session number. If you have more than one SAP window or session open, they are numbered to help you keep track of them. The last item in this section is also displayed in parentheses and is the client number. If you remember, the client was defined earlier in this chapter. It represents a confined set of tables and master data. When working in both a development and a live system environment, this piece of information is helpful to avoid unwanted changes to a production client.

The next rectangular section lists only one bit of information. It identifies the application server that SAP R/3 is running on for this session. This information may be meaningless to you and was probably set up by your system administrator. Just be aware that this is the key to accessing SAP R/3.

The fourth rectangular area displays the status of text input. If the letters OVR are displayed, the keyboard is in type-over mode. This means if you click in the middle of an editable field and start typing, what you type will replace what was in the field. If the letters INS are displayed, the keyboard is in insert mode. This means, of course, that any typed text will be inserted into the already existing text.

CAUTION

Unlike most word processors, SAP users generally work in the overtype (OVR) mode. This is due to the limited length of some fields. When using insert mode (INS) in a short field and the text reaches the end of the field, a warning beep is sounded. No further text can be added until some characters are deleted to make space.

Part

I

Ch

5

Control of this indicator is accomplished by pressing the Insert key on the keyboard. Repeatedly pressing this key toggles the indicator back and forth between INS and OVR.

The last section of the Status Bar, at the far right (usually referred to as the system tray), displays a time element. Normally, this is set to display the time of day. If system performance problems are occurring, however, it can be set to display the system response time in seconds. *Response time* is the amount of time it took to process a transaction. Control of this display is managed through the Options Palette discussed in the section, "Using the Options Palette," earlier in this chapter.

You should now be familiar with the basic elements of the main SAP R/3 screen. Understanding these elements will make basic operation and trouble-shooting easier.

Running Multiple Sessions

Even with a tightly integrated system like SAP R/3, there are times when it is convenient to look at multiple elements handled by the system. For example, even though SAP R/3 can aid in assigning available material to a customer order, many users still prefer to view available inventory. Through the multitasking capabilities of today's computer systems, this is possible.

After logging on to R/3, it is possible to open a second session or *window* where a totally separate SAP transaction can be processed. If fact, it is possible to open a third session and a fourth session—up to a total of six sessions. This is one of the most useful, basic capabilities provided by the R/3 system. Many users find it useful to work with two or three sessions at a time, possibly on completely different tasks (see Figure 5.7).

FIG. 5.7

Multiple sessions running in the SAP R/3 system.

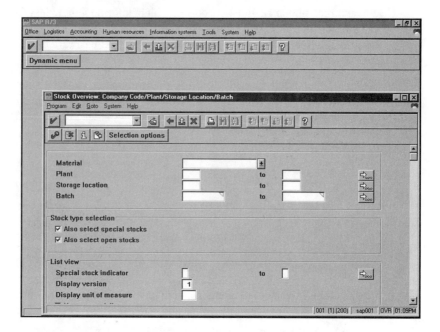

The first thing you probably want to know is how to enact these extra sessions. Select the System menu command and select Create Session from the pull-down menu. A new window will appear with SAP R/3 running and positioned at the main screen.

Be careful, however. Due to the structure of computerized databases, it is not possible for two people, or more specifically two sessions, to be processing the same material. Database locking occurs if an object such as a material definition (known as a material master in SAP) is being edited. This means that a sales order cannot be created for a material if another user, or you in a separate session, is editing the material master.

Fortunately, when you try to process a transaction and database locking blocks you, an error message provides information about who is blocking the transaction. If it ends up being you, in another session, simply switch to that session and back out of the work you are doing that is causing the blocking.

At this point you may be wondering how to switch from one session to another. In Windows 95, you can either select the other session from the Task Bar or use the Alt+Tab key combination. The Alt+Tab key toggles the user through all open windows. Remember that each different session is assigned a number that displays on the Status Bar. This can help you keep track of your sessions.

Logging Off

The last thing to discuss in this chapter is logging off of SAP R/3. After a long day of computing, you should back out of the R/3 system before going home for the night. This is easily accomplished in variety of ways. The quickest way to exit SAP R/3 is to select the System menu option and select Log off from the pull-down menu.

The Log Off dialog box (shown in Figure 5.8) will appear, stating that any unsaved data will be lost and asking if you want to log off. If this is what you want to do, select the Yes button and R/3 will close down. This box always appears when logging off of SAP, whether unsaved data exists or not. Always take care when logging off that all appropriate data has been saved.

FIG. 5.8
The Log Off dialog box allows the user a final option to log off or remain in SAP R/3.

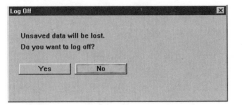

N O T E The final session can be closed down the same way all other sessions were closed, by using the Windows 95 Close button. On the last session closed, the dialog box pictured in Figure 5.8 will still appear. ▪

Another way to log off of the system is to close all but one session using the Windows 95 close box in the upper-right corner of the window. In the remaining session, click the yellow arrow Exit Session button (or press Shift+F3) while in the main SAP R/3 screen. Because there is no further menu path to back out of, SAP prompts the user with the Log Off dialog box. As you can see, there are many ways to log off of the R/3 system.

Moving Forward

This chapter has prepared you to enter the far-reaching avenues of SAP R/3. The enormous capabilities of the system are yet to be covered, but the elements of this chapter are a required first step. Every user, from the 15-year veteran to the absolute beginner, must start with the skills discussed in this chapter. Read on in this book to uncover the true power of the R/3 system and a truly integrated business environment. ●

Part
I

Ch
5

Data Types in SAP R/3

To become familiar with SAP R/3's handling of information, you have to understand the types of data it uses. SAP generally divides data into three types: configuration, master, and transactional data.

Configuration data is static data that directs how the system reacts. Through configuration data, SAP R/3 is set up to perform for the specific functions a customer desires. Next is master data. *Master data* is the high-level definition of a company's resources, including materials, vendors, customers, manufacturing routings, bill of materials, and even a company's General Ledger. The last data type is transactional data. *Transactional data* is the everyday interaction with the system in a live environment. It includes creation of a purchase order, entering a production confirmation on the shop floor, and posting goods issue for a shipment.

This chapter looks at each data type and some of the key elements. You will be introduced to necessary elements in configuration and master data with examples of varying transactions. Through these examples, SAP's handling of data should become clearer.

Configuration

SAP is a complex, integrated software package that is used by companies in many different industries. For obvious reasons, companies in different industries (as well as companies within the same industry) use varying methods to transact business. For example, many consumer goods producers use a make-to-stock production strategy. Industries such as aerospace produce commodities that are customer specific, using a make-to-order production strategy. These varying methods of transacting business are commonly referred to as business processes. Varying business processes are prevalent in all areas of a company, from financials, to production, to sales and distribution.

How then is it possible to use SAP in such a wide variety of companies? The answer is what SAP calls *Configuration*. Configuration enables the SAP software to be tailored to support a company's specific business processes, without modifying the SAP base software.

There is an important distinction to be made between the term Configuration and the terms *Modifications* and *Enhancements*. Configuration refers to setting SAP-supported processing options without making modifications to software code directly. Modifications and Enhancements refer to changing SAP processing by changing software code or adding new software code.

To help manage the effort involved with configuration, SAP provides the *Business Engineer* functionality. The Business Engineer encompasses a set of tools that help guide a company through the difficult process of configuring an SAP system. The tools provided are the Implementation Guide (IMG), Organizational Architect, Business Navigator, and the Business Workflow.

SAP Implementation Guide—IMG

In general terms, the Implementation Guide is a set of configuration steps that must be completed to implement an area of SAP functionality. There are multiple versions of the Implementation Guide called the Reference IMG, the Enterprise IMG, and Project IMG(s). Before an SAP project begins, these versions need to be set up in the system. The relationship between these different versions is depicted in Figure 6.1.

FIG. 6.1
The relationship of the various SAP IMG structures.

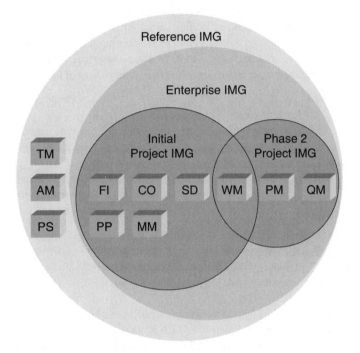

When a new SAP system is first installed, the Reference IMG is the only IMG version that is available. The Reference IMG contains all configuration transactions available for all functionality in the installed version of SAP R/3. This represents the base set of configuration options from which all SAP R/3 functionality can be configured. All other versions of the IMG are derived as subsets of the Reference IMG.

The Enterprise IMG contains only the configuration transactions which are applicable to a specific company's installation of SAP. The Enterprise IMG serves the purpose of filtering out configuration options that will not be needed by a company if certain modules will not be implemented. For example, in Figure 6.1 a company plans to install the Financial Accounting (FI), Controlling (CO), Materials Management (MM), Production Planning (PP), Sales and Distribution (SD), Warehouse Management (WM), Plant Maintenance (PM), and Quality Management (QM) modules. However, the company is not planning to install the Project System (PS), Treasury Management (TM), or Asset Management (AM) modules. There is no need to have the configuration options for these modules available to the project team, so the IMG does not include the modules.

Part

I

Ch

6

N O T E Undocumented feature: The Enterprise IMG can be extended to add configuration for additional modules at any time. Therefore, it is not crucial to create the Enterprise IMG exactly right the first time. ■

A Project IMG contains a subset of the Enterprise IMG configuration transactions that need to be configured to complete a specific project. Most SAP implementations are broken down to roll out the functionality in several phases. For example, many companies choose to implement only the *core* SAP modules for Financial Accounting, Sales and Distribution, Materials Management, and Production Planning initially, and then phase in other *auxiliary* modules such as Plant Maintenance or Warehouse Management in subsequent projects. In this situation, it would be advantageous to have two or more projects—one project for the initial implementation and new projects for each subsequent rollout of functionality.

In the example shown in Figure 6.1, the company chose to install the SAP functionality in two phases, using multiple projects. In the initial project, the company plans to install the FI, CO, MM, SD, and PP modules, as well as some of the WM functionality. A subsequent Phase 2 project of the implementation will add SAP R/3 additional WM, PM, and QM functionality.

N O T E Undocumented feature: To facilitate overall project planning, it is recommended to include all of the SAP modules that will be implemented in the Enterprise IMG. This will help when planning future projects for system upgrades or subsequent project phases. ■

N O T E Undocumented feature: All of the SAP IMG information in an SAP instance is client independent. This means that no matter what SAP client you log in to, the same IMG information is accessed. ■

While technically SAP R/3 configuration can be performed using a Project IMG, the Enterprise IMG, or even the Reference IMG, it is recommended to perform all configuration through the Project IMG. A Project IMG has additional features available to help track and document configuration decisions and configuration status that are not available in the other IMG versions. It may be wise to consider restricting access to the Enterprise IMG and Reference IMG transactions so that all project team members cannot use (or potentially modify) these versions either accidentally or on purpose.

Project IMG Structure

The configuration transactions contained in a project IMG are arranged in a multilevel hierarchy of folders. At the highest level of the hierarchy, the folders roughly match the SAP modules. Consequently, the configuration transactions are grouped in terms of the tasks required to configure an SAP module. Figure 6.2 shows an example of an IMG configuration folder hierarchy.

FIG. 6.2

An example IMG structure.

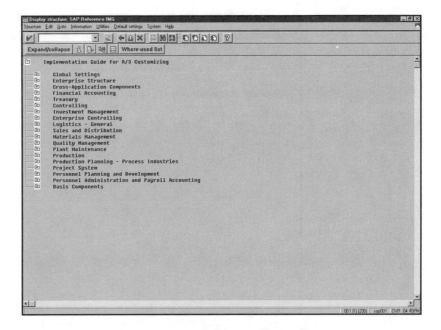

Within an area of functionality to be configured, SAP has attempted to arrange the configuration folders and transactions in the order that the tasks need to be completed from top to bottom. This is not always a strict rule. Many times configuration is an iterative process, where previously completed configuration needs to be revisited based on subsequent decisions. Even so, when in doubt it makes sense to follow the SAP order of configuration tasks.

A Project IMG contains several elements: configuration transactions, configuration help texts, configuration status, configuration documentation, and associated release notes.

Configuration Transactions   Configuration transactions are the heart of the implementation guide; everything else in the IMG is provided to help manage them. Each configuration transaction encompasses the screen(s) used to set the processing options that control a piece of SAP functionality. Configuration transactions are activated by clicking the Execute icon.

The content of configuration transactions varies based on the functionality affected. Some transactions simply allow the maintenance of code tables, such as MRP controllers or purchasing groups. Other transactions are more complex, providing multiple screens of relational data to configure pricing conditions, account determination, MRP plant parameters, and so on.

Insights into how to configure different areas of a business are provided in subsequent chapters of this book.

Configuration Help Texts   Configuration help texts provide online help explaining how configuration affects the SAP processing. The help texts can be displayed in either an SAP text or Windows standard help file format. Configuration help texts are displayed by double-clicking the folder or configuration step text. Figure 6.3 shows an example of a configuration help text displayed using the Windows standard help format.

FIG. 6.3

An example of configuration Help text.

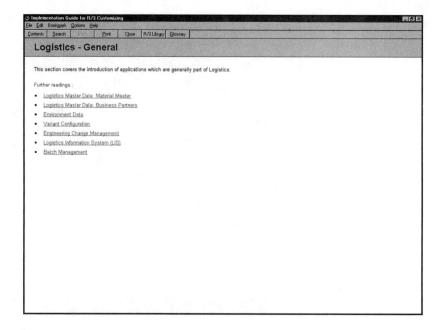

Configuration Status   Configuration status is used to track the current status of the configuration transactions contained in the folder. The status can be recorded in terms of an overall status flag, percent complete, people assigned, and status notes. The status can be maintained at every level of the hierarchy. The configuration status screen is displayed by clicking the status icon. Figure 6.4 shows an example of a configuration status screen, showing the elements that can be tracked.

The overall status flag can be configured to provide user-defined statuses. Standard statuses such as Complete and In Process are provided by SAP. Most projects find it useful to add other meaningful statuses, such as Pending Review or On Hold, based on the project tracking expectations.

Configuration status can be a useful tool for project management only if it is accurately maintained by the project team members. A certain amount of discipline must be instilled in the team to ensure this. The Project IMG can be downloaded into Microsoft Project for a more user-friendly way to use the IMG statuses to monitor project status.

N O T E   Undocumented feature: There is no automatic rollup of status to higher levels based on status changes in lower levels of the hierarchy. Therefore, when all configuration is complete within a folder, it is a manual operation to set the folder status as well as each separate configuration transaction to Complete. ▓

FIG. 6.4

An example configuration status screen.

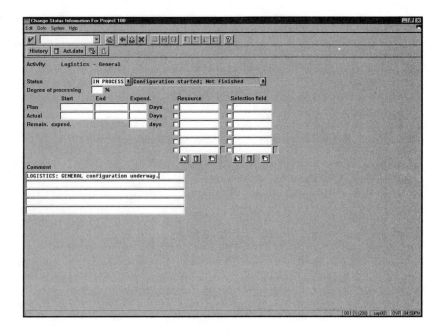

Configuration Documentation   Configuration documentation provides a way of recording additional information for each configuration transaction. The information can be recorded in either SAP long text or by using Microsoft Word in conjunction with a template. Clicking the documentation icon accesses the configuration documentation. Figure 6.5 shows an example of a configuration documentation screen used to record configuration history.

Because the configuration documentation is freeform text, it is a flexible tool that can be used however the project team wants. It is the project team's responsibility to define a standard template for how the documentation will be used. Some projects use this function to record a chronological history of configuration changes. Other projects use it to document configuration decisions. Other projects use it as a notepad to record questions, problems, or concerns. The proper use of this functionality depends on the project's requirement for formal documentation.

Release Notes   Release notes are long text screens explaining functionality that has changed from a previous version of SAP R/3 (see Figure 6.6). This can be useful to help understand configuration of new functionality after a system upgrade.

N O T E   Undocumented feature: The icon for the release note does not appear unless your user settings turn it on by activating the Always Display Release Note Icon check box of the IMG default settings. Once activated, as you drill down in the structure of the IMG, a pointing-hand icon indicates an element with a release note. In addition, other configuration attributes can also be displayed on the screen on the IMG using the user settings. ▨

Part

I

Ch

6

FIG. 6.5

An example of a configuration documentation.

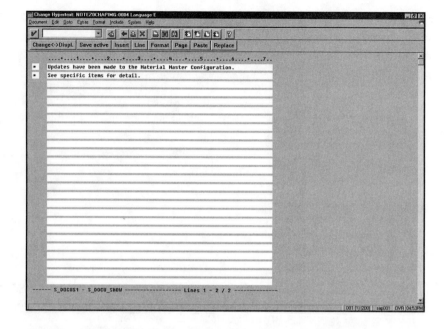

FIG. 6.6

An example of release notes.

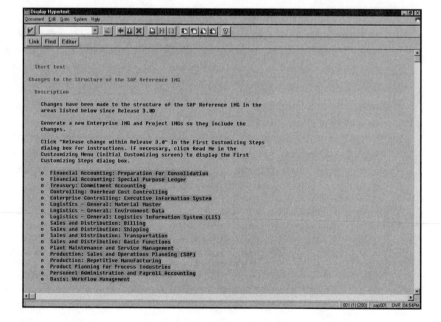

SAP R/3 Organizational Architect

If it is determined that SAP does not support a business process, there are many options to pursue.

■ Check the SAP Online Software Support (OSS) database for a patch or workaround. Chances are that many common problems have been discovered by other projects or are simply the result of software bugs that SAP has already addressed.

■ Check the release notes of future software releases. It is possible that the process will be supported in a higher release of the software.

■ Consider changing the business process. This is not usually a popular option at first glance because it sounds like *business re-engineering*, which was at one time synonymous with terms like *downsizing* and *rightsizing*. However, many companies first ask the question, "Why doesn't SAP support *this* process," without taking a hard look at whether the business could use the SAP-supported process. Companies that are willing to adapt and change quickly to new markets have a competitive edge.

■ Request an enhancement or modification from SAP. If this process makes sense from an industry standpoint, SAP may consider adding code to support the process in future releases.

■ Consider a manual workaround.

■ Custom code and enhancement or modification.

Amazingly, most projects pursue few or none of the above options before accepting the option of custom coding and enhancement.

Base Configuration

SAP comes delivered with a standard configuration that can be used as a starting point. While it is hoped that changes to this configuration can be minimized, a few are absolutely necessary and many more are likely. To make SAP functional for your company, you must define items such as currencies, your factory calendar, and your organizational structure. In the consulting world, this is often called the *base configuration*.

Currencies

SAP's flexible currency configuration allows its customers to track and report various business events in multiple currencies. The six currency types available in SAP's Financial Accounting (FI) module include transaction currency, local currency, group currency, global currency, hard currency, and index-based currency. Transaction currency refers to the currency specified on the document at the time of posting. The currency tracked as the transaction currency is freely definable by the user at the time of entry, given the currency has been defined in SAP. The local currency relates to the currency assigned to the company or company code at the time of its creation. The group currency pertains to the currency assigned to the individual clients established within the SAP environment. In the SAP delivered to clients, this currency comes predefined as German deutsche marks and should be modified as appropriate at the time user-clients are configured.

The global currency is used to facilitate "cross client" transactions. Hard and index currencies are used in areas of high inflation (Brazil or Argentina) or where currency indexing is appropriate (for example, the European Currency Unit in relation to the European Community). A hard or index currency is configured at the country code level and is attached to a company code as a result of its assignment to a country.

Of these six available currencies, the FI module is able to track up to four of them. By default, SAP's FI module tracks the transaction and local currency in its line-item table. In order to track the two additional currencies allowed by FI, the user must define these parallel currencies for a particular company code. Once the parallel currencies are defined, an additional ledger must be created and assigned in order to track and report these currencies on a line-item basis.

Allowing the user to take full advantage of the multicurrency functionality of SAP, an exchange rate table is available to the user (see Figure 6.7). This table can be maintained manually by the user or external data loads can be utilized to provide automated frequent table updates as necessary.

FIG. 6.7

The SAP exchange rate table.

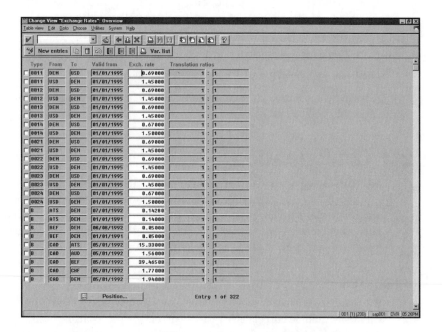

The SAP exchange rate table can capture various exchange rate types depending on the value the user chooses to employ for its transactions. These different rate types include an average exchange rate (M), a selling rate (B), a buying rate (G), or a month-end rate (E), just to name a few. Users are also able to define their own exchange rate types.

Calendar

In many of the SAP modules, calculations are performed that reflect the passage of time. Production planning, for example, is based almost entirely on evaluations of machine and material availability, production and procurement lead-times, inventory movement times, and so on. When dealing with perishable or otherwise dated inventory, warehouse management activities depend greatly on accurate measurement of time. To meet various corporate and legal reporting requirements, financial data processing is typically performed within specified accounting periods and is therefore heavily dependent on an accurate definition of time within the system.

SAP provides a basis for time-related functions in the form of calendars. Through the use of calendars, it is possible to model a corporation's business schedule within the SAP system. For example, corporations whose manufacturing sites do not operate on weekends certainly would not be happy with an MRP-generated production plan that included Saturday and Sunday as normal business days. Such a plan would be unattainable by the manufacturing site since they would always be faced with a 7-day production schedule but only have 5 actual working days in which to accomplish it! In another case, what if the last day of an accounting period happens to fall on a holiday? In reality, it is likely that the period-end reporting would be performed on the preceding business day. Without accurate definition of an appropriate calendar within SAP, the system would not make this adjustment and would miss the actual period-end reporting date.

From these examples, you can see the necessity of accurate SAP calendars. Such calendars are supported in several formats. As is the case with most SAP functionality, these calendars can be easily created and configured to mimic the operating schedule of your organization. Definition of these calendars is performed within the IMG. Because of the widespread influence the calendars have on virtually all of the business functions performed within the system, access to their configuration is typically highly limited.

At a global level, non-client specific calendars can be defined. Such calendars are used to define a high-level schedule, which may be utilized by all clients, companies, and so on, within the organization. If a firm was centrally located within a single country and operated all of its facilities on a single, uniform schedule, one global-level calendar might be sufficient. This is rarely the case for companies large enough to require the services of an ERP system such as SAP. Such firms typically operate in an international environment where it is necessary to accommodate the national, religious, and cultural schedules of many nations. Public holiday calendars and factory calendars defined at the global level within SAP perform this function.

As the name implies, public holiday calendars can be created to define those holidays that are to be regarded as non-business days. For example, by specifying Christmas as a public holiday, that day is excluded from normal business activities by the SAP system. In the case of lead-time calculation for various manufacturing functions, Christmas would not be counted. Production of a material initiated on December 24, which has a scheduled production lead time of one day, would not be scheduled to be completed until December 26.

Part

I

Ch

6

Multiple public holiday calendars can be maintained as necessary to reflect the holiday schedule applicable to different countries. Thus, all operating components of an international organization are not restricted to a single business calendar and can adapt as necessary to their respective countries.

Factory calendars allow a greater level of scheduling detail as they can be defined for each separate location within an organization. Through the definition of factory calendars, each plant within a company can independently apply greater detail to its business schedule than is provided by the holiday calendar alone. The factory calendar does not replace the public holiday calendar, but rather supplements it. The weekly business schedule of the respective plant may be maintained via the factory calendar by specifying which days (Monday, Tuesday, Wednesday, and so on) are business days and which days are not.

It is possible that a plant may not adhere to the same operating schedule perpetually; it may be necessary to allow for cyclical or seasonal variations. For this reason, the definition of a factory calendar includes a validity date range. As necessary, different versions of the factory calendar can be maintained, each with its own validity date range. When performing operations within a plant, such as production scheduling, the factory calendars appropriate for the dates involved are accessed and utilized.

Once created, the factory calendar can be viewed graphically in a typical calendar format (see Figure 6.8). In this display, non-business days are highlighted, making quick evaluations of scheduled operating time more convenient. Non-business days identified via the public holiday calendar are also included in the same manner.

FIG. 6.8

A graphical view of a typical calendar.

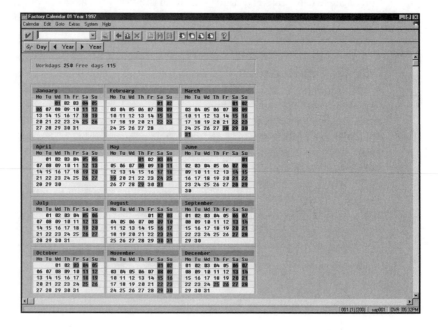

Up to this point, the calendars described have provided a means by which the overall operating schedule of a company or facility is defined. Calendars are also used within the SAP system at a more detailed function level to manage and evaluate ongoing operations. Two such calendars are the planning calendar and the financial calendar.

Within the production planning process, several strategies of demand management and scheduling are available. Included in these are strategies involving the creation and use of planning calendars. Planning calendars allow a great deal of flexibility in defining planning lengths and lot sizes based upon set periods of time. For example, suppose the demand and production characteristics of a particular material suggested that an economical approach to production and inventory management would be to group the demand into time buckets, each of two weeks in length. That is, you would like to total the demand for each two-week period of time into one bucket and then create a single production order to cover it. In addition to this, you would like for the production order to be scheduled such that the required materials were produced and available in inventory by the first Monday of their respective two-week demand bucket. In that way, you could produce the required materials in two-week buckets as desired and would always have them available to fill demand at the beginning of their respective two-week demand period. Through the creation and use of an appropriate planning calendar, you can accomplish this task. As described in this example, the functionality of the planning calendar allows the user to specify flexible planning period lengths that can be used within the production planning process. At the same time, lot sizes may be determined.

Depending on several factors, such as production lead time, the applicable holiday calendar, and operating either ahead of or behind schedule, it is possible that the calculated completion date of a production order would fall on a non-business day. Within the definition of the planning calendar is the desired system response to be applied if this situation occurs. Options exist that can direct the system to displace the production order completion date to either the preceding or following business day, or to not displace the order completion date at all. The latter choice is typically avoided because it would allow the system to plan production operations on days in which the facility is not scheduled to operate.

As with most of the functionality within the Production Planning module, planning calendars are plant-specific. Planning calendars are also defined with respect to validity date ranges. Thus, a specific planning calendar may be available for use in production planning for a discrete period of time, or may be made available indefinitely.

Financial calendars are used largely to assist with the execution of those financial transactions and reporting functions that are repetitive and time-based. Typically, monthly and annual time periods are defined by the financial calendars. However, additional time frames can be defined as desired. Payment runs, dunning runs, end-of-period reporting, and so on are examples of functions whose execution may be directed via a financial calendar. As with many of the financial reporting requirements, the financial calendars are established and maintained at the company level.

Organizational Structures

In the SAP R/3 system, the organizational structure represents the legal and internal framework of a company in which all business transactions are processed. The structure is defined by the following four separate, but integrated, views: Financial Accounting (FI), Controlling (CO), Materials Management (MM), and Sales and Distribution (SD). The four elements common to all organizational structure views are client, company code, plant, and business area.

Financial Accounting (FI) View   The *client* is the highest organizational level in the R/3 system. All areas of a productive R/3 system should be consolidated under one client. The client is one of four organizational elements common to all organizational structure views.

A *company code* is considered a legal entity for external reporting purposes responsible for preparation of financial statements such as a balance sheet, profit and loss statement, and cash flow statement.

Business areas are utilized for flexible financial reporting purposes, such as reporting across company code boundaries. A business area can be defined by such characteristics as geography, plant, and sales area and facilitates the ability to produce internal balance sheets and profit and loss statements as desired by company management.

Controlling (CO) View   A *controlling area* is the highest organizational element defined strictly within CO and represents an organizational unit in which comprehensive management and cost accounting analyses can be performed. Controlling areas can include more than one company code and give management the ability to perform cost, profit, and variance analysis across company-code boundaries. All company codes within a controlling area must utilize the same operational chart of accounts.

Cost centers are the lowest organizational element defined within CO and represent units in which costs are charged, allocated, and ultimately analyzed.

Profit centers are divisions within a controlling area defined for the purpose of profit analysis. Profit center accounting allows a company to generate profit and loss statements using various accounting methods for internal management control.

Materials Management (MM) View   A *purchasing organization* is the organizational unit responsible for purchasing activities for one or more plants, including the generation of purchase orders.

Plants are locations where inventory quantities and values are processed, manufactured, or stored. A plant can be assigned to only one company code, although both company codes and purchasing organizations can have multiple plants assigned to them.

A *storage location* is a unit within a plant utilized for the storage of inventory. Plants can utilize more than one storage location, and storage locations can be utilized by more than one plant.

Sales and Distribution (SD) View   A *sales organization* is the highest level of an organization in which sales are managed—a "selling unit" in a legal sense. Sales organizations are responsible for distributing goods or services, negotiating sales, product liability, and a customer's right of recourse. Regional or industry-sector subdividing of the market can also be carried out with the help of sales organizations. A sales organization can be included in only one company code, although a single company code can have various sales organizations.

Distribution channels are used to provide various ways of supplying customers goods or services. Distribution channels typically are used to represent markets such as wholesale, retail, and direct sales. Sales-specific material master data such as prices, minimum order quantity, minimum delivery quantity, and delivery plant can differ by distribution channel. Customers can be supplied through several distribution channels. A distribution channel can be allocated to one or more sales organizations.

Divisions can be used to represent product groupings. For every division you can make customer-specific agreements such as partial deliveries, pricing, and terms of payment. Within a specific division, you can carry out statistical analysis or set up separate marketing. Divisions can be allocated to one or more sales organizations and distribution channels.

A *sales area* is defined as the combination of sales organization, distribution channel, and division. Management analysis and customer-specific pricing can be done at this level.

Electro Tech Structure

Taking a graphical look at a typical organizational structure across these areas, the working structure of a company is seen. Later in this book, you will take an in-depth look at the fictional company, Electro Tech. To understand how and why an organizational structure is important, Electro Tech's organizational structure is represented in Figure 6.9.

FIG. 6.9
The organizational structure of Electro Tech.

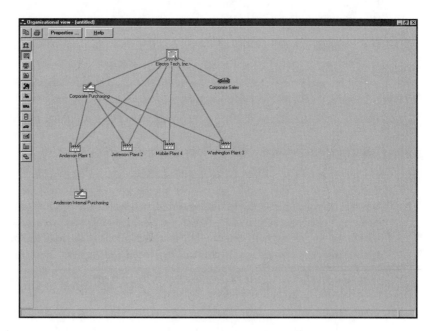

Material Master

The Material Master record in SAP is used to store data relating to all materials tracked in the system. This includes materials bought, sold, produced, and stored by a company. It should be noted that a material has a unique material number designation that is used by all plants that use the material.

The Material Master record is the central repository of data that links together all of the logistics modules in SAP. The different modules in SAP will be discussed in detail later in this book. For now, the logistics modules are listed to illustrate that the Material Master record is utilized throughout the SAP system. The logistics modules include Materials Management, Sales and Distribution, Production Planning, Plant Maintenance, and Quality Management.

Material master data is stored on the different views of the Material Master record. Each view of the Material Master record contains many data fields grouped together with similar data. For example, purchasing data is stored on the Purchasing view, accounting data is stored on the Accounting view, and so on. The different views of the Material Master record will be covered in detail later in this section.

There are several menu paths to navigate to the Material Master screen. This is due to the fact that the Material Master touches all functional modules within SAP. The most commonly used route to access the Material Master is the following menu path: Logistics > Materials Management > Material Master > Material > Create (general) > Immediately.

The screen that appears contains four fields:

- Material is where you enter the number you want to assign to the material.
- Industry sector specifies what type of industry the material will be used in and affects the screens that appear when creating a material.
- Material type is explained at length in this chapter but basically defines if the material is purchased, manufactured, sold, or stored.
- Copy From can be used to copy information from an similar material that already exists.

Material Type

The material type is used to differentiate Material Master records in SAP. The material type identifies how the material is used. More specifically, the material type directs whether a material can be purchased, sold, inventoried, and a number of other functions. Each of these material types has a code assigned to it that identifies the material within SAP R/3. Listed here are the names, associated codes, and brief descriptions of some of the more commonly used material types contained in the standard delivered SAP system.

- Finished Products (FERT)—Materials that are produced by the company to be sold. Examples include computers and radios.
- Semi-finished products (HALB)—Materials that can be procured externally or produced in-house and processed by the company. Examples include circuit boards and subassemblies.

- Raw materials (ROH)—Materials that are procured externally and processed to produce other materials. Examples include chemicals and paper.
- Services (DIEN)—Procured externally and cannot be stored. Examples include overnight delivery services and consulting services.
- Production resources/tools (FHMI)—Materials that are procured externally and used in the manufacture of products. Examples include drills and wrenches.
- Operating supplies (HIBE)—Materials used in day-to-day operations. Examples include light bulbs and pencils.
- Packaging (VERP)—Materials used to transport goods from one location to another. Examples include drums and reusable containers.

Other material types are available in SAP, but the examples previously listed are enough to explain the concept of material types.

In addition to identifying how the material is used, the material type also controls which data views can be stored for a material. For example, raw materials and packaging materials will have a Purchasing view because they are procured externally but will have no Sales view because they are never sold.

Organizational Levels

As mentioned earlier, data on the Material Master record is stored on different views. The data is also stored at different organizational levels, depending on the specific data element. For example, data can be stored at the plant level, the storage location level, or the sales organization level. This is useful if the same material is used at many plants within a company when plant-specific data must be stored. An example of plant-specific data used in SAP is data such as the buyer stored on the Purchasing view. A different buyer at each plant may be responsible for procuring the material. An example of material master data that is not plant specific is the material description, which will be the same for every plant.

Figure 6.10 illustrates the different organizational levels that data can be stored at for the Material Master record. These levels include plant, storage location, valuation type, sales organization, distribution channel, warehouse number, and storage type levels. These levels are explained in greater detail earlier in this chapter in the "Organizational Structures" section.

Material Master Views

Now take a look at the different Material Master views and some of the data contained on each view. You will also see the organizational level at which the data is stored. It should be noted that certain data fields are displayed on many different views. For example, the material number and description is displayed on every view. The organizational level for each specific view is listed in the top portion of the screen. Figure 6.11 lists the different views available on the Material Master record.

Part

I

Ch

6

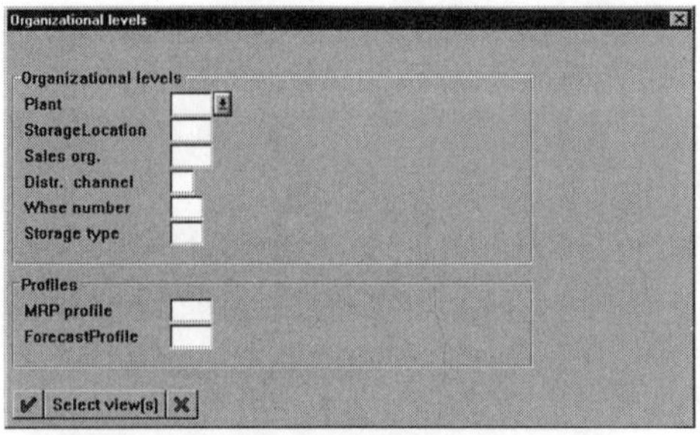

FIG. 6.10

The Organizational Levels pop-up window seen during creation of the Material Master.

FIG. 6.11

The Select view(s) pop-up window as seen during creation of the Material Master.

Basic Data View The Basic Data view contains data that applies to the material at all levels regardless of the plant, sales organization, and so on. Data from the Basic Data view is used throughout SAP in many different modules. Examples of data contained on the Basic Data view are

- Base unit of measure—Identifies how the stock of the material is managed (for example, kilograms, pieces, gallons, and so on).
- Old material number—Can be used to store a material number from a legacy system if one exists, gross weight, net weight, and material description.

This view will exist for all materials.

Sales: Sales Organization Data View This view contains data that is unique to a specific sales organization/distribution channel combination in the company. Data from this view is used on various sales documents for this material. Examples of data contained on this view are

- Sales unit—Identifies how the material is sold (for example, piece, case, dozen, and so on).
- Sales status—Identifies the status of the material from the Sales view (for example, under development, discontinued, and so on).
- Item category group—Used to determine the item category copied to the sales document (for example, standard item, returnable packaging, third-party item, and so on).

Sales: General/Plant Data View   This view contains data that is unique to a specific plant. Data from this view is copied to sales documents for this material. Examples of data contained on this view include

- Transportation group—Used to identify how the material is transported (for example, pallets and liquid form).

- Loading group—Used to identify how the material is handled (for example, forklift, crane, and so on).

N O T E   Both Sales views (Sales Organization and General/Plant) must be stored if the material is going to be sold. SAP will not allow the user to sell a material without these views.

Purchasing View   The Purchasing view contains data that is plant specific. Data from the Purchasing view is copied to purchasing documents (for example, requisitions, purchase orders, and so on) for the material. Examples of data on this view include

- Purchasing group—Identifies the buyer responsible for procuring the material.

- Order unit—Identifies the order unit if it is different from the base unit of measure.

- Source list indicator—Identifies if a source list must be maintained for this material.

- GR processing time—Identifies how long it takes in days to process a goods receipt for this material at the specified plant.

N O T E   It should be noted that a material cannot be purchased in SAP if this view does not exist for the material.

MRP 1 View   The MRP 1 view contains data unique to a specific plant. Data on this view is used to run MRP when planning material requirements. Examples of data on this view are

- MRP type—Identifies how the material is planned.

- MRP controller—Identifies the person responsible for planning material requirements.

- Lot size key—Determines the lot-sizing procedure used to calculate the quantity to be bought or produced.

- Procurement type—Identifies how a material is procured (externally, produced in-house, or both).

MRP 2 View   The MRP 2 view contains data that is unique to a specific plant/storage location combination. Data on this view is used to run MRP when planning material requirements. Most of the data on this screen is plant-specific, but there is a section of the screen containing storage location specific data. The storage location data can be used if a certain storage location is to be excluded from MRP at the plant level. Examples of data on this view include

- Period indicator—Identifies the forecast period.

- Strategy group—Identifies the planning strategy.

- Availability check—Specifies how the system checks availability and generates requirements for the material.

Part

I

Ch

6

Storage View   The Storage view contains data that is unique to a specific plant/storage location combination. Data on this view is used to identify requirements for storing this material in inventory. Examples of data on the Storage view include

- Temperature conditions—Identifies specific temperature requirements for storing the material.
- Container requirements—Identifies the type of container the material must be stored in.
- Total shelf life—Identifies how long the material can be stored.

The Storage Location view must be created if the material is going to be stored as inventory.

Warehouse Management View   This view contains data that is specific to a warehouse within a plant. Warehouse Management enables the user to control inventory at a lower level than at the storage location level. Data on the Warehouse Management view is used to identify more specific storage information. Examples of data on this view are

- Stock removal—Identifies where stock of this material will be pulled from to be issued.
- Stock placement—Specifies where stock will be placed when it is received in the warehouse.
- Minimum and maximum bin quantity.

Quality Management View   The Quality Management view contains plant-specific data. This view is used to store quality data for a material and initiate quality inspection lots in the QM module. Data on this view includes

- MM/PP status—Identifies the usability of a material (for example, blocked for procurement, obsolete, and so on).
- QM inspection data indicator—Identifies if and when inspections will be conducted on the material. (The various inspection types are set up by using the Inspection Type button.)
- QM in procurement indicator—Be careful, this indicator is the only object on the QM view that is at the client-level rather than the plant-level.

The creation of this view is required to use full QM functionality in SAP for a material.

Accounting View   The Accounting view contains plant-specific data. This view is used to store financial data for the material. Data on the view includes

- Currency—Identifies the currency used to value the material.
- Price control—Identifies if the price control used is standard or moving average.
- Standard price and moving average price—Identifies the price of the material.

Costing View   This view contains data that is unique to a specific plant. This view is used to store internal costing data for the material. Data on the Costing view includes

- Product costing indicator—Identifies if product costing is used for the material.
- The variance key—Controls how variances can be calculated.

Vendor Master

You've already seen the Material Master record. Now take a look at the Vendor Master record. The Vendor Master contains information about external suppliers. This information is broken into three sections: general data, accounting data, and purchasing data. You will look at the data maintained in each section a little later in this chapter. Each Vendor Master record has its own unique number and is shared by all departments within the company and all modules in the SAP system. The Materials Management, Production Planning, Quality Management, Sales and Distribution, Plant Maintenance, Quality Management, Service Management, and Financial Accounting modules all may use the Vendor Master for certain transactions.

Similar to the Material Master, the Vendor Master holds information at multiple levels in the SAP hierarchy. Specifically, the Vendor Master tracks information at three distinct hierarchical levels. General data is stored at the client level, accounting data is stored at the company code level, and purchasing data is stored at the purchasing organization level. This division of data serves two purposes. First, it allows separate companies or purchasing organizations within an enterprise to maintain separate data for the same vendor. For example, one company may pay the vendor after 30 days via electronic funds transfer, while another company within the same enterprise may pay by check within 15 days in order to receive a 2% discount.

The second reason for the division of data at the three different hierarchical levels is that it allows the Vendor Master information to be maintained centrally or decentrally. In central maintenance, one individual or department is responsible for entering and maintaining all information in the Vendor Master. They have access to all screens of the Vendor Master and can maintain information at all levels within the SAP hierarchy. If the Vendor Master is maintained decentrally, multiple individuals and departments are responsible for maintaining accurate values in the Vendor Master record. For example, the Purchasing department may maintain the general and purchasing data, while the Accounts Payable department would maintain the accounting data.

When creating a Vendor Master record centrally, nine screens of information are available for maintaining data. If the vendor is to be maintained decentrally, only a subset of these screens is available to any one individual. Look at each of these screens and some of the data contained on each in a little more detail. To navigate to the Vendor Master screen, follow these steps in the menu path: Logistics > Materials Management > Purchasing > Master Data > Vendor > Centrally > Create.

The initial screen seen in Figure 6.12 asks the user to enter the vendor number, company code, purchasing organization, and account group for the vendor. These fields dictate what the Vendor Master record number will be and what levels in the SAP organizational hierarchy will be maintained at this time. If a company code or purchasing organization is not specified, the data fields held at those levels in the SAP hierarchy will not be available for maintenance.

FIG. 6.12

The initial Vendor Master screen.

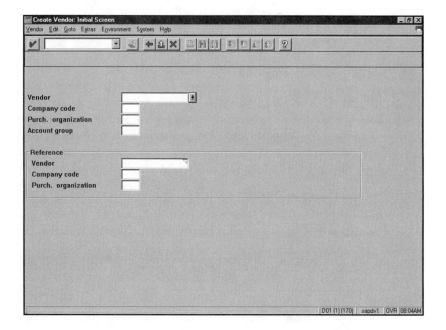

The Vendor Master record number may be defined externally by entering a value on the initial screen or may be defined internally by the system. The account group also must be entered on the initial screen. Once the account group is maintained for a vendor, it cannot be changed except by the system administrator in exceptional cases. When creating a vendor, the initial screen also allows an individual to copy information from an existing Vendor Master record.

The account groups are defined in the SAP system configuration. A standard set of account groups is delivered with the system. These can be modified, deleted, or added to when configuring the software for your specific use. The account group is used to control the number ranges and field statuses. That is, the account group is used to specify fields in the Vendor Master record as mandatory, optional, display only, or suppressed. In addition, the account group specifies the number range(s) allowed for the Vendor Master record.

As mentioned previously, the Vendor Master number can be entered manually when creating a vendor or can be defined by the system. The account group defines which method is used to assign a vendor number. The account group further restricts the number range allowed for the vendor number. A given account group may allow system-assigned numbers between 1000000000 and 1999999999 or externally assigned numbers between A0000 and Z9999, for example.

Vendor Master General Data

The next three screens of the Vendor Master record are the Address screen (see Figure 6.13), Control Data screen (see Figure 6.14), and Payment Transactions screen (see Figure 6.15). The fields on these screens are referred to as general data and are maintained at the client level in the SAP hierarchy. All departments and individuals that use the Vendor Master within the enterprise share the data on these screens. Examples of general data include mailing address, phone and fax numbers, tax information, and bank details.

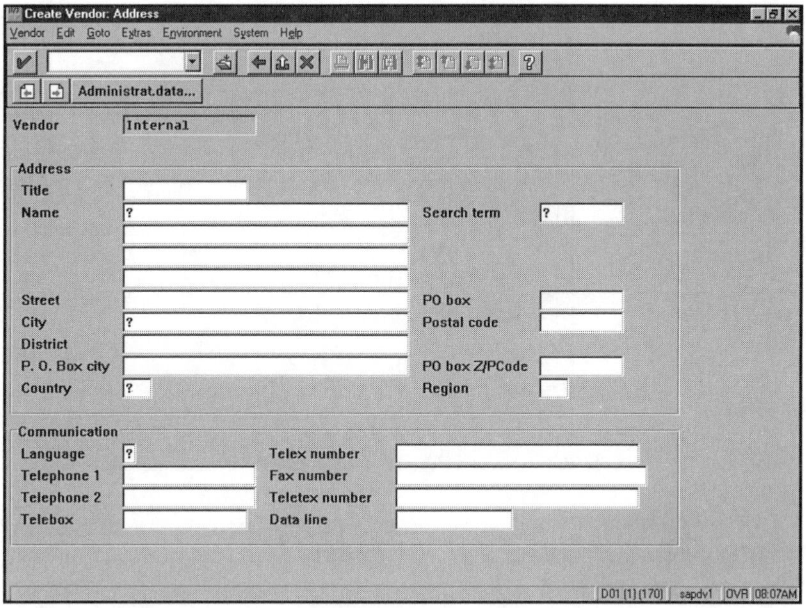

FIG. 6.13

The Vendor Master Address screen.

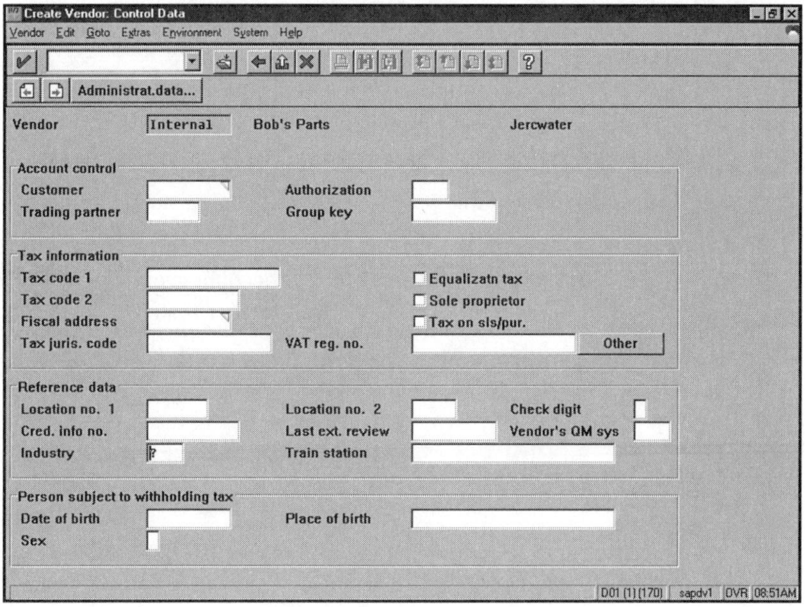

FIG. 6.14

The Vendor Master Control Data screen.

FIG. 6.15

The Vendor Master Payment Transactions screen.

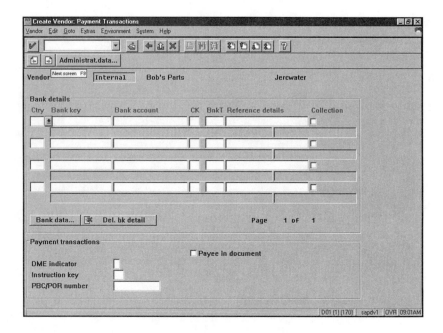

Vendor Master Data by Company Code

The following three screens of data are held at the company code level in the SAP hierarchy and are typically viewed as accounting data. These screens are the Accounting info. screen (see Figure 6.16), the Payment Transactions screen (see Figure 6.17), and the Correspondence screen (see Figure 6.18), respectively. Separate values can be maintained on these screens for each company within an enterprise. Examples of accounting data include General Ledger reconciliation account, payment terms, payment methods, and dunning data.

Vendor Master Data by Purchasing Organization

The final two screens of the Vendor Master hold information at the purchasing organization level. These screens are the Purchasing Data screen (see Figure 6.19) and the Partner Function screen (see Figure 6.20). Examples of data maintained on these screens include payment conditions, vendor control data, and partner functions. Because this information is purchasing-organization specific, separate purchasing organizations within an enterprise can set and maintain different values for the fields on these screens.

FIG. 6.16
The Vendor Master
Accounting Info. screen.

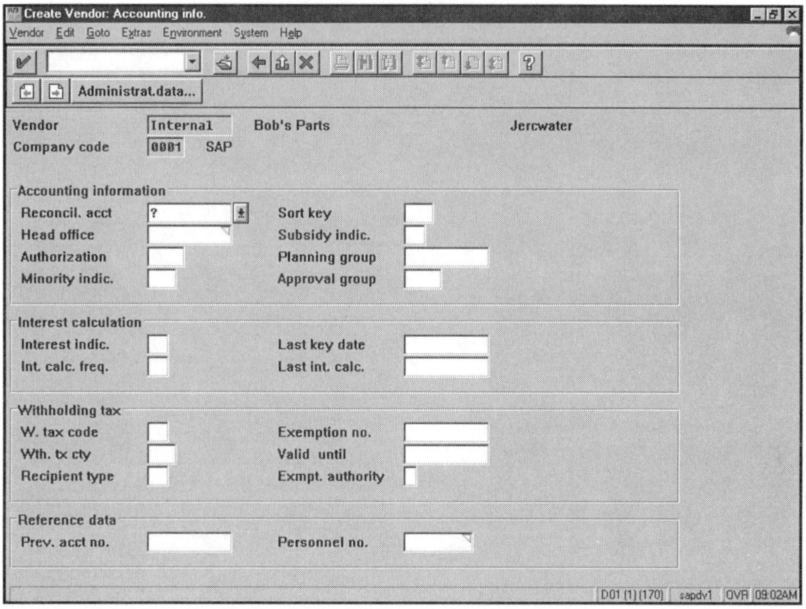

FIG. 6.17
The Vendor Master
Payment Transactions
screen.

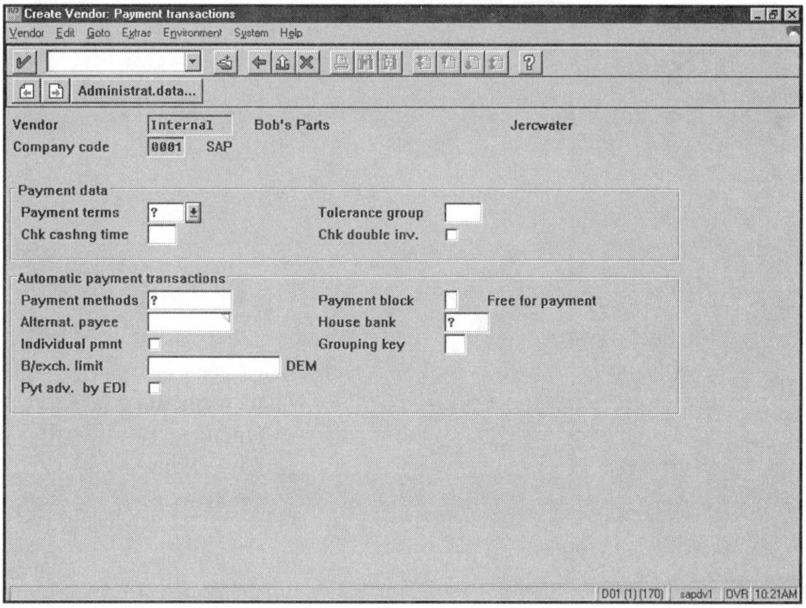

FIG. 6.18

The Vendor Master Correspondence screen.

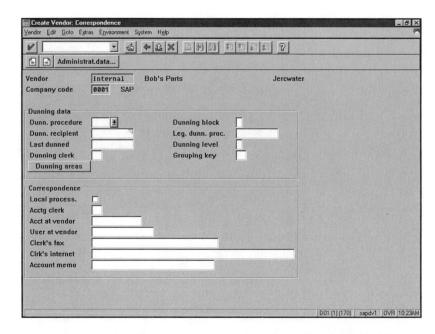

FIG. 6.19

The Vendor Master Purchasing Data screen.

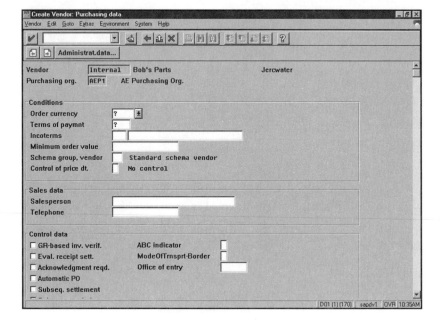

FIG. 6.20

The Vendor Master Partner Functions screen.

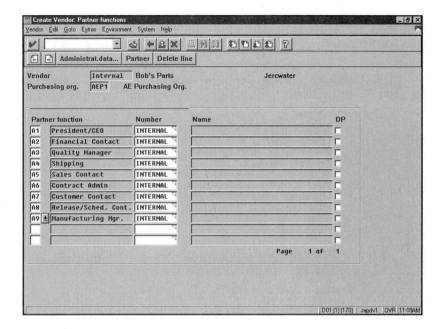

Additional Vendor Master Data

In addition to the data and screens previously mentioned, the SAP system allows you to define data that is relevant only for a vendor subrange, plant, or combination of the two. This gives even more flexibility in allowing different values to be maintained for a single vendor. This functionality is particularly important in the retail industry.

Now that you've looked at what the Vendor Master record is and what types of data are maintained within it, you'll learn how the Vendor Master is used. In general, the information stored in the Vendor Master record is accessed by the system when performing purchasing transactions. When writing a purchase order, for example, the system will check the Vendor Master record to pull an address, information on how to transmit the purchase order, payment terms, and other data into the purchase order. This information can be modified on the purchase order if desired or simply accepted as accurate. Other purchasing documents that reference the Vendor Master include contracts, scheduling agreements, and requests for quotes. These documents will be discussed later.

The Vendor Master serves other purposes besides holding information to be used as default data in purchasing documents. For example, the Vendor Master serves to collect payables. All purchases made from the vendor and outstanding payables to that vendor are captured against the Vendor Master record. This ensures that the Accounts Payable department sends the correct payment to the correct outside suppliers. In addition, the vendor can be blocked for procurement, supply source lists can be created for specific materials, and specific vendor-material relationships can be defined using the Vendor Master record.

Part

I

Ch

6

Customer Master

In SAP, a business partner is any person or legal entity with whom you can conduct business. This may be somebody who provides services and materials to your company (vendors), somebody who buys your product and services (customers), or even the salesperson who markets your company's products (personnel). These business partners have to exist within the organizational structure that you have set up for your company. This section will give you a general overview of the Customer Master, the fields in the master, and how they are used.

A customer can interact with your business in many capacities. It could be a person that you sell to, the person that you ship your product to, or a person who pays for the product. Normally, this is one and the same entity. It could also be three different parties. For an example, I could live in Chicago and order a birthday gift from your company to be shipped directly to my mother in Cleveland, and pay for the purchase with a credit card. In this case, you sold the product to me, shipped it to my mother, and collected payment from my credit card company.

Customer Master Organization

SAP structures each business partner's master data according to the role or capacity that particular business partner plays. The SAP standard system delivers four basic structures for the customer master: sold-to partner, ship-to partner, payer, and bill-to partner. Using the above example, I would be your sold-to partner, my mother would be your ship-to partner, and my credit card company would be both your payer and bill-to partner. If the customer is a large company, its function may be separated by functional departments. The Purchasing department may be the sold-to partner, its offsite plant may be the ship-to partner, and its Accounting department may be the payer and bill-to partner.

Sold-to Partner   Most of the time, a sold-to partner is also a ship-to, a payer, and a bill-to partner. SAP recognizes this fact and assigns a sold-to partner with the other partner functions. As a result, a sold-to partner has the most information stored within its structure. Data stored in the sold-to partner that does not exist within other structures is sales information, such as pricing information and sales office information.

Ship-to Partner   If a customer is designated as the ship-to party only, it will contain information unique to shipping such as unloading dock, dock hours, shipping strategy, transportation zone, preferred shipping plant, and export restrictions.

Payer   Information unique to payer includes terms of payment, billing schedule, payment method (check or wire transfer), and bank information.

Bill-to Partner   The bill-to partner's main function is to provide an address to whom a bill and follow-up correspondence will be sent. Connection to invoice format and electronic data communication may also be kept in this structure.

One-time Customer   You are not required to create a customer master for each of your customers. When it is not necessary to keep individual customer records after a sales transaction occurs (as in the case of a one-time customer), a collective or a dummy master record can be created and used. For example, customers in a geographic area can be designated as collective customers and be assigned a one-time customer number. The one-time Customer Master record will include basic data required for identifying that group of collective customers such as names, countries, and languages. Other information, such as an actual customer name, address, and payment terms, can be captured at the time of order entry.

Customer Master Structure

Similar to a Vendor Master, the various functions for a customer are differentiated by account groups. This ensures that only the necessary screens and fields are displayed for data entry and viewing. In the account group, you can also specify whether the customer numbers are system-assigned or user-assigned, and specify the number range for either assignment.

In addition, the Customer Master is also organized to accommodate the users. The two main user groups for the Customer Master are the Sales and Distribution department and the Accounting department. The Customer Master record can be accessed at three levels and is structured per Figure 6.21.

FIG. 6.21

The Customer Master structure with general data on one level; company code data and Sales and Distribution data on a lower level.

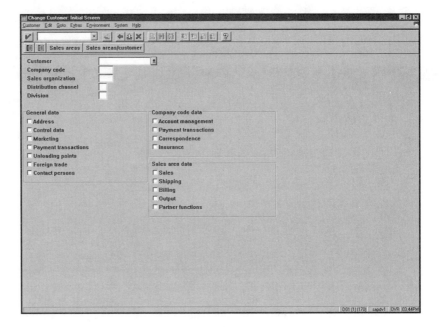

The three levels are described as follows:

- General data includes general information pertaining to the customer as a whole. It does not depend on the company code or sales and distribution factors. Examples include name, address, and telephone number. General data can be accessed through either the Sales and Distribution or the Financial Accounting modules.

- Company code data is important to the Accounting department. It includes data such as account management, payment transaction, dunning procedure, and insurance information.

■ Sales and distribution data is, of course, important to the Sales and Distribution department. Data is unique to a sales area, which is the combination of the sales organization, distribution channel, and division (refer to the "Organizational Structures" section earlier in this chapter for details). It includes data on sales, shipping, billing, output documents, and partner functions.

Creating a Customer Master Record

A Customer Master can be created by either the Accounting or the Sales and Distribution department, through either the Financial Accounting or the Sales and Distribution module. In the following example, you will create a sold-to partner using the Sales and Distribution module. Choose from the menu path: Logistic > Sales and Distribution > Master Data > Business Partners > Sold-to Party > Create > Create, and you will see the screen in Figure 6.22.

FIG. 6.22

The Create Sold-To Party screen.

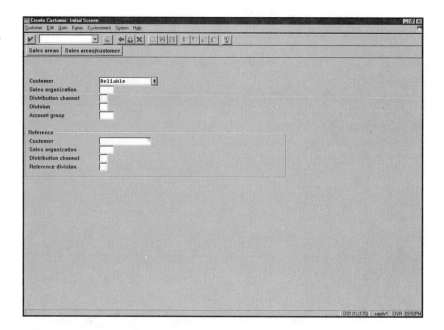

You have to provide the sales area to which this customer will be associated. The Account Group field will default to 0001 for Sold-to Party. The standard SAP system will assign a number for this customer record, so leave the Customer Number field blank.

Following is a list of the screens that will be displayed for input. The list does not represent all fields contained in the Customer Master. By the same token, not all fields listed have to be populated with data before the Customer Master can be used.

Address Screen   The Address screen contains the following fields:

Name: Name of your sold-to partner.

Search Term: A key field with which the customer can be retrieved by using the match code.

Control Data Screen   The Control Data screen contains the following fields:

Vendor:	For your customer who is also a vendor (that is, you buy supplies from him or her and also sell your products to him or her). You can create a Vendor Master for this customer and input the number in this field. There is a similar field in the Vendor Master in which you can input the Customer Master.
Tax Jurisdiction Code:	The code used to determine the sales and use tax rate, if one was applicable to this customer.
Transport Zone:	One of the codes used to determine transportation method and timing for the customer.

Unloading Points Screen   The Unloading Points screen contains the following field:

Goods Receiving Hours:	Times at which your customer receiving dock is open for business. This may be printed on the bill of lading as part of the shipping instruction.

Foreign Trade Screen   The Foreign Trade screen contains the following field:

Table of Denial:	Trade restriction/embargo information can be entered here.

Sales Screen   The Sales screen contains the following field:

Pricing/Statistics:	Price grouping and statistics information can be entered here. This information will feed programs in which prices for the customers can be determined and/or reported.

Shipping Screen   The Shipping screen contains the following fields:

Shipping Condition:	One of the codes to determine shipping strategy for this customer.
Partial Delivery Data:	Indicates whether the customer allows partial delivery for its shipments.

Billing Screen   The Billing screen contains the following fields:

Billing Schedule:	The billing cycle for the customer, for example monthly or weekly billing.
Payment terms:	Cash discount and rate information.
Accounting Assignment Group:	An indicator that can be used to determine revenue account posting in the General Ledger.
Tax Classification:	Code to indicate whether a tax calculation is to be carried out for this customer.

Many of the fields previously listed will be copied to a sales order as an order is taken from the customer. Populating as many of the Customer Master fields provides a time-saving tool, as this data will not have to be input every time a new order is created. At the same time, SAP allows flexibility by allowing users to override the defaulted information in the order.

After the sales and distribution and general data have been entered, the Accounting department has to complete the company code information for this customer. This is done through the Financial Accounting module. You get there by following the menu path: Accounting > Financial Accounting > Accounts Receivable > Master Records > Create (see Figure 6.23).

FIG. 6.23

The Create Customer accounts receivable screen.

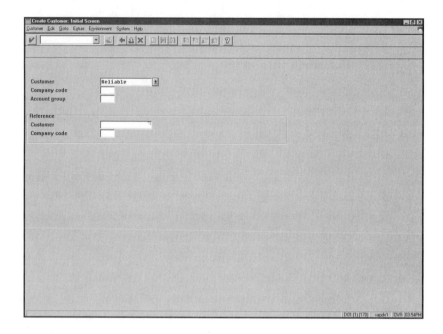

Provide the customer number that was assigned by the system when the sales and distribution data was created. Then press Enter.

Account Management Screen   The Account Management screen contains the following field:

Reconciliation Account: A General Ledger account used to group the A/R subledger accounts.

Payment Transaction Screen   The Payment Transaction screen contains the following field:

Payment Term: Cash discount and rate information. This is the same information entered in the Billing screen, but will be used for invoices created directly in the Financial Accounting module. In contrast, the other Payment Term field will be used when generating an automatic invoice from the Sales and Distribution module.

Correspondence Screen   The Correspondence screen contains the following field:

Dunning Procedure: Code to indicate method and timing of accounts receivable collection correspondence.

Human Resources Master Data

The end-user view for Human Resources information in SAP is the information type, or *infotype* for short. The infotype is unique to the Human Resource module and is nothing more than a grouping of similar data fields, loosely translating into a table, in traditional Information Systems language. (An entry in an infotype would translate into a record on one or many data tables.) A four-digit numeric key identifies infotypes. For example, infotype 0006, the Address infotype, contains the fields relevant to an employee's place of residence, including street, city, state, and zip code. Other examples of infotypes include

0001—Organizational Assignment, which includes such data elements as where the employee is assigned

0002—Personal Data, which includes such data elements as first name, last name, Social Security number, and birth date

0008—Basic Pay, which includes such data elements as earnings codes and amounts

An element of some infotypes is the information subtype, or *subtype* for short. The subtype further breaks down the infotype record. For example, the Address infotype contains subtypes for permanent address, home address, and secondary address. Rather than create a separate infotype record for each address type, the subtype allows for all address types to be stored in one location. Other infotypes that contain subtypes are Recurring Payments and Deductions and Additional Payments.

There are three methods for updating Human Resource infotype records.

The first method is single screen maintenance, which is used for maintaining the fields of an individual infotype. The user goes directly to the infotype for the individual employee and updates the relevant information. An example would be updating an individual employee's address change in the Address infotype.

The second method is via personnel events. A personnel event is a process that requires the user to create or update multiple infotypes in order to complete the event. For example, the hiring event may incorporate the Organizational Assignment, Event, Address, Personal Data, Benefits, Planned Working Time, and Basic Pay infotypes. Each of these infotypes will be called up for input automatically when the hiring event is processed in SAP. The infotypes are processed in a logical sequence. An additional feature of SAP is the dynamic event, where certain screens may be called up based upon information entered for an employee. For example, if you enter in the Personal Data infotype that Joe Smith is married, the Family/Related Persons infotype will automatically be called up for input as well.

The final method for updating infoytpe records is via the fast entry function. This method allows the user to maintain an infotype for multiple employees at the same time, using one screen. Lists of personnel numbers can be created either manually or generated using specified selection criteria.

Part
I

Ch
6

In SAP, when you update an infotype, the old information is not deleted; rather, it is kept as historical information. Each infotype record contains a validity period, meaning a to and from date, during which the associated employee data is legitimate. Therefore, an employee may have multiple records for an infotype, but the validity period indicates which record(s) are currently active. SAP uses time constraints to define the relationship between multiple infotype records for an employee. The three time constraints are described as follows:

Time Constraint 1 requires that at any given point in a person's employment, only one record may be valid for the infotype. Periods of validity cannot overlap, and when a new record is created, the previous one is delimited, or ended, at the begin date of the new record. One valid record must always exist for the employee. This time constraint applies particularly to personal data and organizational assignment. An example is the Basic Pay infotype. An employee may have only one standard pay rate at a given time.

Time Constraint 2 requires that at any point in time, no more than one valid record may exist. Overlaps are not allowed, and the existence of a record is not obligatory. When a new record is created, the previous one is delimited if necessary. An example is the Family/Related Persons infotype, for the spouse subtype. When last checked, employees were only allowed to have one spouse at a time.

Time Constraint 3 allows any number of records to be valid at any given time. Individual records do not affect one another. An example is the Family/Related Persons, when entering information for children. Time Constraint 3 allows for more than one child to be stored in the system.

The most commonly used infotypes are grouped together according to their content and are contained in menus. SAP delivers standard system menus, such as the Basic Personnel Data and Gross Payroll; however, the client may customize menus to suit the job functions performed by the various Human Resources functions and roles. This customization is accommodated in the Implementation Guide.

Some of the infotypes that constitute Human Resource master data are

- Events (briefly described previously in this section) are groups of related infotypes that can be used for the following: hiring an employee, changing an employee's pay, changing an employee's organizational assignment, or changing an employee's status. When the Personnel Event infotype 0000 is initiated, a series of infotypes are automatically pulled up for input into the system.

- The Organizational Assignment infotype 0001 defines how the employee fits into the company structure and personnel administrative structure. The information defined here includes the employee's job, position, and organization unit. In addition, the employee can be assigned to a cost center in this infotype. When integration between the SAP submodules of Personnel Planning and Development and Personnel Administration is active, you can have the system default the job and organizational unit according to the employee's position assignment.

- The Personal Data infotype stores data for an individual employee. This infotype is comprised of the following information: the employee's name, including first name, last name, name at birth, name by which the employee is known, initials, academic title, name prefixes, and name suffixes. Also included is date of birth, place of birth, nationality and language, number of children, and marital status.

■ The Address infotype consists of data that describes where an employee lives such as street, city, state, and zip code. SAP can conduct validity checks on allowable zip codes for the indicated state. This infotype also has several subtypes, such as Permanent, Temporary, and Mailing.

■ An employee's working schedule is recorded on the Planned Working Time infotype (0007). This infotype also defines how the employee's time is processed—either exception reporting or complete reporting of time information. This infotype is required to calculate basic pay and must always be recorded before the Basic Pay infotype.

■ Base salary information is recorded on the Basic Pay infotype (0008). Using the Planned Working Time infotype, the SAP system calculates an employee's annual, monthly, biweekly, weekly, and daily wage amounts. To eliminate data entry errors, you have the ability to default the pay rates using pay scale grades and levels.

■ The Payroll Status infotype is created automatically when the employee is hired. It provides the data that relates to when the employee's last pay was processed through the SAP system and the starting date of allowable calculation of retroactive pay. This infotype also has a field that indicates the need for retroactive calculation when an infotype such as Basic Pay has been changed with a validity date before the last payroll run.

Walking through this hiring event, realize that as a customer of SAP, you have the ability to build your hiring event to meet your business practice needs. You can add as many infotypes to the process or have as few infotypes as those previously listed. The main thing to realize is that the information you put in a system is the information you will get out of a system.

The General Ledger

General Ledger (G/L) accounts are the backbone for the entire SAP system. All transactions that affect external reporting requirements are reflected in G/L accounts. For instance, a goods receipt (MM) will increase the inventory account, just as billing a customer (SD) will increase the receivable account.

G/L accounts are ultimately used to produce reports to meet legal requirements (that is, balance sheets, profit and loss statements, and cash flow statements). The G/L accounts identify what types of expenses and income make up a company's business. Using G/L accounts, each transaction can be classified as revenue, expense, liability, and so on. Within these broad sections, G/L accounts identify specifics; for instance, within the expense category, wages would be tracked separately from benefit expenses.

Each G/L account has two control levels that must be created before posting to the account. The two sections are the chart of accounts section and the company code section. The chart of accounts section is only created once for each G/L account number. The company code section, however, must be created for each company that needs to post to the account.

Part
I

Ch
6

Chart of Accounts Level Data

The chart of accounts control section contains general data about the account including name, account type, and account group (see Figure 6.24). This data applies to all companies that use the account.

FIG. 6.24

The initial data entry screen for creating a G/L account, Create G/L Account: Control Ch/Accts.

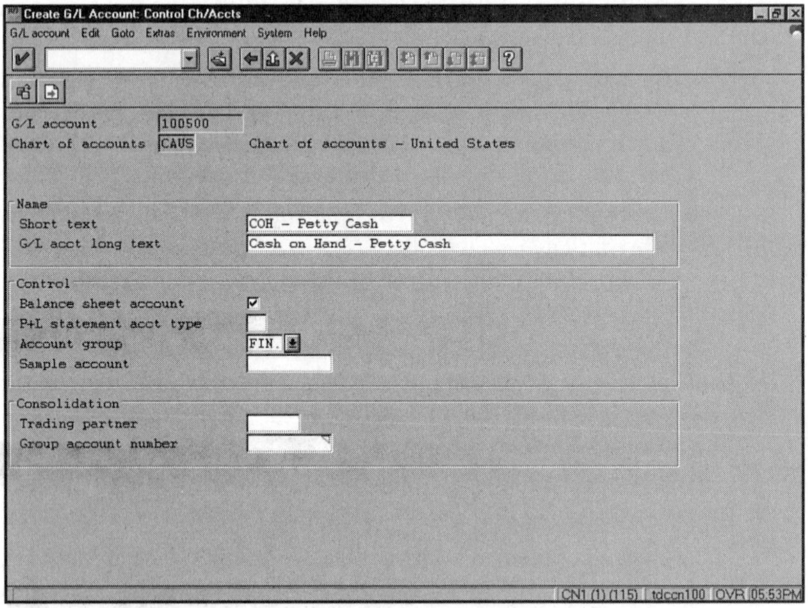

The Short Text field is used for drop-down lists of available accounts. It should be descriptive enough to indicate to the user which account is appropriate. When space permits, the G/L Acct Long Text field is used for the account description.

There are two fields to choose from to determine the account type. Only one field must be completed to continue creating the master data. The first field, Balance Sheet Account, indicates that the account is a balance sheet account. As such, its balances will not be cleared out at the end of each fiscal year. The next field, P+L Statement Acct Type, however, defines the account as a profit and loss account. The indicator in this field determines the retained earnings account to which the account will be carried forward.

The account group defines both the valid account number range and the field status for the master data creation. The number ranges are used to logically group different types of accounts. So, account group cash accounts, for instance, could identify a range of accounts from 100000 through 150000. To set up a cash account using this account group, the account number would have to be in the range between 100000 and 150000. Additionally, the account group also identifies which fields will be suppressed, required, or optional during the entry of the company code control section. For example, the cash account group can require that the field Relevant to Cash Flow be checked. This will ensure that all accounts in the cash account group will have the field checked.

Company Code Level Data

The company code control section identifies company code-specific settings for the account (see Figure 6.25). These settings are established for every company that needs to post to the account. The account control section includes fields to determine the account currency and the tax category as well as whether the account can be posted to in a foreign currency.

FIG. 6.25

The initial data entry screen for creating a G/L account, Create G/L Account: Control Comp. Code.

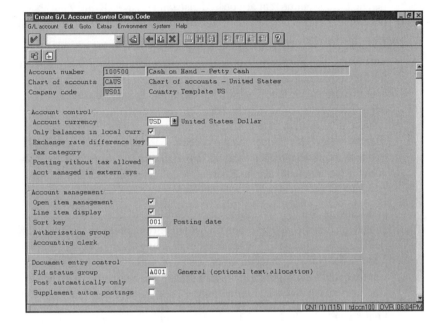

Currency The first editable field in this section is Account Currency. This field identifies the currency to which the system will post transactions. The currency will typically match that of the company's local currency. However, if a U.S. company had a Canadian bank account, for instance, the account currency should be Canadian dollars. The field Only balances in local curr. is selected if no transaction should be posted to the account in a foreign currency.

Tax Category The Tax Category field determines what types of taxes can be posted to this account. For instance, a revenue account should only allow output taxes (for example, sales tax) and not input taxes (for example, use tax). All categories can be permitted on the account by indicating an * in this field.

Open Item Management The field labeled Open Item Management determines whether the account can use SAP clearing functionality. Postings to accounts managed on an open item basis can be cleared from the account. This is commonly used in A/P, A/R, and clearing accounts. In the example of an A/P account, a credit entry is initially posted to the account to identify the amount due to the vendor. At the time of payment, a corresponding debit is posted to the A/P account to reduce the amount due. With open item management functionality, the two equal and offsetting amounts are cleared so that future reports on the account do display the values. Therefore, only the items that are open remain on the account display.

Part

I

Ch

6

Line Item Display   The Line Item Display indicator determines whether the individual line items that are posted to the account can be displayed through reports. For the most part, the indicator should be selected so that line item display is possible during reporting. The line item display allows the user to drill down from an account balance to the individual documents that were posted to the account. Reconciliation accounts, however, should not have line item display selected. Reconciliation accounts, such as A/P and A/R, are meant to keep balances in FI for detailed transactions that are posted elsewhere. An A/P entry, for example, is posted to a vendor account and only that balance is brought into the A/P reconciliation account. The vendor accounts contain the details behind the A/P balance.

Sort Key   The Sort Key field defines posting data that the system will capture in the Allocation field on a document. The Allocation field can then be used in reporting to sort data. The cost center value, for instance, can be indicated as the sort key on certain expense accounts. Reports on those accounts can be sorted by the Allocation field in which the cost center is populated. The Allocation field is also used for automatic clearing of accounts. Clearing accounts, such as the goods receipt/invoice receipt (GR/IR) account, captures the offset entries of both goods receipts and invoice entries. The amounts should match and balance to zero. The GR/IR account can automatically be cleared based on the value in the Allocation field. In this case, the purchase order number would likely be the sort key value.

Field Status Group   The Field Status Group field has the most impact on the transactions posted against the account. The field status group identifies which fields are suppressed, required, or optional during transaction data entry. This indicator forces the users to enter values into the fields that have been identified as required in the field status group. For instance, Cost Center could be required for accounts that must be posted to a cost center. Additionally, accounts to which cost accounting does not apply could have the Cost Center field suppressed.

Post Automatically Only   The Post Automatically Only field prevents users from manually making entries to an account. Accounts that have this indicator selected can be posted to from other modules (for example, MM and SD). The GR/IR account previously mentioned is a good example of this. Entries made to the GR/IR account are generated by SAP to balance an entry. The goods are marked as received, creating a debit entry to inventory, but that information alone would generate a one-sided entry. SAP automatically posts the credit entry offset to the GR/IR account.

Most of the transactions made from other modules have an impact on the financial records of a company; therefore, many SAP transactions create a posting to G/L accounts. It is through these accounts that a company can report to outside investors the financial position of the company. For this reason, the G/L accounts really are the backbone of the SAP system.

Transactional Data

Once the SAP R/3 system is configured and the appropriate master data is set up, it's time to go to work. This statement isn't intended to oversimplify the configuration and master data set-ups, rather it is intended to point out that the ultimate goal of implementing SAP R/3 is to run a business. Running a business means entering data or, in other terms, conducting business transactions.

Transactional data is the dynamic data. It encompasses the system inputs that represent all work such as entering a purchase order or sales order, entering a confirmation of production activities, or posting a goods movement. Several such transactions will be discussed in detail in later chapters of this book.

In Review

Hopefully, this chapter has demonstrated that there is a significant difference in the three data types used in SAP. When implementing R/3, the three data types somewhat blend together. Generally, the data is utilized in the order presented. Configuration, specifically base configuration, comes first. Next, master data is loaded into the system, and lastly, transactional data is processed. Obviously, changes and additions can occur to any of the three types of data at any time.

You are now ready to meet Electro Tech, the fictional company you will use in your case studies. The company will be introduced, and the type of configuration, master, and transactional data it encounters on a daily basis will be defined. The data of doing business is also the data used in SAP. ●

Part

I

Ch

6

Meet Electro Tech, Inc.

As explained in the "Understanding the Book's Approach" section of the Introduction, you are now going to be introduced to Electro Tech. Electro Tech is a fictional company, created from the collection of a variety of true-life business practices. While not intended to represent any one company, it is intended to represent the reality that exists in many companies today. Through the analysis of Electro Tech's strengths and weaknesses, the advantages SAP R/3 can provide will be demonstrated.

Introducing Electro Tech

Electro Tech is approximately a 500 million dollar manufacturer of industrial electrical components and factory automation products. It has been in business since the late 1950s, demonstrating consistent growth through the '60s, '70s, and '80s. Electro Tech is not unique in the successes it has had or the problems it faces. Declining customer satisfaction with delayed shipments, high quality failure rates, and increasing inventory levels are just a few of the difficulties facing Electro Tech.

To understand how these problems came about, and the difficulties in conquering them, you must first understand how Electro Tech grew through the years. By understanding the source of Electro Tech's problems, you can also understand how SAP can help.

The Company History

As previously stated, Electro Tech makes electronic components for industry power systems as well as factory automation products. The company has prospered through new product development and a strong market presence. Electro Tech originally sprang from engineering roots through the development of low-priced, long-lasting electrical components. As the company grew, top engineers moved into management and supervisory positions dealing with manufacturing, quality management, and even human resources.

Over time, inevitably, there was a need for information. Payroll had to be automated, invoicing couldn't remain a manual operation. Inventory reporting grew so big that the tubs and tubs of inventory cards that had to be updated everyday took so much time and were so inaccurate that Electro Tech required a complete inventory of all operations each month just to make the inventory balances on the cards accurate for the succeeding month.

Early attempts were made by the Management Information Systems department to capture Electro Tech's key information. Homespun programs written in COBOL or FORTRAN for mainframe systems allowed specific groupings of information to be collected. Due to budgetary constraints and staffing limitations, systems for each department were constructed at different times, often in varying program code or on varying hardware platforms. Data collection was empowered, but cross-functional integration was lost. This was a typical problem for industry during the late 1970s and 1980s.

A Gradual Awakening of the Technology Age

Slowly, as Electro Tech's management became aware of what their competition and customers were doing with information, they added budget requests for MIS activities to their meetings. Additional MIS resources were hired; primarily these people were programmers with systems backgrounds or recent graduates trained in the latest computer program languages. As this area began to grow, some existing employees chose to alter their career paths to grab available management positions in the information systems arena.

As business complexity grew, as government increased its requirements of business for supplying information, as customers needed knowledge from their suppliers, the first homegrown systems began to strain. New code was developed and old code was changed. Documentation of the requirement of these systems took on a more complex dimension as the career paths of information specialists actually heated up, and the original programmers were promoted or left the company.

The perception began to be refined that information is an asset of the company. As important as the wonder programmers and system analysts were, they were transient; the systems were here forever. The company had to develop a knowledge base that wasn't specific to a valued employee. Staffs grew again.

There was still a perception that no software developed by strangers outside of the company could actually be used and software developed internally would be better. It was not possible for a generic computer package to encompass the subtle nuances of Electro Tech's business. Information engineering was judged as just another form of engineering and Electro Tech was founded on engineering roots.

Then came the financial packages—standalone software that replaced the manual general ledger. Accounts Payable systems came from the same vendors that had the same chart of accounts as the general ledger (the company's first integrated applications). Accounts Receivable was next. Using the order entry information, a standalone Receivables package was the pride of the company—it was the first package that actually had colors other than green or yellow.

After the budget was expanded, the VP of Sales and Marketing went on a two-year sales campaign to get a state-of-the-art order entry system that worked on a minicomputer. The data generated could be passed to the mainframe software with some work by the MIS staff.

While all of this was occurring, Electro Tech enjoyed the economics of the '70s and '80s. The global economy was developing and Electro Tech began to build plants in Thailand and Western Europe. These plants used the same engineering principles as the American plants. In most cases, the engineers modified existing plants, updating them for the latest equipment and technology, finding the closest suppliers of this equipment and building as they did in the U.S.

By this time, the personal computer was available and the Engineering departments at Electro Tech had the budgets to purchase the first PCs in the company. When the engineers discovered Visicalc and Lotus 1-2-3, their project accounting and control became automated. In wasn't unusual to see floppy disks from all over the world appearing on projects to help the project engineers and managers with their detailed paperwork.

Part

I

Ch

7

As prices decreased, the Accounting department finally found the advantages of these personal computers and began using them extensively. Manufacturing supervisors, quality engineers, and HR personnel collected isolated bits of data. Decisions were made from the data available in a disjointed collection of databases and spreadsheets. Imperfect decisions resulted from incomplete information. These decisions, while intended to better the company, have contributed to the many problems Electro Tech faces today.

Now, yet another problem faces Electro Tech. Its many separate, homespun computer systems are not year-2000 compliant. Accounting systems, purchasing systems, inventory systems, and production planning systems are all in jeopardy. Estimates have placed the cost of correcting these systems approaching millions of dollars. These costs are only half the problem. Long-term contracts already require manual intervention and management due to year-2000 problems.

The Complete Electro Tech Picture

To complete the fictional picture of Electro Tech, you must finally examine its geographic structure. As previously explained, Electro Tech is a Midwestern company. Its corporate office housing the Controlling Management, Customer Service Organization, MIS functions, and R&D activities is located in Cincinnati, OH. Four manufacturing facilities are spread throughout the Midwest with the largest plant located in Anderson, IN. From the four facilities, they service customers across the U.S. and in Europe.

The Electro Tech story is not uncommon in industry today. It represents a typical evolution carried out in many companies. The boon the business-consulting world has seen in the late 1980s and 1990s can be directly related to similar stories. Companies worldwide have recognized that their managerial structures are often weighted with people experienced with a single discipline, whether it be engineers, programmers, accountants, or MBAs. For this reason, many companies have sought outside resources to help re-engineer business practices and to upgrade information systems. Electro Tech has chosen SAP R/3 as one power tool for resolving both of these problems. ●

The Customer Service Desk

A Day-in-the-life of the Customer Service Desk

In this chapter

A typical day-in-the-life of a customer service representative at Electro Tech

The working structure of Electro Tech, and how the lack of information flow from one work group to another can cause service problems and incur added costs

The lack of integration between homespun computer systems, and how this lack of integration has caused problems

The first example you will examine is a typical day at the Customer Service department of Electro Tech. The job of a Customer Service Representative (CSR) is to be the interface between the customer and Electro Tech. The CSR may talk to both the customer and the manufacturing facility daily in an attempt to assure quality service and on-time delivery. Unfortunately for many CSRs, changing customer demands and manufacturing schedules don't always match. From this example, you will see how SAP R/3 can help.

Understanding the Customer Service Desk

As you look at the Customer Service department of Electro Tech, you see a typical business environment—an open area full of cubicles, each equipped with a dumb terminal attached to the mainframe and a multiline telephone. The outer wall contains the offices of managers for varying customer service functions. The Electro Tech Customer Service department is open Monday through Friday 7:00 a.m. to 8:00 p.m. EST. An overutilized emergency number is available to Electro Tech's "A" customers on evenings and weeks.

Looking at a typical day in the Customer Service department, you meet Bob Peters. Bob has been working at the order desk of Electro Tech for about five years after working for Electro Tech as a summer intern. He was involved in the latest upgrade of the Customer First project that added some badly needed functions to Electro Tech's home-grown Order Management system—simply called *Order It*.

About five years ago, customers began to complain that they never knew for certain when they would receive their orders. The CSR would give a customer a delivery date, but when the buyers called in to ask about their orders, often another seven days was added to the delivery time. The causes of these delays varied and often seemed complex, but the bottom line was customer dissatisfaction.

Bob was part of the team that developed an improvement to the system. Today, every production run scheduled at the factory over the succeeding two weeks is sent to the order clerks by fax. Along with this report, the MIS department prints out the daily plant and distribution center inventory report for each of the order clerks. Now, when the customers call, Bob is armed with the latest inventory and the latest production schedule. It is a "perfect" system. Customer complaints were cut in half and every time a customer called on the status of the order, Bob could give a specific date, not just the typical "five working days from tomorrow" that he relied in the past.

The Players

The following is a list of the employees involved in the Electro Tech customer service example.

- Bob Peters—Customer Service Representative
- Sam Soot—Customer from Reliable Manufactures
- Bryan Luther—Plant Production Scheduler
- Frank Brewer—Quality Control Analyst

- Brad Tuttle—Technical Services Manager
- Laurie Stewart—Warehouse and Ship Dock Manager

The Situation

On this Monday morning, Bob arrives at his desk about 15 minutes before his shift. Because it's a Midwestern company, the early order desk shift covers East Coast time. The second shift is set up to cover orders later in the day arriving from the West Coast.

Gradually, the rest of the early shift arrives and arms themselves for the day. Bob pulls the latest copy of the plant inventory report off the printer, cuts the margins off so he can fit it on his desk, and pulls out his red, green, and yellow markers so that he can mark up the report once customer calls and plant changes are called in. This is necessary because the *Order It* system is not integrated with the production scheduling or inventory systems that the manufacturing facilities use.

Bob answers his phone and finds himself talking to Sam Soot of Reliable Manufactures. Sam is calling to check the status of order SH1000655 at the request of his manufacturing manager. Apparently, Reliable's customer requested an emergency shipment in five days, but the equipment used to manufacture Reliable's best-selling product is down due to automation system problems. The parts necessary to fix the problem were included in order SH1000655, which is now a week late.

Bob has been through this so many times that he instinctively goes into his routine. He explains that order SH1000655 is delayed because part number A1Z1, a current sensor with relay output used in automation systems, is behind manufacturing schedule but is due off the line later today. Bob guesses and adds one day for packaging and test time, and then tells Sam the order could be shipped the day after tomorrow (Wednesday).

The Problem

Bob feels pretty good and begins to update the system's Date Required By Customer field to Wednesday, when the buyer responds with concern. Sam says, "Excuse me, but we've called two times in the last week and have received the same treatment. You guys either don't know what is going on or you feel you can treat us customers as if we don't have customers that we care about. I'll take that date, but you better make sure that the stuff gets to us or it's the last order you get from us. We are already evaluating alternate vendors."

Bob had been through this before as well. His training had been very effective in pointing out that the Order Desk is the most important part of the company—the buck stops there. He is personally and professionally responsible for appeasing the customer—making the customer feel that Electro Tech is looking at him or her as if he or she is the only customer Electro Tech has.

Bob apologizes and explains that all of his reports show that this order is going to be there. He assures Sam that he will make a special call to the plant to ensure that everything is OK. He confirms Sam's telephone number and tells him he will call if there are any problems with the order. Bob then thanks Sam for calling and assures him that Reliable is an honored customer.

After Bob enters the new delivery date in the system, he fills out his log. Bob's biggest decision is whether to use the yellow pen for a caution or the red pen for alert. Bob decides on the yellow pen.

The morning progresses at a similar pace. Bob enters several new orders and deals with other customers' concerns about delivery dates and quality problems. By 11:00 a.m. the next shift is helping to eat into the volume, and the East Coast is out to lunch. Bob decides to check on some of his action items. He calls Bryan Luther, the Plant Production Scheduler, to check on the orders in question so far.

Bryan is the main point of contact for CSRs with questions about the plant's schedule. In his production-scheduling role, he has to balance the sales order demand with the plant's production. Bob begins to run down his list of red and yellow line items when Bryan informs him that preventative maintenance over the weekend has them a day-and-a-half behind schedule in the department that manufactures the A1Z1 current sensors with relay output.

After a long pause, Bob says, "You can't be serious, Bryan. I just got off the phone with the buyer at Reliable and assured him that we'd have the order to them. Can you shut down the maintenance until we get the order out?" Bryan explains that it's too late. "The maintenance is almost complete now, but it will take most of the remainder of the day to get the equipment buttoned up and running." He also reminds Bob that the preventative maintenance will help prevent future problems and more order delays.

Bob has been down this road before also and knows that his only chance is the off-spec list. This is a special list generated from the plant inventory system. Every Friday, the plant QC department reviews the inventory of material that is marginally off-spec and places a potential distribution on it. Sometimes, if the right customer called, it is possible to match the customer requirements with some production made off-spec.

Bob finds the list and begins to review the pages of material for the product A1Z1. Finally, a lucky break. The off-spec report shows lot 970114A of 50 pieces on quality hold. Bob looks at the distribution and finds Frank Brewer as the QC Analyst of Record. Bob picks up the phone and hits the speed dial for the plant QC Lab.

At the other end of the line Bob hears, "QC Lab, this is Frank." Bob says, "Hi Frank, it's Bob Peters. I need your help with a lot of A1Z1s that are on the off-spec report." This is a familiar conversation; in fact, too familiar to both Bob and Frank. Bob explains his dilemma with Reliable and steers Frank to the lot of A1Z1s he has listed on the off-spec report. Normally, the lab tries to provide possible outlets for marginal material when it is listed on the off-spec report, but occasionally no outlet can be determined so the QC Analyst of Record is listed. This allows CSRs to contact the correct person in shortage situations. The specific details of the shortage and marginal material can be reviewed to see if they fit together. It is this circumstance that has brought Bob and Frank together.

Frank accesses the QC computer system to determine the problem with lot 970114A. The current sensors have specifications related to their capability to detect and react to changes in current load. The specification problem is related to the sensitivity of the sensors. They have an adjustable trip set point that is listed to have a +/- 2% range. Frank explains that the lot in question tested + 2% and – 2.3%. Bob says that seems like a minor difference and asks if the units can be released for Reliable. Frank explains that the variance in the spec may be acceptable to Reliable, but he can't release the lot without speaking to the technical service representative to Reliable.

Frank explains that the problem is with the Certificate of Compliance that is sent out with most shipments. The certificate typically lists the test results for trip point, and, if Reliable is given the exact manufacturing spec, they will reject the lot upon delivery. Frank tells Bob that the specifications that have been given to the customer are maintained by Technical Services so he will have to call them to check Reliable's file. Bob says he understands, but asks Frank to check with Technical Services immediately and get back with him as soon as possible. Frank agrees, as he too has been trained that the customer comes first.

Frank hangs up the phone and immediately picks it back up to call Brad Tuttle, Technical Services Manager for the current sensor/relay division. Brad came up through the ranks of the company and has worked in Technical Services for the last five years. Frank enjoys working with him because he knows Brad understands the balance between quality, customer satisfaction, and business decisions. Brad answers the phone, and after the normal polite discussion, Frank explains the problem with lot 970114A and Reliable.

Brad understands the difficult situation Bob and Frank are trying to resolve. "Let me check the file on Reliable, Frank," Brad says. Frank can hear the opening and closing of file drawers and the rattling of paperwork. After a moment, Frank hears Brad say, "Good news, Frank. Reliable has a spec of plus or minus 3%. Beyond that though, they don't require that trip point results be reported on the Certificate of Compliance." Frank is thrilled to hear that, but feels silly that he bothered Brad on something that isn't even reported to the customer. Frank thanks Brad for his help and hangs up to call Bob back. After several attempts to get through to Bob, Frank leaves a voice mail that the lot of A1Z1s can go to Reliable. Another crisis avoided, or so it seems.

The next business day begins with Bob checking his voice mail. He is relieved to hear the message from Frank and makes a note to follow up and thank him. Again, the morning progresses with nonstop action. Bob thinks business must be good because his phone is always ringing, yet he is concerned about the number of calls he gets dealing with late shipments or product problems. About halfway through the morning a break in the action occurs, and Bob gives Frank a quick call.

"Frank, thanks for the help yesterday," says Bob as he hears that familiar voice on the phone. "You're welcome," replies Frank. Bob goes on to explain how getting that shipment out will save the Reliable account and that if Frank hadn't made sure lot 970114A was sent on the shipment, nothing could have avoided a lost customer. Frank, puzzled by Bob's choice of words, explains that he left the voice mail for Bob yesterday and updated the off-spec report for printing on Friday but he hadn't spoken to anyone at the shipping dock. He had assumed that Bob would take care of that through the *Order It* system.

Bob's stomach begins to churn at the realization that the Reliable order hasn't shipped yet. "Frank, are you telling me you didn't call the dock to tell them which lot to use?" asks Bob. Frank explains that he didn't realize he was expected to talk to the shipping dock. The reason he had tried to call Bob several times, and eventually left a voice mail, was so Bob could talk to the appropriate people. There was more than a materials issue involved here. The proper transportation had to be lined up for a rush shipment. Frank didn't know if any special packing requirements had been agreed to with Reliable. A number of other issues could exist. Frank reminds Bob that these were issues that Customer Service normally coordinated. Bob knows Frank is right, but is still upset by the whole situation.

The Solution

Ending the conversation abruptly, Bob hangs up the phone and immediately calls the manager of the warehouse and shipping dock, Laurie Stewart. Laurie is amazing to those who know her well. She never appears rattled, even when the walls seem to be falling in around her. And somehow, she always manages to get the job done. Laurie listens carefully as Bob explains the situation with Reliable and how the shipment has to go out today. Laurie takes the situation in stride and agrees to get the lot shipped as soon as she has shipping instructions specifying the carrier and the Certificate of Compliance from the lab. Bob agrees to have the updated order with carrier instructions printed out in the plant's office area and to have the lab get the Certificate of Compliance ready. Laurie agrees to swing by the lab and office area before lunch to pick up both documents. She assures Bob that if both items are ready by lunch, she will have no difficulty getting the sensors sent out for overnight delivery. This is an added cost that Electro Tech has to eat. They normally ship second-day delivery, but this shipment has to go express.

As Laurie promised, she makes the rounds just before lunch and is able to collect the appropriate documents. This is necessary because the mainframe system the *Order It* system runs on can only print to one printer at the plant. A clerk then pulls orders off the printer, faxes copies to the lab so they can create Certificates of Compliance, and separates the orders for the two shipping docks at the plant. The lab uses a word processor to make the Certificates of Compliance, and the LAN that Electro Tech was installing does not yet reach the dock. This means that two or three times a day, Laurie has to stop in the lab to pick up the completed certificates.

Later that day, the control sensors are shipped and another crisis has passed. Some unexpected cost is incurred, and a few people have jumped through hoops to get the job done, but isn't that what you have to do to satisfy the customer?

The Assessment

Taking a look at this case example, there are several "opportunities for improvement." In many companies this scenario would be viewed as a success story. Any extra effort that results in customer satisfaction must be a good thing, right? Well, not always. If you examine this "Day-in-the-life of the CSR," several problems can be identified. Many of these problems are the result of inaccurate or untimely information. More importantly, several of these activities result in additional cost being incurred.

If you step back and examine the work processes and system tools involved this case study, the following problems present themselves:

- The lack of integration between the *Order It* system and the plant scheduling system can result in improper delivery dates being promised.

- The lack of integration between the *Order It* system and the plant inventory system can result in improper delivery dates being promised.

- Plant maintenance activities are manually scheduled, so they are not adequately reflected in plant scheduling or order delivery scheduling.

- The complete manufacturing cycle time is misunderstood. The packaging and test time are not formally included in the production planning cycle, forcing customer service representatives to "guess" at these additional lead times.

- Printed reports used by multiple people create a situation where overcommitment can occur because two CSRs promise the same items based on data that is not real-time.

- Product specifications and customer requirements differ. Lack of common information available to all parties has made matching available material to allowable customers difficult.

- Inventory and warehouse systems are not real-time with sales and quality systems.

- Simple plant logistics of where information prints or is stored creates added workload.

Part
II

Ch
8

CHAPTER 9

Making the Move from Customer Service Past to SAP R/3

In this chapter

How to define and maintain a scope related to sales and distribution activities

How breaking the entire business process into five levels helps build a clearer definition of required activities

The content of the Sales and Distribution section of the SAP R/3 Implementation Guide

The SAP R/3 Business Navigator and how it aids in defining business processes

Now that you have met the Electro Tech Customer Service Desk, you must examine the issues it must face in implementing SAP R/3. The preceding chapters painted a picture of a struggling company with an honorable past and a potentially strong future. To realize this future, Electro Tech has recognized a need to modernize. This may seem odd for a company that makes parts for automated manufacturing equipment. It is not the manufacturing equipment that needs modernization, however. The information systems and business practices are what need to be updated.

Electro Tech believes that implementing the R/3 system will help it realize its potentially bright future. Fortunately, Electro Tech also recognizes that change must start from within but is often aided by outside forces. Management has decided to implement SAP R/3 with the assistance of a consulting firm whose charge is to guide the transformation process and help establish the necessary SAP R/3 configuration for the company.

Understanding Sales and Distribution

No area of a business interacts with the customer in quite the same way that a Customer Service department does. While the salesperson may maintain constant contact with the purchasing agent, and the technical representative may demonstrate a product's virtues to the production staff, it is the Customer Service Representative (CSR) who places the company's integrity and reputation on the line each and every time a promise date is made or a product's price is quoted.

Additionally, no other area of the enterprise interacts with the other departments within a company with the same frequency as the Customer Service department. As you have seen in the Electro Tech case study, it is the CSRs who must juggle the complex areas of production scheduling, inventory, packaging, shipping times, and customer-specific product specifications. They must also consider a host of other variable items such as foreign country regulations, carrier availability, credit limits, prices, and taxes to meet the ever-changing customer order demand. Problems that occur during a shipment or with a product's performance that result in a product return or a credit situation are initiated with the same CSR.

These daily interactions between the CSR and the other areas of the enterprise often result in an "always been done that way" environment. Want to know when something will be ready to be packaged for shipment? Make a call to Bryan at the scheduling desk. Need to know if an order shipped and by what carrier? Call Laurie in shipping. Need an MSDS for a specific product? Get the customer's address and fax the request to Joanne over in the corporate headquarters lab. All too often, CSRs' effectiveness is not dependent upon how they interpret all the complex data at their disposal and how they use it to offer a customer accurate information, but in the strength of their inter-company interpersonal relationships.

Introducing the integration of SAP and the lack of need for this voice-to-voice dependency for an answer can be difficult for a Customer Service department. The reason the volume of internal phone calls became a necessary part of fulfilling a customer's request was because of the lack of reliable information from the computer systems. Assuring a new SAP user that the delivery date proposed by the SAP order entry system is accurate and has taken into account all variables is tantamount to blind faith.

To assist in avoiding the problems often encountered in an SD (System Development) implementation, and to get away from the "always been done that way" resistance, it is necessary to apply a decision making structure which will steer those involved away from current strategies and towards a vision of best practice. The use of Business Process Simulation (BPS) techniques provides such a structure. The BPS approach will be described at length later in the "Business Process Simulation" section of this chapter. To this point, the Sales and Distribution module of SAP has mostly been addressed in terms of its impact on the Customer Service department and its benefits to the customer order process. To be complete, the functions of customer order shipment (those being picking, carrier selection, inventory relief, and transport), and customer order billing (those being pricing, tax calculation, and transfer of data to the Accounts Receivable and Profitability Analysis areas of SAP) are also incorporated into the SD module and will be covered in much detail as order processing going forward.

The Scope

The scope of an SD implementation will vary greatly from implementation to implementation. While the basics of Order Entry, Customer Shipment, and Billing are necessary to complete what is considered the "SD Life Cycle," an ever-increasing number of bells and whistles accompany each SAP release (see Figure 9.1).

FIG. 9.1
SAP SD Life Cycle
Process.

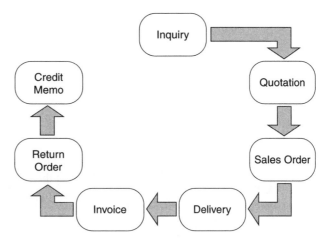

The checklist in Figure 9.2 can be used to determine the high-level scope of an SAP SD installation.

It is tempting to scope SD with complete functionality. After all, as the argument goes, isn't bigger better? When it comes to piles of money, yes. But in the world of SAP, not necessarily. One needs to remember that this functionality list is designed to meet the needs of many diverse industries operating under equally as many diverse business circumstances.

FIG. 9.2

The functionality checklist.

Master Data

a. Organizational Data (Hierarchy)
b. Business Partners
    (Customer Master & Related Configuration)
c. Customer Hierarchies
d. Customer-Material Information Records
e. Material Master
f. Material Determination (Substitution)
g. Material Listing/Exclusions
h. Pricing
i. Discounts/surcharges
j. Freight
k. Taxes

Sales Order Processing

a. Sales Order Types
    (Sales, Returns, Credits)
b. Sales Document Output
c. Backorder Processing
d. Credit Check
e. Availability Check
f. Rebate Agreement
g. Foreign Trade
h. Sales Promotions/Deals
i. Document Blocks
j. Special Instruction Text
k. Sales Analysis(SIS)Reporting

Delivery Processing

a. Delivery Types
b. Shipping Output
c. Picking
d. Packing
e. Carrier Selection/Route Selection
f. Transportation

Billing Processing

a. Billing Types
b. Billing Output
c. Billing Schedules
d. Account Determination
e. Terms of Payment

For instance, SAP's Foreign Trade capabilities can be a wonderful and productive tool for a company that does a respectable amount of business overseas. However, this complex functionality cannot be implemented without a significant investment in current process research, configuration development, and end user training. Generally speaking, it's probably not a worthwhile piece to implement in order to save a few minutes for the occasional foreign customer's order.

At a high management level, definition of the project scope is essential. BSWs that will eventually define the sales and distribution processes down to the actual transaction level cannot be adequately conducted without a clear and consistent scope definition. Consistency of scope definition is a common source of large problems within an SAP implementation process. An inconsistent scope definition is essentially a moving target and is sometimes referred to as *scope creep*. Initially, it would appear somewhat simple to avoid scope creep. Simply define the areas to be affected and the desired time frame. This view is common in the early stages of many implementations and, unfortunately, indicative of a low appreciation for the level of integration that exists between the SAP modules.

As the sales and distribution activities are examined in greater and greater detail during the BSW process, their impact on other areas of the organization become increasingly visible. If these interactions were not identified initially, during the scope definition portion of the project, it often becomes necessary to subsequently modify the scope. Thus, scope creep occurs. The bad news does not end here. Following a change of scope, it is often necessary to revisit decisions previously derived to determine if they are still applicable. If not, these decisions must be modified, possibly affecting other subsequent process decisions and the overall scope. This decision making spiral can go on and on. The result is a continually changing project scope and an iterative decision making process that does not produce a usable business plan. Individuals involved in these situations can quickly become discouraged by their organization's apparent inability to reach firm decisions.

The amount of expected daily transactional data and the number of end users will impact the time to implement the functionality determined by the scope. In an environment of long manufacturing lead times and few orders, the available to promise (ATP) development necessary will be less than that of a short lead time, high-demand product industry. Likewise, in a relatively stable marketplace, the pricing development need will be less than that of a highly competitive and volatile industry.

Part
II
Ch
9

Oftentimes, the scope and implementation approach seen as most desirable from a materials management viewpoint (for example, a plant-by-plant rollout) is nullified by the need to offer sales and distribution information (for example, product availability across multiple plants). Just as a CSR's job in the pre-SAP environment brings him or her into constant contact with other areas of the enterprise, an SD installation is dependent on the other areas of SAP being implemented. Only through a tightly integrated scope development process can the level of SD functionality desired versus the level of SD functionality required to achieve a company's objectives be determined.

The Basic Team Definition

The issues discussed thus far help define the desired characteristics of potential BPS team members. Company representatives form the nucleus of the BPS process. Without knowledgeable representation for each element of SD functionality desired, the BPS process becomes compromised. While various types of consultants are frequently involved, it is the company or client representatives who must claim the process decisions made as their own. After all, the consultants will eventually move on to other projects, leaving the entire burden of managing the post-SAP Sales and Distribution activities to the company. Oddly enough, this is often a difficult issue to firmly establish in the minds of BPS team members, both company and consultant. It is all too easy for company representatives to view the SAP implementation as something that is being done by visiting consultants for them.

It is essential that company representatives view themselves as the process owners throughout the SAP implementation process. For Electro Tech, Bob Peters would make an excellent choice for the BSW team. Bob has been involved in past system developments and seems to understand the CSR role thoroughly. While a consultant may recommend a new approach to the process of credit checking and order release, it is the employees (BPS team members) that must stand behind the process in a productive environment. Bob brings the knowledge needed to assist in these decisions.

In order to achieve success throughout the BPS process, company involvement should consist of a small number of individuals who are able to provide full representation of the functional areas involved. In the case of Sales and Distribution, this may include CSRs, pricing analysts,

Shipping department personnel, and billing specialists. For Electro Tech, Bob Peters and others involved in customer service activities would be logical choices for BPS team members. While creating a list of the "best and brightest" individuals for each piece of SD functionality being implemented, it is easy to end up with a lengthy list of individuals whose involvement is desired. Caution must be exercised when creating a BPS team as its size may actually detract from the process because large groups generally have a harder time reaching decisions than do smaller ones. Somewhere exists a manageable balance between effectiveness and size.

Selection of suitable people to the BPS team has a lot to do with reducing the number of people required. More than anything else, the ability of those individuals selected to make decisions is key. Few things in the SAP implementation process are more frustrating than to place together experienced, knowledgeable company representatives only to find that they are unwilling to commit to process decisions within their own areas of expertise. It is possible that an occasional poor decision will be harmful to the overall BPS process. It is a certainty that indecision will always be harmful. This situation occurs frequently and is often an indication of waning support from upper management on previous decisions and projects. The BPS team members must know that they have the support of their upper management levels in order to feel comfortable with their roles in the SAP implementation process. For example, an extremely effective CSR may not perform well on an order entry team if he does not have the capacity to make decisions that would alter the current process of order entry.

In order to gain and maintain this support from upper management, the BPS team members must possess excellent communication skills. Their ability to create suitable Sales and Distribution processes during the BPS sessions means little if they are unable to communicate the value of their plans to their superiors. In most cases, upper management representatives are mainly interested in the overall strategy to be applied, the costs incurred by the switch to this strategy, and the benefits expected from it. BPS team members must be able to represent their decisions within these criteria. At the same time, BPS team members will often be called upon to describe day-to-day business transactions to individuals at more operational levels.

Lastly, BPS team members must possess an inherent desire to derive and apply improved solutions. The Sales and Distribution module within SAP offers a great deal of information and structure to the processes of Order Entry and Shipping and Billing, but it requires an equally great amount of well-organized data to perform. In many cases, the amount of data required by SAP to perform the desired tasks is much greater than that of current systems, and the efforts required to acquire and manage this data prove to be discouraging to those involved. Team members will need constant reminding that the current systems are not up to the necessities of the marketplace (after all, why replace a system that works?) and that the advantages of SAP, once installed, will outweigh the hard work necessary to implement it.

Business Process Simulation

As previously mentioned, the approach of tackling the scope of an SAP implementation can be a daunting task. The use of BPS techniques provides a flexible structure that maximizes company input while insuring that all necessary system activities take place.

Level 1: Enterprisewide

Looking at an SAP implementation from an enterprisewide viewpoint, relationships between business functions can be seen. These relationships are depicted by a Level 1 flow diagram. The derivation of post-SAP Sales and Distribution processes is a complex task. As such, it is helpful to separate this process into several smaller, more manageable activities. A structure divided into four distinct levels has proven successful in the endeavor (see Figure 9.3).

FIG. 9.3
This Level 1 diagram of business process shows Sales as a piece of the entire enterprise.

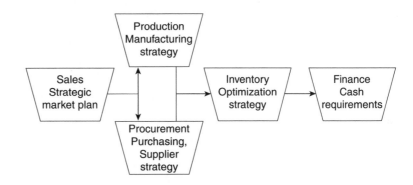

Generally speaking, the functionality of Sales and Distribution can be broken down into high-level processes. This is represented as a Level 2 flow diagram.

Level 2: Intra-Function Process Flows

Within a company like Electro Tech, the inner workings of the various departments are depicted by Level 2 flows. For example, the functions of the Sales department are called out in a Level 2 flow. This is where the broad integration points between the various modules in SAP begin to take shape.

Based upon your current knowledge of how Electro Tech operates, the Level 2 process flow would likely depict business functions performed by Sales and Distribution. Examining Level 2, you can see exactly how these business functions must come together (see Figure 9.4).

FIG. 9.4
Level 2 diagram of the Sales business process.

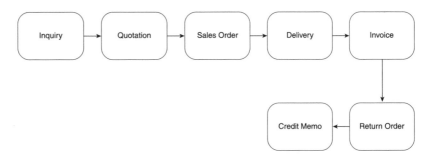

Level 3: Intra-Function Process Flows

Using the BPS methodology, each of the main areas—Order Entry, Shipping, and Billing—can be considered separate Level 3 activities. As an example of a Level 3 process flow for Electro Tech's Sales department, see Figures 9.5, 9.6, and 9.7.

FIG. 9.5

Level 3 flow for Order Entry.

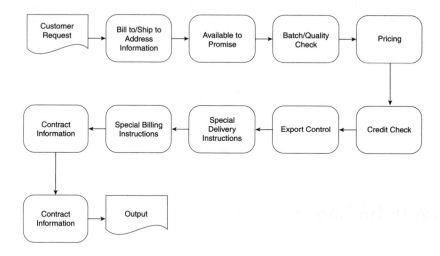

FIG. 9.6

Level 3 flow for Shipping.

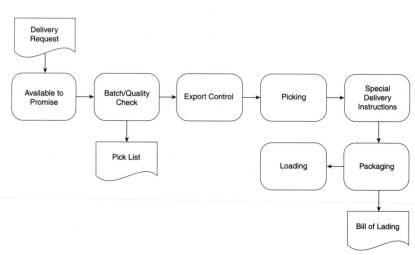

FIG. 9.7
Level 3 flow for Billing.

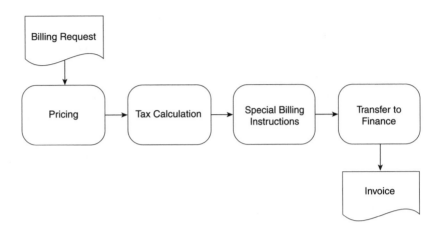

Part

II

Ch

9

Level 4: Transactions

By examining the Level 3 diagrams, the Level 4 processes become clear. Take each job task contained in the Level 3 flow diagram and develop a detailed flow of the job steps (see Figure 9.8).

FIG. 9.8
Availability checking flow.

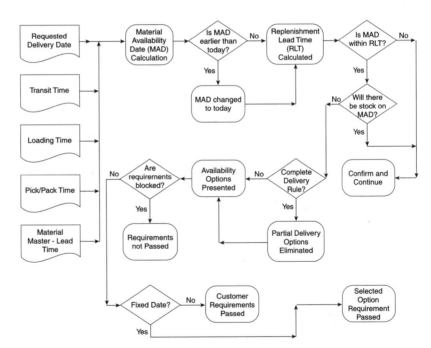

As-is and To-be Flows

Each of the flow diagrams describe SAP's complete functionality. When using the BPS process, these diagrams are considered reference flows and should not be used as a starting point for analysis of the current as-is or to-be environments. To fully realize the benefits of the BPS methodology, the enterprise should begin the flow diagram activities at the highest level from scratch (see Figure 9.9).

FIG. 9.9

Electro Tech's Level 4 flow.

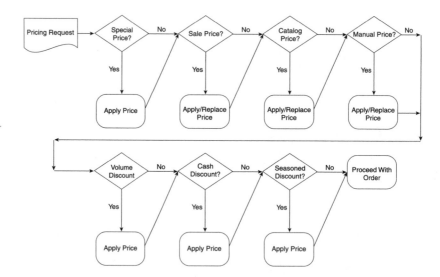

Comparing Figure 9.9 to SAP's business process, it is clear that Electro Tech is not operating in an SAP environment. This does not mean that Electro Tech's process needs tuning or that SAP cannot help improve it. It merely points out the folly in using SAP's flow diagrams to represent any current business situation.

Through analysis, SAP discovery and decision making for the enterprise will create a vision of the business process described in the to-be situation. Whether called *re-engineering* or *brainstorming* or *visioning* the end result, if applied properly, is the same: a more efficient way to perform a task. It is only after this step is complete that an enterprise is ready to apply SAP to its business environment.

Core Business Process

Using the BPS process to determine key Level 4 activities results in a different approach for each SD implementation. While certain basic elements are consistent across all installations (for example, order entry as a Level 3 process) the Level 4 detail is where the detailed differences occur. No two companies or industries will use the functionality in quite the same way. Some of the most complex areas of SAP, in fact, may be fairly straightforward to implement when looked at as business process flows.

How to implement each of the following areas will be covered in detail in Chapter 10, "Sales and Distribution Functionality with SAP R/3." This chapter will describe some of the most common problems associated with using the BPS methodology, as well as some ideas for making the BPS proceed smoothly.

Availability Checking (ATP)

No area of SD is as difficult to implement as Availability Checking. From an SAP integration point of view, as well as a business change perspective, offering the CSR accurate and reliable Available to Promise information is a challenge. Every company's wish list of SAP functionality includes accurate ATP information. However, even under the best implementation scenarios, few companies are able to implement the business process discipline necessary to maintain it.

Offering true and complete ATP to a Customer Service Representative requires accurate views of current inventory levels, manufacturing schedules, expected purchasing receipts, safety stocks, current order demand, capacity planning, manufacturing equipment down time, point-to-point transit times, packaging times, carrier availability, plant schedules, customer receiving schedules, product allocation priorities, and customer product specifications. In order for all of these components to be accurate, the people responsible for the related business functions (the production scheduler, shipping manager, and so on) must perform their tasks accurately and in a timely manner. The BPS team members responsible for providing ATP must understand SAP's functionality and limitations and be able to apply them to the current business practices. These same team members must also be willing to make the argument to the enterprise that drastic changes should occur in many departments and jobs.

Oftentimes, requiring drastic change to a department in order to achieve this high level of accountability causes friction within the BPS team and can result in replicating the current approach of phone calls and guesswork using SAP. Staying focused on the goals of the ATP BPS activities, those being better information for the customer and less time spent gathering information, will help to ease the fears that some departments or persons may feel about giving up the control they currently have. In order for the benefits of SAP's ATP functionality to be gained, the complex components previously listed must be broken down and quantified. The information offered to a customer regarding product availability is only as good as the data entered into the system. Business practices that allow vital information to remain *hidden* in departments, such as purchasing or scheduling, cannot occur under SAP without negatively affecting the benefits received.

Pricing

In a perfect business environment, the price quoted to a customer via the system matches the price quote offered from the salesperson, and the entire process does not involve the CSR to a large degree. SAP's pricing functionality fully supports this view. As in the case of ATP (seen previously), this does not come without the price of accurate data input and departmental accountability.

As a pricing BPS proceeds, the typical scenario that develops regarding pricing is that a group of people from a department with a mystical sounding name such as Competitive Marketing Analysis and Execution are in charge of providing the numbers used for quotations and billing purposes. Using a large number of spreadsheets and graphs, these people stay in contact with the salespeople and are in charge of entering the proper data into the current system environment. An experienced, organized, and logical CSR will most likely not be able to decipher the formulas and criteria used in product pricing.

A BPS team examining pricing needs to have a member of this group as an active player. This person must understand the criterion used to derive a customer's price and be able to explain it in a manner that can be replicated. This person must also be willing to accept that there may be a more efficient manner in which to collect, store, and analyze pricing information. Information is power within any organization—financial information most of all. As a result, gathering this information and translating it to SAP through the use of a BPS will be difficult, as it probably won't easily be shared. Introducing a team to examine the processes and job functions of a pricing group can often result in a fear of job loss through automation and may end in a memo that reads in part, "Due to the confidential nature of the information...interface to current systems is necessary...manual procedures will remain in place..." being distributed throughout the organization.

SAP's pricing functionality is extremely flexible and powerful. A BPS team must assure those people concerned with keeping pricing information confidential that it will remain so. The message that is important to send, entirely because it will be proven true, is that quantifying and organizing current pricing schemas into SAP will yield a tremendous amount of information, as well as eliminate a large number of errors and problems.

Credit Checking

Through the integration of SD with the financial information provided from Accounts Receivable, SAP's credit checking functionality can provide the CSR with a great deal of information during order entry.

A BPS team examining this process within a company must be willing to

- Establish criteria for credit limits.
- Create business rules regarding order release for customers exceeding their credit limit.
- Define applicable tolerance levels.
- Determine what the response to the CSR will be during order entry for a customer order that exceeds the limit.

Again, having access to confidential financial information oftentimes results in a closed environment within an organization. Researching and documenting the current procedure, and creating the desired results in SAP, can be frustrating. The fear of job loss through automation is high in a Credit department due to the clerical nature of a large number of tasks. It is not uncommon to find that a multimillion dollar organization performs credit checks on customer orders via a daily order report, which is compared against an Excel spreadsheet using a calculator.

Sales Information System

As with all of SAP's Information Systems (IS), the data presented for analysis is only as good as the data requested. BPSs that examine current reports should not be surprised to discover that 50%+ of all reports generated on paper daily are not looked at by a single soul.

If the BPS team recommends that reporting be automated and online, it is to be expected that a great deal of resistance will be met. A large number of people, especially those who have been working since before the advent of the PC, find it comforting to be armed with large paper reports. Arguments about accuracy and timeliness will fall on deaf ears, and the cycle of daily batch reporting will continue if the team members do not have the authority to make decisions.

SAP's Sales Information System can provide a wealth of sales-related data. Sales reports, financial reports, shipment timeliness, and so on can all be generated using simple online transactions. Data is up-to-the-minute and presented in a format chosen by the requester. SAP is quick to demonstrate its reporting capabilities, including color charts and graphs, during the sales cycle. Be warned, however, that generating data for all the supplied reports can take up precious disk space and processing time. This BPS team should be concerned with creating and providing only the reports necessary for all the implemented business functions to perform.

Text

Call them Special Instructions, Customer Text, or Order Information, they all mean the same thing and they are always a necessity of SD processes: free form text that prints on documents or is displayed to the user. All customers expect them, and all Customer Service Reps want them. SAP is extremely flexible in the area of text, but, as in most things SAP, nothing comes easy. Conversion of current system instructions into SAP oftentimes becomes one of the messiest data conversions. Establishing the rules for displaying and printing can often lead to the rewriting of forms and documents.

The BPS team responsible for Special Instruction text must critically examine the current system's functionality in order to determine exactly what is needed when using SAP. Providing information to the CSR during order entry or to the shipping dock via the Pick List can be very valuable if used correctly. Used incorrectly, information becomes counterproductive. Having meaningless messages pop up on screen while entering an order can be distracting and annoying. It may also result in the CSR *Entering through* them by repeatedly pressing the Enter key to get to the data input portion of order entry and thereby missing some important information.

SAP Business Navigator

To assist in process definition, SAP provides the Business Navigator (see Figure 9.10). In R/3 V3.0, the Business Navigator is essentially a graphical depiction of the decision logic tree reflected in the base SAP configuration. The process diagrams mentioned under "Business Process Simulation," earlier in this chapter, are similar to the Business Navigator's output, with additional information regarding logic and integration added.

The Navigator is often used as an initial training aid to help companies grasp a more physical understanding of the logic and transactions within SAP. The effectiveness of the Navigator becomes increasingly apparent as the company discovers the need to configure the system to better suit its needs. The Navigator can then be used for its intended purpose, as a flexible business strategy modeling tool. By examining the many decision and action steps depicted by the Navigator, the company is forced to map out desired business practices in great detail.

FIG. 9.10

SAP R/3's Navigator.

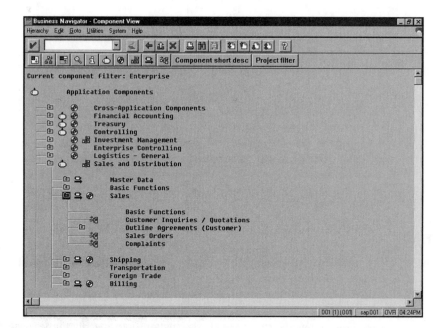

Such detail is necessary if subsequent configuration of the system's response is to be accomplished correctly and efficiently.

Oftentimes, the Business Navigator is ignored or forgotten during the implementation process. Once a company becomes involved in the definition of its own processes, it is easy to become buried in details and forget that a structured model exists. This is unfortunate, since the Navigator's purpose is to provide a decision-making path such that total confusion and information overload is avoided for the company.

As in the case of configuration, it is extremely unlikely that the initial decision tree depicted in the SAP Business Navigator is immediately suitable to a specific organization. This is assumed. Therefore, the Navigator may be modified as necessary to reflect the company's desired decision logic. Again, SAP configuration-related tools are intended to allow the system to support the company's desired operating modes. They follow the company's desired structure. They do not impose a structure upon the company.

Implementation Guide (IMG)

The Implementation Guide (IMG) is an SAP tool that is provided to ease the actual act of system configuration (see Figure 9.11). In effect, the IMG is nothing more than a graphical front end to the configuration tables. It is organized in a hierarchy of business functions and allows the company to quickly drill down to the configuration settings of specific transactions.

FIG. 9.11
The SD Implementation Guide.

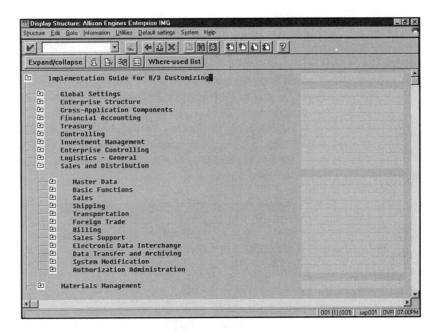

The IMG allows the company to select, or even create, desired configuration options that will direct the system's response. The IMG does not necessarily assist the company with process definition decisions, but rather provides the method by which existing process definition decisions can be enabled within the system.

Within most modules, including Sales and Distribution, use of the IMG and actual system configuration may elicit a variety of responses and problems from the company. Because of the broad scope that configuration changes may have, such actions must be taken with care. When modifying configuration settings, the user is not necessarily affecting one discrete activity. It is quite possible, and likely, that any change to the system configuration affects many activities in many modules. Thus, a substantial level of understanding of the SAP system is generally helpful. This fact often contributes to a hesitance of the company to explore the possibilities contained within the IMG. As a result, the company may not fully examine system capabilities and form the opinion that SAP is limited in its capabilities and unsuitable for a desired function. Some companies have gone so far as to then utilize several additional software packages, each for a specific task, in conjunction with SAP and never realized that SAP had every bit of the capability they required all along. They never realized that the additional cost and complications incurred in the process of combining several unrelated systems with the SAP system were unnecessary.

SAP is delivered and installed with a single IMG directory called the *Enterprise IMG*. The Enterprise IMG contains every configuration item available for all SAP modules. It is possible, and even recommended, that each SAP implementation project create Project IMGs. These Project IMGs are partial or full copies of the Enterprise IMG. The advantages of a Project IMG versus the Enterprise IMG is that only those relevant areas of the Enterprise IMG are copied into the Project IMG. For example, if an SAP project has been scoped to not include the Plant Maintenance (PM) functionality, all of the items associated with PM could not be copied into the Project IMG. As a result, the configuration for PM will not be explored nor seen as a to-do.

In addition to providing a navigation tool to configuration, the IMG can serve as a documentation tool for tracking changes to the configuration as well as the decision making process behind the change/no change to the SAP delivered system. Through the use of status codes, all configuration items in the Project IMG can be marked as Completed, Awaiting Decision, OK as Delivered, or anything the project team decides upon to describe an item (see Figure 9.12). When the IMG is displayed, the status can be displayed as well. At a glance, it is possible to judge the completeness of the configuration effort.

FIG. 9.12
IMG with status
codes displayed.

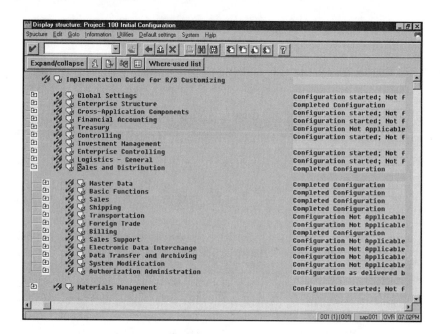

Interfaces

Due to the integrated nature of SAP, all modules interact with other modules. Sales and Distribution is no exception. The following SD processes do not operate in a vacuum, and, in fact, need to be developed jointly with the areas described. It is worth noting that most of the following list of highly integrated functionality consist of items mentioned earlier in this chapter (under "Core Business Process") as areas within an SD implementation that can become difficult to install.

Availability Checking—Materials Management/Production Planning

Without accurate inventory information and current manufacturing/purchasing schedules, the Order Entry Availability Check will not provide the CSR with the necessary information to provide a customer with a date. Bob Peters will be left to his reports and colored markers.

Transfer of Order Requirements—Materials Management/ Production Planning

In order to make sense of the demand generated by Order processing, the areas of MRP/MPS must be configured to handle the data, and the enterprise must have processes in place to communicate problems and changes to the manufacturing/purchasing schedules.

Credit Checking—Finance

Without accurate Account Receivable data, performing a credit check during order entry can lead to incorrect decisions. Processes for applying customer payments to outstanding balances must be in place for this functionality to provide worthwhile information to the CSR. Additionally, changing market factors and customer relationships may result in changing credit limits for customers. This data must be reflected in the SAP customer master file in order to be reflected in the check.

Material Shipments—Materials Management and Finance

When a customer order is shipped, a number of inventory actions occur. These actions, while dependent on the SD process, need to be developed in conjunction with the MM and FI modules of the implementation. Relieving inventory, in this case both physically and financially, impacts the cost of goods sold and the MRP processes tracking stock. To insure that the proper General Ledger accounts recognize the shipment, and that the inventory stores reflect the loss of material, requires integrated process development.

Material Returns—Materials Management and Finance

Incorrect shipments or damaged goods are often causes of material returns. As in the case of material shipments, material returns processes need to be developed jointly with the FI and MM elements of the implementation team. In order to insure that the accurate inventory stores and the proper financial accounts recognize the return, an integrated development team is needed.

Application of Taxes and Pricing—Finance

Sales revenue is often tracked separately from that related to taxes or freight, even though each of these components make up a customer invoice. In order to insure that all accounts receivable balances are reflected accurately in the General Ledger, pricing and tax applications to sales orders and invoices needs to be developed in tandem with the FI processes for the same.

Successful BPS

The approach that has been reviewed here guides Electro Tech through the implementation process. It helps recognize all key aspects of the Customer Service function, while providing a systematic approach to configuring SAP. A great many factors can negatively influence an SAP implementation, but none more so than decision making or, rather, a lack of quality decision making. Undergoing any change to business processes will result in the need for decisions. Whether the decision is related to the performance of a specific job function or to the makeup of a data field on a master file, management cannot assume a "hands-off" posture during an SAP implementation.

As a result of the hard work of management, the BPS team, any contributing users, and the probable consultant experience, a configured system with appropriate scripts is delivered. The next chapter looks at what a configured system is and allows through the execution of scripts. This is not the "why" of SAP R/3, but it certainly is the "how." ●

CHAPTER 10

Sales and Distribution Functionality with SAP R/3

Now that you have examined Electro Tech as a company and you have looked at what steps are necessary to move it from an environment of outdated, nonintegrated systems to one using SAP, you can examine the work processes used with SAP. This chapter examines, first and foremost, the work process of a customer service representative like Bob Peters of Electro Tech. You will also look at the complementary work processes such as monitoring inventory, quality certificates, and accounts receivable.

Understanding Sales and Distribution

As mentioned in Chapter 9, "Making the Move from Customer Service Past to SAP R/3," the Sales and Distribution module can be summed up as a three-step process considered to be the SD (Sales and Distribution) life cycle. This chapter focuses on how to perform each of these processes: Order Entry, Shipping, and Billing.

Order Entry

One of the simplest tasks to accomplish in SAP, but one that often requires the most ambitious decision making and configuration efforts, is Order Entry. While SAP is delivered fully capable of accepting orders, pricing them, and checking availability of materials, every implementation will have the need to make changes to this delivered system. It is doubtful that Electro Tech's needs for product pricing would be the same as the pharmaceutical industry or an oil refining company. Order Entry, in SAP terms, is a lot more than just capturing customer requirements. Through the integration built into the system, the act of entering an order has implications in the areas of scheduling, purchasing, receivables, and forecasting. Unless all of these areas are developed with the same business goals in mind, any orders entered into the system might not be compatible with the processes in these areas (and little, if any, benefit will be achieved).

To enter an order into SAP, the following menu path is used:

Menu Path: Logistics > Sales/Distribution > Sales > Order > Create
Transaction Code: VA01

The screen in Figure 10.1 appears.

Only a few pieces of data are needed before an order can be taken. Using the pull-down menu, one can see that SAP comes delivered with numerous types of orders. From Returns (Order Type RA) to Consignment Orders (Order Type KE), this single transaction is used to capture almost all customer sales requirements. This section will focus on Order Type OR (Standard Order). While the Order Type OR behaves differently than other order types offered via this transaction, one must remember that almost everything in this area is configurable and can be changed to suit the needs of the organization.

The Sales Organization, Distribution Channel, and Division fields should be entered here in accordance with the decisions made as part of the enterprise.

FIG. 10.1

Sales order creation screen.

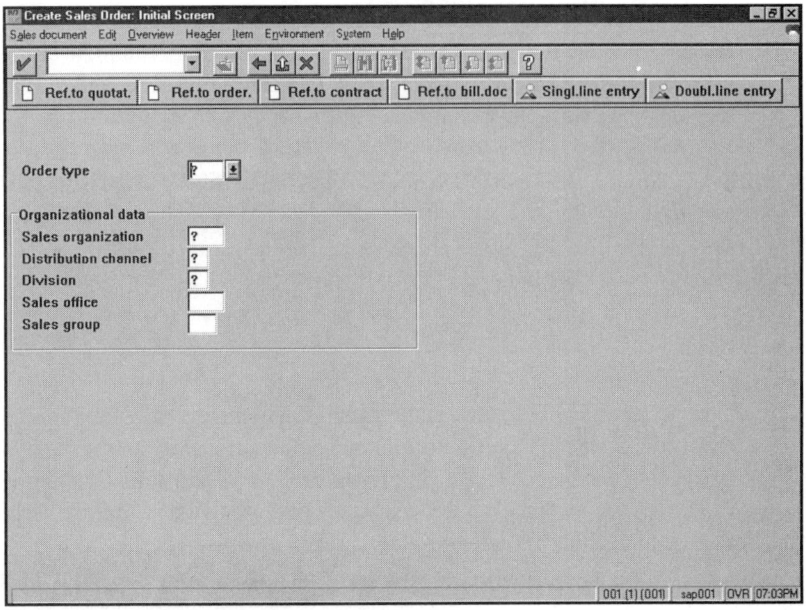

Depending on the type of data to be entered, the selection made on this screen (Single Line Entry, Business Data, and so on) is designed to minimize entry. Figure 10.2 shows the Double-Line Entry view for entering a sales order. Through configuration, any of the entry screens can be made the default when the Enter key is pressed.

FIG. 10.2

Sales order entry, Double-Line Entry view.

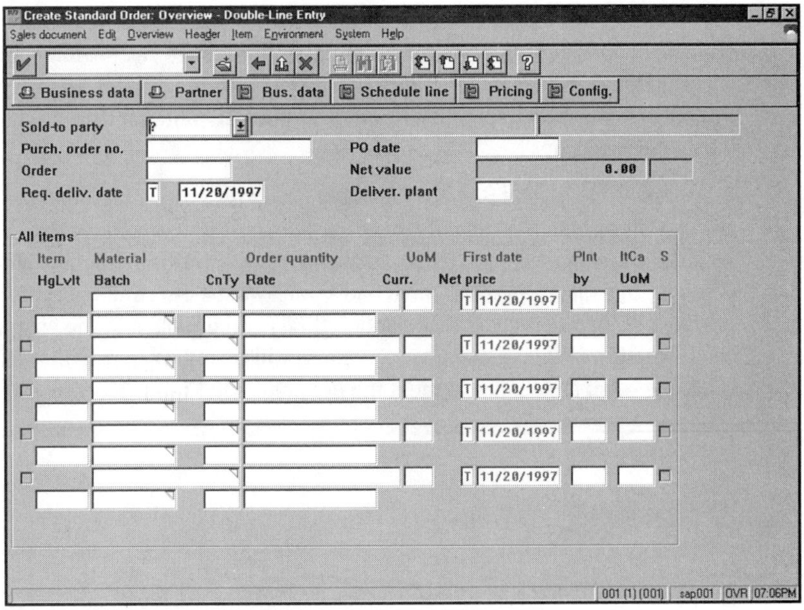

The first piece of information required, regardless of the entry screen, is the Sold-to Party. As discussed earlier in Chapter 6, "Data Types in SAP R/3," multiple ship-to addresses can be associated with a single Sold-to Party. If this is the case, SAP will prompt for selection of a single Ship-to via a pop-up list (see Figure 10.3).

FIG. 10.3

Pop-up dialog box for Ship-to Party.

Depending on configuration settings and the makeup of the Customer Master, the SAP system may prompt via messages for additional data entries prior to the ability to enter materials. A single date can be entered as Requested Delivery Date and will apply to all items entered, or it can be left empty and each item can have a separate date. Additionally, the system can be configured to default this date based on a set of established criteria.

When a material is entered, along with a Quantity and Shipping Plant, a number of things occur *behind the scenes*. Depending on business decisions and configuration made, these steps may provide the CSR with information, halt processing, and send information to another SAP module. The three most complex results of material entry are: Availability Checking, Pricing, and Credit Checking. Each will be discussed in the sections that follow.

Availability Checking   Availability Checking within SAP is a two-step process. The first calculation made is that of the internal time necessary to manufacture/purchase the item and provide it as available to the shipping dock. The second calculation is that of the time necessary to pick, pack, load, and ship the item. Due to both of these calculations being made, SAP requests that the delivery date for each item be entered into the system. In many companies, the delivery date is considered the date available at the plant and not the date the material will arrive at a customer's facility.

To see the full range of SAP's Availability Checking, you should enter a quantity for an item that is well beyond the capabilities of purchasing and manufacturing. Dependent upon rules established, certain areas of inventory and production (for example, stock levels, existing demand, manufacturing lead-time, and so on) will be checked to see if the customer demand can be met. Additionally, transportation time from the plant to the customer will be added into the calculation. When it cannot, the system will react by offering the CSR a number of choices—all in an attempt to meet the demand (see Figure 10.4).

FIG. 10.4

The Availability Control screen for standard order entry.

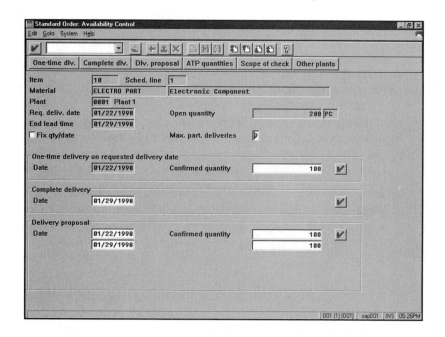

When the requested item and quantity are not fully available on the date requested, the system will react by bringing up the Availability Control shown in Figure 10.4. Along the top portion of the window is information about the customer and the material requested. The lower portion contains the following information:

- One-time Delivery On Requested Delivery Date—The system will offer the CSR the choice of delivering whatever quantity is available on the requested delivery date. This option may return a quantity of 0. No attempts will be made to deliver the remainder if this option is chosen.

- Complete Delivery—The system will offer the CSR the choice of delivering the full quantity on a date determined by the system. Using lead times for manufacturing/ purchasing, existing demand, forecasts, and other time factors, the system will calculate when the full amount requested will be available. If the CSR chooses this option, the originally requested date will be retained for reporting purposes, but the customer will receive acknowledgment of his order on the date proposed. If the scope of the Availability Check (see following) does not include lead times, this option will not appear.

- Delivery Proposal—The last option offered affords a mix of the previous choices. Taking into account all of the same inventory factors previously described, the system will calculate when any of the requested amount will be made available, and on what dates, and offer this information to the CSR in the form of a schedule. Choosing this option will break down the customer's request into many requests, based on the information returned.

Regardless of the choice made on this Availability Screen, the Order Demand created will be for the full amount requested on the date requested. While the system has already determined the enterprise's inability to meet this date, the factors that make up the determination may change. If they do, SAP offers the ability to run Rescheduling in an attempt to meet the customer's original quantity and date. To prevent this, and to create the demand on the dates chosen, a selection option is presented on the Availability Screen. Selecting the fixed date and quantity option (Fix Qty/Date) is an acceptance by the customer to deliver on the dates proposed and not on the dates requested. The system will overwrite the customer's original requested delivery date and pass that information on as if it was the customer's request. Rescheduling will have no effect on orders that have the fixed date and quantity indicator selected.

When Order Demand is created during Order Entry, the material and quantity requirements become visible immediately in the Materials Management module. The requirements can then be used in MRP/MPS. For that reason, the creation of Order Demand is referred to as the *Transfer of Requirements*.

The Availability Screen also allows the CSR to gather additional information about the material being offered and to pose new scenarios to the customer. From this screen, the availability of the material in other plants can be accessed. Due to processing constraints, this is not automatically performed in cases of non-availability for the material at the original plant on the original date. To do this, the CSR can select the Other plants button to be presented with a selection list of all plants for which the material is valid (see Figure 10.5). When a plant is selected, the quantity available in *unrestricted stock* is displayed. The plant cannot be changed via this function. The CSR must return to one of the overview screens to change the plant.

FIG. 10.5

The Plant Selection pop-up dialog box.

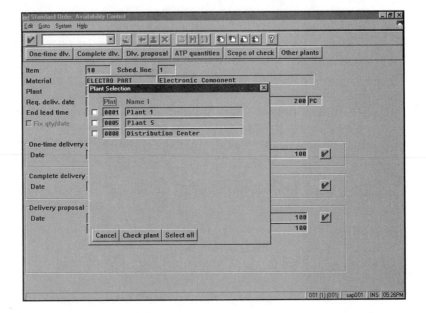

The determination rules behind the Availability Check can be accessed from this window as well. Via the selection button Scope of check, the components that make up the current check (what inventory stores, lead times, and so on) can be seen. This information might prove beneficial to a CSR in emergency situations. If, for example, safety stock is not included in the general check, the CSR can access the safety stock levels and follow the process designed to access this material.

The external time calculation (that of transportation time) is dependent upon the route assigned to an order item. Via configuration, each customer as well as each plant can be assigned to a *Transportation Zone*. These zones may be as broad as those used by UPS or FedEx, or they may be as narrow of those used by the USPS. Along with the transportation zone, the shipping conditions indicator from the Customer Master is also used to calculate the route to be assigned to an item.

The Route is an open field on the order and can be changed by the CSR. In many businesses, it is desirable to override the calculated Route because customers may opt to pick up material at the facility, and therefore no transportation time needs to be calculated. In these cases, a Route with 0 time assigned is created in configuration and procedures established so that the CSR can assign this Route to order items during order entry.

At any time after the Availability Check has occurred, the CSR can see what date(s) the system has returned as delivery dates for an item.

Menu Path: Item > Schedule Lines > Quantities/Dates

The CSR will see the requested dates and amounts as well as what SAP states as possible. Each schedule line operates as an independent entity in the downstream SD processes of Shipping. Each schedule line is actually made up of a number of dates. By selecting any schedule line and pressing the Shipping Details button, the dates in Figure 10.6 are displayed.

- Delivery Date—The date calculated for arrival at the customer's facility. This is the date returned by the Availability Check.

- Material Availability Date—The date that the material must be available for the processes of picking, packing, loading, and transport. The system determines this date by subtracting the time necessary for each of those activities from the delivery date.

- Loading Date—The date that picking and packing must be completed so that the goods can be loaded for shipment to the customer. The system determines this date by subtracting the time necessary for the activities of loading and transporting from the delivery date.

- Goods Issue Date—The date that the material must leave the plant in order to arrive at the customer's location on the delivery date. The system determines this date by subtracting the transport time of the route from the delivery date.

- Transportation Scheduling Date—The date that the Shipping department must begin arranging transportation to insure that a carrier is available on the goods issue date. The system determines this date by subtracting the planning time of the route from the goods issue date.

FIG. 10.6

The Shipping Details screen for a sales order item.

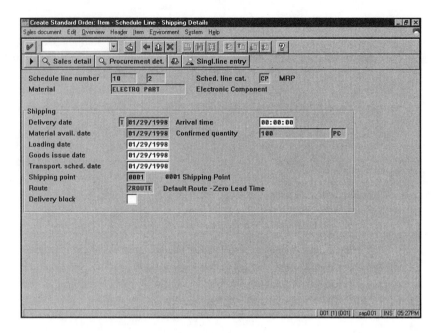

Through the use of these date fields, the CSR can provide the customer with an accurate picture of expected delivery date. This is a powerful customer relations tool. The integration of SAP gives the CSR the best possible projection of all dates involved, rather than depending on a best guess. With this at hand, the CSR can deal with other customer-related questions such as pricing.

Pricing   Product Pricing is potentially the most complex area of Sales and Distribution. What makes this complexity worthwhile to fully explore and configure is its flexibility. Want to offer a 2 percent discount to all customers in Utah when they order on Mondays for orders above $10,000? With a little work, SAP makes that happen automatically and applies the discount to any other pricing elements dictated by the system on each order item. Figure 10.7 shows a typical item pricing screen in SAP.

Pricing in SAP is a *building block* technique. A product's price is determined by adding or subtracting different components. Each of these components is called a *condition*. All of the potential conditions for an item can be seen via the screen in Figure 10.6. Select the individual item by clicking the selection indicator (check box) in front of the line and follow the path:

> **Menu Path:** Item > Pricing

Using F4 on the Conditions column will bring up a list of all potentially applicable conditions for an item. This screen also shows the pricing procedure used to determine which set of conditions might apply. Each of the potential conditions must be assigned to the pricing procedure used. Pricing procedures are determined via a combination of an indicator set on the order type and the Customer Master. As a result, the pricing for the same customer placing a Standard Order can be different than that of a Return Order. By creating this building of conditions through a pricing procedure, each price can be assured to be determined or manually applied in the proper sequence (see Figure 10.8). This sequencing is done in order to apply discounts and surcharges to the applicable components (typically price) and not to others (typically taxes and freight).

FIG. 10.7
Item pricing screen.

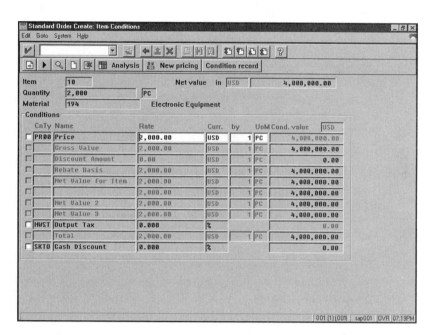

FIG. 10.8
The Price Conditions screen.

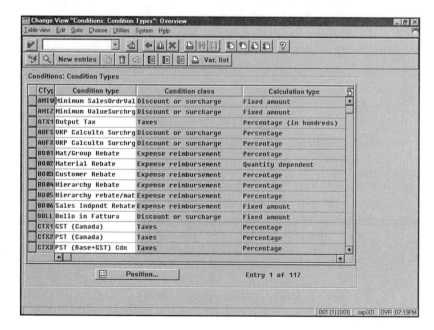

In configuration, the rules that apply to each condition are set. These rules make up the steps leading to the item's total price. Each condition can be determined automatically or applied manually. For example, the discount scenario previously listed would typically be set as an automatic condition. If all the criteria were met by the item (customer in Utah, order on a Monday, and so on), the discount would be applied in the pricing equation at the determined spot. Manual conditions typically consist of add-ons or discounts applied on a case-by-case basis at the discretion of the CSR or Sales Representative.

Creating the criteria for application (the customer in Utah, for example) is done via Condition tables and Condition records. A Condition table establishes the criteria to be determined (in the previous example this includes day of week, state, and amount of order). The Condition record, which is created via Sales and Distribution Master data and not configuration, is where the assignment of a 2 percent discount is made to Utah, Monday, and $10,000.

Conditions may also apply to an order as a whole and not just a single item. The applicable conditions for an order header can be seen via the path:

Menu Path: Header > Pricing

These conditions are usually those for volume discounts, freight, and taxes. All Conditions must be established in configuration as Header or Item related.

The advantages to creating conditions in the system prior to order entry are many:

- Most importantly, it ensures an accurate and consistent approach to the information given to a customer.
- It eliminates the need for Price Catalogs and homemade spreadsheets tracking profit projections.
- Mass price changes (such as percentage increases) can be entered into the system at any time, as all conditions are date activated. This eliminates problems synching the Pricing department with Sales and Order Entry when a change in pricing is to occur.

Additionally, if pricing is applied automatically during order entry and agreed upon by the customer at that time, the CSR has more time free during the day to handle other problems that might apply to an order and doesn't spend as much time tracking down quotes left on contracts and other paperwork.

Credit Checking   Once an order's items are fully priced, a net value for the entire order is calculated. This can be seen in Figure 10.9.

If desired and configured, a Credit Check can be performed on the order prior to it being saved. The rules behind calculating the credit limit and the response by the system if it is exceeded are established in configuration. In addition to the value of the new order, the amount in outstanding Accounts Receivable (A/R), the values of existing orders and deliveries, and any payments due to a customer may be applied against the established credit limit. *Tolerance limits*, either percentages or fixed value, may be established for individual customers as well.

FIG. 10.9
Main order entry page
with the order Net Value
filled in.

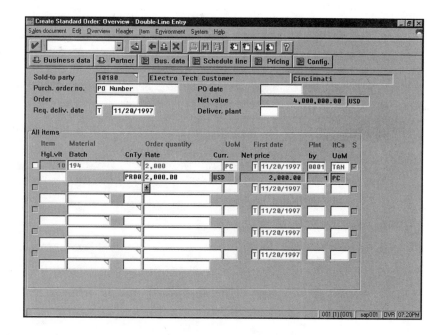

If the total credit limit is exceeded by the value of this new order, a number of options exist for the decision-makers. A message may be displayed informing the CSR that the limit is exceeded. This message may be purely informative, it may contain the exact amount of overage, or it may prevent further processing of the order altogether. It is possible, through customer grouping, to have different results for different customers.

Based on your organization's needs and financial policies, it may not be practical to inform the CSR of the A/R status of the customer. In these cases, SAP offers the ability to *hold* orders behind-the-scenes. A block is placed on all orders exceeding the credit limit rules, and a report is generated online by those responsible for examining the situation. Via this report and a special transaction, the block can be removed.

Credit Checking is a direct, real-time interface with the Financial module of SAP. Credit Limits are established for a customer via the financial entry screens of the Customer Master record. Accounts Receivable and Payable are accessed in determining if an order is over the established limit. Without an accurately updated FI system, the SD Credit Checking functionality could become a difficult obstacle to order entry.

Required Fields Depending on your enterprise's needs, certain information above and beyond that previously described may be necessary for an order or for an item. For example, it may be beneficial for your organization to track the name and phone number of the customer's purchasing agent. Or maybe there is a need to know a reason behind placing a Return Order. SAP can be configured to perform an *incompletion check*, to look for data requirements, such as these, prior to accepting an order. Each Order Type and Item Type (described later in the section "Item Categories/Schedule Line Categories") is assigned a value called an Incompletion Procedure.

Within configuration for Orders and Items, each Incompletion Procedure is a list of all available entry fields (see Figure 10.10). By assigning the appropriate status group, any field can be made mandatory during order entry.

FIG. 10.10

The Incompletion Procedure list.

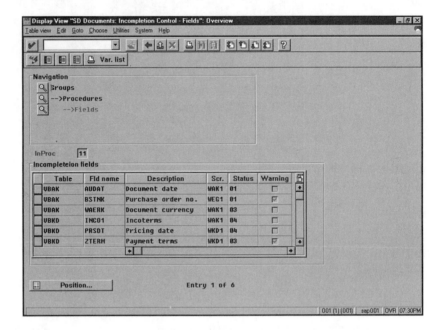

Two things occur as a result of making a field mandatory during order entry. First, the fields made mandatory appear with ? in them when the order is taken (see Figure 10.11).

Second, if an order is saved that has not had all of the mandatory entries made, the SAP system will return an informative message to the CSR (see Figure 10.12).

When this message is displayed, the CSR has the option of saving the incomplete order or entering the necessary data. Saving an incomplete order prevents the transfer of requirements, as well as preventing the order amount from appearing in any Credit Check calculations. If the CSR chooses the option to complete the data entry, a selection screen detailing the missing data is displayed (see Figure 10.13).

After all the necessary data is entered, the system will return a message to that effect. An incompletion check can be performed manually at any time in the order entry/change process. This is done as follows:

Menu Path: Edit > Incompletion Log

The incompletion procedures for the order and each item will be accessed and each mandatory data field checked. The same incompletion message seen while saving an order will occur if the check's result is positive or negative.

FIG. 10.11
Mandatory non-filled in fields.

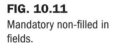

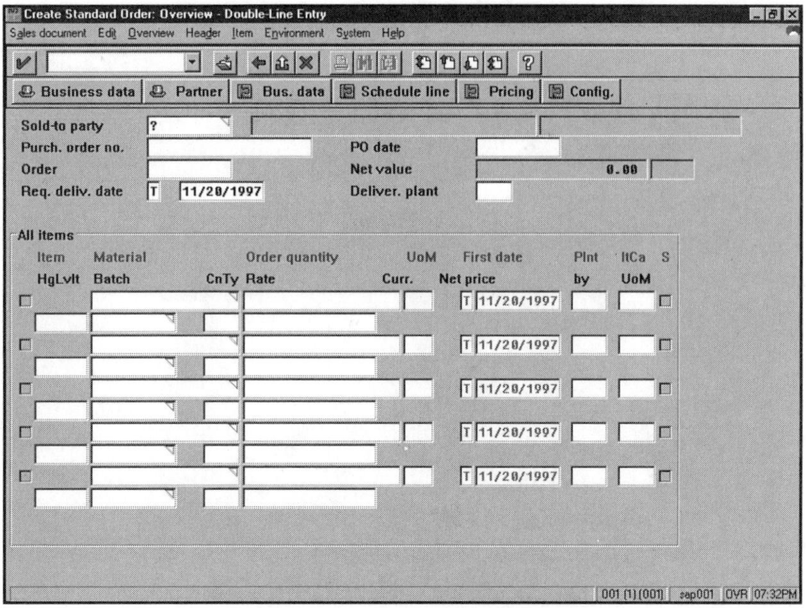

FIG. 10.12
Error message pop-up.

Item Categories/Schedule Line Categories In order to offer an element of additional item level control, each item entered on an order is automatically assigned an Item Category (see Figure 10.14). This assignment occurs based on a combination of the order type and the material entered. Each Item Category controls how an item reacts in its interfacing with the other modules, as well as within the SD arena.

As seen in Figure 10.14, the Item Category controls whether the item can be priced, costed, picked, returned, and invoiced. What this control affords the SAP user is the ability to enter a single item on many different order types, all with different results. It may be beneficial to perform costing on all Standard Orders so that profitability can be calculated, but this same functionality may not be needed on a Credit Memo Request Order.

As mentioned during the Availability Check discussion, each Schedule Line generated during the Availability Check operates as an independent demand line in the downstream SD process of shipping. The Schedule Line category assigned to each line, via a combination of the Item Category and an indicator on the Material Master, is where the control for performing an Availability Check and the Transfer of Requirements occurs.

Part

II

Ch

10

FIG. 10.13

Process missing data screen.

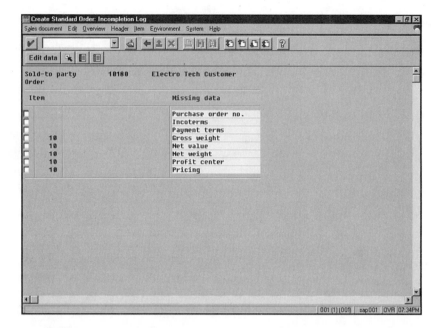

FIG. 10.14

Item Category Control.

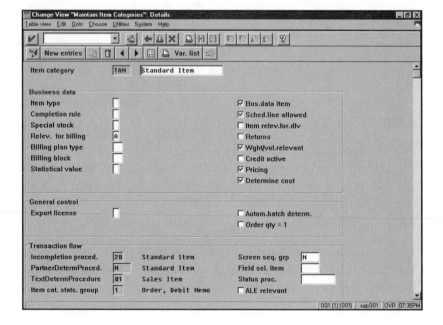

As seen in Figure 10.15, each Schedule Line category is assigned a Movement Type. This Movement Type controls the financial and physical inventory movement made when this item is shipped.

FIG. 10.15

The Maintain Schedule Line Categories screen showing the assigned movement type.

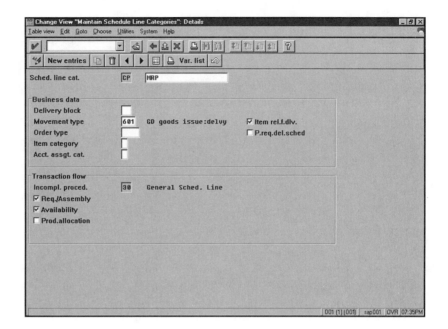

Shipping

Sales and Distribution is more than Order Entry and its associated processes. As SD itself implies, Distribution is an important piece of the puzzle. It is through the processing of Delivery Documents that the processes of Picking, Packing, and Customer Shipment occur. It is the order, however, that controls how and when the Delivery Document will be processed. This section will concentrate on the data that makes the Shipping process occur.

Each Schedule Line operates as a single piece of information in Shipping. From the Shipping screen follow this path:

Menu Path: Item > Business Data > [Schedule line] button > [Shipping det.] button

Other information that may be needed to make a customer shipment, such as total weight, can be seen (see Figure 10.16).

For each Schedule Line, assignments for Plant and Shipping Point are made. The Plant is the physical or logical point where the inventory is stored. The Shipping Point is the physical or logical point that controls customer shipments. All paperwork associated with the Delivery Document (Pick List and so on) is generated at a Shipping Point. Within configuration, Shipping Points are created and assigned to a combination of Plant, the Loading Group indicator of the Material Master, and the Shipping Conditions indicator of the Customer Master.

Part

II

Ch

10

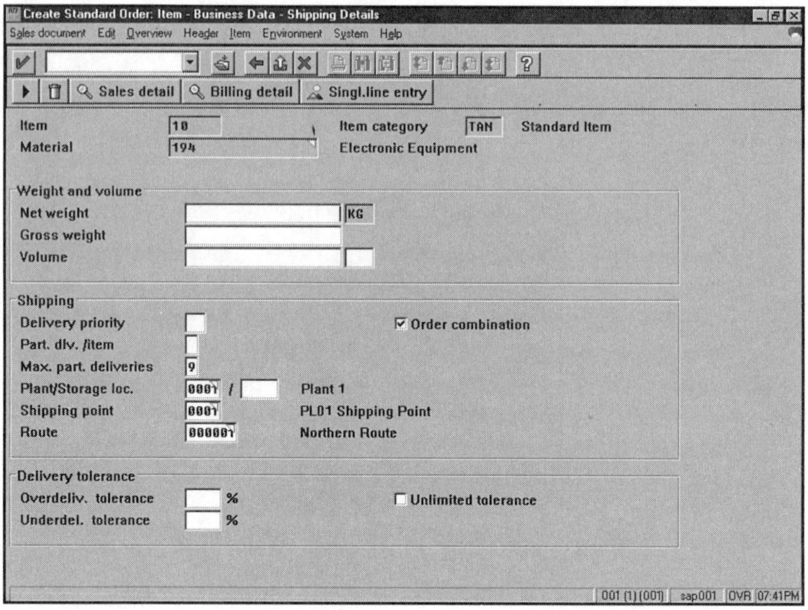

FIG. 10.16

Shipping data screen.

Billing

In order to complete the SD life cycle, billing must be carried out for shipped orders. Use the following path from the main order screen:

Menu Path: Item > Business Data > Billing detail button

Controls that apply to the billing of each order line item can be seen and changed. This information includes payment terms, special rules about invoicing, and tax determination.

If pricing is not agreed upon or calculated for an item, the CSR can enter a Billing Block on this screen. The order demand will be created as normal, and the item will be shipped. However, no invoice will be created until this block is removed. There is a special transaction within SAP to see all order items with Billing Blocks on them.

Menu Path: Logistics > Sales/Distribution > Sales > Order > Release for Billing

Transaction Code: V.23

Through configuration, multiple blocks can be created, each with an independent description. From the generated list, the user can edit any of the line items presented and remove the block.

Output

The SAP Order is considered an *internal document*. That means the information entered into the order is for internal processing purposes only. Oftentimes, the customer or the Sales Representative requires a paper copy of the order for verification purposes. This is accomplished through the use of Output. A list of all available Order Output can be seen from the following menu path:

Menu Path: Header > Output

Output is assigned via an Output Procedure (similar to a Pricing Procedure) that is assigned to the Order Type in configuration. As a result, different Output Types can be established for different types of order processing (see Figure 10.17).

FIG. 10.17
Output list for order processing.

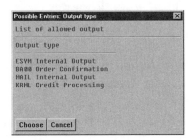

Selecting a type of output from this list provides for the hard copy to be created. Through configuration, additional types of output can be created and assigned to orders. There are a number of options the CSR must choose from when selecting an Output Type from the menu. These options are listed as follows:

- Output Medium—Output does not necessarily mean printout. Output can be a fax, an EDI transmission, or an onscreen display. By selecting the proper Medium from the Output selection screen, the CSR will receive the desired result.

- Send Time—If there is no immediate need to create the output, the CSR can select a Timing option to delay the creation. Creating Output requires processing time, and in high-volume areas like Order Entry it may not be beneficial to the processes to have to wait for output to be created. The time is set via the Further Data button.

Text

One of the most requested requirements for SAP Order Entry is the use of free form text to capture internal manufacturing directions and order-specific delivery information. Few industries or companies can make do without this functionality. SAP is very flexible in this area, and, with minor configuration effort, can provide limitless entry space for special instructions. Via a Text Procedure (similar to a Pricing Procedure), Text Conditions are assigned in configuration to order types and Item Categories. The Text Types allowed for the order can be seen from the following:

Menu Path: Header > Text

The individual order items text fields can be seen via the following:

Menu Path: Item > Texts

Part
II

Ch
10

All the Text Conditions on an order are created and controlled within configuration. This control consists of setting the rules for transfer of the information to the Delivery Documents, the Billing Document, and any associated Output (an order acknowledgment, for example) with these documents. It would not make sense to provide Shipping Instructions on an Invoice or Purchase Order information on the Picking List, although both types of information need to be captured during the order entry process.

When entering text into a Text Type, more room is available than is displayed onscreen. By double-clicking any displayed Text Type, a full screen is displayed. Using page-up and page-down commands, this text space is limited to 9999 lines. If text beyond the additional space is entered, an indicator will be selected informing anyone displaying the order that more than the displayed text applies.

Deliveries

After an order has been completed and the first of the items is ready for shipment, the item is considered *due*. Typically, a Shipping Point processes all Due Delivery Documents on a daily basis. The menu path is as follows:

> **Menu Path:** Logistics > Sales/Distribution > Shipping > Delivery > Process Delivery Due List
>
> **Transaction Code**: VL04

The Delivery Due List process scans all open order line items to return a list of items that are ready for shipment according to the earliest of the following dates for a line item: Material Availability Date or Transportation Planning Date.

From this screen (see Figure 10.18), the user has the option of creating all Delivery Documents for the list or creating them singly. When a Delivery Document is created, the control of the order has transferred from Customer Service/Sales to the Shipping Dock. Any attempt to make changes to an order that has a delivery created will return a message to the CSR informing him that downstream SD processing has occurred for the order. For this reason, as well as practicality, deliveries are usually not created until the last minute. Since the requirements have been transferred via the Schedule Lines, there is no business need to inform the Picking and Shipping departments of the order prior to their need to remove the inventory from the plant or contact a carrier. Depending on your organization's need for data verification, this process can occur via a background batch program and might need no human intervention.

Based on settings in configuration, an Availability Check can occur before a Delivery Document is created. If your enterprise desires this functionality, the same components that make up the Order Entry Availability Check can be selected. For deliveries, it makes sense to limit the scope of the check to stock and materials already in process. As deliveries are usually created immediately prior to the shipment, use of purchasing/manufacturing lead times does not add any value to the Availability Check.

FIG. 10.18

The Delivery Due List.

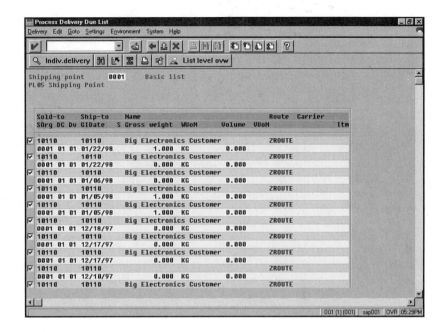

The Delivery Document, like the Order Document, is considered an *internal document*. Pick lists, shipping paperwork, and so on are all associated Outputs to the Delivery Document. The Delivery Document is the centralized data storehouse for all Shipping activities. Having created a Delivery Document does not mean that goods or services have been delivered. It is the means by which shipping paperwork is created.

Picking

The first step in completing a shipment to a customer is the picking of material from inventory and staging it for shipment. When the delivery is created, Output can generate a Pick List informing the Shipping department of the material needed. To confirm that material has been picked for a delivery, follow the menu path:

Menu Path: Overview > Picking

Confirmation of picking removes the picked quantity from available stock and reserves it for the individual delivery. As a result, Availability Checks that only look at *unrestricted stock* will not include this quantity in their calculations. On the Picking screen, each of the Delivery Document's items is listed similarly to the Order Entry Double Line entry screen (see Figure 10.19).

The quantity to be delivered is listed along with the plant the material should be removed from. The storage location of the material, as well as the picked quantity, needs to be entered for each item picked.

Part

II

Ch

10

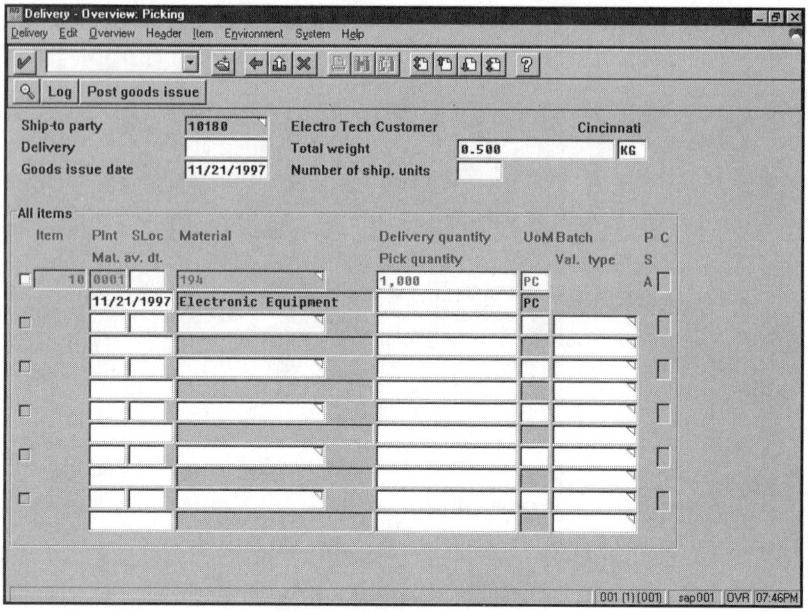

FIG. 10.19
The delivery Picking screen.

Storage Location

Storage Locations exist to offer a finer element of control to Inventory Management. Picking, and subsequent inventory relief, must occur from a Plant/Storage Location combination. Based on configuration settings and an enterprise's business need, it is possible to have the Storage Location default into the Delivery Document. A list of valid Storage Locations for a material can be seen by clicking in the SLoc field, shown in Figure 10.19, and selecting F4. This list is not an Availability Check. An Availability Check occurs on the Storage Location level during creation of the Delivery Document only if automated Storage Location assignment is turned on. If a Storage Location is entered as the Picking Location and insufficient stock is available, the Goods Issue step (see section that follows) of Shipment processing will return an error. The Delivery Document can be saved after Picking confirmation is complete.

Goods Issue

Once an item has been picked and is ready to be released to the customer, a goods issue must be performed. From the Delivery (delivery change path), the operator is offered a goods issue button. Clicking this button for a Delivery that is not fully picked will return an error message to the user.

The Goods Issue button is also available on the Picking Confirmation screen. If the policies developed for using SAP allow Picking and Issuing to be a single process, they can be accomplished immediately after one another. SAP will access an internal Availability Check that looks only at unrestricted stock within the Storage Location before goods issue can occur. If the stock is not available, an error message will be returned to the user.

According to the inventory rules established in configuration for the movement type associated with the Schedule Line being shipped, the Goods Issue process will relieve the physical and financial inventory burden from the plant and place it against the specified Cost of Goods Sold account. This financial shift can be seen in Figure 10.20.

FIG. 10.20
A material document for a Goods Issue.

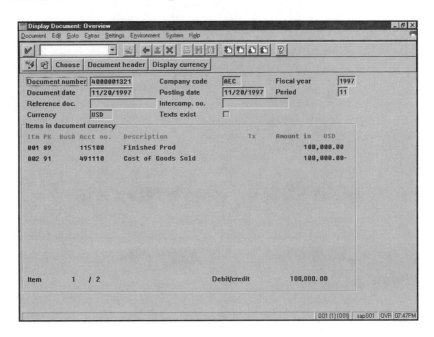

Partial Shipments

Sometimes, due to many factors, the quantity of an item to be picked and issued is not available, although the Availability Check states that it is. Or perhaps, due to a shortage of material, the full amount of material requested by the customer will not be shipped. If a Delivery has been created, making the change to Quantity or Date on the Order Document will not affect the Delivery Quantity for the line item. If these situations occur, the business needs to examine the timeliness and accuracy of all inventory data as well as additional order demand. Additionally, a policy needs to exist for short-shipping a Delivery. If it is desired to ship a portion of the requested amount of material via a Delivery and ship the remainder at a later time, this can be accomplished during the Picking confirmation step (see previous section). When the Picking Quantity is entered in to the field, the Delivery Quantity must be adjusted to agree (see Figure 10.21).

When the Goods Issue step occurs, the quantity requested but not shipped is returned to control of Customer Service/Sales and can be modified as necessary. Any subsequent run of the Delivery Due List will show the remainder as well.

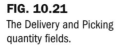

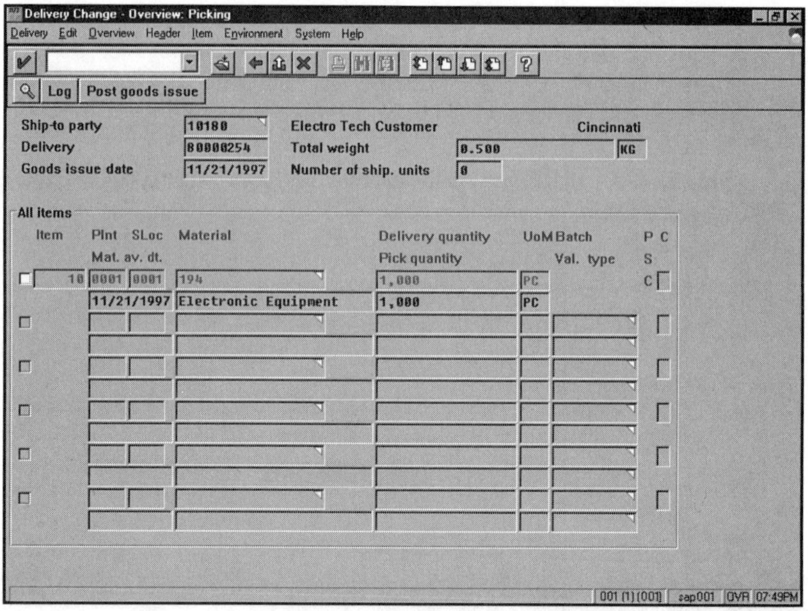

FIG. 10.21

The Delivery and Picking quantity fields.

Invoicing

The last step in the SD life cycle is Invoicing. If all the processes of Order Entry and Shipping have been completed without error, Invoicing should be a simple task to perform. A Billing Due List can be created:

> **Menu Path:** Logistics > Sales/Distribution > Billing > Billing Document > Billing Due List
>
> **Transaction Code:** VF04

Similar to the Delivery Due List, the Billing Due List process scans all delivered line items to return a list of items ready to be billed. It is possible to combine many shipments to a single customer into a single invoice. Using settings on the Customer Master, as well as in Billing configurations, the rules behind consolidation can be established.

As with the Delivery Due List, a single invoice can be created from the result of the process or the entire invoice can be created at once. Depending on your organization's need for data validation, the Invoicing program can be run via a background batch process and may need no human intervention.

Pricing

Based on rules established in configuration, Pricing may be carried out anew in the Billing Document, transferred from the Order, or a combination of both (prices transferred, but taxes recalculated). This control is established per Item category of the referenced document. For example, if a Billing Document is to be created for a Goods Issued Delivery Document, the

Delivery is considered the reference document. Item categories, as described earlier in this chapter, are carried forward from the sales order into the Delivery automatically. If established as manual, pricing conditions can be entered or changed via the following path:

Menu Path: Item > Pricing

Selection of how pricing will be carried out is controlled through the Pricing type, as seen in Figure 10.22.

FIG. 10.22
Pricing type selection screen.

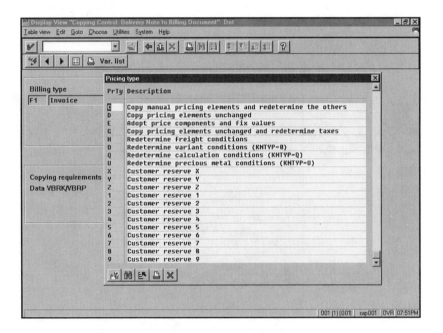

Part

II

Ch

10

Viewing Inventory and Planned Production

The Availability Checking that is available in SAP is a useful and powerful tool. It allows for automated determination of when material will be available. Even with this capability, every once in a while a CSR needs to view the available inventory and planned manufacturing manually. SAP provides two commonly used views of inventory and planned production: the Stock Overview and the Stock/Requirements List.

Stock Overview

The Stock Overview in SAP is the means by which to view stock of a material across all organizational levels—some companies call this tool an *inventory display* in their legacy systems. At its most basic, the Stock Overview allows you to determine *what* is *where*.

The Stock Overview allows you to view the breakdown of a material's stock in varying formats and for different levels of the organization, depending on the parameters input in the selection screen. For example, you can view material for a single plant, for all plants, or for a selection of plants. You have the same selection options for Storage Location and Batch.

Navigation to the Stock Requirements List   There are many menu paths that lead to the Stock Overview, which seems appropriate because there are many people in an organization in different functional areas who all have need, at one time or another, to view the stock situation of a given material (see Figure 10.23). I will list the most common menu path here:

> **Menu Path:** Logistics > Materials Management > Inventory Management > Environment > Stock > Stock Overview

> **Transaction Code:** MMBE

FIG. 10.23

The Stock Overview input screen.

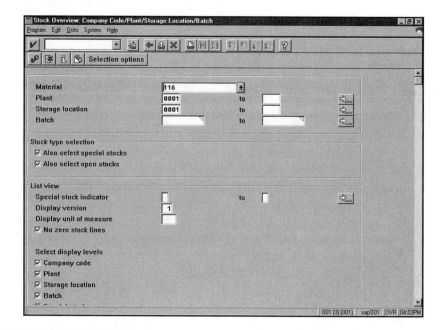

Once at the Stock Overview input screen, the minimum information that is required is the Material number. If this is the only input and all other defaults are accepted, the result will be a stock breakdown for the material at all organization levels:

- Client
- Company Code
- Plant
- Storage Location
- Batch

The material will have stock lines for each plant, each storage location within each plant, and each batch within each storage location. So, if the material exists only at one company code but at multiple plants each with multiple storage locations and batches, the result of the query will be quite lengthy.

In order to narrow your search, you can enter selection criteria that will limit the organizational levels that are shown. In the Input Parameter screen, you can enter the Plant, or range of plants, the Storage Location, or range of storage locations, and Batch, or range of batches for which you would like to have the stock information. For example if you would like to see only the stock for a particular storage location within a plant, enter the Plant and Storage Location in addition to the Material number. If the material is subject to batch management, but you don't want to see batches within the storage location, deselect the Batch indicator (and the Special Stock indicator, see next paragraph) in the List View, Select Display Levels box of the input screen. (If the material is not subject to batch management, there is no need to deselect the Batch indicator; since no batches exist for the material, none will be listed.) The result of this query will only include the plant and storage location stock.

The function of the List View, Select Display Levels box is to limit the organizational levels that are displayed. If you would like to view the stock of a material at the plant level for all plants, ensure no specific plants are entered in the Plant input field, and deselect the Storage Location, Batch, and Special Stock indicators. The result of the query will be a stock line for each plant that has stock information for the material. The reason all indicators below Storage Location should be deselected is because the organizational levels are hierarchical; if you don't deselect them, a warning will be issued informing you that the display levels will be extended hierarchically. In other words, you can't view the stock at the Storage Location level unless you're also viewing the Plant level. In the hierarchy, Storage Locations belong to Plants.

Once you determine the selection criteria and click the Execute button, the result of the query will include several columns, or *buckets*, of stock information (see Figure 10.24). There are three buckets to a screen, so in order to see more information, you have to click the black Right Arrow button. The order, number, and content of the columns are configurable. The standard configuration includes five windows with three columns each (not all of which contain information and at least one column that repeats twice). Again, you can change the order in which the columns appear, add new columns, and take others out completely, depending on your company's needs.

N O T E   If you have the need to transfer material from one plant to another using stock transport orders, there is at least one logical change to make to the standard configuration. Add the Stock In Transit column (Field Name TRAME) to one of the windows. The IMG transaction for this configuration is OMBG. ■

Stock Buckets in the Stock Overview Screen   Each of the columns in the Stock Overview is considered to be one of two types of information: either on-hand stock or open stock. On-hand stock includes all the stock that is currently owned by the company, regardless of its status (more on status later). On-hand stock buckets include Unrestricted Use, Quality Inspection, Blocked Stock, and Transfer (Plant). Open stock buckets include Reserved, Open (purchase order) Quantity, and Goods Receipt Blocked Stock.

FIG. 10.24
The Stock Overview screen.

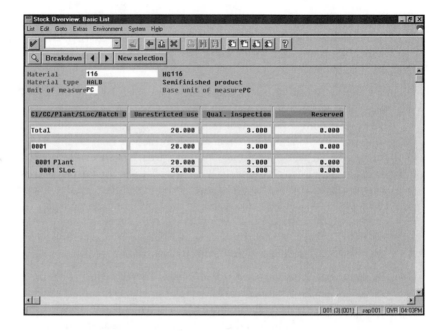

The status of a material has to do either with whether or not the material is available for use in production, or whether or not MRP considers the material available for use in its planning calculations. If material is in the Unrestricted Use bucket of the Stock Overview, the material is considered usable by the system. The material may be issued to production, and MRP considers it as available stock. Blocked stock and stock in Quality Inspection, on the other hand, are more restricted. Material in the Blocked Stock bucket, although it is technically possible to issue to production, may be flagged in MRP configuration as not being available for MRP. Material in the Quality Inspection bucket (where an inspection lot exists for the material) may not be issued to production until the inspector makes the usage decision that moves the material from QI stock to Unrestricted Use.

The Stock Overview also includes *special* stock of a material that exists. Special stock includes consignment stock for a customer, material provided to a vendor (for subcontracting work), vendor consignment stock, project stock, and sales order stock. Special stock is considered special because of the fact that it must be managed separately either for reasons of ownership or location. For example, vendor consignment stock is physically in house, but is not owned by your company until it is consumed. Material provided to a vendor is owned by your company, but is physically located at your vendor. An interesting thing about special stock is that it is listed in the query under the particular organizational level to which it belongs. For example, vendor consignment stock is in a storage location, so it is listed under the storage location in which it resides. Also, material provided to a vendor still belongs to the plant, but is not in a storage location in-house, so it is listed under the plant that owns it.

Once in the query itself, it is possible to change which material's stock is displayed without returning to the input screen by typing in the new Material number in the white Material field and clicking the New Selection button. The resulting query will display the stock of the new material for the same organizational levels originally selected. It is also possible to change the unit of measure in which the stock is displayed (if the material has multiple units of measure) without exiting the query screen by typing in the alternate unit in the white Unit Of Measure field, and clicking the New Selection button. The system will convert the stock display from the original unit of measure to the alternate using the conversions entered in the Material Master.

 TIP If you double-click a stock quantity or an organizational level in the query screen (or single-click and then click the Magnifying Glass button), a window listing all columns in the Stock Overview plus additional buckets not included in the Stock Overview will appear.

Stock/Requirements List

In addition to the Stock Overview, the user can review the Stock/Requirements List for information about a specific material. The Stock/Requirements List displays the most up-to-date situation of stocks and requirements for a material. It contains scheduled receipt dates and quantities, available quantity, purchase order numbers, production order numbers, and various other useful data.

The Stock/Requirements List differs from the Stock Overview in that it contains data relating to future availability and requirements for a material, while the Stock Overview focuses on the current stock situation. In addition, the Stock/Requirements List allows the user to perform numerous update functions, while the Stock Overview simply allows the user to view stock data in the system.

Navigation to the Stock Requirements Screen   The Stock/Requirements List can be accessed via numerous menu paths. One of those paths is as follows:

> **Menu Path:** Logistics > Materials Management > Inventory Management > Environment > Stock > Stock/rqmts. List
>
> **Transaction Code:** MD04

Utilizing this SAP menu path will take the user to the screen in Figure 10.25.

The user should input the Material number and Plant and press Enter to view the Stock/Requirements List: Individual Lines screen, as displayed in Figure 10.26.

The data displayed on the Stock/Requirements List is collected from many different modules in the SAP system. Purchase requisitions and purchase orders created manually in Purchasing are displayed on the list. Planned orders, purchase requisitions, schedule lines, and production orders created automatically when MRP is run are also contained on the list. In addition, dependent and independent requirements created in Demand Management are displayed on the list.

The Stock/Requirements List: Individual Lines screen displays the dates of all known current and future requirements for a specific material. In addition, the available quantity of the material based on the requirements is calculated and displayed on this screen.

FIG. 10.25

The Stock/Requirements List screen.

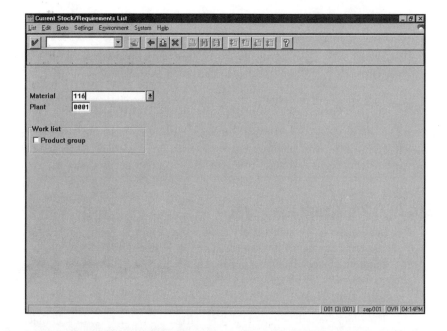

FIG. 10.26

The Stock/Requirements List: Individual Lines screen.

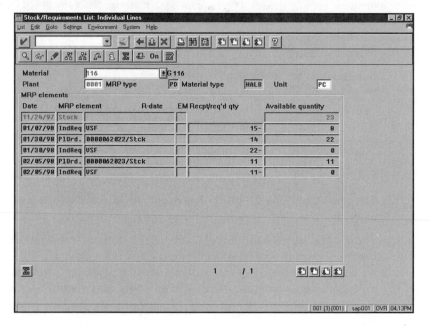

The following data fields are contained on this screen:

- Material—Identifies the material number of the material being reviewed.
- Plant—Identifies the plant the material requirements listed on the screen apply to.

■ MRP type—Key that determines how the material is planned. For example, manual reorder point planning, automatic reorder point planning, forecast-based planning, and so on.

■ Material type—Identifies the type of the material. For example, raw material, finished good, packaging, and so on.

■ Unit—The unit of measure for the displayed material.

■ Date—Date that indicates when a material has been received or when a material requirement exists.

■ MRP element—Abbreviation for the MRP element. MRP elements include: plant stock, customer requirement, planned independent requirements, planned orders, purchase orders, production order, and so on.

■ MRP element detail data—The data contained in this field will vary, depending on the MRP element. This field often contains a number identifying the MRP element (for example, purchase requisition number and R-date).

■ EM—Exception Message number that refers to an exception message generated when MRP is executed for the material. Examples of common exception messages include: "Start date in the past" and "Safety stock level exceeded."

■ Recpt/req'd qty—Identifies either the incoming quantity received or the quantity required, depending on the MRP element.

■ Available quantity—Quantity available on the specified date, based on current warehouse stock, receipts, and issues.

Functionality of the Stock Requirements Screen   Now that you have an understanding of the data on this screen, review some of the functions that can be performed. The following are only a few of the many activities that can be performed on this screen:

■ *Check the available quantity for a specific date.* This could be done before entering a new order if the Customer Service Representative wants to make sure enough stock will be available to satisfy the order.

■ *Check the status of a specific customer requirement.* Bob from Customer Service could have checked this list for the Reliable Manufacturers order described in Chapter 8, "A Day-in-the-life of the Customer Service Desk."

■ *Select a specific line item and use the SAP menu path Edit > Add to view more information relating to the item.* This additional information could be the production order that will create the material to satisfy a specific customer requirement. Referring back to the example from Chapter 8 again, Bob could have checked the production order that was to produce the parts for the Reliable Manufacturers order to see if it was complete or had been rescheduled. This would have given him real-time information rather than dated information on a printed report.

■ *Convert purchase requisitions into purchase orders.* Depending on the settings in MRP, the purchase requisitions generated by running MRP may need to be manually converted to purchase orders by the buyer.

■ *Convert planned orders into production orders.* For materials produced in-house, the planned orders generated by running MRP may need to be manually converted into production orders by the production controller.

This list is only a sample of the functions that can be performed on this screen. It should be noted that not all of the activities just listed relate to Customer Service. They were included in this section to highlight how many different modules in SAP can utilize the same screen. This screen will also be utilized by many different people within the organization. Some of these people include: Customer Service Representatives, buyers, planners, inventory managers, and production controllers.

After reading this section, you should understand the difference between the Stock Overview and the Stock/Requirements List, and when each of the screens should be utilized. The Stock Overview is used when the user would like a snapshot of the current stock situation. The Stock/Requirements List should be accessed when the user needs information about all the requirements for a specific material.

Using Quality Certificates in SAP

In today's world of cost control and smaller staffs, it is commonplace for the customer in a supplier/customer relationship to request or even demand documentation stating that the delivered materials conform to some set of standards. By having the supplier perform testing and certify the material's adherence to agreed upon standards, the customer lowers the cost for conducting incoming inspection of goods. These documents often relate to who bears the responsibility (cost or legal) if a problem occurs related to the delivered goods. Whatever the intent of the certification document, it is a real-life issue in many industries.

The more common names of these documents are Certificate of Analysis or Certificate of Compliance. The content differs slightly from company to company, but the purpose is to certify the quality of the material shipped. At a header level, these certificates often include information such as material number, batch number, date of manufacture, expiration date, and shipping date, to name a few. The body of the certificate normally includes the test conducted, the agreed-upon specification for the test, the method used for testing, and the test's result. Other information that may be included is the type(s) of certification(s) the supplier has achieved, references to governmental requirements, and signatures by authorized personnel.

Once the certificate is defined, the method of providing the certificates comes into play. Typical methods of delivery are fax, mail, or sent with the shipment. The delivery method is normally specified by the customer to fit his business practices.

If you look back at the Electro Tech situation for the shipment to Reliable, a certificate was to accompany the shipment. Laurie Stewart had to go to the lab to get the certificate before the shipment could leave. The Technical Service group held the specifications for the customer. The *Quality Certificate* system was not integrated with the *Sales* system, so requirements for a certificate had to be passed manually. Several disjointed systems and business practices constituted the Electro Tech certification process.

SAP provides a means of creating customized certifications with minimal effort. A certificate does not have to contain data from an inspection; rather it can state that the material was produced under certain guidelines. In contrast, the certificates could contain any number of characteristics. The decision is up to you and your customers.

Layout Sets

If, based on an agreement with a customer, you need to provide specific certification results, you must define certain aspects of the reporting. A member of the quality planning organization will need to create what is known as a layout set. A layout set in SAP is a predefined form used to generate a specific output. A sample layout set, QM_QCERT_01, is provided as a starting point for creating the output that meets the customer's requirements.

To maintain a layout set for a quality certificate, follow the menu path:

> **Menu Path:** Logistics > Quality Management > Quality Certificates > Certificate Profile > Process Layout Set
>
> **Transaction Code:** SE71

The screen that appears allows you to define the name and language of the layout set (see Figure 10.27).

FIG. 10.27

Initial screen for selection of a layout set.

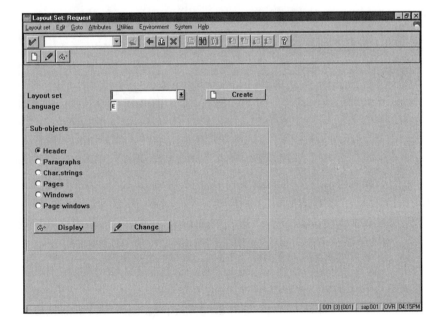

The initial setup of layout sets is often a job in itself (see Figure 10.28). It can be quite elaborate or very simple, but the following elements can be defined:

- Header
- Paragraph
- Character strings
- Pages
- Windows
- Page windows

FIG. 10.28
Layout set maintenance screen.

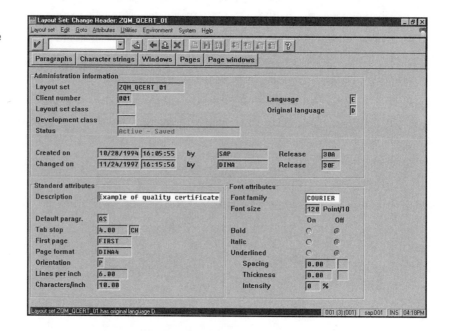

Certificate Profiles

The next step in the process is creating a certificate profile. The profile determines the status and the usage of the certificate. What this means is that the profile defines where the data is pulled from and when the certificate can be generated. More specifically, the exact characteristics that need to be reported are defined through the certificate profile. The certificate profile is the link between the material and customer.

The steps for creating a certificate profile are found with the following path:

Menu Path: Logistics > Quality Management > Quality Certificates > Certificate Profile > Create

Transaction Code: QC01

At the initial screen a name must be assigned to the profile (see Figure 10.29). This name can be any alphanumeric name but should help distinguish the specific use of the profile. You must also specify a certificate type. Certificate types are defined through configuration.

FIG. 10.29

Initial screen for entering a certificate profile.

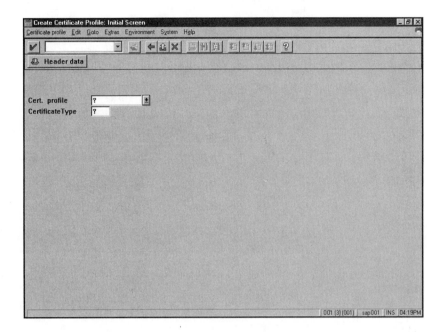

The main screen for defining quality certificate profiles asks for a layout set name, general information for looking up the profile such as Search Field and Short Text, and various requirements for selecting the correct inspection lot from which to extract information (see Figure 10.30).

Once the header data has been defined, click the Characs button to define what characteristics should be used on the certificate. Enter a line item number and select whether characteristic category Master Inspection characteristics or General characteristics should be used. Press Enter and you will be prompted to provide a plant and characteristic. The Characteristic Data box will appear (see Figure 10.31).

Enter the appropriate data and repeat for as many characteristics as necessary. Save the profile.

Certificate Recipient

The last step of the process is to define the recipients for the certificate. The certificate recipient defines when a certificate should be produced and who will receive it. The "who" can be any number of people involved in the receipt of the shipment. The customer buyer, dock supervisor, or any number of other individuals can be the certificate recipient. Multiple recipients can be defined.

Part

II

Ch

10

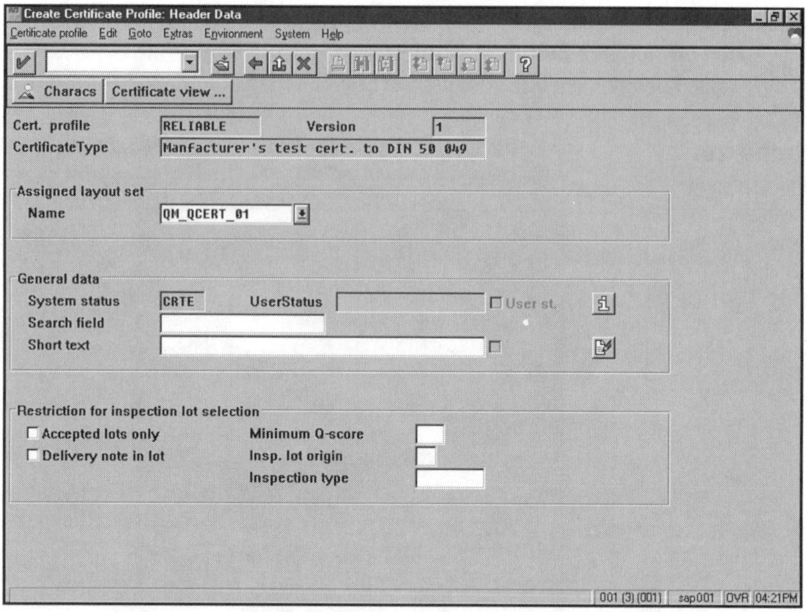

FIG. 10.30

The Create Certificate Profile: Header Data screen.

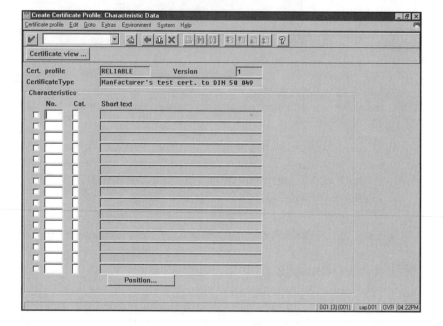

FIG. 10.31

The Characteristic Data box.

To set up a certificate recipient, use the following menu path:

Menu Path: Logistics > Quality Management > Quality Certificates > Cert. Recipient > Create

Transaction Code: VV21

The screen that appears is used to define the output type, which is the type of document to be generated. Click the Key Combination button to continue. Define the sales organization and appropriate customer information including what medium, timing, and language to generate the document (see Figure 10.32).

FIG. 10.32

Maintenance screen for certificate recipient.

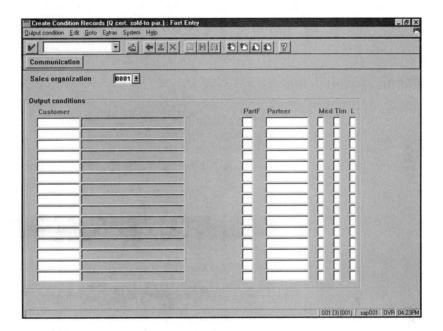

Part

II

Ch

10

Generating the Certificate

Quality certificates can be generated for a delivery, inspection lot, or batch. To create a certificate for an inspection lot, proceed as follows:

> **Menu Path:** Logistics > Quality Management > Quality Certificates > Certificate Creation > For Inspection Lot
>
> **Transaction Code:** QC21

Specify the inspection lot for which you want to create a certificate. Choose a recipient and specify the certificate profile information. Execute the function and a Print Controller box will appear. The certificate can be previewed onscreen or printed.

Financial Management for Sales and Distribution

In the Customer Service discussion of Electro Tech in Chapter 8, the lack of integration between the *Order It* system and Financials could create data inconsistency. If Sales and Financials are not integrated, business functions will need to be entered twice, once in each area. This could result in an inability to effectively service customers by creating incorrect invoices, causing lost discounts, or sending faulty overdue notices. How can Electro Tech's utilization of SAP R/3 prevent such problems?

The integration between Sales and Financials within SAP R/3 provides real-time account postings. This powerful capability to automatically post to Finished Goods, Revenue, and Accounts Receivable accounts ensures that external reporting requirements are met with minimal intervention by the user. The resulting financial statements contain accurate data gathered in real-time by the system, and the negative effects upon customer service are minimized.

Within SAP R/3, a number of business functions within Sales and Distribution affect Financial Accounting.

Goods Issue/Delivery to Customer

Creation of a Delivery Document and triggering of the goods issue within Sales simultaneously trigger a number of actions. As the goods issue (movement type) occurs, the finished goods stock is reduced by the quantity of the goods issue. An accounting document is automatically created to reflect the goods issue. The posted amounts consist of the goods issue quantity multiplied by the price (usually standard price) specified in the Material Master record (Accounting screen).

The following example shows the Accounting Document with a debit to Cost of Goods Sold (profit and loss account) and a credit to Finished Goods Inventory (Balance Sheet account):

10 pieces @ $10 standard price

Debit	Cost of Goods Sold	100
Credit	Finished Goods Inventory	100

This data can be viewed, as seen in Figure 10.33, by displaying the Accounting Document as explained in the "Display Document" section later in this chapter.

FIG. 10.33

The Goods Issue Accounting Document.

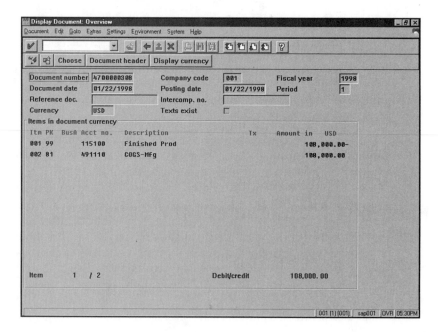

Creation of a Billing Document

Creation of a Billing Document (invoice) within Sales simultaneously triggers automatic creation of a Financial Accounting Document (Accounts Receivable). The posted amounts consist of the goods issue quantity multiplied by the price specified in Sales Order.

The following example shows the Accounting Document for a customer invoice with a debit to the Customer subledger/Accounts Receivable (Balance Sheet account) and a credit to Sales (profit and loss account):

10 pieces @ $20 (from Sales Order)

| Debit | Customer—Accounts Receivable | 200 |
| Credit | Sales Revenue | 200 |

This data can be viewed, as seen in Figure 10.34, by displaying the Accounting Document as explained in the "Display Document" section later in this chapter.

FIG. 10.34

The Accounting Document for customer invoice.

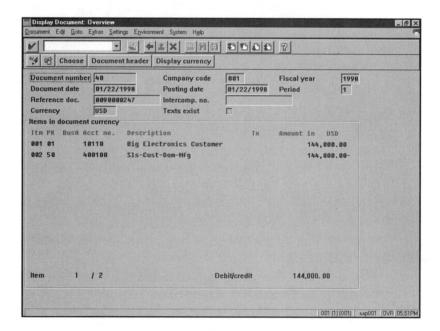

Within SAP R/3, a number of useful functions are performed in the Accounts Receivable area of Financial Accounting. A few of the major functions are listed in the following sections.

Customer Payment

Receiving payment from the customer is a relatively easy task within SAP R/3. The fact that the creation of the Billing Document in Sales automatically transfers to Financials allows for payment to be applied with reduced effort by the Accounts Receivable clerk. In a non-integrated system, the clerk may be left to create the invoice before paying it.

The following example shows the Accounting Document for a customer payment with a debit to cash (Balance Sheet account) and a credit to the Customer subledger/Accounts Receivable (Balance Sheet account):

Debit	Cash	200
Credit	Customer—Accounts Receivable	200

This data can be viewed, as seen in Figure 10.35, by displaying the Accounting Document as explained in the following section, "Display Document."

FIG. 10.35

The Accounting Document for customer payment.

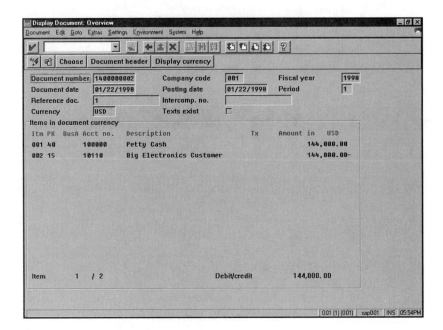

Display Document

This function allows the user to display a document that has been previously created in the system. This can be useful if a customer inquires as to the status of an invoice. Those invoices that have been paid will appear with a clearing document (Payment Document) number attached.

In addition, a document may be viewed in Change mode. While in Change mode, the user may edit various fields in the document. Keep in mind that posting dates, posting keys, and amounts may not be changed.

To display a document such as the ones discussed in the previous three sections of this chapter, follow the menu path:

Menu Path: Accounting > Financial Accounting > Accounts Receivable > Document > Display

Transaction Code: FB03

The major screen fields (see Figure 10.36) are as follows:

- Document Number—Number of the accounting document you want to display
- Company Code—The organizational definition of the company in which the document was posted
- Fiscal Year—The 12 month period for which the company defines a balance sheet

FIG. 10.36

The Display Document: Initial screen.

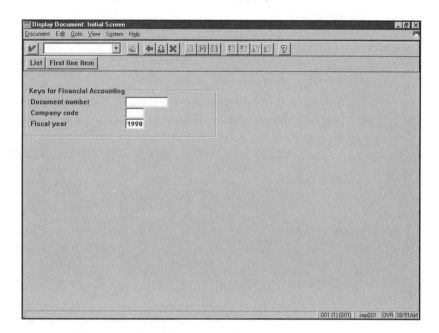

If the Document number is not known, you can look up the document by clicking the List button in the upper-left corner of the screen. The screen that appears allows you to specify certain criteria to limit the scope of the document search. The Document type field will limit the search to a specific type of Accounting Document. For example, the Goods issue/Delivery Document is type WL. The Billing Doc. transfer is type RV, and the Customer Payment Document is DZ.

Display Account Balances

This function allows the user to display the balance in a customer's account. The balance is comprised of all previously posted entries to the customer account.

The customer account may be viewed in either Account Balance mode or Line Item mode.

Account Balance The Account Balance mode displays the following:

- The opening carry forward balance
- The debit and credit balances for each posting period

- The balance per posting period
- The accumulated year-to-date balance

Line Item   To display individual line items from the Account Balance screen, double-click any period credit, debit, or balance. The line items that comprise the balance will be displayed.

> **Menu Path:** Accounting > Financial Accounting > Accounts Receivable > Account > Display Balances
>
> **Transaction Code:** FD10

The major screen fields (see Figure 10.37) are as follows:

- Customer—The customer account number
- Company Code—The legal entity for which the financial transaction is taking place
- Fiscal Year—The legal fiscal year in which the document was created

FIG. 10.37

The Customer: Initial Screen Balances Display.

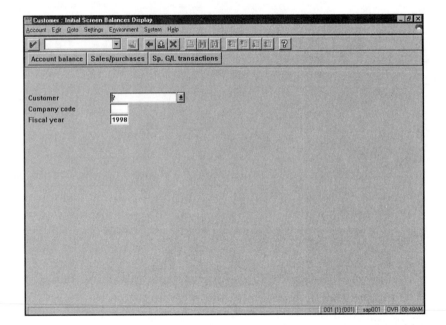

Dunning

Dunning is the process of sending customers a reminder that they owe your organization money for overdue invoices. During the dunning procedure the system searches for overdue invoices and prints notices to the customer. The layout and text for the notice are determined during system configuration.

Dunning is carried out via the Dunning program. The program determines the following:

■ The accounts and items to be dunned

■ The dunning level of the account

■ The dunning notice based on the dunning level

The menu path is as follows:

> **Menu Path:** Accounting > Financial Accounting > Accounts Receivable > Periodic Processing > Dunning
>
> **Transaction Code:** F150

The major screen fields are as follows:

■ Run Date—The date on which the dunning program is run

■ Identification—The legal entity for which the financial transaction is taking place

Customer Service Desk with SAP R/3

Now it's time to examine is a typical day at the Customer Service department of Electro Tech using SAP R/3. The job of a Customer Service Representative (CSR) is to be the interface between the customer and Electro Tech. Supplied with the right tools, the CSR can stop problems before they begin by not overcommitting when shipments can be made. Also, aided by the systems integration, additional service activities like certification of materials and invoicing can be accomplished easily and accurately.

Understanding the Customer Service Desk with SAP R/3

The Customer Service department of Electro Tech has now successfully implemented SAP R/3. As you look around the room, you still see an open area full of cubicles. The most obvious change in the surroundings is that instead of dumb terminals, there are now personal computers at each station. Multi-line telephones are still standard issue, but the constant ring has leveled to a normal work pace. There has also been a noticeable drop in the stacks of paper that fill the room.

As you recall, the Electro Tech Customer Service department is open Monday through Friday 7:00 a.m. to 8:00 p.m. EST. Looking at a typical day in the Customer Service department, you meet Bob Peters, who has been working at the order desk of Electro Tech for about five years. Bob was a participant in the BPS process to install SAP R/3 and understands the capabilities of the new system.

The Players

The following is a list of the employees involved in the Electro Tech customer service example.

- Bob Peters—Customer Service Representative
- Sam Soot—Customer from Reliable Manufactures
- Bryan Luther—Plant Production Scheduler
- Frank Brewer—Quality Control Analyst
- Laurie Stewart—Warehouse and Ship Dock Manager

The Situation

Before SAP was implemented, CSRs would give a customer a delivery date but often had to add days to the delivery date after the fact. Electro Tech's practice had been to never turn away an order. If a customer asked for a delivery within the established lead times, it was still accepted. When the delivery could not be made, it was delayed and customer satisfaction was on the decline.

Since the SAP go-live date, customers' complaints about delayed orders have slowly declined. The world isn't perfect, so delays still happen. But there has been a decided downward trend. The difference seems to be the use of SAP's availability-checking capabilities. Now when a customer calls in to place an order, an automatic availability check determines if the requested delivery date can be met. If it can, the order is confirmed. If it cannot be met, the CSR is given a delivery proposal that provides options. The total delivery date is determined based on inventory and planned production. Optionally, if a partial delivery can be made, the system will propose two delivery dates: a partial delivery based on the requested delivery date, and a subsequent delivery as production allows.

At first customers were upset by the fact that Electro Tech was refusing to accept orders within advertised lead times. Through the combined effort of the sales force and the CSRs, customers began to accept that Electro Tech's previous practice of overcommitting delivery dates only hurt in the long run. As customers began to accept the delivery proposals, they realized that deliveries became more regular.

SAP's Approach

It is Monday morning and Bob arrives at his desk about 15 minutes before his shift. Because it's a Midwestern company, the early order desk shift has to cover East Coast time. The second shift is set up to cover orders later in the day arriving from the West Coast.

Before SAP, Bob would pull out the latest copy of the plant inventory report and mark it with red, green, and yellow markers based on customer orders and the plant changes. This was necessary because the *Order It* system was not integrated with the production scheduling or inventory systems that the manufacturing facilities used. With the integration provided by SAP, this was no longer necessary. In fact, online reports and system integration points allow Bob to work almost completely without printed reports. The data is in the system and accessible.

On this morning, Bob answers his ringing phone and finds himself talking to Sam Soot of Reliable Manufactures. Sam is calling to place an order for 100 units of part A1Z1, a current sensor with relay output. Sam requests a delivery in four days. Bob enters the sold-to customer information and confirms with Sam the proper ship-to location. When he enters the item, quantity, and requested delivery date, the system responds with a delivery proposal. Based on the available stock, planned production, pick, pack, and ship times, only 37 units can be delivered within four days. The balance of the order can be delivered the end of next week. Based on this information, Bob explains to Sam that he can have the two partial shipments or he can wait until the end of next week and have a single complete shipment.

Sam is concerned but understands that Bob is providing the realistic options. He asks if he can put Bob on hold while he contacts his production manager. After a moment, Sam returns to say that Reliable would prefer to have the two partial shipments. The 37 available units will allow Reliable to meet a last-minute order that they received.

Bob continues to process the order. With the new system he can do pricing and credit checking on-the-fly. Pricing for Reliable on the A1Z1 offers a discount on orders of 100 or more. In the case of this order, the system automatically determines that the discount applies.

As the pricing is automatically determined, Bob thinks back to the BPS activities in which he was involved. Determining the necessary conditions to activate automatic pricing was no easy task. The system configuration took a lot of work to nail down, but with the contributions of the sales team and the support of management, it was realized.

Bob also likes the credit-checking capabilities SAP provides. Reliable has been a very good customer for a number of years, and no problem occurs in processing the order. Other customers have not been as fortunate. The credit-checking features let Bob know if the line of credit for a customer has been exceeded.

Bob finishes processing the order by running an incompleteness check. Between what is entered by Bob and the information that is pulled in from configuration and master data, the order is complete. Bob saves the order and thanks Sam for the business.

Later in the morning, a lull in the action gives Bob a chance to think about what Electro Tech has accomplished. He realizes that he hardly ever speaks to Bryan Luther or Frank Brewer any more. They talk occasionally to clarify information entered on a specific order, but for the most part, the integration of the Production Planning, Quality Management, and the Sales and Distribution modules allows all parties to get any information they might need without a phone call.

Bob decides to pick up the phone and call Frank to see how things are going for the plant. Frank answers the lab phone and almost doesn't recognize Bob's voice. "Hey Frank, it's Bob. How's it going?" asks Bob. Frank is surprised to hear from Bob and, due to old habits, says hello with a bit of apprehension. Bob assures him that this is strictly a social call and that he is more interested in how the lab likes the new computer system than he is in tracking some problem.

Frank explains that the lab likes the new system. There were a few problems in the beginning, getting everyone familiar with the required transactions, but it is smoothing out now. He says that he personally likes the quality certificate features. The number of problems associated with certificates has dropped substantially.

His past headaches of customizing the data reported on a certificate for a specific customer have been simplified. Through batch determination, the system can select lots that fit customer specification, and by using output determination, certificates can be automatically faxed or sent by EDI.

It wasn't all that easy converting to SAP, though. Frank tells Bob that setting up the certificate profiles and recipients was not an easy task. Since their legacy data was either poor or non-existent, lots of work had to be done to clean up or establish data. The quality management team worked long hours during the BPS process to get ready to go live, but it was time well spent.

He knows Laurie Stewart is happy with the new system, too. She doesn't have to make trip after trip to the lab to pick up certificates. The new LAN setup and output configuration allow the certificates to print at the dock when the delivery is processed.

Frank thanks Bob for the call and tells him to stay in touch, at least on a social basis. The conversation reminds Bob of the time they had to track down material for Reliable and, even after finding material on the off spec report, almost missed the shipment because it wasn't arranged. As he hangs up, he thinks of how SAP helps Electro Tech monitor shipments also.

The delivery due list is processed by the plant daily. It allows them to plan deliveries in an orderly, timely manner. If a situation does occur where expected product availability doesn't happen, processing the delivery due list can again point this out. Unlike the sales order check, the delivery due list availability check is typically limited to stock only, but it allows for monitoring material shortages.

Laurie Stewart processes the delivery due list. Material is chosen, removed from the available unrestricted stock, and reserved for the individual delivery. All necessary paperwork is printed out, material is shipped, and the Goods Issue is posted.

After shipment has occurred, invoicing can occur. This is processed in much the same way that the delivery is. The billing due list can create invoices based on settings in Master Data.

Thinking over the process, Bob realized that SAP has added organization to Electro Tech's business practices. The products that the company sold have not changed. The customers who bought the materials have not changed. Even the documentation needed to enter, ship, and certify a product have not changed. What has changed is the addition of a tight integration in these processes that allows them to function more efficiently. Yes, problems still occur, but with less frequency and easier resolution.

The Assessment

Comparing the life of a Customer Service Representative prior to SAP to post-SAP highlights some of the advantages the system provides. Most obvious is the decrease in firefighting. The system allows for information to be shared. Accessibility to information allows people to make better decisions. Better decisions generally lead to reduced cost.

If you step back and examine the work processes and system tools involved this case study, the following advantages present themselves:

- The tight integration between the PP, IM, and SD modules allows for accurate availability checking to occur automatically. This helps avoid overcommitting to customers and increases customer satisfaction.
- The stock requirements list provides at-a-glance information on planned production, inventory, and sales demand.
- Managing quality certifications to customers is improved through automated batch and output determination.
- The delivery due list ensures that shipments are not missed because a phone call was not made or a paper order was misplaced.
- Integration of the modules ensures that material is not doubly committed, as could have occurred with the paper system Electro Tech employed prior to SAP.
- Invoicing activities are directly tied to shipping activities.
- Simple plant logistics of where information prints or is stored is simplified.

Production Planning and Execution

CHAPTER 12

A Day-in-the-life of Production Planning and Execution

In this chapter

A typical day-in-the-life of a Plant Production Scheduler at Electro Tech

The working structure of Electro Tech and how the lack of information flow from one work group to another can cause service problems and incur added costs

The lack of integration between homespun computer systems and how this lack of integration has caused problems

How maintenance activities impact production activities

How supply problems impact production activities

How failure to adhere to or even respect the production schedule can cause customer problems

In the first example, you looked at a typical day at the Customer Service department of Electro Tech. During that example you met Bryan Luther, the Plant Production Scheduler. In that short moment, you began to see the problems facing the manufacturing facility. The scheduling of multiple manufacturing lines, the coordination of maintenance tasks, and supply problems are just a few of the challenges facing Electro Tech. This chapter takes a closer look at these activities to understand the problems and opportunities present at Electro Tech, Inc.

Understanding Production Scheduling

Bryan Luther has been with Electro Tech for 23 years. He has an MBA in plant operations but rarely gets to use his skills. Crisis management might have been a more appropriate educational background. Bryan is charged with the task of managing the material inputs and outputs of Electro Tech's largest manufacturing facility—a difficult task, made somewhat manageable by the MRP software he runs on his PC.

Every morning around 7:30, Bryan arrives at the plant and begins the process of determining what happened overnight by calling the various area supervisors. His goal is to determine how far off schedule the various manufacturing lines are. This is a necessary activity because it is rare that the schedule is maintained. Equipment problems, material shortages, and even failure to follow the schedule all contribute to Bryan's morning ritual.

The Players

The following is a list of the employees involved in the Electro Tech production example:

- Bryan Luther—Plant Production Scheduler
- Dave Jackson—Area Supervisor, Manufacturing Line 4
- Marge Houlihan—Plant Manager
- Irving Mayer—Maintenance Manager
- Matt Carlton—Mechanic
- Tom Norr—Maintenance Supervisor
- Ted Goldfield—Purchasing

The Situation

The seemingly simple task of determining what has slipped on the schedule is not easy at all. The area supervisors who hold the information Bryan needs so badly are busy trying to get equipment running or tracking down components needed for their manufacturing areas. Engulfed by their own problems, they don't respond to Bryan's voice mail messages or pages quickly.

Slowly, as the morning progresses, the information starts to flow into Bryan's desk—a phone call from one area supervisor, an email from another, while some appear in person to report the plant status. Around 9:00 a.m., Dave Jackson, the area supervisor for Manufacturing Line 4, the line that produces the A1Z1 current sensors, appears at Bryan's office door.

Dave is a young, hard-working person who cares about what happens within his department and the company he works for. He has a degree in business, which includes specialized training in supervision. Dave has managed to earn the respect of both his hourly employees and his management. Specifically, Bryan has come to respect Dave because his morning visits have become a regular occurrence. Whether the news is good or bad, Dave stops by to let Bryan know where things stand.

Dave explains that maintenance delays over the weekend have his department approximately a day-and-a-half behind schedule. Both Bryan and Dave know that this will impact several products in the automated production equipment line. Manufacturing Line 4 produces a whole line of current sensors, some of which go into the higher-level assemblies that Electro Tech sells. Dave proposes changes to the schedule, based on where the maintenance stands and what components he has available. The proposed changes primarily shorten the run quantities of the items on the schedule. A few items are deleted because Dave notices there is some available inventory, and these items have longer set-up times than other subassemblies.

Bryan reviews the suggested changes quickly, based on customer orders he knows are in jeopardy. After making a few minor changes, he agrees with Dave's proposal and tells him to move forward. He promises to update the schedule, based on their discussion, and have a new schedule printed and in Dave's mailbox later that afternoon. Dave agrees and heads to his department to implement the schedule changes.

As the morning moves forward, both Bryan and Dave move to put their plan into action. Bryan is slowed by the onslaught of phone calls from Customer Service Representatives (CSRs) trying to determine the status of their orders. Bob Peters is just one of many trying to track down items manufactured on Manufacturing Line 4. Some overzealous CSRs who aren't lucky enough to find material on the off-spec report, and who are dissatisfied by the answers Bryan gives, try calling the plant manager to complain.

The plant manager, Marge Houlihan, understands that the calls are a natural reaction but is bothered that the CSRs have become accustomed to calling her when they are dissatisfied by the answers her staff gives. The delays are not Bryan Luther's fault, and calls to the plant manager will not change the fact that, once again, the plant has fallen behind schedule. On this occasion, however, Marge is disturbed by the number of calls she is receiving and decides to get Bryan Luther, Dave Jackson, and the maintenance manager, Irving Mayer, together to determine what caused the delays on Line 4.

Irving Mayer is new to Electro Tech. He was hired, after an extensive interview process, because of his years of maintenance experience. The quality that differentiated him was that his last company used the same maintenance software that Electro Tech was using. Irving also has experience in manufacturing plants. He knows the credo: KEEP THE EQUIPMENT RUNNING. He has been getting used to his staff and labor resources and has been enjoying his work at Electro Tech.

Although it is still too early in his reign, Irving is anticipating the ability to do more predictive and preventive maintenance. In fact, he has targeted the old manufacturing lines in the Current Sensor department as a likely first target to show the effects of preventive maintenance. The first Preventive Maintenance Order (he designed it himself) went out last Friday. Line 4 went down over the weekend.

At 2:30 p.m., Irving, Bryan, and Dave assemble in Marge's conference room at her request. Bryan is still in the midst of trying to update the schedule per the changes he and Dave decided on earlier. The impromptu meeting is just one of several interferences that is blocking his progress. Irving isn't sure what the meeting is about, but he has a feeling that the delays in maintenance over the weekend will come up.

Marge sits quietly as the group filters in and sits. Once everyone is in place, she closes the door and starts the meeting with a simple question, "Gentlemen, once again I have received numerous phone calls from our Customer Service department about shipment delays. The complaints all seem to center around the items scheduled on Manufacturing Line 4. Can anyone explain what the problem is?" The group sits quietly for a few seconds, waiting to see who will speak first. Bryan Luther starts off with a quick explanation.

The Problem

"Marge, you are correct. Line 4 is behind schedule, but Dave and I have worked out adjustments to try to meet as many shipments as possible," Bryan says. He goes on to explain that the delays were caused by maintenance activities that ran long over the weekend. The items produced on Line 4 are in very high demand and when a day-and-a-half was lost, it caused problems.

Marge listens carefully as Bryan explains the problem. Both Irving and Dave sit quietly, waiting to see how Marge will react. Irving especially cringes as Bryan mentions the maintenance delays over the previous weekend. Irving knows that Marge supported preventive maintenance activities but knows his first attempt at using his newly designed maintenance work orders hadn't gone well. Marge turns to Irving and asks what went wrong to cause a day-and-a-half delay.

Irving explains that, going into the weekend, he had already laid out specific plans including personnel. Irving had assigned the best personnel in his organization to the Line 4 overhaul. He had pulled them from other places in the plant—and that annoyed some managers—but this was a critical step in moving Electro Tech's preventive maintenance activities into the future, and it had to be a success. The maintenance was to start at the end of second shift Friday night and be complete for first shift Sunday morning. Unfortunately, due to two different problems, the work wasn't completed until midday today, Monday.

The two problems his team had encountered were absenteeism and missing parts. On third shift Friday night, Matt Carlton, a mechanic, called in sick. Irving went on to explain that Matt was a competent mechanic but that he had a history of absenteeism, and this one hurt. Matt and another mechanic were scheduled to open the equipment up and when Matt didn't show, it slowed the progress. In fact, the other mechanics scheduled to come in on first shift Saturday had to help open up the equipment rather than work on it.

Marge, familiar with Matt Carlton's record, acknowledges Irving's problem with some understanding. She explains that she will speak to HR and find out where his record stands to see if disciplinary action is warranted. Then she asks Irving what else had slowed the maintenance work. She says, "You mentioned two problems slowed your work over the weekend. What was the second problem?"

Irving feels somewhat embarrassed by the second issue. In a plant that manufactures plant automation parts, he has to admit that maintenance activities were slowed because the correct replacement parts weren't available. Irving explains, "One of the motors on the line uses a custom-fitted belt, and we were out of the belt. We realized this late Saturday afternoon and had to rush order it in, but it didn't arrive until the beginning of the second shift on Sunday." For the first time in the meeting, Marge becomes noticeably aggravated by this admission.

"How did we go into a major maintenance job without having the correct replacement parts lined up?" Marge asks. Irving explains that only one motor in the whole plant uses the custom belt. He also explains that he, too, was confused by the fact that the part was missing. Irving had asked the supervisor who coordinated parts for the weekend repair why this part was missing. The supervisor, Tom Norr, said he had personally filled out a requisition for the missing part earlier in the week. He assumed it had come in and was available. Irving adds that while this was a costly assumption on Tom's part, there seemed to be a mix-up in Purchasing about the requisition and the needed delivery date.

Marge, not wanting to make too big a deal over an honest mistake, asks Irving to follow up with Ted Goldfield in Purchasing to determine the cause of the delay. She then asks the group what is being done to avoid future problems. Again, after a short pause, Bryan Luther is the first to speak. Bryan acknowledges the need for preventive maintenance activities but is concerned about the way the recent run was scheduled. He describes the current plant scheduling approach as being in monthly buckets. Only two of the weeks are considered firm, but the plan goes out a month. The maintenance activities over the weekend were scheduled on one week's notice, right in the middle of a monthly cycle.

At this statement, Dave Jackson perks up in agreement. Dave explains that he has also encountered problems with the late notice given for the maintenance activities. He had already scheduled workers for the line and had to find filler work for them when the line became unavailable. This is an added cost that he doesn't want to incur on a regular basis.

Marge asks the group how the maintenance activities were established and communicated among themselves. Irving immediately speaks up, saying that he had tried to work in maintenance activities several times but was always put off by the department. In this case, he worked up the plan and communicated it to Bryan and Dave as a must, not an option. He did emphasize that both Bryan and Dave had been verbally notified, however. Bryan and Dave agree that Irving had tried to schedule other maintenance activities and had pushed the latest effort through.

The Solution

Marge sits thinking for a moment. She is concerned about what she has heard but cannot offer an immediate solution. There is no question that Manufacturing Line 4 is at or near capacity but also needs preventive maintenance. Lacking a tactically advantageous solution herself,

Marge challenges the three to find a better way to schedule preventive maintenance. Bryan and Dave are asked to be more flexible in their scheduling of the maintenance activities. Irving is asked to provide advanced notice whenever possible and to make certain that the activities are properly staged. First and foremost, the three are asked to communicate with each other in an attempt to avoid further problems.

Marge agrees to support these efforts and says she will deal with the complaints from Customer Service. Bryan, Dave, and Irving agree to work out a mutually tolerable solution for future maintenance activities. With that, the meeting concludes.

Bryan Luther returns to his desk to find four messages from CSRs inquiring about orders they have submitted. There is also a message from one of the other area supervisors about problems on his manufacturing line. Bryan wonders if there is a simple solution to the problems Electro Tech faces. With that, he sits down at his PC and finally finishes updating the schedule with the changes he and Dave had agreed to hours before. Finally, at 4:00 p.m., a revised schedule is distributed to the area supervisors' mailboxes. The process began at 7:30 a.m. and, over eight hours later, is complete—at least until tomorrow.

The Assessment

As in the customer service example, there are several opportunities for improvement with this planning study. The delays in the manufacturing schedule were caused by a number of problems including HR and Purchasing, but most obviously centered around a poor understanding of scheduling. The complete picture of Maintenance, Purchasing, Human Resources, and Manufacturing demands must be considered in plant scheduling activities.

If you step back and examine the work processes and system tools involved in this case study, the following problems present themselves:

- Production scheduling is reacting to the occurrences in the plant, not proactively scheduling it.
- The CSRs don't have information available to them, so they make numerous phone calls on the same matter.
- Maintenance activities are not integrated with plant scheduling.
- Purchasing activities are not integrated with either maintenance or plant scheduling.
- Word-of-mouth is the link between departments.
- Changes to the schedule are based on gut reactions, not demand management.

CHAPTER 13

Making the Move from Production Planning Past to SAP R/3

In this chapter

How to define and maintain a scope related to production planning and execution activities

How breaking the entire business process into five levels helps build a clearer definition of required activities

The content of the production section of the SAP R/3 Implementation Guide

The SAP R/3 Business Navigator and how it aids in defining business processes

You have looked at some of the difficulties that Electro Tech faces in coordinating production scheduling with sales demand, maintenance activities, and material availability. These are not unique problems, and there are many ways to overcome them. Here, you will look at how SAP R/3 provides a powerful set of tools that enable a company to understand and control its production activities.

The process discussed here is the same as that presented in Chapter 9, "Making the Move from Customer Service Past to SAP R/3,"—analyze the current business process, re-engineer as necessary, map activities to SAP R/3 functions, document process and procedural changes, adjust organizational structure to streamline processes, and obtain agreement on the new operating practices. Some people may think this sounds simple. Others say that it's easy to list these steps but impossible to enact them. This chapter is based on real-life application of these practices.

Understanding Production

Within the production environment, the transition from pre-SAP to post-SAP often requires several procedural and culture changes. It is not uncommon for a production organization to be unsatisfied with its current operating mode, exhibit a large degree of agreement on the desired future operating mode, but have no clear concept of how to bridge the gap between the two. A large contributor to this dilemma is the attempt of a production organization to create an improved strategy based upon the same elements that led to the current operating mode. As has been said many times, when faced with unknowns, people will very often apply a "go with what you know" approach to their decisions. This is completely destructive to the goal of determining an improved production strategy. The same people, applying the same overall method of decision making, will undoubtedly re-create the same situations they are trying to outgrow.

The "go with what you know" philosophy is embedded in the Electro Tech organization. Decisions are made based on "what they know" and not on a structured analysis of information. While they want to improve their scheduling practices, knee-jerk reactions to the pressing issue creates schedule problems rather than solving them. Even specific projects directed at improving schedule performance have resulted in little or no success. To assist in avoiding this common and costly project result, it is necessary to apply a decision-making structure that will steer those involved away from current strategies and toward the desired result. The use of the Business Process Simulation (BPS) technique provides such a structure.

Production Planning BPSs provide a forum in which a structured view of current procedures, desired results, and the steps in between can be created. This focus can be applied at several levels of the production processes, beginning with a broad, overall view and working down to the actual, individual transactions necessary to support it. Along the way, internal procedures necessary to support the overall strategy are derived and implemented. Perhaps more importantly, the numerous integration points between production planning activities and the rest of the organization can be itemized and controlled.

The Scope

To successfully accomplish such a task requires several commitments from many directions. One of the earliest commitments necessary involves the definition of the scope of the project relative to the production planning processes. As with many data elements utilized in SAP, scope may be thought of as consisting of two qualities: area of validity and time frame. Time frame seems somewhat self-explanatory. As a result, it is often easy to minimize the attention paid to this scope element. Time frame essentially poses the question, "What is to be included within the project within a specified period of time?" Depending upon the organization involved, it may be possible (or even necessary) to place the transition of all production planning processes into an SAP environment within one time frame. For instance, a manufacturing firm with a single plant, or very few plants, may find it advantageous to restructure their entire production planning strategy as a single entity. This is especially true if the multiple plants are heavily dependent on each other for daily operation. Such a firm may derive no benefit from separate "waves" of production implementations of SAP. In fact, a single process review and system implementation may serve to simplify the entire process by avoiding the need to maintain old systems, create "bridges" between SAP and legacy planning systems, and train employees on multiple planning systems. The Electro Tech structure would be conducive with this approach. While they operate multiple plants making a variety of products, there are dependencies throughout the organization.

Another manufacturing firm with many manufacturing sites, each of which operates largely independently of the others, may find great benefit and little pain in breaking the SAP implementation into several waves. Such an approach may allow the use of one manufacturing site implementation to be managed on a smaller scale and then utilized as a model for subsequent implementations. Depending on the level of interaction between the multiple manufacturing sites, the inconveniences caused by maintaining several planning systems may be minimal.

Area of validity is an element of the project scope that has proven to be difficult for organizations to control. The area of validity refers to a definition of the production planning functions and their respective departments that will be addressed within an SAP implementation. An organization with very few manufacturing sites or departments is likely to include all manufacturing operations within the project scope, while an organization with many large, unrelated divisions may find it advantageous to limit its project scope to specific departments or plants and leave other portions of the organization unchanged.

By combining these two qualities—time frame and area of validity—the production planning scope may be defined. Examples of scope definitions may include all manufacturing functions at once (essentially a production planning "big bang"), plants 1 and 2 during wave 1, plant 1 only in wave 1, and so on.

At a high management level, definition of the project scope is essential. BPS activities that will eventually define the production planning processes down to the actual transaction level cannot be adequately conducted without a clear and consistent scope definition. For Electro Tech, upper management such as Marge Houlihan, the Plant Manager, and others involved in production planning and sales activities must commit to a constant scope. Inconsistency of scope definition is a common source of large problems within the production planning SAP implementation process. An inconsistent scope definition is essentially a moving target and is sometimes referred to as *scope creep*. Initially, it would appear somewhat simple to avoid scope creep. Simply define the areas to be affected and the desired time frame. This view is common in the early stages of many implementations and, unfortunately, indicative of a low appreciation for the level of integration that exists between the SAP modules.

As the production planning activities are examined in greater and greater detail during the BPS process, their impact on other areas of the organization become increasingly visible. If these interactions were not identified initially during the scope definition portion of the project, it often becomes necessary to subsequently modify the scope. Thus, scope creep occurs. The bad news does not end here. Following a change of scope, it is often necessary to revisit decisions previously derived to determine if they are still applicable. If not, these decisions must be modified, possibly affecting other subsequent process decisions and the overall scope. This decision-making spiral can go on and on. The result is a continually changing project scope and an iterative decision-making process that does not produce a usable business plan. Individuals involved in these situations can quickly become discouraged by their organization's apparent inability to reach firm decisions.

Often, observing existing gaps in the business processes can easily identify the area of validity of the implementation scope. Your brief examination of Electro Tech's current operating mode provides this information clearly. The need for Sales and Distribution (SD) information is evident by the difficulties experienced by Bob Peters and Bryan Luther when researching the status of a crucial order. It is again made visible by the difficulties incurred in verifying the subsequent shipment of that same order. Bob's daily task of hand-marking the production status printout with colored markers suggests that greater integration of *real-time* Production Planning (PP) information into the overall operation would be helpful. Bob's call to Frank Brewer for help in identifying usable off-spec material implies that a stronger link to Quality Management (QM) data should be considered. This call also suggests a need for Electro Tech management to review the basic concepts of quality in manufacturing and perhaps the legality of shipping off-spec material, but that's another story entirely. Finally, Bob's surprise when he learned that the ongoing maintenance activities had severely and adversely affected the plant's ability to serve the customer highlights a possible need for the inclusion of Plant Maintenance (PM) data into the overall project.

The Basic Team Definition

The issues discussed thus far help define the desired characteristics of potential BPS team members. While various types of consultants are frequently involved, it is the company or company representatives who must claim the process decisions made as their own. Company representatives form the nucleus of the BPS process. After all, the consultants will eventually move on to other projects, leaving the entire burden of managing the post-SAP production planning activities to the company. Oddly enough, this is often a difficult issue to firmly establish in the minds of BPS team members, both company and consultant. It is all too easy for company representatives to view the SAP implementation as something that is being done by visiting consultants for them. It is essential that company representatives view themselves as the process owners throughout the SAP implementation process. This is especially true when dealing with the industry-specific production methods and standards that exist within manufacturing.

In order to achieve success throughout the BPS process, representatives of the company should consist of a small number of individuals who are able to provide full representation of the functional areas involved. In the case of production planning for Electro Tech, this would include planners such as Bryan Luther, who represents various departments, shop floor staff like Dave Jackson, and procurement individuals who must align purchase activities with production planning. Ted Goldfield or Cindy Kendall, who you will meet in later chapters, might fill the procurement role. It is easy to end up with a lengthy list of individuals whose involvement is desired. This may actually detract from the process, as large groups generally have a harder time reaching decisions than do smaller ones. Somewhere there is a manageable balance between effectiveness and size.

Selection of suitable people to the BPS team has a lot to do with reducing the number of people required. More than anything else, the ability of those individuals selected to make decisions is key. Few things in the SAP implementation process are more frustrating than to place together experienced, knowledgeable company representatives only to find that they are unwilling to commit to process decisions within their own areas of expertise. It is possible that an occasional poor decision will be harmful to the overall BPS process. It is a certainty that indecision will always be harmful. This situation occurs frequently and is often an indication of waning support from upper management on previous decisions and projects. The BPS team members must know that they have the support of their upper management levels in order to feel comfortable with their roles in the SAP implementation process.

In order to gain and maintain this support from upper management, the BPS team members must possess excellent communication skills. Their ability to derive suitable production planning processes during the BPS sessions means little if they are unable to communicate the value of their plans to their superiors. In most cases, upper management representatives are mainly interested in the overall strategy to be applied, the costs incurred by the switch to this strategy, and the benefits expected from it. BPS team members must be able to represent their decisions within these criteria. At the same time, BPS team members will often be called upon to describe the day-to-day business transactions to individuals at more operational levels.

Lastly, BPS team members must possess an inherent desire to derive and apply improved solutions. The Production Planning module within SAP offers a great deal of structure to the production environment, but it requires an equally great amount of well-organized data to perform. In many cases, the amount of data required by SAP is much greater than that of legacy systems, and the efforts required to acquire and manage this data prove to be discouraging to those involved. As the saying goes, "There's no such thing as a free lunch!"

Business Process Simulation

The derivation of the post-SAP production planning structure is a complex process. As such, it is helpful to separate this mountainous task into several manageable levels. A process whereby the structure is derived into four distinct levels has proven to promote success in this large endeavor.

Level 1: Enterprisewide

The overall SAP implementation is viewed from an enterprisewide vantage point. Relationships between separate business requirements are depicted.

In the case of the example firm Electro Tech, the Level 1 flow would depict the overall business functions of the firm but in a little more detail (see Figure 13.1). If, at some time in the future, the organization expands horizontally, this will most likely be displayed within the Level 1 process flow.

FIG. 13.1

An example of a Level 1 process flow.

Level 2: Inter-Function Process Flows

Within a company, the relationships between the business functions are depicted in Level 2 flows. For example, the link between Sales forecast and Production Planning or between Production Planning and Production Execution are specified.

Based upon your current knowledge of Electro Tech's operating modes, the Level 2 process flow would likely depict a complex interaction between the various functions performed by Sales Forecasting, Production Planning, and the Shop Floor. Deeper examination of each area's operations would likely present further areas of interaction (see Figure 13.2).

Level 3: Intra-Function Process Flows

Within each specific department, such as Production Planning or Sales, the process flows are derived.

As an example, a Level 3 process flow for Electro Tech's Production Planning department would likely depict the receipt of demand data, scheduling of production to accommodate demand, verification of available machine and labor capacity, scheduling of items to be reworked, and so on (see Figure 13.3).

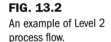

FIG. 13.2
An example of Level 2 process flow.

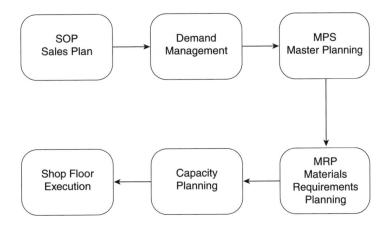

FIG. 13.3
An example of a Level 3 process flow.

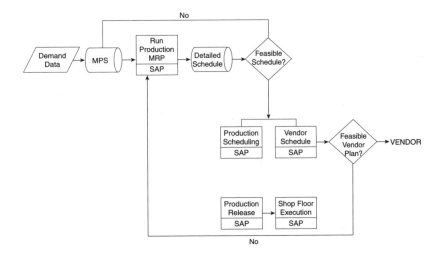

Level 4: Transactions

For each action described within the applicable Level 3 process flow, the actual transactions to be performed are presented as shown in Figure 13.4.

Level 1 and Level 2 process flows are largely determined at a middle to upper management level. In this way, the desired high-level operating strategies for the entire enterprise are specified. These strategies serve as guidelines for the derivation of the necessary Level 3 and Level 4 process flows. The real meat of the BPS process occurs in the derivation of the Level 3 and Level 4 flows. It is here where the actual business transactions are defined and the links between them are specified.

Part
III

Ch
13

FIG. 13.4

An example of a Level 4 process flow.

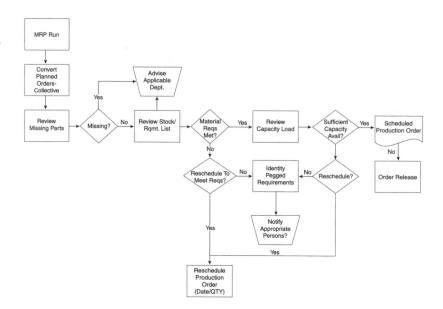

Because of the large number of issues at hand, record keeping becomes an increasingly important element of the BPS process. Prior to the initiation of Level 3 activities, the creation of a suitable BPS workbook can prove to be an enormous subsequent timesaver. Through the use of such a workbook, the intended scope and direction of the BPS sessions can be better controlled. In essence, the workbook serves as a BPS roadmap. However, the workbook itself is to be considered a living document, subject to modification as necessary.

Hopefully, modification to a BPS workbook will consist of additions of detail rather than gross changes. This issue deserves some additional consideration. When properly established, the entire business process can be examined through the combination of many BPS workbooks. For example, Production Planning processes are described in one workbook. Sales processes are described in another workbook. Integration points between the two areas are identified in both workbooks. When planning activities require input from Sales, this input is indicated on the appropriate Production Planning Level 3 process flow. The corresponding output of information from Sales to Production Planning is indicated on the appropriate Sales Level 3 process flow. In this way, each area's internal processes can be defined, along with the necessary integration points. This provides a method by which gaps in the overall process are identified.

Since it is therefore not possible for a BPS team, such as Production Planning, to operate completely independently of the rest of the SAP implementation, it is essential that a certain level of discipline be applied to the process. Adherence to the overall implementation methodology is key. Within each BPS session, adherence to discipline is often most difficult regarding the levels of the process. The temptation is great to evaluate a Level 2 issue and then allow the same discussion to immediately drive down to the SAP transaction level, which is a Level 4 discussion. For example, a Production Planning BPS team that wants to identify Level 2 concerns may initially discuss the fact that their actions will undoubtedly affect the shop floor activities. Rather than moving on to other Level 2 areas of integration, the discussion will then become centered on exactly how planning will affect shop floor execution. Inevitably, some member of the team will then begin discussing the specific existing SAP transactions and the question will arise: "What does SAP do for this situation?" In an instant, the discussion has disintegrated from a structured design of a Level 2 flow to an open forum, which derives nothing other than each team member's guesses as to SAP's standard configuration capabilities.

Without careful attention to the project implementation plan, this situation repeats itself over and over, in many different BPSs. The result is a lack of progress, despite a large investment of time on the part of everyone involved, and the general impression that the implementation task is too large to ever be successfully accomplished. Depression sets in for the BPS team members, and progress slows further. It is a scenario that has unnecessarily lengthened many SAP implementations.

A company's dependence on SAP's initial configuration deserves additional discussion. Historically, business management software packages have been fairly rigid in nature. Following the installation, it was necessary for the company to modify their procedures to accommodate the structure forced upon them by the software. As a result, the company was not given the flexibility or responsibility to fully define its own procedures. This mindset often exists on the part of an organization when implementing SAP. As much as the broad configuration capabilities of SAP are discussed, it is often the case that the company just doesn't understand the implications present. With the freedom granted by SAP's broad configuration capabilities comes a large responsibility to adequately define the desired business practices up front, prior to any concern over the software's capabilities or limitations. This task is a difficult one in any organization and is a task that most members of an organization are not accustomed to performing. A common response to process definition difficulties is for the company to assume that there exists an "SAP solution" to their issues that should be adopted simply on the belief that "SAP handles it that way." Nothing is further removed from the desired direction of an SAP system implementation. The SAP system's broad configuration capabilities are intended to enable a company's desired business practices, not direct its structure. SAP configuration is intended to follow the company's business plan, not lead it.

Production planning activities highlight this condition very well. By definition, production planning issues are tied directly to the characteristics of the end product. Chemical processes may involve reaction times, perishable products, and temperature concerns. Aircraft production may involve long component lead-times, high component value, and make-to-order strategies. Textile production may be well suited for repetitive manufacturing methods. Each type of production has its own set of characteristics that should be supported by the planning software package. To assume that SAP immediately offers a ready-to-use solution for each type of planning issue is overly optimistic. What is not overly optimistic is to assume that SAP can be configured to support a wide variety of production planning strategies, *after* those strategies have been clearly derived by the company.

If they are not organized in their approach, the management staff of Electro Tech is perfectly poised to miss this crucial item. In their current condition, they are discouraged and frustrated with their mode of operation. While they realize that there must be a more structured manner with which to organize their business activities, they are intimidated by the apparent enormity of the problem. If they do not apply a great deal of self-discipline and logic to the situation, they will make an extremely costly leap of desperation. They will pursue an SAP implementation based on the belief that the system itself will provide control structure and overall business strategies, which they lack.

Scheduling Reality

By their very composition and nature, computerized business management systems, such as SAP, operate in a purely quantitative manner. They access discrete segments of data that they have been given, they perform operations per a logic path that has been configured, and they present the conclusions. That's it. They do not respond to anything that has not been quantified or lies outside of a given logic path. Or, to phrase this concept in a slightly different manner more pertinent to production scheduling, the scheduling information produced by the system will be a direct result of the data and strategies that were input.

This sounds like a simple, direct concept that does not introduce controversy into the scheduling process. In fact, it is, as long as an assumption is made that the master data contained within the system reflects reality. Unfortunately, for many production organizations, this assumption is a very tough one to live up to. For a variety of reasons, master data may often be largely detached from the actual material and process characteristics.

Within the Electro Tech example, you have already witnessed this problem. Unrealistic assumptions used to formulate Irving Mayer's preventive maintenance schedules affected daily scheduled production rates. Subsequently, commitments to customer orders were jeopardized, along with both Bryan's and Irving's opportunities for future advancement.

Common Sources of Master Data Inaccuracy

When production processes are initially created, estimates of their expected characteristics are usually derived. In many cases, such estimates are required in order to justify the creation and funding of the process itself. Expected production rates, maintenance requirements, operator skill level requirements, and so on, are specified and serve as the initial master data set for the respective process. Oftentimes, this initial set of master data reflects an extremely optimistic view of the anticipated process characteristics such that the process owner will be able to gain approval for its implementation more easily. Following implementation of the process, it is likely that the actual operating characteristics differ from those anticipated. Yet, in many cases, the follow-up action of updating the process master data to reflect actual characteristics is not accomplished. Resources aimed at process justification have moved on to the next "new" project and are not dedicated to maintaining those already approved and implemented. As a result, the original process master data, which differs from subsequent actual data, is retained. Each time the process is scheduled, it is scheduled per the original master data. Each time the process is performed, the actual results depict a lower performance level than that which was scheduled.

This is not an uncommon scenario. The result is an apparent inability to attain scheduled performance due to poor shop floor performance. It is possible that the production processes themselves require modification and that the performance level initially depicted is attainable. However, until such improvements are verified, to continue to schedule overly optimistic values is a poor business strategy.

This example suggests that inaccurate scheduling data could result at the time of the creation of new processes. What about those shop floor operations that have existed for years without significant change? Is it safe to assume that the system master data for these processes accurately reflects their performance characteristics? Without a continual, concentrated effort at data management and control, the answer is "No." Just because a process has existed for a long period of time does not say anything about the validity of the data used to schedule it. In fact, master data relevant to mature processes is often taken for granted. It is not uncommon to hear production schedulers or shop floor supervisors discuss how they are aware of the actual completion time of a specific task despite the time indicated on the production schedule. "We know how long that job is scheduled for and also we know how long it really takes," may be heard frequently within production shops across the country. Yet, these same shops may have no defined process to update the master data on a regular basis. They are, in effect, relying on the individuals in the shops to bridge the gap between scheduled performance and reality.

Derivation of Factual Master Data

Statistical data is often helpful to verify or refute perceptions about actual process capabilities. Unfortunately, Statistical Processing Control (SPC) techniques are often misunderstood and applied incorrectly. When properly established, SPC techniques can provide a great deal of information regarding the long-term characteristics of a manufacturing process, the impact specific external events may have on that process, the repeatability of the process, and so on.

The long-term view of process characteristics provided by SPC techniques is especially important to the production scheduling arena. All too often, a process is evaluated based on only one or two trials. The result is then taken to represent the long-term capability of the process. It is unlikely that one or two test cases of any process provide a sufficient sample from which to base large generalizations. Furthermore, it is highly likely that the test cases performed were conducted under conditions more optimal than those normally present in the shop environment.

Because SPC techniques are largely quantitative in nature, they fit well into the scheme of an SAP implementation. When used correctly, the view of process capabilities they provide is an invaluable tool in establishing the master data to be used throughout the SAP system, especially in the area of production planning. Through SPC, the influence of personal perceptions, politics, and agendas may be reduced, leaving quantitative data suitable for use by the SAP system.

Master Data Revision Difficulties

More than any other item, the magnitude of the task and the lack of suitable resources is presented as the primary reason why cleanup of master data is not accomplished prior to use within SAP. This is a frequent but very shortsighted view of the issue. There is no doubt that the resources required to adequately maintain master data in a current and secure manner are substantial for any department or firm. However, the benefits gained by this activity are many times greater than the costs incurred.

Master data is the one consistent focal point of all production scheduling activities within SAP. Conclusions resulting from use of the master data are continually produced in Manufacturing, Sales, Accounting, Human Resources, and so on. The effort required to update master data may be large, depending on the current status of the organization. The resources required to track down and correct the hundreds or even thousands of daily transactions, which are based upon the incorrect master data, are often found to be too large to contemplate. The decision of whether or not to dedicate resources to the control of master data in production scheduling is a matter of "pay me now or pay me later," with the latter payment being so high that it is essentially impossible to perform.

Corrections or updates to scheduling master data may receive attention from a more managerial or political direction. Suppose the master data for an item incorrectly indicates that production requires 25 days per unit, even though the actual production process for the item requires 30 days per unit. At the same time, suppose that Sales has secured a large, seemingly profitable contract based upon the firm's ability to supply one unit every 25 days to an important customer. After the units are scheduled, it becomes painfully evident to the scheduler that all the units will be delivered late. In response to this, the scheduler is likely to pursue one of two choices. Either the actual production time of the unit must be immediately shortened to 25 days, or the master data must be modified such that 30 days per unit is reflected by the production schedule. In either case, a conflict will immediately result. A sudden change in production time from 30 days to 25 days will likely receive some resistance from the Production departments involved because this change probably will increase their daily workload. An update of the scheduling master data to reflect the actual production time of 30 days will receive a strong reaction from Sales or Customer Service, since the production schedule will be unable to meet their commitments to the customer. At some level within the organization, a political battle will ensue between Sales and Production, with the production scheduler sitting in the middle.

There are many other examples of situations such as these, all with the common theme of *reality*. Prior to use of any ERP system for production scheduling functions such as SAP, master data must be reviewed and maintained such that it may be used to model reality. This is a key point that cannot be overemphasized. Allowing unrealistic master data to exist and to be utilized in the business processes modeled and tracked by SAP will produce inaccurate and misleading results. This issue must be addressed at a high level of management during the early stages of an SAP implementation. Benefits anticipated from the use of SAP within production scheduling (or any other area of a company) will not be realized if a continual effort is not maintained to keep factual master data.

SAP Business Navigator

To assist in process definition, SAP provides the Business Navigator. In R/3 V3.0 the Business Navigator is essentially a graphical depiction of the decision logic tree reflected in the base SAP configuration (see Figure 13.5).

FIG. 13.5

Sample of SAP R/3's Navigator.

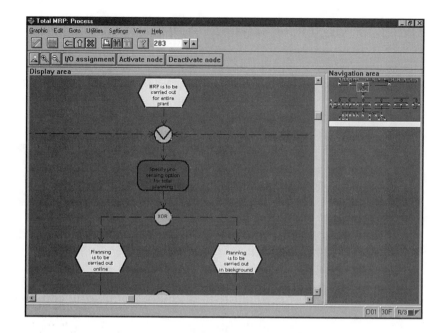

The Navigator is often used as an initial training aid to help companies grasp a more physical understanding of the logic and transactions within SAP. The effectiveness of the Navigator becomes increasingly apparent as the company discovers the need to configure the system to better suit its needs. The Navigator can then be used for its intended purpose, as a flexible business process modeling tool. By examining the many decision and action steps depicted by the Navigator, the company is forced to map out desired business practices in great detail. Such detail is necessary if subsequent configuration of the system's response is to be accomplished correctly and efficiently.

Oftentimes, the Business Navigator is ignored or forgotten during the implementation process. Once the companies become involved in the definition of their own processes, it is easy to become buried in detail and forget that a structured model exists. This is unfortunate since the Navigator's purpose is to provide a decision-making path such that total confusion and information overload is avoided.

As in the case of configuration, it is extremely unlikely that the initial decision tree depicted in the SAP Business Navigator is immediately suitable to a specific organization. This is assumed. Therefore, the Navigator can be modified as necessary to reflect the company's desired decision logic. Again, SAP configuration-related tools are intended to allow the system to support the company's desired operating modes. They follow the company's desired structure. They do not impose a structure upon the company.

Part

III

Ch

13

Implementation Guide (IMG)

The Implementation Guide (IMG) is an SAP tool that is provided to ease the actual act of system configuration. In effect, the IMG is nothing more than a graphical front-end to the configuration tables (see Figure 13.6). It is organized in a hierarchy of business functions and allows the company to quickly (well, usually quickly) drill-down to the configuration settings of specific transactions.

FIG. 13.6

The SAP R/3 Production IMG.

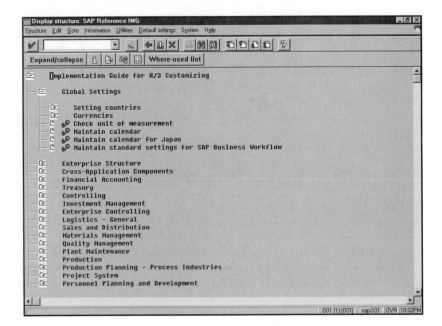

The IMG allows the company to select, or even create, desired configuration options, which will direct the system's response. The IMG does not necessarily assist the company with process definition decisions, but rather provides the method by which existing process definition decisions can be enabled within the system.

Within most modules, including Production Planning, use of the IMG and actual system configuration may elicit a variety of responses and problems from the company. Because of the broad scope that configuration changes may have, such actions must be taken with care. When modifying configuration settings, the user is not necessarily affecting one discrete activity. It is quite possible, and likely, that any change to the system configuration affects many activities in many modules. Thus, a substantial level of understanding of the SAP system is generally helpful. This fact often contributes to a hesitance of the company to explore the possibilities contained within the IMG. As a result, the company may not fully examine system capabilities and form the opinion that SAP is limited in its capabilities and unsuitable for a desired function. Some companies have gone so far as to then utilize several additional software packages, each for a specific task, in conjunction with SAP, never realizing that SAP had every bit of the capability they required all along. They never realize that the additional cost and complications incurred in the process of combining several unrelated systems with the SAP system were unnecessary.

Integration Points

As you have seen in the Electro Tech case studies thus far, production planning touches many different areas of the business. In the Sales and Distribution case study, you saw how production schedule changes directly impacted the customer service performance of Electro Tech. Similarly, you have seen how plant maintenance activities can adversely affect the production schedule. The term *Supply Chain* is commonly used to represent the process of converting raw materials into a delivered product. The case studies are meant to demonstrate that if any link in the chain is broken, the strength of the organization suffers. Oddly enough, non-integrated computer systems are like having all the links of the chain without any of them being connected.

In the course of conducting BPS activities, each team must consider integration points. The Production Planning team must interact with the Sales and Distribution team, the Quality Management team, and the Costing and the Plant Maintenance teams, to name a few. This is often difficult for experienced industrial people who are used to working within their own departments or business functions. Considering the far-reaching implications of a production planning decision doesn't fit the "firefighting" mold these people are often familiar with.

This book reviews several key business areas and how BPS activities can transpire for that given function. It is important to remember that each module of SAP that is being implemented warrants a similar approach. One or more BPS teams are usually needed to properly acknowledge, define, and address the necessary business concerns. Note that more than one team may be necessary per module. Looking at the PP module, it is very typical for one team to address MPS while another addresses MRP. There is almost always a team specific to production execution on the shop floor.

What a company accomplishes through an SAP implementation depends on what it puts into it. Commitment and time are requirements. The success at the end of the process is well worth it, however.

CHAPTER 14

Production Planning and Execution Functionality with SAP R/3

In this chapter

The Production Planning (PP) module of SAP provides a fully functional suite of production planning and shop floor execution transactions. Like the rest of the SAP system, the PP module is built on the concept of developing a plan and then enacting it. The planning starts with the setup of a variety of master data discussed in Chapter 6, "Data Types in SAP R/3." Once the master data is defined, demand from sales operations feeds the production planning process. These planning techniques feed the shop floor that executes the plan.

Understanding Production Planning

It is difficult to present a general overview of the SAP production planning process. The production planning functionality is a highly flexible collection of submodules and functionality that can be linked together to form a coherent planning and scheduling process. Every SAP implementation has the opportunity to use some or all of the SAP planning functionality, resulting in a production planning process tailored to meet a company's needs.

For example, Figure 14.1 depicts an example of how the functional submodules in the SAP Production Planning system can be used. The sales representatives create sales plans in the Sales and Operations (SOP) module. These sales plans are then copied into Demand Management by the master production scheduler and smoothed out from weekly buckets into daily buckets. Once the master plan (in Demand Management) is satisfactory, master production scheduling is performed, followed by detailed material requirements planning. The detailed material requirements are fed into the capacity planning system for finite production scheduling and dispatching.

This process would be applicable for a company that has accurate sales forecast information based on sales account representative feedback from customers, or some form of accurate market predictors. The production environment would typically be a job shop with relatively expensive finished goods being produced in a complex manufacturing and assembly process.

FIG. 14.1

Sample SAP production planning process.

Sales Plan
[SOP]

⬇

Independent Requirements
[Demand Management]

⬇

Master Plan
[MPS]

⬇

Material Requirements Plan
[MRP]

⬇

Dispatch Schedule
[Capacity Planning]

In contrast, another installation can use the planning process depicted in Figure 14.2. The Materials Forecast module is executed to produce forecasted requirements based on historical sales data applied to a statistical forecasting algorithm. These forecasted requirements are fed into the Material Requirements Planning module to generate a weekly run schedule.

This planning process would be applicable to a company that produces high volume products in an assembly line facility, where product mix and changeover minimization are the driving factors in scheduling.

FIG. 14.2
Alternative SAP
production planning
process.

These examples pose two distinctly different production planning processes that can be modeled in SAP. However, SAP is not limited to only two processes. The Production Planning module supports the following submodules and processing options, which can be linked into flexible planning processes (see Table 14.1).

Table 14.1   Production Planning Functionality

Production Planning Submodules	Processing Options
Sales and Operations Planning	Product Group Planning
	Create Sales Plan
	Create Production Plan
	Rough-Cut Capacity Planning
Demand Management	Transfer from SOP Plan
	Transfer from Materials Forecast
	Manage Independent Requirements
	Manage Customer Requirements
Consumption-Based Planning	Reorder Point Planning
	Materials Forecasting
Master Production Scheduling	Product Group Scheduling
	Interactive Planning

Part
III

Ch
14

continues

Table 14.1 Continued

Production Planning Submodules	Processing Options
Material Requirements Planning	Basic Date Scheduling
	Detailed Lead Time Scheduling
Capacity Planning	Detailed Capacity Planning
	Rate-Based Capacity Planning
	Aggregate Capacity Planning
	Dispatching
Shop Floor Execution	Production Order Scheduling
	Repetitive Manufacturing
	Production Planning for the Process Industries
	Kanban Scheduling
Long-term Planning	Multiple Independent Planning Scenarios

Some system and practical constraints limit the possible combinations of these submodules and processing options. However, SAP allows the production planning process to be defined differently for each plant, each production line, each department, or even for each manufactured component. For example, a plant may have a kanban cell in one department and a repetitive assembly line in another. Each of these areas could have a different production planning process in SAP.

To define multiple production planning processes, most implementations segregate groups of materials that are planned in a similar manner. Using the Electro Tech example, the industrial electronic components are produced on a repetitive assembly line. The factory automation products are made in a job shop manner, in small lots. Spare parts for both industrial components and automation products are produced, in addition to the components needed for assembly into finished parts. Each of these three groups (Industrial, Automation, and Spares) can have a different scheduling process in SAP.

The flexibility available in the SAP Production Planning functionality creates a myriad of possible production planning processes. To help explain the possibilities, this section describes how to use each of the production planning submodules:

- Sales and Operations Planning
- Materials Forecasting
- Demand Management
- Master Production Scheduling
- Material Requirements Planning

- Capacity Planning
- Long-term Planning
- Shop Floor Execution

Each submodule is explained in terms of how to use the functionality, along with an explanation of the inputs that can feed into the submodule, and an explanation of follow-on functionality that can be used to process the results. Knowing this information allows one to construct the possible production planning processes.

Sales and Operations Planning

The need for effective sales and operations planning has become an increasing reality in the customer age. In noncompetitive or monopolistic markets, producers can dictate lead times with customers, accepting orders only outside of production lead time. In competitive markets, however, customers are no longer content placing orders far in advance and waiting for full or published lead times to receive the product. As market competition increases, the producer who can react to customer demand the quickest often wins the battle for the customer. In these competitive markets, sales and operations planning is used to anticipate future demand so that production can begin before customer orders are placed.

Consider the fictional company Electro Tech. In the beginning, Electro Tech was a pioneer in the market for industrial electronic components and factory automation products. In the 1950s and 1960s, this was an emerging market. Customers accepted long lead times because Electro Tech's products were engineered to meet the specific requirements for each installation. This proved to be a very lucrative business for Electro Tech, and the company grew dramatically.

However, in the 1970s and 1980s, the market began to change. Industrial electronics became the standard for production facilities. Factory automation, which was pioneered for large automotive manufacturing assembly lines, found applications in small-scale production lines, from automotive components to assembly operations. With the market explosion came increased competition. Also, widespread use triggered the adoption of industry standards.

By the late 1980s and 1990s, the customer focus shifted from engineer-to-order solutions to programmable configurations that could meet many customer's requirements. As the market matured, Electro Tech lost some of its competitive advantage. Other competitors began offering similar products with shorter lead times than Electro Tech's. In response to the market pressure, Electro Tech began booking orders within production lead times. Very quickly, the Manufacturing department started to fall behind, and orders were shipped increasingly late.

Sales and Operations Planning in SAP encompasses several different techniques that can be used to help forecast sales demand in environments where customer-quoted lead times are less than manufacturing lead times. However, companies that have the luxury of accepting customer orders at full manufacturing lead time are not forced to use this functionality. For this situation, SAP provides make-to-order and engineer-to-order production strategies.

Part
III

Ch
14

Using the SOP Planning Table

Sales and Operations Planning provides a link between the sales forecasting and master production scheduling processes. It allows information to be shared online between the Sales department and Production Scheduling to keep each up-to-date with the latest information.

The planning table is the SAP vehicle for recording and sharing this information. The standard SAP planning table is an integrated spreadsheet, used to record a sales plan, and a production plan. There can be multiple versions of the planning table for a given material or product group, but only one of these planning tables is active at any point in time. Only the active planning table can be used to transfer the SOP plan to Demand Management for further processing.

To access the planning table for a material, execute the following menu path:

> **Menu Path:** Logistics > Production > SOP > Planning > For Material > Change
>
> **Transaction Code:** MC88

The system will display a selection screen to choose which SOP plan to maintain. SOP plans can be created specifically for a material or product group. Product groups represent a collection of materials, as will be explained later. Enter the appropriate data into the Material/Product Group and Plant fields, as explained in Table 14.2, and click the Active version button.

Table 14.2   Data Fields for the Planning Table

Field	Value	Description
Material/Product	Enter a material number	Material number or Group product group for which the SOP plan will be created
Plant	Enter a plant	Plant in which the material or product group is being planned
Active Version	Select button	Select to maintain the active version of the SOP plan

Once the fields on the selection screen have been correctly entered, press the Enter key. The SOP planning table will appear. Figure 14.3 shows an example of a standard SOP planning table. The columns represent time periods such as days, weeks, or months.

The rows represent information that can be used to help synchronize the production plan with the sales forecast:

- Sales—Displays the sales plan. This row represents the forecast of anticipated sales for an item during each time period. If the SOP plan is for a specific material, the values in the sales line represent the amount forecast to be sold for that material. If the SOP plan is for a product group, the values represent the aggregate amount forecasted for all materials in the product group. The sales plan can be used directly as the basis for creating the Demand Management requirements, which directly feed into MRP. If this is the case, the rest of the rows in the SOP plan do not need to be entered, unless further processing (such as Rough-Cut Capacity Planning) will be performed in SOP.

FIG. 14.3
A Standard SOP Planning Table.

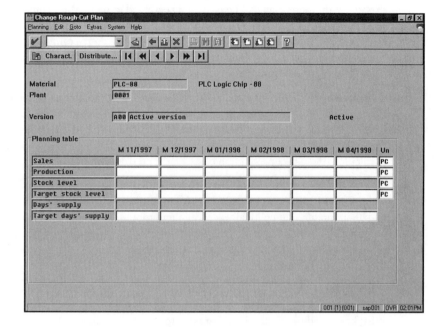

- Production—Represents the production plan. This row represents the target quantity that the production facility will be required to produce.

- Stock Level—A display-only row representing the difference between the production plan and the sales plan. In effect, this shows the net inventory gain/loss that will be incurred if the sales plan and production plan hold true in reality.

N O T E Undocumented Feature—Stock Level should not be confused with safety stock. Safety stock levels are maintained on the Material Master and planned by the MRP modules. With net-requirements planning, MRP will still eventually net out the inventory level to zero (or the Material Master safety stock level), even if a stock level is maintained in the SOP plan. ▦

- Target Stock Level—Represents an alternative way to create the production plan. Instead of entering it directly, a target stock level can be entered, and the production plan can be calculated to meet these values.

- Days' Supply—A display-only row representing the number of days the stock level will last if the sales plan and production plan hold true in reality.

- Target Days' Supply—Represents an alternative way to create the production plan. Instead of entering it directly, a target days' supply can be entered, and the production plan can be calculated to meet these values.

Part
III

Ch
14

Understanding the Sales Plan Importance

The sales plan is the heart of the Sales and Operations Planning functionality. As previously explained, the sales plan can be passed directly to Demand Management and can be the only portion of SOP used in the planning process. Even if the production plan is used in SOP, the sales plan is the basis for comparison and validation. Keep in mind that the sales plan has direct correlation to what the production facility will produce. Therefore, the sales plan should be kept as accurate and up-to-date as possible.

To demonstrate the importance of the sales plan, examine Electro Tech. Once a year, the Electro Tech budgeting process required each product line to create the sales plan for the next fiscal year. Each production department also submitted a budget, including overhead and direct production costs, for the following year. Some of the better departments actually attempted to calculate the direct production costs based on the sales plan, instead of the standard last-year-plus-ten-percent calculation.

Once the budgeting process was completed, the original sales plan and departmental budgets had been modified to politically acceptable numbers, and the sales plan was passed to the master planner. The sales plan was the target for production, until the first orders were in jeopardy of shipping late. John sold customer X these parts. Jim sold customer Y these parts. But neither John nor Jim changed the sales plan. So within weeks, the master planner was working off of an outdated sales plan. Eventually, the plan was just ignored because it was obviously wrong, and scheduling reverted back to backorder processing and firefighting.

What happened to Electro Tech happens to many companies. The Sales department is measured against their sales targets, and Production is measured against on-time deliveries. However, should Production be held responsible if the sales plan is inaccurate? By recording and facilitating the transfer of information between Sales and Production, SAP allows the measurement of realistic performance measurements—sales forecast versus actual orders, actual production completion dates versus planned production end dates, total value of inventory. By providing information such as this, departments can be held accountable for the actions within their control.

To reiterate, the sales plan has direct implications on what the production facility will produce. Therefore, proper procedures and performance measurements should be put in place to ensure that the sales forecast is kept accurate and up-to-date.

Creating the Sales Plan Manually

The easiest way to create a sales plan is to create it manually. This simply involves typing the anticipated sales figures into the sales plan lines. This method is usually used if the sales representatives are entering the sales plan based on their own judgment, or if an external system is used to gather data and generate the future sales plan.

The manual method of creating or changing a sales plan is always an option, even if one of the automated creation methods described in this chapter is used. For example, if the original sales plan is generated via the forecasting functionality, it can be modified manually for any time period. Therefore, the automated creation methods can provide a good base sales plan from which the final sales plan can be manually created.

Copying Data from the Sales Information System   There is another planning mechanism in the Sales and Distribution module known as the Sales Information System, which can be used to capture forecasted sales information. If this mechanism is used, the information can be transferred from SIS by using the following menu path from within an SOP planning table:

> **Menu Path:** Edit > Create Sales Plan > Tsfr Plan from SIS

A pop-up box will appear where you must specify the Info structure, Version, and dates for the SIS plan to be copied. Clicking Continue will copy the values into your sales plan.

Copying Data from the CO/PA Module   There is another module in SAP known as the Controlling/Profitability Analysis module in which a forecasted plan can be created, usually for budgeting reasons. The CO/PA plan can also be copied into the SOP planning table as a starting point for the sales plan. To transfer the CO/PA plan, use the following menu path from within an SOP planning table:

> **Menu Path:** Edit > Create Sales Plan > Transfer Plan from SIS

A pop-up box will appear where you must specify the Version and dates for the CO/PA plan to be copied. Clicking Continue will copy the values into your sales plan.

Forecasting the Sales Plan

Another powerful tool to aid in the creation of the sales plan in SAP is the integrated forecasting functionality. The forecasting function uses a set of statistical algorithms to calculate the future forecast based on the historical sales data. A detailed description of the forecasting algorithms and their usage is presented in the materials forecast sections later in this chapter. The parameters used in the statistical forecasting algorithms are stored on the forecasting view of the material master. To create the sales plan using the forecasting function, use the following menu path from within an SOP planning table:

> **Menu Path:** Edit > Create Sales Plan > Forecast

At the Forecast pop-up box, select the proper forecast model and click the Perform Forecast button. At the next pop-up box, enter the appropriate forecast model parameters and click the Perform Forecast button. Copy the results into the plan.

Creating a Production Plan

The overall goal for the production plan is to meet the sales plan in the time period needed. In many cases, it is better to smooth out the production plan so that the factory is not overutilized during some periods and underutilized in others. In either case, the production plan that is developed in SOP can be transferred to Demand Management to be used by MRP as the requirements that will drive production.

Part
III
Ch
14

Creating the Production Plan Manually Just like the sales plan, the easiest way to create a production plan is to create it manually. This involves simply typing the planned production quantities into the production plan lines.

Creating the Production Plan Synchronous to Sales The production plan can be created synchronous to sales, whereby the sales plan is simply copied into the production plan. This is done using the following menu path from the SOP planning table:

Menu Path: Edit > Create Production Plan > Synchronous to Sales

Creating the Production Plan with Zero Stock Level The production plan can also be created using the zero stock level function, whereby any existing stock levels will be subtracted from the sales plan when creating the production plan. This is done using the following menu path from the SOP planning table:

Menu Path: Edit > Create Production Plan > Stock Level = Zero

Creating the Production Plan Targeting Stock Level Another way to create the production plan is by entering the stock level line of the planning table and using the target stock level function. The production plan is calculated by adding the sales plan and the target stock level. To execute this function, use the following menu path from within the SOP planning table:

Menu Path: Edit > Create Production Plan > Target Stock Level

Creating the Production Plan Targeting Days' Supply The last way to create the production plan is by entering the days' supply line of the planning table and using the target days' supply function. This function first recalculates stock level line based on the target days' supply line. Then the production plan is calculated by adding the sales plan and the stock level. To do this, use the following menu path from within the SOP planning table:

Menu Path: Edit > Create Production Plan > Target Days' Supply

Rough-Cut Capacity Planning

Within the Sales and Operations Planning module, functionality exists to perform rough-cut capacity planning. The purpose of rough-cut capacity planning in SAP is to provide a quick sanity check of the SOP production plan against key production resources that the plan requires. These key resources can be maintained independent of the production routing in rough-cut capacity profiles.

The goal of the production plan, as previously mentioned, is to meet the sales plan. Often, this is not possible due to realistic production constraints such as materials, labor, bottleneck machines, or cash flow. Using rough-cut capacity planning, these constraints can be identified early in the production planning process, before the factory has committed to an unachievable master plan. Additionally, this practice should provide identification of these constraints early enough that action can be taken to avoid the constraints. The scheduling process can become proactive instead of reactive.

For example, in Electro Tech there are several production bottlenecks that repeatedly cause products to ship late. An automotive customer has large orders every year corresponding to the retooling of its assembly lines. However, in Electro Tech's current scheduling process, there is no visibility to the load placed on these bottlenecks ahead of time.

Using rough-cut capacity planning, Electro Tech will be able to monitor the effects of the production plan on these bottleneck resources. The load on these resources is displayed immediately to the master scheduler as the SOP production plan is created or changed. Using this information, the master scheduler can quickly adjust the production plan to smooth out the load across the key resources by building ahead or making capacity adjustments before the factory gets overloaded.

To display the rough-cut capacity plan in an SOP planning table, execute the following menu:

Menu Path: Edit > Capacity Situation > Rough-Cut Planning > Show

The rough-cut capacity planning functionality splits the SOP planning table into two sections (see Figure 14.4). At the top is the original SOP planning table, just as before. Underneath that, the resource load section displays the resulting loads on key resources based on the current production plan line. As changes are made in the production plan, the resource loads are automatically recalculated and redisplayed.

FIG. 14.4

Example rough-cut capacity plan.

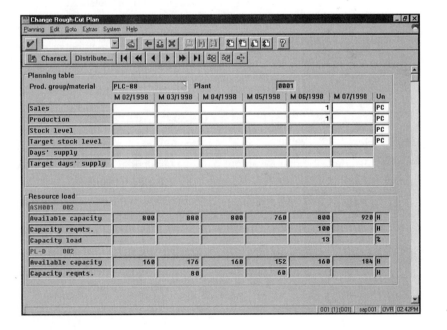

Part

III

Ch

14

Rough-Cut Capacity Profiles

The resources displayed in the resource load section are based on a rough-cut capacity profile that is created for the material or product group being planned. The rough-cut capacity profile must be maintained separately from the production routing. This allows the rough-cut capacity profile to maintain only the production resources that are of interest to the master scheduler. The types of resources that can be added to a rough-cut capacity profile are flexible, including bottleneck work centers representing machines or labor, key materials, key tools, and costs.

Unfortunately, there is no automated way in the current SAP software to update the rough-cut capacity profile based on changes to the actual production routings. This maintenance must be done manually. Keep in mind that the rough-cut capacities do not have to be maintained 100% accurately to be effective. Accuracy is achieved in the detailed capacity plan during MRP. The purpose of rough-cut capacity planning is to get a quick, rough estimate of the feasibility of the master plan with regard to the common resource constraints.

N O T E Undocumented Feature—One way to help build the rough-cut capacity profiles is to use the Long-term Planning (LTP) functionality. To calculate resource requirements for all levels of a complex multilevel BOM item, create a separate planning scenario in LTP and create demand for a quantity of one for the item. Through the LTP-detailed capacity planning functionality, the aggregate capacity load on the bottleneck work centers can be displayed in time-phased buckets. This capacity information can be used as the basis for creating the rough-cut capacity profile. ▨

To create a rough-cut capacity profile for a material, use the following menu paths:

> **Menu Path:** Logistics > Production > SOP > Tools > Rough-cut Plng Prfl. > Create
>
> **Transaction Code: MC35**

The system displays a selection screen to choose the material or product group for which the rough-cut capacity profile is being created. Enter the fields from Table 14.3 into the selection screen.

Table 14.3 Data Fields for a Rough-Cut Capacity Profile

Field	Value	Description
Material	Enter a material number	Key that identifies the material for which you want to create a planning profile
Plant	Enter a plant	Plant in which the material is being planned

Once this information is correctly entered, press the Enter key to proceed with creating the rough-cut planning profile. The General data screen is displayed next to record header-level data about the planning profile. Fill in the fields on the General data screen as described in Table 14.4.

Table 14.4 Data Fields on the General View of a Rough-Cut Capacity Profile

Field	Value	Description
Time Span (workdays)	Enter **30 days**	This identifies how many workdays are in each capacity-planning time period in the planning profile. Periods are usually 5 or 7 days for weekly planning, 20 or 30 days for monthly planning (depending on plant schedule) of 5- or 7-day workweeks).
Status of plan	Enter **4** (Released for order and costing)	The Status key identifies what transactions in the system will be allowed to access the planning profile.
Usage	Enter **1**	The Usage key allows prioritization of planning profiles in the case that multiple profiles are needed. For example, profiles might be created for usage's production and engineering. The system can be configured to first look for production profiles, and next look for engineering profiles.
From lot size	Enter **1** (Production)	Minimum lot size for which this planning profile is valid. (Leaving this value blank can cause inconsistencies during rough-cut capacity planning. Always enter a value.)
To lot size	Enter **999,999**	Maximum lot size for which this planning profile is valid.

Once this information is correctly entered, click the Continue button to proceed with creating the rough-cut planning profile. The Rough-Cut Planning Profile screen is displayed next to record resource requirements for the planning profile.

Figure 14.5 shows an example of a rough-cut planning profile screen. The resources are entered vertically in the first column of the spreadsheet, and the requirements for those resources are entered in the horizontal planning periods defined by the time-span field. The spreadsheet can be scrolled to the right to enter more planning periods than can be displayed on the screen at once.

As new resources are entered, a pop-up box will appear to gather additional information about the new resource. The resources must be created as one of four different resource types—work centers, materials, production resources/tools, or costs. An SAP master data record must exist for the resource of the type that is being referenced in the planning profile. For example, if Production Line D references a work center, a work center (such as PL-D) must already exist in the system.

Some planners are initially confused about how the requirements in the planning profiles are staggered, because the entry of these requirements is somewhat counter-intuitive. The key point to remember is that the requirements are backward-scheduled from the last planning period that has requirements in the profile.

For example, Figure 14.5 shows the Final Assembly resource with requirements in the fourth planning period and Production Line D with requirements in the first and third planning periods. In rough-cut capacity planning, if one PLC-88 is planned in May, this will load the Final Assembly resource in May and Production Line D in February and April, based on the resource requirements. The requirements are backward-scheduled from the date of the latest requirement.

FIG. 14.5

Sample rough-cut planning profile.

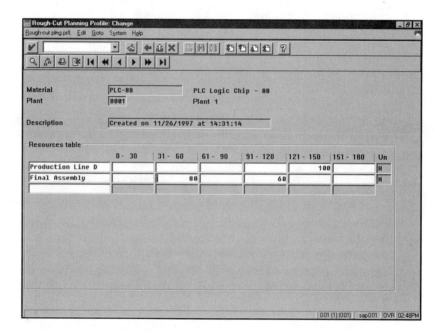

Detailed Capacity Planning in SOP

SOP also provides functionality for performing detailed capacity planning within the SOP plan. At first glance, this functionality sounds like a very powerful tool. However, the usefulness of this feature is hampered by some practical realities in most circumstances.

The theory is to use the actual production routing to generate capacity loads across all resources in the routing for the planned item. This works exactly as advertised. However, the following points are sometimes overlooked when discussing this functionality:

■ The capacities are based only on the plan for the end-item being planned. This is fine for single-level BOM products. However, for multilevel BOM products, there is no way to aggregate the capacity loads placed on the factory for production of lower-level components into the plan, unless every level of the BOM is planned in SOP.

- Many master scheduled items are complex assemblies requiring complex routings. The detailed loads across every specific work center are not as important to the master scheduler as the total loads across departments or key bottleneck work centers. Looking at all the detail makes it hard to see the forest for the trees.

- Rough-cut capacity planning is most beneficial when requirements are planned for key resources. These key resources, such as cost, material, or labor are not always related 1:1 to specific routed operations and would not be planned using detailed capacity planning in SOP.

At this point, detailed capacity planning in SOP is not a very useful tool.

Demand Management

Demand management is used to consolidate and refine the independent requirements for specific materials. This is another example of a term for which there is a mismatch between the commonly accepted definition and the SAP functionality. As commonly defined, demand management is the function of recognizing all demands for a product, including forecasts, customer orders, interplant orders, and service parts requirements. Within SAP Demand Management, however, only independent requirements are managed. Customer requirements are managed in sales order management, part of the Sales and Distribution module.

The output of demand management is referred to as the *demand program*. It consists of a list of independent requirements for each material, specifying the quantities and dates the material is needed. SAP supports multiple independent requirement versions, which can be used for comparisons and simulations. Each of these versions can be marked as active or inactive. Active independent requirement versions create the demand program that is fed into MRP for the operative planning run. The inactive independent requirement versions can be passed to the long-term planning functionality to run MRP simulations.

Multiple versions of the planned independent requirements can be useful for segregating and managing different components of demand. For example, the sales demand for some products at Electro Tech is composed of direct sales and warranty replacement. The sales force plans the direct sales via SOP planning tables, but the warranty replacement demand is calculated manually based on reliability data and total number of units in service. To segregate this demand, one demand management version could be reserved for direct sales demand and another for warranty demand. The combination of demand between these two demand management versions becomes the total independent requirement that would be passed to MRP for detailed planning.

Demand Management serves as a link between the forecasting tools and MRP. Data from the materials forecast, SOP sales plans, and SOP production plans can be copied into Demand Management to create independent requirements. As the data is copied, it can also be automatically or manually split into finer time buckets. For example, if the SOP plan is maintained in months, the independent requirements can be distributed into weekly or daily requirements. This can help to smooth the manufacturing plan that will be created by MRP.

Part

III

Ch

14

Creating Planned Independent Requirements

To create planned independent requirements for a material, use the following menu path:

>**Menu Path:** Logistics > Production > Master Planning >Demand Management >
>Planned Indep. Reqmts > Create

>**Transaction Code:** MD61

On the initial screen, a material, plant, and version must be entered. Once these fields have been filled in, press Enter, and the schedule line screen will be displayed. Requirements can be created manually by filling in the requirements date and planned quantity fields. Each line represents a separate requirement quantity that will be passed to MRP for detailed planning (see Figure 14.6).

FIG. 14.6

Creating planned independent requirements.

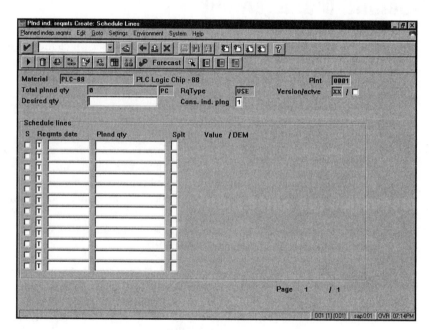

Copying the SOP Sales Plan

The independent requirements can be created by copying the information from an SOP sales plan. This can be done from within the Create Planned Independent Requirements transaction shown in Figure 14.6. To copy the SOP sales plan, use the following menu path:

>**Menu Path:** Edit > Copy Requirements > Sales Plan > Copy Completely

This function will copy the contents of the active sales plan into the independent requirements version currently being created. If the system is configured to perform automatic splitting, the requirements from the sales plan will be split according to the splitting logic as they are copied.

Copying the SOP Production Plan

Alternatively, the independent requirements can be created by copying the information from an SOP production plan. This can be done from within the Create Planned Independent Requirements transaction shown in Figure 14.6. To copy the SOP production plan, use the following menu path:

Menu Path: Edit > Copy Requirements > Production Plan > Copy Completely

This function will copy the contents of the active production plan into the independent requirements version currently being created. If the system is configured to perform automatic splitting, the requirements from the production plan will be split according to the splitting logic as they are copied.

Copying the Materials Forecast

Copying the information from the materials forecast can also create independent requirements. This can be done from within the Create Planned Independent Requirements transaction shown in Figure 14.6. To copy the materials forecast, use the following menu path:

Menu Path: Edit > Copy Requirements > Forecast > Copy Complete Forec

This function will copy the contents of the materials forecast into the independent requirements version currently being created. If the system is configured to perform automatic splitting, the requirements from the materials forecast will be split according to the splitting logic as they are copied.

Product Group Planning

SAP provides a flexible hierarchy called product groups that can be used within Sales and Operations Planning to plan at aggregate levels. The aggregate plans can then be broken down and distributed (disaggregated) to the lower levels of the hierarchy, and eventually to the lowest-level materials that will be produced.

This functionality is useful in planning situations where product families can be forecast with greater confidence than individual items in the product family. For example, an automobile manufacturer can forecast the total number of light trucks that will be sold in the third and forth quarter of next year more accurately than how many green, air-conditioned trucks will be sold. It is more important to forecast the total number of light trucks because decisions about how many of the common long lead items are needed, such as the chassis, are not affected by what color the trucks are eventually painted. Decisions about exactly which options are to be assembled onto each truck can be delayed until much later in the planning cycle.

The use of product groups in SAP is very helpful in the planning cycle. You can define any number of product groups and in varying structures. A product group can be part of the hierarchies of another product group. To create a product group, use the following menu paths:

Menu Path: Logistics > Production > SOP > Product Group > Create
Transaction Code: MC84

Part

III

Ch

14

The system displays a selection screen to choose which material or product group for which the rough-cut capacity profile is being created. Enter the fields from Table 14.5 into the selection screen.

Table 14.5 Data Fields for the Creation of a Product Group

Field	Value	Description
Product Group	Enter identifier	Key that will uniquely identify the product group you are creating
Product Group Description	Enter a text description	Text description of the product group
Plant	Enter a plant	Plant in which the product group will be planned
UOM	Enter a unit of measure	The default unit that the product group will use when planning
Members	Choose materials	Indicator that determines whether the members of the product group are materials or other product groups

Once this information is correctly entered, press the Enter key to proceed with creating the product group. The General data screen is displayed next to record header-level data about the planning profile. Fill in the fields on the General data screen seen in Figure 14.7.

FIG. 14.7
Sample product group.

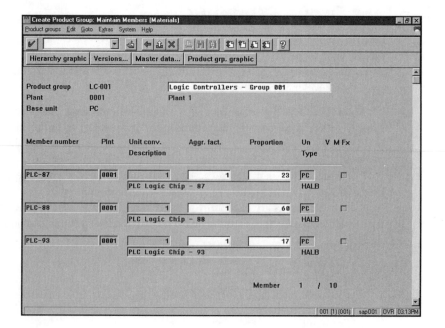

Forecasting

Forecasting in SAP is an ambiguous term that must be clarified. The common definition of forecasting is an estimate of future demand, whether the estimate is based on subjective means or based on a mathematical formula. This definition would include Sales and Operation Planning as part of forecasting. However, in SAP terms, forecasting is reserved specifically for functionality that calculates future expectations, based on order history, by using statistical forecasting algorithms.

The SAP forecasting functionality can be executed in several different areas of the system. The forecasting functionality is integrated within the Material Master, within the Material Forecasting module, within the Sales and Operations Plan, and within Demand Management. While the same algorithms are used to calculate the forecast for each of these areas, there are substantial differences in the business processes that are enabled via the use of forecasting within these different areas.

For example, if the forecast is run directly in the Material Forecasting module, the results can be read directly by MRP as requirements. Alternatively, the forecast could be created using the Forecasting module and then copied into the SOP module for rough-cut capacity planning prior to passing the SOP plan to MRP as requirements. Another option would be to copy the forecasting results directly in Demand Management to create independent requirements that then feed into MRP.

All these options are ways to use the forecasting functionality. The best use of the forecasting functionality depends on what overall planning process makes sense for your company. Ask the following:

■ Do all forecasted materials need to be part of SOP planning to make rough-cut capacity planning valid?

■ Would sales representatives forecast more accurately if they used statistically calculated forecasts as a basis?

■ Will the entire production volume be forecast, or is there dependent demand mixed with forecasted demand for the materials?

There are numerous process decisions that affect how the forecasting functionality should be used.

The forecasting algorithms can calculate three outputs that are of use in other production planning functionality:

First, the forecasted requirements are calculated. These requirements can be forecasted in monthly, weekly, daily, or fiscal accounting time periods.

Second, the forecast can calculate a safety stock level, based on the past statistical deviation, the lead time, and the customer service level percentage.

Third, the forecast can calculate a reorder point level. (The exact formulas that SAP uses to calculate these values are explained in detail in the SAP online help.)

Generally, the forecasting functionality needs to be executed as part of the planning process prior to the MRP run because all three of the outputs described earlier have an effect on the MRP run. The exact timing of the forecast depends on several factors, including length of the forecasting time buckets, time required to process forecasting exceptions, number of forecasted MPS parts versus forecasted MRP materials, and the subsequent timing of the MPS and MRP runs.

Executing a Material Forecast

For many implementations, the most effective way to carry out the forecasting of materials is using the total forecast run functionality. This function uses a single transaction to trigger the forecasting of a large group of materials. The transaction can be executed online or in batch mode on a periodic basis.

To execute a total forecast for a group of materials, use the following menu paths:

> **Menu Path:** Logistics > Production > Master Planning > Materials Forecast > Forecast > Total Forecast > Execute
>
> **Transaction Code:** MP38

The system displays a selection screen to choose the total forecast parameters, as shown in Figure 14.8. Enter the fields from Table 14.6 into the selection screen.

FIG. 14.8

Executing a total forecast.

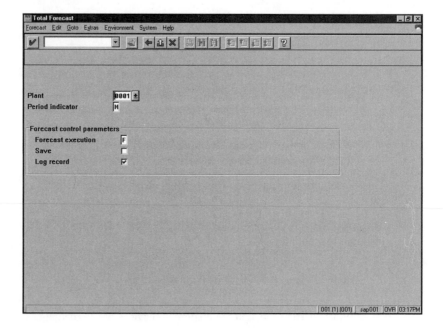

Table 14.6   Parameters for a Total Forecast Run

Field	Value	Description
Plant	Enter a plant	Plant in which the materials will be forecast.
Period Indicator	Enter **M**	Key specifying a forecasting time period, such as days, weeks, or months. Only materials in the specified plant with the selected period indicator on the Material Master forecasting view will be forecast.
Forecast Execution	Enter **F**	This field controls whether the forecast will be carried out starting in the current period (A), or in the following period (F).
Save	Leave blank	This flag controls whether the forecast will be run as a simulation to review the results (leave blank) or will actually execute and save the forecast results (enter an **X**).
Log Record	Select	Indicator that specifies whether a detailed log is generated displaying the forecasting results for each material in the forecasting run.

Press the Enter key to execute the forecast. The system will respond with a warning message to "check input parameters." Press Enter again to confirm that the total forecast should be executed using the entered parameters. The system next responds with a message box stating "Total forecast to be started. Please press ENTER." Press Enter again to finally begin the forecasting run.

When the total forecast run is complete, a log will be displayed detailing the results for all materials that were forecast in the run.

Processing Forecast Exceptions

After a forecasting run has been executed, it is the responsibility of the planner to review any forecast errors that occurred. This is done using the forecast reprocessing functionality.

For example, Electro Tech has just introduced a new programmable logic controller, and it is ready to begin full production. Several new components now need to be purchased, and it is decided that, because they are inexpensive, low-level components, the replenishment will be forecast. When the Material Masters are set up for these components, they are copied from existing materials that are similar, but when the forecast is carried out, the new components all end up with forecasting errors.

To determine what caused the errors for the new materials, the planner would use the forecast reprocessing function by executing the following menu paths:

Menu Path: Logistics > Production > Master Planning > Materials Forecast > Forecast > Total Forecast > Reprocess

Transaction Code: MP33

On the screen that appears for reprocessing the forecast, you must supply the fields seen in Table 14.7.

Table 14.7   Data Fields for Reprocessing a Forecast

Field	Value	Description
Plant	Enter a plant	Plant in which the materials were forecast.
MRP Controller	Enter an MRP controller	MRP controller responsible for planning a collection of materials.
Period Indicator	Select M	Key specifying a forecasting time period, such as days, weeks, or months. Only materials in the specified plant with the selected period indicator on the material master forecasting view will be displayed.
Error Class Selection	Select all error classes	Grouping of possible errors from the forecasting run used to narrow down the reprocessing list by displaying only materials with a certain error class.

When the selection screen has been completed, press the Enter key. The forecast reprocessing screen is displayed, listing all materials for which messages were generated during the last total forecasting run that meet the selection criteria applied from the initial screen. An example of the forecast reprocessing screen is displayed in Figure 14.9.

To reprocess a material in the reprocessing screen, either double-click the material or place the cursor on the line and click the Choose button. This will activate the Execute Forecast: Parameter Overview screen. This is actually a subscreen of the transaction for executing a forecast of a single material, accessed also via the following menu path:

Menu Path: Logistics > Production > Master Planning > Materials Forecast > Forecast > Individual Forecast > Execute

Transaction Code: MP30

To get more information about the forecasting error from the Parameter Overview screen select the following menu path:

Menu Path: Extras > Messages

FIG. 14.9

Processing forecasting errors.

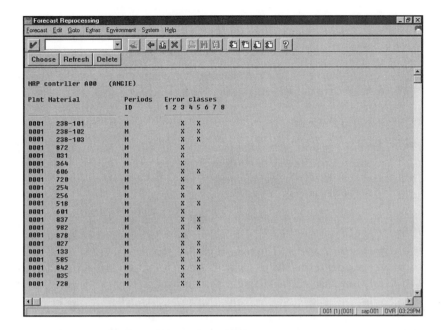

A screen titled Display Exception/Process Messages will be displayed. This screen will display a long text description of the forecast exception message. There are numerous possible exception messages, some of which are merely informational, some of which require specific action to fix an error. Planners will quickly learn how to react to the common messages that occur frequently based on their planning process. Even so, most implementations create a detailed reference document to explain what action(s) to take for each possible error. This is helpful to train new planners, and as reference for existing planners when uncommon errors arise.

Back to the Electro Tech example, the materials all show a message number 11—"No historical data exists." Recognizing that these are new components, the planner realizes that there could not be any consumption history. The planner could go to the Material Master and manually enter consumption history and reforecast the material. Instead, the planner decides that there are existing components that are similar to the new components that would serve as a good *reference history* for forecasting the new components. The Material Master Forecasting view is changed to add the reference material, and the material is reforecast.

Executing a Forecast from the Material Master

Sometimes it is easier to execute the forecasting function directly from the Material Master on an individual basis. This is especially true when forecasting parameters are being added or modified, and the planner wants to immediately see the effect of the new settings.

To execute the forecast from the Material Master, the planner must first access the forecasting view of the Material Master. (There are many different ways for the planner to get to this—from the Change Material Master, the MRP list, the Stock Requirements list, and so on.

Part
III

Ch
14

The point is that when executing the forecast from the Material Master, the planner is usually already in the Material Master to modify the forecasting parameters.) From the Material Master Forecasting view, click the Execute Forecast button at the bottom of the screen.

A pop-up screen is displayed allowing the planner to change the forecasting model. The model defaults from the Material Master Forecasting view, so there is usually no reason to change the parameters, unless the forecast is being run to try a different model. Click the button labeled Perform Forecast.

Another pop-up screen is displayed allowing the planner to change the forecasting parameters associated with the model from the previous screen. Again, click the button labeled Perform Forecast. This will trigger the execution of the forecast calculation based on the model and parameters selected.

An example of the resulting forecast is shown in Figure 14.10. The screen displays the original forecast, representing the values that the system calculated based on the forecast model and parameters entered. The column labeled corrected forecast (CoeeFvstVI) can be changed by the planner to modify the forecast manually for any time period. If a field is corrected, then the *fixed* indicator will be set, indicating that any subsequent forecasting runs will not overwrite the value.

FIG. 14.10

Example Material
Master forecast results.

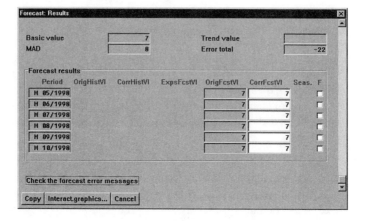

The forecast results are not actually saved unless the Copy button is clicked.

Executing a Forecast in SOP

Another way to use the forecasting functionality is from within the Sales and Operations Planning module. This feature is useful to provide the planner an alternative way to start the sales and operations planning process, instead of relying completely on subjective projections of future demand. The planner can use the forecasting functionality to allow the system to calculate the sales plan based on the forecasting algorithms.

To forecast the sales plan, the planner must be creating or changing the SOP plan for the material. Select the following menu path:

Menu Path: Edit > Create Sales Plan > Forecast

A pop-up screen is displayed allowing the planner to change the forecasting model. The model defaults from the Material Master forecasting view, so there is usually no reason to change the parameters, unless the forecast is being run to try a different model. Click the button labeled Perform Forecast.

Another pop-up screen is displayed allowing the planner to change the forecasting parameters associated with the model from the previous screen. Again, click the button labeled Perform Forecast. This will trigger the execution of the forecast calculation based on the model and parameters selected.

An example of the resulting forecast is shown in Figure 14.11. The screen displays the original forecast, representing the values that the system calculated based on the forecast model and parameters entered. The column labeled corrected forecast (CorrFcstVI) can be changed by the planner to modify the forecast manually for any time period. If a field is corrected, then the *fixed* indicator will be set, indicating that any subsequent forecasting runs will not overwrite the value.

FIG. 14.11

Example SOP plan forecast results.

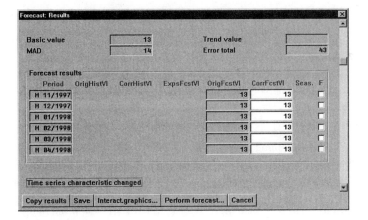

To copy the forecast results to the SOP plan, click the Copy Results button. This will update the sales plan row with the results from the forecast calculation.

One major advantage to using the forecasting functionality within SOP is the ability to forecast based on different consumption segments. This is only possible when using a flexible planning SOP table. In all other areas of the system, the forecast is based on the total historical consumption of the material within a specific plant. Sometimes this is not the best situation.

For example, Electro Tech has the following forecasting dilemma. Some of the components that are used in the finished product are also sold as spare parts to service products if they break or wear out. Therefore, the demands for these components come from two different

Part
III

Ch
14

sources: dependent demand based on the final product schedule and spare parts demand. Electro Tech needs to forecast the spare parts demand based on the sales history for the spare parts only, and then add in the dependent demand from the production requirements for the finished product. This segregation of demand history can be accomplished using SOP flexible planning.

A flexible planning hierarchy can be created based on the different sales divisions (or other Sales and Distribution-related hierarchy fields). By using a different sales division for spare parts versus finished products, the actual sales are recorded in different consumption accounts. When planning in SOP using a flexible planning table, the plans are created for each sales division. When forecasting for one of those plans, the historical values used are only the sales of one specific sales division.

Scheduling

Scheduling is the process by which an achievable plan is derived that directs the actual manufacture of the firm's products. Within SAP, the purpose of the scheduling functions is to evaluate capacity, material, inventory, and process characteristics in order to derive production schedules that accommodate material requirements. Those are two very long ways of saying that scheduling strives to produce workable manufacturing plans that meet customer requirements. This is something that Electro Tech very much lacks in their present mode. Rather than following a logically established plan, Electro Tech has fallen into the practice of scheduling by exception, also commonly referred to as *firefighting*. Shortage situations are given top priority, whether they warrant it or not. In most cases, these shortage situations are continually generated due to the lack of scheduling logic being previously applied. Unrealistic commitments on the part of Sales or Customer Service, loose control of the production processes themselves, and overly optimistic views of plant maintenance requirements are all contributing factors to Electro Tech's current scheduling difficulties.

Through the scheduling tools contained within SAP, many of these difficulties can be minimized or eliminated altogether. Material Requirements Planning (MRP) logic forms the heart of SAP's scheduling capabilities. Through the use of detailed master data pertaining to virtually all elements of manufacturing, procurement, material inventory status, material demand information, and desired service level, MRP drives toward a solution that will guarantee material availability.

As it represents the heart of production scheduling in SAP, a brief reminder of basic MRP logic may be helpful. MRP logic operates by scheduling necessary production and procurement to accommodate demand at a specified material level. Production master data regarding such items as the time, equipment, and labor requirements for production at that level are utilized to schedule the necessary orders. If present (as indicated in the product's bill of material), dependent requirements are then placed as appropriate at the next lower material level. Again, necessary production and procurement to accommodate this lower-level demand is scheduled. Again, if present, dependent requirements are placed as appropriate at the next lower material level. This process is repeated downward throughout the end-item's bill of material until the lowest level of materials is reached. By beginning this process with the end-item's requirement date and working backwards (downwards) through the end-item's bill of materials, a production schedule can be derived that will provide each level of material at the appropriate time. Of course, this is assuming that any schedules created will be adhered to by the Shop Floor or Purchasing departments. Yes, that's often a huge assumption, but you need to use it for now. Schedule nonconformance is another issue altogether.

Master Production Scheduling

MRP activities are often divided into two groups within SAP: Master Production Scheduling (MPS) and Material Requirements Planning (MRP). The two function in a nearly identical manner, with one exception. MPS operates within only one level of the Bill of Material (BOM), while MRP can be utilized throughout all levels of a material's BOM. Thus, if MPS is run on a material, the necessary orders are planned at that level; dependent requirements (if any) are placed on the next BOM level down, and then the process stops.

If MPS is utilized, it is usually applied at the end-item level, the highest level of the BOM. Materials can then be scheduled at the end-item level only, without always forcing the system to schedule downward through potentially large BOMs. Many firms find this helpful as it allows them to more easily formulate rough schedules for their end-item, or high-value materials.

MPS can be executed in a variety of ways. The scope of the scheduling run can include all MPS level materials within a plant, or can be limited to a single material. A scheduling run that encompasses all materials within a plant is referred to as an *MPS Total Planning* run.

For each material scheduled during an MPS run, the depth of the scheduling function performed can be specified. The planning run can be configured to completely reschedule all planned orders or only those that need to be modified since the previous scheduling run.

A user can activate MPS at virtually any point in time with the appropriate system access. Large MPS jobs, such as total planning runs, can generate very large processing demands on the system. When initiated online, these data-intensive runs can negatively impact overall system performance and cause inconvenience to other users. To avoid this common problem, it is possible to conduct total planning runs as background jobs. In addition to operating in the background, these jobs can be scheduled to take place automatically during periods of low system demand, such as late evenings or weekends.

A background MPS total planning run is generally initiated via the following menu path:

> **Menu Path:** Logistics > Production > Master Planning > MPS > MPS > Total Planning > As Background Job
>
> **Transaction Code:** MDBS

The system will then display a list of planning variants that are available for running MPS. These planning variants are nothing more than previously saved specifications of the MPS run to be performed. The variants will include the settings shown in Table 14.7.

Part

III

Ch

14

Table 14.7 Settings for the MPS Variant

Field	Value	Description	Required Entry?
Plant	Enter applicable plant code.	Plant involved in MPS run.	Yes
Processing Key	Typically NETCH. Other choices are available.	Net Change. Leaves previously scheduled items unchanged unless a change is necessary. Creates new schedule items where necessary.	Yes
Create Purchase Req.	Typically 1 (Purchase Requisitions). Other choices are available.	Determines whether or not purchase requisitions will automatically be created as appropriate for externally procured items.	Yes
Delivery Schedules	Typically 3 (Schedule Lines). Other choices are available.	Determines whether or not delivery schedules will be created for externally procured items.	Yes
Create MRP List	Typically 1 (MRP List). Other choices are available.	Determines whether or not an MRP list will be generated and saved following the scheduling run.	Yes

Field	Value	Description	Required Entry?
Planning Mode	Typically 1 (Reactivate Planning Dates). Other choices are available.	Determines whether or not existing planning dates (from previous scheduling runs) will be maintained or deleted and then rescheduled.	Yes
Scheduling	Typically 2 (Lead Time Scheduling).	Specifies whether scheduling will be performed per basic dates (Material Master data-based) or per lead time scheduling (routing data based).	Yes

Other data entry options may be available. The previous table highlights the data entry most critical to defining the MPS planning run.

If you desire to view or modify the settings contained within an existing planning variant, you can do so by clicking once within the variant name and then clicking the Show/Change Variant button. However, confirm the reason for the variant's existence and format prior to arbitrarily modifying it.

If the specifications contained with the variant are found to be satisfactory, it can be activated immediately by clicking once within the variant name and then clicking the Immediate button. If the variant is found to be satisfactory but a scheduling run at a later time is desired, click once within the variant name and then once within the appropriate button. Again, it may be wise to schedule total planning MPS runs to activate during nonpeak system times.

During MPS runs in the background, all users can continue to utilize the SAP system. However, be aware that all information accessed during an MPS run represents the last saved status just prior to the initiation of the run. No schedule data will be updated by the system until the MPS run has completed.

Material Requirements Planning

If the previous discussion of MPS did not cause you too many problems, this discussion of Material Requirements Planning (MRP) will seem to be very redundant. That's good, because in many ways, it is redundant. Execution of MRP runs are virtually identical to the execution of

Part
III

Ch
14

MPS runs. It is the scope of the run that can vary significantly. Where MPS runs are, by definition, limited to only one layer within a material's BOM, the MRP run has no such restriction. If desired, MRP can be executed on a material such that every level of the material's components are scheduled downward through the BOM.

As is the case with MPS, MRP can be executed in a variety of ways. The scope of the scheduling run can include all MRP level materials within a plant or can be limited to a single material. A scheduling run that encompasses all materials within a plant is again referred to as an MRP Total Planning run.

For each material scheduled during an MRP run, the depth of the scheduling function performed can be specified. The planning run can be configured to completely reschedule all planned orders or only those that need to be modified since the previous scheduling run.

A user can activate MRP at virtually any point in time with the appropriate system access. Large MRP jobs, such as total planning runs, can generate very large processing demands on the system. When initiated online, these data intensive runs can negatively impact overall system performance and cause inconvenience to other users. To avoid this common problem, it is possible to conduct total planning runs as background jobs. In addition to operating in the background, these jobs can be scheduled to take place automatically during periods of low system demand, such as late evenings or weekends.

Whereas MPS runs on individual materials can be executed relatively infrequently as compared to total planning runs, MRP runs on individual materials are quite common. It is often desirable to evaluate a specific material's schedule in great detail, but inconvenient to reschedule an entire plant in order to accomplish this. Therefore, individual MRP runs are frequently utilized. Since the general steps necessary to accomplish an MPS total planning run were already depicted, a single-item MRP run will be described here.

An online MRP single item, multilevel planning run is generally initiated via the following menu path:

> **Menu Path:** Logistics > Production > MRP > MRP > Single-item, Multi-lvl
>
> **Transaction Code:** MD02

The system will then display a data entry screen that contains several data entry fields, including those described in Table 14.8. Notice that the MRP run specifications entered here are virtually identical to those utilized in the MPS run previously described.

Table 14.8 Data Parameters for an MRP Run

Field	Value	Description	Required Entry?
Plant	Enter applicable plant code.	Plant involved in MPS run.	Yes

Field	Value	Description	Required Entry?
Processing Key	Typically NETCH. Other choices are available.	Net Change. Leaves previously scheduled items unchanged unless a change is necessary. Creates new schedule items where necessary.	Yes
Create Purchase Req.	Typically 1 (Purchase Requisitions). Other choices are available.	Determines whether or not purchase requisitions will automatically be created as appropriate for externally procured items.	Yes
Delivery Schedules	Typically 3 (Schedule Lines). Other choices are available.	Determines whether or not delivery schedules will be created for externally procured items.	Yes
Create MRP List	Typically 1 (MRP List). Other choices are available.	Determines whether or not an MRP list will be generated and saved following the scheduling run.	Yes
Planning Mode	Typically 1 (Reactivate Planning Dates). Other choices are available.	Determines whether or not existing planning dates (from previous scheduling runs) will be maintained or deleted and then rescheduled.	Yes

continues

Table 14.8 Continued

Field	Value	Description	Required Entry?
Scheduling	Typically 2 (Lead Time Scheduling).	Specifies whether scheduling will be performed per basic dates (Material Master data based) or per lead time scheduling (routing data based).	Yes

Planning Results Display

The activities planned during the MPS or MRP run for a specific material are presented in the form of *planned orders* or *purchase requisitions*. Typically, planned orders are created for items that are to be produced internally.

Purchase requisitions are created for items that will be procured externally. Following their creation during an MPS or MRP run, purchase requisitions are generally addressed by a Purchasing department and have little further direct involvement with production planning.

Planned orders, on the other hand, represent the first step toward an actual production schedule for the shop floor. As such, planned orders remain very much within the domain of production planning.

Following the completion of an MPS or MRP run, the resulting planned orders and purchase requisitions can be viewed in several ways. The most common methods to view these scheduling run results are through either the MRP List or the Stock Requirements List. Each of these lists are depicted in Figures 14.12 and 14.13.

As shown, both of these lists are virtually identical in their representation of the material schedule status. Each list depicts current stock, material requirements, planned receipts, exception messages, and anticipated available inventory. In fact, it is impossible from these figures to identify any significant differences between them. These two lists *do* differ in one very key manner. While both are created during the MPS or MRP run, only the Stock Requirements List is active to represent changes that occur at any time *after* the MPS or MRP run. At the instant the MPS or MRP run is completed for a specific material, both the MRP List and the Stock Requirements List for that material reflect the same information.

Following that point in time, any changes to supply, demand, or inventory data pertaining to that material are immediately reflected in the Stock Requirements List. None of these subsequent changes are reflected in the MRP List. The MRP List remains fixed and is updated only by a subsequent MPS or MRP run on that same material. Thus, the MRP List always reflects the status as of the time of the most recent MPS or MRP run for that material. This subtle difference needs to be clear to the user.

FIG. 14.12
Stock Requirements
List.

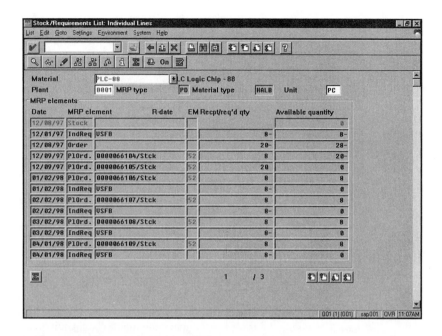

FIG. 14.13
Corresponding MRP
List.

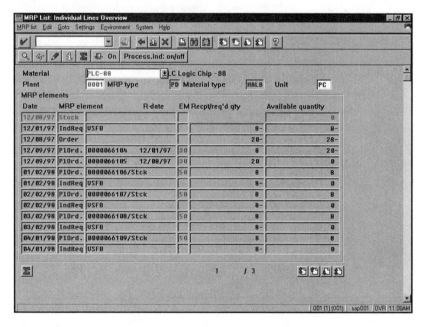

If current information regarding a material's plan is desired, the Stock Requirements List should be used. If historical information is desired regarding the material's plan as of the most recent scheduling run, whenever that occurred, the MRP List is available to provide this information. Because of the high degree of similarity between these two lists, care should be applied to make sure that the correct list is viewed. It is easy to get the two confused.

Accessing the Stock Requirements List can be accomplished via a variety of menu paths. A typical path utilized by Production Planning personnel to view this list for a single material is the following:

> **Menu Path:** Logistics > Production > MRP > Evaluations > Stock/Reqmts List
>
> **Transaction Code:** MD04

In a similar manner, the MRP List for a single material can be viewed by following this menu path:

> **Menu Path:** Logistics > Production > MRP > Evaluations > MRP List—Material
>
> **Transaction Code:** MD05

Planned Orders

Planned orders typically exist in one of two possible statuses: *unfirmed* and *firmed*. Typically, the planned orders created during the scheduling run are created as unfirmed planned orders. The concept of firmed versus unfirmed refers to whether or not the planned orders can be *automatically* modified during subsequent scheduling runs. Unfirmed planned orders are susceptible to automatic modifications. Firmed orders cannot be automatically modified.

For example, suppose during an MRP run, several unfirmed planned orders are created in order to meet forecast demand. Several days later, assume that the demand that necessitated the creation of the planned orders in the first place is increased by the Sales department. When MRP is run again, this increase in demand will be evaluated and the unfirmed planned orders will be modified as appropriate to meet the increased demand. In this way, unfirmed planned orders require little manual maintenance by the Production Planning personnel since they will continually be updated during scheduling runs.

In this example, it appears that unfirmed orders are very desirable because they are largely self-maintaining. In many instances, however, it may be advantageous to *lock* a planned order such that subsequent scheduling runs do not modify it.

Looking back to the previous example, suppose that the Production Planner decides to manually increase the quantity of a planned order by one unit. Ideally, this would never be necessary because MRP and MPS would always schedule the correct quantities. But suppose the Production Planner has no faith in the shop's ability to adhere to a schedule or in Sales's ability to adhere to an agreed-upon sales plan, and just wants to create a little insurance against fate by having one extra unit in stock.

Electro Tech's scheduler, Bryan Luther, has already experienced this scenario and would be a likely candidate to perform this type of change to many of the system-generated planned orders. If the planned orders are manually changed but left in an unfirmed status, the next scheduling run would evaluate the planned orders, determine that an excessive number of units were planned, and then return the planned orders back to their original condition. To avoid this situation, the SAP system is configured such that *any* manual changes to planned orders immediately changes their status to firmed. A manual change in order quantity was used to illustrate this concept. A manual change in date for the planned order results in automatic firming of the planned order as well.

As with many functions within SAP, there exists more than one way to view and modify planned orders. The following menu path will take the user directly to the planned order display or change screens:

> **Menu Path:** Logistics > Production > MRP > Planned Order > Change (or Display) > Individual Display or Display > Collective Display)
>
> **Transaction Code:** MD12, MD13, MD16

When viewing a planned order in the change mode (see Figure 14.14), data fields that can be modified will appear with a white background. Data fields that cannot be modified will be displayed with a gray background.

FIG. 14.14

Planned order header screen in change mode.

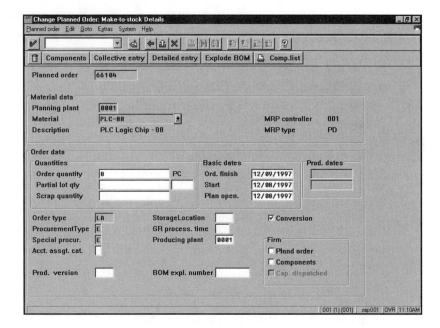

As expected, when viewing a planned order in the display mode, all data fields are presented with a gray background, indicating that they cannot be modified.

Following any changes to a planned order, the status of the order is automatically changed to firmed. Planned orders, which have been firmed, can be easily identified from within the planned order header or by reviewing the MRP List or Stock Requirements List for a particular material (see Figure 14.15). Firm planned orders are denoted by an asterisk (*) at the end of the planned order number line.

Part

III

Ch

14

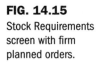

FIG. 14.15
Stock Requirements
screen with firm
planned orders.

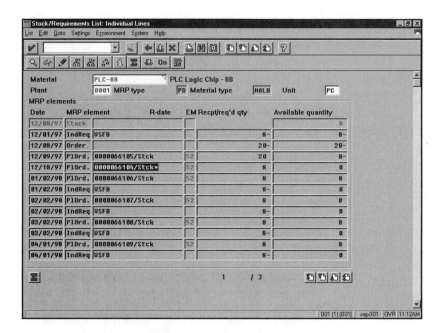

In many situations, it would be very helpful if planned orders were automatically firmed by the system at a specified point in time in the future. For example, suppose a planned order for a specific material is created today with a planned start time six months from now. At the same time, suppose that the production lead time for this material is 30 days. Because the anticipated start time for the planned order is well beyond the production lead time, there is no immediate need to firm the planned order at this time. In fact, it is actually advantageous to leave the planned order unfirmed. If left unfirmed, the planned order will be automatically modified, if necessary, by subsequent MRP runs. Now, assume that several months pass and the current date moves closer to the planned start date of the planned order. At some point in time, it will become helpful to firm the order. This action serves to add stability to the near-term production schedule by guarding against automatic changes very close to the planned start date of the order.

The tool utilized to trigger firming of planned orders a specified number of days prior to production is known as a *time fence*. If desired, a time fence can be established within the Material Master for each material to be scheduled via MPS or MRP.

Production Orders

Planned orders are typically the result of an MRP run and serve to provide an initial production schedule. However, planned orders do not contain the complete set of data necessary for the production shop floor. Therefore, they are useful only in scheduling activities and cannot be used to direct and confirm actual production operations. Production orders are necessary for these activities. Production orders are complete information packages that contain all of the necessary data to support a shop floor schedule and provide a method to confirm operations performed.

Creation of Production Orders from Planned Orders

While production orders can be manually created at any time, they are most often created with a direct reference to a planned order. The process is commonly referred to as *planned order conversion*. During conversion, data already contained within a planned order is copied into a production order. This data typically includes material number, quantity, planned production dates, and plant. After this data is copied into the production order, additional information is accessed and added. A list of components necessary for the production order is generated automatically by accessing the appropriate BOM. A task list (routing) is generated by accessing the appropriate routing master. If desired, component material availability checks can be automatically performed at this point to determine whether or not the required materials will be available in sufficient quantities to allow completion of the production order. Pricing and creation of an order settlement rule are also performed during the creation of the production order.

The conversion of planned orders into production orders can be accomplished individually or collectively. When converting a single planned order, a common menu path originates from within either the Stock Requirements List or MRP List for the respective material:

> **Menu Path:** Logistics > Production > MRP > Evaluations > Stock/Reqmts List
>
> **Transaction Code:** MD04

After the appropriate Stock Requirements List or MRP List is displayed, double-clicking the desired planned order will lead to the screen shown in Figure 14.16.

FIG. 14.16

The planned order/ production order screen.

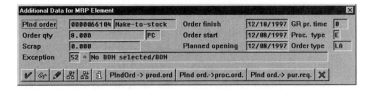

Clicking the Plnd Ord. → Prod.Ord. button immediately creates a production order based on the planned order selected. If difficulties are encountered by the system during this process, the appropriate information, warning, or error messages will be displayed.

Individual conversion of planned orders into production orders is a very thorough process but requires a great deal of time and is therefore impractical for most production schedulers on a day-to-day basis. A more efficient approach is the use of collective order conversion. In this process, the production scheduler first uses a search routine to identify those planned orders for which conversion is desired. Then the system automatically progresses through the conversion process for each planned order involved. If problems are encountered, the system prompts the scheduler for input as necessary.

The collective planned order conversion process can be accessed via the following menu path:

> **Menu Path:** Logistics > Production > MRP > Planned Order > Convert > Prod. Ord. > Collect. Conversion
>
> **Transaction Code:** CO41

Part

III

Ch

14

At this point, the system will prompt the user for search criteria to be used in identifying those planned orders that are to be converted into production orders. The data entries in Table 14.9 may be helpful.

Table 14.9   Data Fields for the Collective Conversion of Planned Orders

Field	Value	Description	Required Entry?
Plant	Enter Plant Code	Plant in which planned orders exist.	Yes
MRP Controller	Desired MRP Controller	Limits order selection to only those created by MRP Controller.	Yes
From Opening Date	Earliest planned order start date desired	Earliest planned order start date to be included in search.	No
To Opening Date	Latest planned order start date desired	Latest planned order start date to be included in search.	No
Sales Order	Sales Order number	Limits order selection to only those linked to Sales Order(s).	No
Material	Material number	Limits order selection to only those relevant to the selected material number(s).	No

Field	Value	Description	Required Entry?
Order Type	Production Order Type	Directs conversion from planned orders to specific type of production order.	Yes

After entering the desired planned order search criteria, click the Enter button. The search will be performed and the resulting planned orders will be displayed. Select those orders to be converted by clicking within their respective boxes. If all orders displayed are to be converted, this can be more quickly accomplished via the menu command Edit > Select All.

Another option is by clicking the Select All button.

The actual conversion process is then enacted by clicking the Save icon. Those planned orders selected will be sequentially converted into production orders.

Order Change

With respect to MRP, production orders behave similarly to firmed planned orders. That is, they are not subject to automatic modification as the result of a subsequent MPS or MRP run. Production orders remain fixed until modified by a user. Manual modification or deletion of a production order can be performed at virtually any time prior to release of the order (order release itself will be discussed in a moment). As with many planned or production order processes, the production order change process is often initiated in the Stock Requirements List as indicated here:

> **Menu Path:** Logistics > Production > MRP > Evaluations > Stock/Reqmts List
>
> **Transaction Code:** MD04

Select the desired production order by clicking it within the appropriate Stock Requirements List. Then, click the Order Change icon, which looks like a writing pencil. Once within the production order while in the change mode, fields that can be modified are displayed with a white background. Fields that cannot be modified are displayed with a gray background.

After making the desired changes, save the production order by clicking the Save icon, which looks like a file folder. Depending on the configuration settings, the system can reschedule the modified order as it is being saved. This is generally a desirable configuration setup because virtually any changes made will necessitate a scheduling change in either this order itself or other orders that are somehow pegged to it.

Part

III

Ch

14

Order Deletion

Deletion of the production order is also accomplished from within the order itself while in the change mode. After the order is opened in the change mode, it can be deleted as follows:

Menu Path: Order > Functions > Deletion Flag > Activate

Setting the deletion flag causes the order to be completely disregarded by the system. However, the order itself is not actually erased. If desired, the deletion flag can be deactivated, making the order active once again.

Order Release

The creation of production orders, whether accomplished via conversion from planned orders or otherwise, results in a complete information package intended to direct the manufacture of a specific material on the shop floor. All the necessary data items, such as a component list or task list, are linked together in one data package. However, the order cannot be acted on by the shop floor until it is released. The act of releasing a production order causes several changes. Prior to release of a production order, it is not possible for anyone in the organization to enter confirmations against either individual operations or the entire order. Generally, the printing of paperwork on the shop floor is tied to the order release process. So, prior to order release, there is no printed documentation available to the shop floor personnel to initiate their activities.

N O T E Inspection lots, necessary to collect and evaluate quality control information resulting from the production order, are not created within the system until the order release is carried out.

The order release process can trigger an additional component material Availability check. An Availability check performed at this point in the process can differ from checks performed previously. For example, during production order creation, it was mentioned that a check of component availability could be performed. Because a production order can often be created many weeks or months prior to its scheduled start date, it might be helpful to perform an Availability check at that time that examines both current stock and planned receipt of the component materials.

Far in advance of a production order's start date, it is not uncommon to find that component materials are not already in stock, but will be produced or procured by the time that they are needed in the production order. Thus, an Availability check, which includes both of these categories, would be appropriate. Much closer to the scheduled start date of the production order, the order release is typically carried out. At this time, a material Availability check, which still includes planned receipts, may not provide useful information.

If the order release is carried out very close to the scheduled start date of the production order, an Availability check, which only examines current stock, may be appropriate. Such a check would simply indicate whether or not the necessary components are actually available at that moment. If materials are available in stock, the production order can be accomplished as scheduled. If materials are not available in stock, the system would then indicate that there are missing parts, even if planned receipts exist. In this way, the scheduler or shop floor supervisor is notified that components, which were expected to be in inventory, are not yet present. With this information, the order release can be delayed or the production order itself can be rescheduled to avoid release of an order to the shop floor that will be impossible to complete due to a lack of component material.

All these characteristics of the order release process serve to further increase a scheduler's or supervisor's control over the shop floor activities. This serves to reinforce the overall business process by reducing the ease with which individual production shops can deviate from the overall schedule and work on what they want, when they want. Withholding the printed shop documents until orders are released reduces the chance that shops will be working ahead on some operations or entire orders. By restricting the shop floor's ability to confirm operations until an order is released, this type of control is further enhanced. This is especially true if the compensation of shop floor personnel is directly linked to conformance to the schedule. The incentive to work on operations outside of those scheduled and released is removed. Of course, this same restriction places a much greater emphasis on generating an appropriate and efficient schedule in the first place.

Individual Order Release   Release of production orders can be accomplished individually or collectively. The release process is considered a change to a production order and is therefore accessed in a manner similar to order change procedures previously discussed. An example of the path leading to the release of an individual production order is the following:

> **Menu Path:** Logistics > Production > MRP > Evaluations > Stock/Reqmts List
>
> **Transaction Code:** MD04

Select the desired production order by clicking it within the appropriate Stock Requirements List. Then, click the Order Change icon. Once within the production order while in the change mode, fields that can be modified are displayed with a white background. Fields that cannot be modified are displayed with a gray background.

Order release can be accessed via Order > Functions > Release.

Save the production order by clicking the Save icon. Depending on the configuration settings, the system can again reschedule the modified order as it is being saved.

Collective Order Release   Depending on the number of production orders involved at any given time, it is likely that releasing the orders individually will prove to be a time-consuming and laborious process. Collective order releases can be utilized to speed this task. Collective order release is typically initiated as follows:

> **Menu Path:** Logistics > Production > Production Control > Order > Release > Collective Release > Execute
>
> **Transaction Code:** CO05

At this point, the system will prompt the user for search criteria to be used in identifying those production orders that will be proposed for release. The data entries in Table 14.10 can be helpful.

Part
III

Ch
14

Table 14.10 Search Criteria for Collective Order Release

Field	Value	Description	Required?
Order Type	Select from list. PP01 is typically selected.	Order type differentiates orders by their configured characteristics.	Yes
Plant	Desired plant code.	Plant in which desired orders exist.	Yes
MRP Controller	Desired MRP Controller.	Limits order selection to only those created by MRP Controller.	No
Production Scheduler	Desired Production Scheduler.	Limits order selection to only those assigned to the specific Production Scheduler.	No
Material	Material Number.	Limits order selection to only those pertaining to a specific material.	No
Order	Order Number.	Limits order selection to order number(s) indicated.	No
Date Selection	Schedule Order Release Date(s).	Limits order selection to those with scheduled release date within specified range.	No (very useful order selection criteria)

After entering the desired search criteria, click the Execute button. A list of production orders that meet the selection criteria will be displayed. Select those orders to be released by clicking within their respective boxes. If all orders displayed are to be released, this can be more quickly accomplished via the menu command Edit > Select > Select All.

The selected orders are then sequentially released by clicking the Release button. Depending on the user's desired system configuration, any difficulties encountered by the system during the release process will be presented as warning or error messages. As always, the user has the option of proceeding through warning messages. Error messages will stop the release process until the problem is corrected.

Capacity Evaluation

Capacity evaluation discussions generally revolve around work centers. As such, a general description of work center capacities may be helpful. For each work center defined within SAP, available capacities can be specified in various categories. The most common capacity categories utilized are machine and labor. Detailed information can be included for each category. This concept can be easily depicted via an example relating back to Electro Tech.

Suppose that somewhere within Electro Tech's production operations is a material number stamping process. For each item produced, a machine is used to imprint the material number on the object itself. Assume that two operators are required to run the machine: one to load the materials into the front of the machine and another to remove stamped materials from the back of the machine. Now, assume that this process is scheduled to be available (running) Monday through Friday, two shifts per day. The third shift each day is to be utilized for any machine maintenance that may be required. For the machine itself, assume that a shift consists of eight available hours. For each of the operators, lunch and other break time will reduce their available hours per shift. Available capacities can then be calculated as shown in Figure 14.17.

FIG. 14.17

An example of capacity evaluation.

Machine:

Machines:	1
Days per week:	5
Shifts per day:	2
Hours per shift:	8
Total Available Machine Capacity:	1 x 5 x 2 x 8 = <u>80 hours/week</u>

Labor:

People:	2
Days per week:	5
Shifts per day:	2
Hours per shift:	7 (8 – .5 hour lunch – .25 hour break – .25 break)
Total Available Labor Capacity:	2 x 5 x 2 x 7 = <u>140 hours/week</u>

In this example, the available machine hours are 80 and the available labor hours are 140. This information is helpful because it will be used to evaluate the feasibility of the production schedule across this particular work center.

Part

III

Ch

14

Following the creation of production orders (and planned orders if lead time scheduling is utilized) the requirements on each work center referenced in the routing are scheduled and totaled automatically within the system. A comparison between the total hours available and the total hours required within a specified time frame, usually a week, can then be viewed.

The capacity situation can be viewed in a variety of ways. Generally, capacity is viewed by work center and capacity category. While an overall capacity evaluation is always possible, the large amount of data can make a meaningful evaluation impossible. Periods of capacity overload or backlog can be identified separately because these types of conditions are usually high priority items to production schedulers and denote areas of potential schedule conflicts.

In general, capacity evaluations can be initiated via the following menu path:

Menu Path: Logistics > Production > Capacity Planning

Transaction Code: CM00

From this point, overall work center load, overload, backlog, and so on can be evaluated. To review overall load, proceed with the menu path Evaluation > Work Center View > Load, and then supply the data entries in Table 14.11.

Table 14.11   Data Fields for Capacity Evaluations on a Work Center

Field	Value	Description	Required Entry?
Work Center	Work center to be examined	Limits review to work center indicated. If left blank, all work centers will be included.	Yes, if Work Center Category entry not made.
Work Center Category	Work Center Category code	Limits review to those work centers managed by the indicated group.	Yes, if a specific work center is not indicated above.
Location	Location code	Specifies location for which work center evaluation is to be performed.	Yes.

After entering the necessary data, click the Enter button. For each work center and capacity category that falls within the specified guidelines, a table similar to that shown in Figure 14.18 will be displayed.

FIG. 14.18
Work center load evaluation.

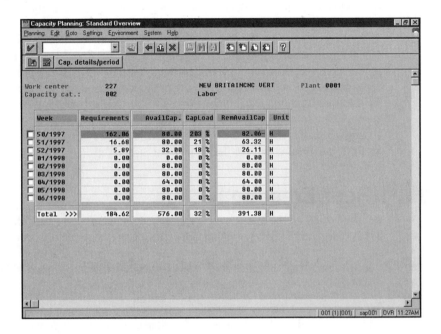

The columns in the table are described in Table 14.12.

Table 14.12   Definitions for Output of Capacity Evaluations on a Work Center

Column	Description
Week	Self-explanatory time guide
Requirements	Workload placed on work center and capacity category by the existing production schedule
Available Capacity	Total hours available within the respective time period
Capacity Load %	Percentage of available capacity loaded by existing production schedule
Remaining Available Capacity	Unused available capacity within the respective time period
Units	Units of capacity measure—typically hours

Periods that indicate over 100% Capacity Load are frequently of concern because they indicate a scheduled overload for that capacity category. Will the SAP system allow this to happen? The answer depends on whether a logic known as *finite scheduling* is being applied.

Part
III

Ch
14

Finite scheduling refers to a system-imposed restriction that prevents automatic generation of a production schedule that results in work center overloads. When applying finite scheduling logic, the creation of production orders and planned orders (if lead-time scheduling is used) is suspended each time a work center overload would result. Scheduling of the order in question is suspended and the user must manually alleviate the overload condition. Then automatic scheduling is resumed. This sequence of events repeats itself, as necessary, throughout the scheduling process. While finite scheduling serves to prevent creation of scheduled work center overloads, the magnitude of data that must be manually managed can be very large, depending on the scope and depth of the production schedule. For this reason, finite scheduling is frequently not utilized. *Infinite* scheduling is applied, allowing the SAP system to generate work center overload situations. Following the generation of a production schedule, the Scheduling staff is then faced with the responsibility of evaluating the overload conditions and manually performing capacity leveling as necessary.

Shop Floor Execution

Once the order has been released to the shop floor and, if necessary, shop floor paperwork has been printed, work can begin. A manufacturing process can be very complicated or very simple, but, regardless of the process, there are some basics that apply to almost all. Generally, a manufacturing facility takes raw materials and converts them to a salable product through the addition of labor, machine processing, and knowledge.

All these activities have costs associated with them. Understanding the cost of raw materials, skilled labor, and machine time is the first step to understanding manufacturing costs and relating them to pricing and, ultimately, profitability.

Within SAP, the production order functions as a cost collector. As material, labor, and machine time is consumed, costs are collected through the production order. At the same time, a *lien* is placed on the capacity of the required machines. This excludes them from use in the manufacture of other products for the needed block of time. How, though, does the production order know what amount of labor to collect or how long a machine ran and when it can be released for use? Each operation can have a standard time assigned to it that estimates the time necessary to complete the operation; but to gain accurate costing, actual time should be collected. This is accomplished through what SAP calls a *completion confirmation*.

A completion confirmation is used to report the number of good pieces manufactured or the *yield* of the operation. It also provides for reporting the number of pieces scrapped on an operation or the pieces requiring rework. The labor time used to manufacture the pieces and the machine time required to complete the task are known as *activities*. Activities are defined through the standard value key associated with a work center. Up to six activities can be defined within a standard value key so, in addition to labor time, items like setup time, machine time, and tear-down time can be collected.

In addition to yield and activity times, additional items that can be recorded are personnel data, work center, goods movements (automatically or manually), and confirmation text. If the Quality Management module is also being utilized, inspection results can also be recorded at inspection operations.

N O T E Quality operations can be defined in the production routing just like production operations. They allow for the recording of in-process inspection results including limited SPC charting. To see how inspection results are recorded in SAP, see the section "Results Recording" in Chapter 18, "Purchasing Functionality with SAP R/3." ■

In SAP, you can confirm objects at different levels. An entire order can be confirmed or just one operation of the order. The following is a complete list of items that can be confirmed:

- An order
- An operation
- A sub-operation
- An individual capacity of an operation
- An individual capacity of a sub-operation

Take Electro Tech as an example—it requires employees to report yield and activities. This means that at the completion of key operations, employees enter yield count, scrap count (if appropriate), rework count (if appropriate), setup time, labor time, and machine time. This means that not all operations are confirmed but, on selected operations, entry is required.

Control of Production Confirmation

SAP allows for control of which operation must be confirmed through a control key assigned to each operation. The control key defines several elements of how the operation functions including printing, scheduling activities, and the confirmation requirements.

N O T E Controls keys are defined though configuration of SAP. The system comes delivered with a wide variety of control keys. If these do not satisfy your needs then create new one(s) that start with a Z. Do not change the delivered SAP control keys because many different task list types can use these control keys. Also, upgrades of the software can overwrite your changes if the new keys do not start with an X, Y, or Z. ■

The confirmation options available in SAP are as follows:

- Milestone
- Confirmation required
- Confirmation possible but not required
- Confirmation not possible

As these options suggest, it is possible to require or disallow the entry of a confirmation for a given operation. The most powerful setting might be setting an operation as a milestone. A milestone will disallow confirmation of subsequent operations prior to confirmation of the milestone. In this manner, key manufacturing steps or quality operation can be marked as required, so they are not intentionally or unintentionally bypassed.

Part
III

Ch
14

> **CAUTION**
>
> Once any partial confirmation has occurred at a milestone operation, full confirmation can occur at a subsequent operation. In other words, if a production order for 10 pieces is sent to the shop floor and 1 piece is confirmed at milestone operation 0010, then all 10 pieces can be confirmed at operation 0020. This is true even if the remaining 9 pieces have never been reported as clearing operation 0010.

Entering a Production Confirmation

Once the appropriate operations to confirm have been established, you must decide how they will be confirmed. SAP offers a variety of methods to confirm work on the shop floor. The three primary options are the following:

- Time ticket confirmation
- Time event confirmation
- Collective time ticket confirmation

The difference in these methods is how the information is collected rather than what information is collected. A standard time ticket reporting is the entry of yield and activity time for work completed. The time event confirmation allows for an operator to sign in with a start time for the work task and sign out when the work is complete. SAP calculates the activity time and the operator specifies the yield.

Some shop floors still prefer to avoid having operators go to a terminal after every operation so they utilize collective time ticket entry. This method allows entry of a number of confirmations at once by using individual confirmation numbers that identify the material, order number, and operation.

> **CAUTION**
>
> When using collective confirmations, the activities are calculated based on the entered yield quantity and the planned standard values. This means actual time is not captured.

To demonstrate the base functionality of SAP, you will examine only the time ticket confirmation in this chapter. To enter a time ticket confirmation, follow this path:

> **Menu Path:** Logistics > Production > Production Control > Confirmation > Enter > For Operation > Time Ticket
>
> **Transaction Code:** CO11

The initial screen for entry of a time ticket, shown in Figure 14.19, allows for selecting the appropriate operation in several ways. The Confirmation number is assigned when the order is created. This number is unique to a combination of material, order number, and operation. By entering the confirmation number, the specific operation to confirm is selected.

If the Confirmation number is not known, a combination of the Order number, Operation, and, if appropriate, Sub-operation can be used. If the Order number is not known, the Selection button can be used to look up the Order number by using information such as material or work center. After the appropriate criteria have been provided, press Enter to continue.

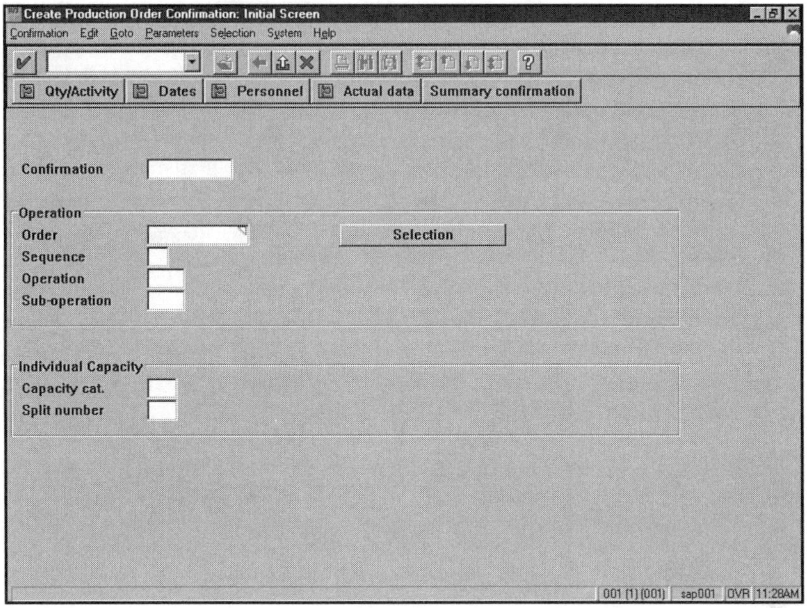

FIG. 14.19
The initial screen for a time ticket confirmation.

[Screenshot: Create Production Order Confirmation: Initial Screen

Menu bar: Confirmation Edit Goto Parameters Selection System Help

Toolbar buttons: Qty/Activity | Dates | Personnel | Actual data | Summary confirmation

Confirmation [   ]

Operation
Order   [   ]   [Selection]
Sequence   [ ]
Operation [ ]
Sub-operation [ ]

Individual Capacity
Capacity cat. [ ]
Split number [ ]

Status bar: 001 (1) (001)   sap001   OVR 11:28AM]

There are several possible views for entering a time ticket confirmation:

- Quantity/Activity
- Dates
- Personnel data
- Qty/Activity/Forecst

You are going to focus only on the most commonly used view—Quantity/Activity.

The Quantity/Activity view is the most commonly used view, but it lacks a lot of the fields available on the other views (see Figure 14.20). Enter the number of good pieces to confirm in the Yield to Conf. field. Enter the number of rejected pieces in the Scrap field and the number of defective pieces in the Rework field. A Reason code is also available to trigger follow-up activities for the rework quantity such as the creation of a rework order.

The activity times can also be entered. As explained earlier in the case of Electro Tech, setup, labor, machine, and tear-down time are reported. Finally, select the appropriate radio button stating whether the confirmation is a partial, final, or auto-final confirmation. If all the pieces have been completed, select the Final Confirm. button. If only some of the pieces have been completed, Partial Conf. should be selected. If the operator does not know if all the parts have

Part
III

Ch
14

been completed, selecting the Aut.fin.confirm indicator calculates whether the expected yield has been reached. If the yield entered through one or more confirmations equals the expected yield based on order quantity and confirmation tolerances, a final confirmation is recorded. If the entered yield does not calculate to the desired quantity, a partial confirmation is recorded.

FIG. 14.20

The Quantity/Activity confirmation screen.

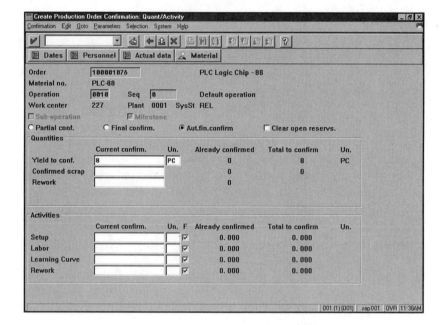

N O T E This discussion of production confirmations has adhered to the assumption of working in the discrete manufacturing environment. If the PP-PI modules were utilized, interactive process instruction sheets can be set up that allow operators to have work instructions passed to them automatically while confirming work and recording results all through the PI sheet. ■

Goods Movements and Confirmations

Activity times are not the only financial consideration associated with manufacturing. The consumption of raw materials and the delivery of final material to inventory both have a dollar value associated with them. In SAP, the confirmation of an operation can both consume raw materials and deliver finished goods to storage.

The consumption of raw materials automatically based on a production confirmation is called *backflushing*. By confirming an order or operation, raw materials can be automatically backflushed based on quantities called out in the Bill of Material (BOM) and the routing. Raw materials or components on the BOM are allocated to consuming operations in the routing. When the order is created, this relationship is copied into the order. When an operation is confirmed, the system will automatically post a goods issue of the components allocated to the operation, assuming the Backflushing Indicator has been set.

The Backflushing Indicator can be set in one of three places:

- The Material Master on the MRP 2 view
- In the work center in the basic data setup
- In the routing, at the component allocation screen

When the order is created, the Backflush Indicator is copied from one of these three master data sources. When a confirmation is entered for an operation with components allocated to it, the inventory is consumed from the specified supply area to the production order and the appropriate material cost is collected through the production order.

You may want the manufactured product to be placed into inventory at the end of the manufacturing cycle. This, too, can be handled automatically in SAP. Through the definition of the control key discussed earlier in this chapter, you can specify that an automatic goods receipt should take place when an operation is confirmed. An automatic goods receipt can only be posted once per production order. Since goods receipts are typically done at the end of the manufacturing cycle, the last operation of the routing should have a different control key than all the others. This control key should be configured to post an automatic goods receipt.

N O T E Automatic goods receipts cannot be carried out for either coproducts or serialized parts.

If backflushing and automatic goods receipts are not desired, these transactions can be carried out through the normal inventory management transactions allowed in SAP. If an error occurs in a goods movement, such as there is not enough material in inventory when the backflush occurs, you can process the failed goods movements either directly in the confirmation transaction, or in a separate transaction for processing goods movements with errors.

Order Completion

Confirmation of production order operations constitutes the most common manner of completing each production order. The logic behind this process and a general description of the system tools to support it are discussed in other chapters. An additional method of closing a production order, a *technical completion*, applies within the context of this chapter and needs to be presented here.

As mentioned earlier, the release of a production order generally triggers the printing of shop paperwork and allows operation confirmations to be entered. Suppose that a production order is reviewed by the appropriate scheduler, found to be correct, and then released to the shop floor. Upon receipt of the printed material pertinent to the production order, work is initiated on the shop floor and the first few operations within the order are confirmed.

Now, suppose that information is received stating that this particular production order should not be completed. Perhaps Engineering has determined that this particular design is flawed and should no longer be produced. Or possibly, Sales has learned that the customer for which this particular production order was scheduled has filed bankruptcy and will not accept (or pay

Part

III

Ch

14

for) any further deliveries. An initial response on the part of Scheduling or Production might be to simply delete the production order. This is generally unacceptable from an accounting or tracking point of view because material and labor costs would have already been incurred by the operations already confirmed. Simply deleting these costs from the books would lead to inaccurate, not to mention possibly illegal, accounting results.

The solution to this type of situation provided by SAP is known as a *technical completion*. By technically completing a production order, any confirmations already entered are maintained, but future operations are essentially removed from the production schedule. The order is closed without yielding a product. More importantly, any aspect of the production planning system no longer considers the planned receipt of material from this production order. Because shop paperwork was printed during the order release process, it will be necessary to manually retract it following the technical completion of a production order. Otherwise, a production shop could inadvertently continue to expend labor and machine resources on a production order that should not be completed.

Technical completions are generally performed on individual production orders per the following menu path:

> **Menu Path:** Logistics > Production > Production control > Order > Change
>
> **Transaction Code:** CO02

After selecting the desired production order, follow Order > Functions > Restrict Processing > Technically Complete.

The blue status line within the production order header will be updated with the abbreviation TECO, indicating that the order has been technically completed.

Purchase Orders

Virtually all of the discussions presented within this chapter have dealt with internally manufactured materials and their respective production orders. Externally procured materials are scheduled in largely the same manner. In fact, up through the point of the MRP run, there is little difference at all. It is after this point in the production planning process that differences become more visible. Obviously, planned orders for procured materials are not converted into production orders. In fact, it is possible to avoid the creation of planned orders altogether and instruct the MRP run to generate purchase requisitions directly. These requisitions are subsequently converted into purchase orders.

Further discussions and much more detailed information regarding the scheduling of externally procured materials are addressed in Chapter 18.

Plant Maintenance

Oftentimes, management can lose sight of the role plant maintenance can play within the organization. As with Electro Tech, it appears that Irving's predecessor relegated maintenance to strictly a reactive repair service organization. It doesn't have to be, nor should it be this way.

On-time shipments depend on consistent and reliable equipment availability. Without this consistency, the company can incur excess costs.

These costs come in the form of schedule changes causing excessive and unplanned changeovers. This is not only true for the piece of equipment that may have broken down, but for those operations upstream as well as downstream. Often, companies counter the effects of equipment downtime with excess capacity or excess inventory. Again, these are expensive alternatives to the real solution: properly repairing and regularly maintaining a machine at its planned status and thus preventing unnecessary interruptions to the operation. Inconsistent production resulting from persistent and regularly occurring breakage and adjustments can be reduced and controlled through regular or preventive maintenance.

Regular maintenance within SAP's Plant Maintenance module is handled through the creation and scheduling of maintenance plans. While regular maintenance plans are most often developed to maximize the useful life of an asset and decrease the frequency of breakdown, they can serve other purposes as well. In addition to providing consistent production capabilities, maintenance plans are developed to improve the quality of production. For instance, it has been determined that a product's quality can be adversely affected by the condition of the equipment producing the product. The more consistent the condition of the equipment, the more consistent the final product produced from that equipment. Maintenance plans can be created to maintain this consistency.

Also, warranties are often based on service conditions requiring equipment be maintained to the manufacturers' requirements. Maintenance plans acknowledge a company's awareness of these maintenance requirements. Execution of these plans is also documented through the Plant Maintenance system's reporting capabilities. Similarly, maintenance plans can be created to address legal regulations. Government regulations, as they relate to worker safety and environmental protection, must be adhered to. Maintenance plans can ensure that the company stays in compliance with these requirements.

The competition created by the world economy has dictated that companies continue to pursue the elimination of waste and ultimately reduce the cost of their product. Plant maintenance hasn't always believed it could contribute significantly in this area. Through the application of SAP's maintenance-planning capabilities, maintenance costs can be reduced. Initially, maintenance costs will rise from the introduction of regular maintenance plans and procedures. As machine breakdowns become less frequent, it should become evident that the cost of regular maintenance is much lower than the cost of repeatedly repairing equipment. Also, regular maintenance plans provide maintenance planners and dispatchers the information necessary to plan a higher percentage of their crews' work. Such planning capability provides more efficient work sequencing and logical operation consolidation. This can ultimately reduce maintenance costs through the increase of planning efficiency. Normally, reductions of planning and maintenance trade personnel should be realized.

Lastly, regular maintenance plans require the standardization and documentation of the work to be performed through maintenance items. Maintenance items within SAP's Plant Maintenance module incorporate task lists with detailed operational information. Do not fail to review this data on a regular basis. Performed properly with a cross-functional team, this exercise

Part
III

Ch
14

should ensure the accuracy of the task data, further standardize the work for each piece of equipment, and possibly identify those tasks that might be performed internal to the machines operation by the operator. This would transfer maintenance efforts currently performed external to machine operations, causing downtime to the machines internal runtime. Costs will once again be reduced.

Creating a Maintenance Plan

SAP Plant Maintenance supports the creation of two types of maintenance plans: time-based plans and counter-based plans.

Time-based plans are created when the work must be carried out at key dates or specific intervals of a factory or Gregorian calendar. This type of plan should be applied to applications with level demand or noncritical pieces of equipment requiring low-cost tasks. For example, use time-based maintenance plans with pumps or motors that run consistently without experiencing any peaks or valleys in demand or usage. Also, insignificant or nonbottleneck pieces of equipment may not warrant the regular monitoring required to support counter-based planning, the second type of maintenance planning.

Counter-based planning triggers the execution of maintenance tasks based upon one or multiple counters. Once a counter has exceeded a predetermined value, the plan creates an order to be carried out. These counters track such measures as the number of hours a piece of equipment has run. Other examples would be the number of gallons pumped or miles driven. This type of planning requires the recording of counter measurements and thus additional labor requirements upon the maintenance function. Use of these types of plans should be limited to equipment experiencing varying levels of use over time. In particular, it is recommended that counter-based plans are developed for production constraining or bottleneck pieces of equipment.

You can also set up maintenance plans for equipment where multiple counters exist simultaneously. The plan can be set to trigger a work order to be carried out whether tripped by the first counter or last counter of the group.

The scope of this section assumes that all maintenance items, and thus corresponding maintenance task lists, technical object assignment, and strategies, have been created. At this point, you will learn how to create and schedule both a time-based as well as a counter-based plan.

Creating a Time-Based Maintenance Plan   To create a time-based maintenance plan, use the following path:

> **Menu Path:** Logistics > Plant Maintenance > Maintenance Planning > Prev.maint.plans > Create
>
> **Transaction Code:** IP01

Complete the following steps:

1. The system will automatically assign a number to the plan unless you are using external numbering. If this is the case, enter an appropriate number.

2. Enter an appropriate time-based (key date, factory, or Gregorian calendar) maintenance strategy.

3. Press Enter and you will be on the Maintenance Schedule screen.

4. For future reference, it is advisable to document (via the text tools) a description of the plan and its intended purpose. The system will facilitate both a short as well as a long text. Enter your text as necessary.

5. At this point, you need to adjust the scheduling parameters. Choosing the Goto function in the toolbar and selecting Sched Parameters can perform this. You are currently on the Selection Criteria screen. Proceed until complete.

6. To complete the maintenance plan, you must assign one or more maintenance items to the plan. You should be on the Maintenance Schedule screen once again. At this point, select Edit > Select MaintItem to pull up another Selection Criteria screen. You will need to make a number of entries to limit the maintenance items that can be assigned to your plan. The maintenance items to be assigned must share the same strategy and not be assigned to any other maintenance plans. To generate the maintenance item possibilities select Program > Execute from the menu bar.

7. From this list, you can select the maintenance items to be assigned to your plan in one of two ways. You can either place the cursor on the appropriate maintenance item and select the Choose button or select the Edit > Choose command from the menu bar. The system will copy all of the items you have chosen into your maintenance plan.

8. To complete the maintenance plan, we must save it. Select MaintPlan > Save from the menu bar or click the Save button.

Creating a Counter-Based Maintenance Plan To create a counter-based maintenance plan, use the following path:

> **Menu Path:** Logistics > Plant Maintenance > Maintenance Planning > Prev.maint.plans > Create

> **Transaction Code:** IP01

Complete the following steps:

1. The system will automatically assign a number to the plan unless you are using external numbering. If this is the case, enter an appropriate number.

2. Enter an appropriate performance-based maintenance strategy.

3. Press Enter and you will be on the Maintenance Schedule screen.

4. Enter the counter from which the measurement document readings will trigger the scheduling of an order.

5. For future reference, it is advisable to document (via the text tools) a description of the plan and its intended purpose. The system will facilitate both a short as well as a long text. Enter your text as necessary.

6. At this point, you need to adjust the scheduling parameters. Choosing the Goto function in the toolbar and selecting Sched Parameters can perform this. You are currently on the Selection Criteria screen. Proceed until complete.

Part
III

Ch
14

7. To complete the maintenance plan, you must assign one or more maintenance items to the plan. You should be on the Maintenance Schedule screen once again. At this point, select Edit > Select MaintItem to pull up another Selection Criteria screen. You will need to make a number of entries to limit the maintenance items that can be assigned to your plan. The maintenance items to be assigned must share the same strategy and not be assigned to any other maintenance plans. To generate the maintenance item possibilities, select Program > Execute from the menu bar.

8. You can select from this list the maintenance items to be assigned to your plan one of two ways. You can either place the cursor on the appropriate maintenance item and select the Choose button or select the Edit > Choose command from the menu bar. The system will copy all of the items you have chosen into your maintenance plan.

9. To complete the maintenance plan, we must save it. Select MaintPlan > Save from the menu bar or click the Save button.

Creating a Multiple Counter-Based Plan   To create a multiple counter-based maintenance plan, use the following path:

> **Menu Path:** Logistics > Plant Maintenance > Maintenance Planning > Prev.maint.plans > Create

> **Transaction Code:** IP01

Complete the following steps:

1. The system will automatically assign a number to the plan unless you are using external numbering. If this is the case, enter an appropriate number.

2. Select Enter without entering a maintenance strategy. You will receive a warning that you are about to create a multiple counter plan.

3. Press Enter *again*. You will be on the Maintenance Schedule screen.

4. For future reference, it is advisable to document (via the text tools) a description of the plan and its intended purpose. The system will facilitate both a short as well as a long text. Enter your text as necessary.

5. You must now create a maintenance cycle.

6. At this point, you need to adjust the scheduling parameters. Choosing the Goto function in the toolbar and selecting Sched Parameters can perform this. You are currently on the Selection Criteria screen. Proceed until complete.

7. To complete the maintenance plan, you must assign one or more maintenance items to the plan. You should be on the Maintenance Schedule screen once again. At this point, select Edit > Select MaintItem to pull up another Selection Criteria screen. You will need to make a number of entries to limit the maintenance items that can be assigned to your plan. The maintenance items to be assigned must share the same strategy and not be assigned to any other maintenance plans. To generate the maintenance item possibilities, select Program > Execute from the menu bar.

8. You can select from this list the maintenance items to be assigned to your plan one of two ways. You can either place the cursor on the appropriate maintenance item and select the

Choose button or select the Edit > Choose command from the menu bar. The system will copy all of the items you have chosen into your maintenance plan.

9. To complete the maintenance plan, we must save it. Select MaintPlan > Save from the menu bar or click the Save button.

Scheduling a Time-Based Maintenance Plan Initially   To schedule a time-based maintenance plan for the first time, follow this path:

> **Menu Path:** Logistics > Plant Maintenance > Maintenance Planning
>
> **Transaction Code:** IP00

Complete the following steps:

1. From the menu bar, choose Prev.maint.plans > Schedule.
2. Enter the maintenance plan to be scheduled and press Enter.
3. From the menu bar, choose Edit > Start to schedule the plan.
4. A Start of Cycle field will appear at this point. Enter the date when you want the scheduling to start. Based upon the previously maintained scheduling parameters and packages from the maintenance item, call dates and planned dates will be calculated.
5. Save the plan by selecting from the menu bar MaintPlan > Save or click the Save button.

Scheduling a Counter-Based Maintenance Plan Initially   To schedule your counter-based plan for the first time, proceed as follows:

> **Menu Path:** Logistics > Plant Maintenance >Maintenance Planning
>
> **Transaction Code:** IP00

Complete the following steps:

1. From the menu bar, choose Prev.maint.plans > Schedule.
2. Enter the maintenance plan to be scheduled and press Enter.
3. From the menu bar, choose Edit > Start to schedule the plan.
4. A Start of Cycle field will appear at this point. Enter the counter reading that would appear at the time you want the system to start scheduling the plan. Select Enter. A planned date and call date are calculated by the system, taking into account the existing maintenance packages, scheduling parameters, the annual estimate for the counter unit of measure, and the counter reading at the time of the cycle.
5. Save the plan by selecting from the menu bar MaintPlan > Save or click the Save button.

Scheduling a Multiple Counter-Based Maintenance Plan Initially   To schedule your multiple counter-based plan for the first time, proceed as follows:

> **Menu Path:** Logistics > Plant Maintenance >Maintenance Planning >
>
> **Transaction Code:** IP00

Part
III

Ch
14

Complete the following steps:

1. From the menu bar, choose Prev.maint.plans > Schedule.
2. Enter the maintenance plan to be scheduled and press Enter.
3. From the menu bar, choose Edit > Start to schedule the plan.
4. Using the current date as the start date, the system will automatically calculate planned dates and call dates, taking into account the existing maintenance packages, scheduling parameters, the annual estimate for the counter unit of measure, and the counter readings at the time of the cycle. The planned date used to create a maintenance order depends upon the operation type for the maintenance plan. Or operation types dictate the system create a maintenance order based upon the earliest of the multiple planned dates. And operation types dictate the latest of the multiple planned dates be used.
5. Save the plan by selecting from the menu bar MaintPlan > Save or click the Save button.

Production in the Real World—Human Resources

SAP has excellent production planning and execution tools available. Keep in mind, however, that these systems are only as good as their application. Adherence to schedule, timely reporting of working, updating inventory as needed, and enacting a preventive maintenance plan are aided by SAP, but they are carried out by employees. The system can help direct and empower your workforce, but not manage it.

The definition and maintenance of personnel activities is no small task. All companies, from the smallest start-up shop to the largest global conglomerate, must deal with personnel issues like payroll, benefits, recruitment, organizational management, and employee records. Even in this time of high-tech advancements, people still make a company run.

SAP's HR module is one of many very good personnel packages available today. Unlike most other HR packages, however, the HR module integrates seamlessly to the other functional modules of SAP. This means that payroll, benefits, and travel expense tracking have hooks to the FI/CO modules as needed. Likewise, the PP and PM modules feed employee information back to HR. This real-time integration to the various parts of your business is what makes SAP's HR module so appealing.

In Chapter 12, "A Day-in-the-life of Production Planning and Execution," you learned about Matt Carlton. Matt was a maintenance worker at Electro Tech. Recent problems had created a situation where a review of Matt's employee records was needed. Here you will take a look at the capabilities of HR within SAP.

Time Tracking

Time recording allows you to enter employee time data for working time, leave, business trips, and substitutions. This data can be entered as clock times or in hours and can contain account assignment specifications for other SAP applications.

There are basically two different methods of entering employee time data in the SAP system:

- Negative Time Recording—Recording exceptions to the normal working schedule
- Positive Time Recording—Recording all attendance and absences, as well as any exceptions to the normal work schedule

You can record actual times in one of three ways:

Automatic recording—The actual times are recorded at front-end time recording terminals and uploaded to the SAP system. Employees record their clock-in and clock-out times (actual times) electronically at the time recording terminals by using a time recording ID card. This data is then imported to the SAP system and processed using the time evaluation program.

Manual entry in time infotypes—Use of a time recording system is not mandatory because you can also record actual times manually into time infotypes for individual employees. Time data can be entered in hours or as clock times. A calendar entry option allows you to enter employee time data for longer periods of time. The list entry function is provided in a number of time infotypes and allows you to enter several records for one employee. Fast entry facilitates your day-to-day operations by offering a special entry screen where you can enter different time infotype records for different employees.

Manual time tracking CATS (Cross Application Time Sheet)—The functionality of this new component will enable time recording to be performed in the following applications:

- CO: internal activity allocation
- HR: attendance, absences
- MM-SRV: service
- PM/PS/SM: completion confirmations
- Travel expenses
- Withdrawals of materials

Absences

In the Absences infotype (2001), you can enter the times during which an employee is absent from work. An employee in the HR system is regarded as absent if he or she does not work the planned working hours stipulated in the personal work schedule.

Absences are divided into absence types:

- General absences
- Absences with quota deduction
- Absences relating to a work incapacity

Attendances

Attendances in the HR system define or supplement an employee's personal work schedule. Attendances are recorded in the Attendance infotype (2002). Typical attendances are business trips, off-site work, and training courses.

Part
III

Ch
14

Attendances are divided into attendance types:

■ General attendances

■ Attendances with quota deduction

Reporting

A central feature of the HR system is its ability to maintain data histories. When you enter new, up-to-date data in the system, the existing data is not deleted, but delimited according to its validity period. This allows you to run evaluations and reports at any time for current data, as well as past or future data.

Within the Time Management module, you can generate reports based on monthly work schedule and employee absence/attendance data. Each report retrieves relevant data from the database and displays information for evaluation.

There are work schedule reports:

Personal Work Schedule Report—This report displays an overview of an employee's most important working time data and time infotype records.

Daily Work Schedule Report—This report displays individual daily work schedules, including planned working time and breaks.

There are absence/attendance reports:

Attendances Report—This report generates an overview of an employee's attendances. Planned days and hours are displayed, as well as actual days and hours worked.

Attendance Check Report—You can use this report to obtain an overview of all employees who are at work or absent with a reason at any specific time. You can refer to the list to ascertain which employees are at work at the time of the evaluation, which are running late, and which are absent without having given prior notification. The evaluation is based on the time events recorded by the employee at the time recording terminal and the records in the Attendances (2002) and Absences (2001) infotypes. If you activate the Evaluate Work Schedule field on the report selection screen, you also obtain a list of employees who should be at work at the time of evaluation according to their personal work schedules, but are neither at work nor have notified you that they would be absent. In the standard system, you can refer to the following information to see when the employee is likely to be at work on the current day:

• Last clock-in entry, if you use time recording systems

• Off-site work records, if you use time recording systems

• Recorded absences, both full-day absences and absences of less than one workday

• Recorded attendance, such as business trips

Graphic Attendance/Absence Overview Report—This report generates a graphic overview of attendance and absence data for the specified group. This allows you to display any exceptions to work schedules in a graphic for all employees in a particular department.

Absences Report—You can use this report to summarize and classify absences.

Leave Report—You can refer to employee leave data to generate an overview of anticipated or actual absences for leave.

CHAPTER 15

Production Planning and Execution with SAP R/3

In this chapter

A typical day-in-the-life of a plant production scheduler at Electro Tech

The working structure of Electro Tech and how the information flow from one work group to another has been improved with SAP R/3

How maintenance scheduling is worked into the production scheduling activities

How MRP planning addresses both internal and external sources

How the integration of customer demand feeds the production planning activities, and how the stock requirements list allows for quick viewing of the balance between supply and demand

You have already looked at a typical day in the Customer Service Department of Electro Tech using SAP. During that example, you saw how SAP diminished the constant phone calls between Bob Peters, the CSR, and Bryan Luther, the Plant Scheduler. You have also seen the problems facing the manufacturing facility without an integrated production planning system. The scheduling of multiple manufacturing lines, the coordination of maintenance tasks, and supply problems are just a few of the problems that faced Electro Tech. This chapter takes a close look at the production planning activities to understand how SAP R/3 enables the functionality desperately needed at Electro Tech, Inc.

Understanding Production Scheduling with SAP R/3

In Chapter 12, "A Day-in-the-life of Production Planning and Execution," you met Bryan Luther, who has been with Electro Tech for 23 years and has an MBA in Plant Operations. Since the implementation of SAP, Bryan has actually begun to feel that he and his group schedule the plant instead of the plant scheduling their lives. Crisis management has been on the decline and proactive planning on the rise. Bryan was a contributing member of the production planning BPS team. He is pleased with the integration of the new computer system; a far cry above the MRP software he had run on his PC.

Every morning around 8:00 a.m., Bryan arrives at the plant and begins the process of determining what happened overnight. Now, instead of solely chasing the problems that occurred on the shop floor, he looks at new demands from sales. He can run several reports to examine what confirmations have taken place on the shop floor. Similarly, he can look at new orders entered in the system. His goal is to determine if there are production orders that need adjustment or an unexpected demand on the plant. This is a necessary activity because the world isn't perfect, whether a company is running SAP or not. Equipment problems, material shortages due to a failed vendor delivery, and even failure to follow the schedule can still occur, so the process must be monitored. Fortunately, with SAP's PP module, this does not require the tracking down of overworked area supervisors, nor are constant calls to the CSRs necessary. Monitoring the progress of a production order on the shop floor or new sales orders can be done from any SAP-capable computer in the building.

The Players

The following is a list of the employees involved in the Electro Tech production example:

- Bryan Luther—Plant MRP Controller
- Dave Jackson—Area Supervisor Manufacturing Line 4
- Marge Houlihan—Plant Manager
- Irving Mayer—Maintenance Manager
- Ted Goldfield—Purchasing

The Situation

The task of determining what changes need to be made to the schedule is much simpler now. Area supervisors like Dave Jackson, who used to hold the information on handwritten forms, now look up the status of orders on the system. Bryan Luther looks at the same information from his terminal. The ability to look at this information electronically allows Bryan the opportunity to do his job—schedule the plant.

The structure of Bryan's department changed somewhat during the implementation of SAP. That was something that surprised him. Going in he thought of SAP as a piece of software, so he couldn't see why that would cause his department to change. As he worked through the BPS process with the other team members, he realized that much of what they were doing was determining the best way to manage the scheduling process, with or without SAP. This did cause the redefinition of jobs. Even Bryan's title changed from Production Scheduler to MRP Controller. He is one of three MRP Controllers for the plant and has a two person staff created from pulling "troubleshooters" from the floor. These troubleshooters are now titled Production Schedulers.

At first this seemed like a large staff for the scheduling function, but with SAP up and running, it made more sense to him. The idea was to front-load the planning process. By creating the best possible manufacturing plan, the number of problems that arose from enacting the plan would decrease. After all, if Electro Tech was installing just another piece of software with the same job roles and same business practices, why bother? Automating a process that doesn't work well only produces problems faster.

SAP's Approach

Each morning, Bryan runs a series of reports for the sections of the plant for which he is responsible. Other MRP Controllers do the same. These reports address whether orders that were due to be completed were actually finished. He can also look at a list of all orders that are under his control. If an order is determined to be behind schedule, it can be individually rescheduled from its current status to the new expected completion date. The rescheduled order then can be looked at on the Stock Requirements List to see if the change affected the supply and demand picture. If a problem is discovered, a production scheduler can work with the area supervisor to shorten lead times and bring the material back on schedule, or the CSR can be notified in advance of the delay.

On a weekly basis, new schedules are generated to adjust to the changing supply and demand picture. Some parts are managed at the highest level through MPS runs, while others are managed through a complete bill-of-material explosion through MRP. The weekly scheduling bucket was also determined during the BPS process. Previously, scheduling was done on a bi-monthly basis that produced a schedule with two firm weeks and two soft weeks. The schedules were distributed on paper via the company mail system, and changes were made daily.

Changes still may occur daily, but they are based on the absolute, most current information available through the system. The changes are reflected on the reports the area supervisors use to manage the manufacturing lines. The ability to look at production orders against a manufacturing line or work center also allows Bryan Luther to monitor what orders are affected by unexpected equipment outages.

If a piece of equipment has been down, affecting several production orders, a list can be generated for all open production orders that contain that work center. The orders then can be individually rescheduled or rerouted, if necessary. These unexpected outages occasionally still cause problems with delayed shipments, but, with the improving preventive maintenance practices in the plant, outages are on the decline, too.

Irving Mayer's maintenance group has adopted SAP's preventive maintenance planning system. By mixing the use of both time-based and counter-based preventive maintenance plans, Irving's staff has been able to keep control of the varying life cycles of their equipment. Before SAP, they were using only time-based planning techniques, and these were not being adhered to. The addition of counter-based plans on some of the high-use equipment has allowed them to be proactive rather than reactive. At the same time, using counter-based planning on some of the low-use equipment has allowed them to spread their preventive maintenance activities. This has reduced cost and provided much needed additional resources.

Because no substantial preventive maintenance activities were observed before Irving's arrival, the initial process of creating a preventive maintenance program has only been strengthened by the added SAP capabilities. Irving has won the continued support of Marge Houlihan, the Plant Manager. Marge knows that SAP has helped Electro Tech run the plant better, but if she does not support the preventive maintenance activities that SAP plans, there is little use in doing it.

Having an online planning system for preventive maintenance has helped Bryan Luther, too. He has the ability to view but not change Irving's maintenance plans. This allows him to adjust the overall plant schedule based on the maintenance schedule. Irving also uses SAP's mail system to inform Bryan of changes to the maintenance plan. In some of the added SAP functionality Electro Tech is looking at implementing, Irving hopes to automate the notification of maintenance plan status changes via Workflow. Both Irving and Bryan are satisfied with the advantages they have realized using SAP R/3.

As Bryan converts planned orders to production orders for the week, Dave Jackson stops by his office to see how things are going. Dave's visits used to be more regular, but since SAP went live, they have slowed. Because the system allows Dave to see what Bryan has scheduled and allows Bryan to see how Dave's area is performing, the required daily appearances have been eliminated. Dave still stops in occasionally to say hello.

As they talk, Bryan asks how things are going on the shop floor with SAP. Bryan knows that this was one of the toughest areas to implement. Before SAP, the operators reported their production activities during a shift change meeting. The shift supervisors recorded the information on Operator Performance forms. The supervisors then keyed the information into a PC application that MIS had written for them. When the operators were required to enter their activities into SAP, they initially fought the idea.

Dave told Bryan that many of the operators were scared of the idea of using a computer. Others thought management was trying to monitor their work to compare performances and would discipline those who did not meet the expectations. Dave and the other area supervisors had to address these concerns during training. They not only explained how the information would help them manage schedules better, they flow diagrammed both processes to highlight the inefficiencies of the paper system. With time and some pushing, the operators slowly came around.

That wasn't the only problem they had to overcome, though. Because they had never used an integrated system, they overlooked one advantage. Originally, they planned to allow operators to enter the production confirmations for the day at the end of the shift. During the testing phase of the BPS process, they realized that many of the management and planning tools they had designed depended on real-time data. For this process to be effective, they needed confirmations entered when the work was completed, rather than at the end of the shift. There were problems with reporting out of order, and backflushing occurred when milestones were confirmed. It took a lot of work and some added discipline, but the benefit was worth it in the end.

Dave's pager goes off, so he excuses himself to see what's up. As Bryan thinks about their conversation, he wonders if other areas had similar problems. He remembers an earlier discussion with Ted Goldfield from Purchasing. Ted's group absolutely loved the benefits they received from SAP. The automatic creation of purchase requisitions for Bryan's MRP runs really helped them. No more comparing printed inventory reports to the printed schedule to determine what to order. No more lost or misrouted requisitions because they are now totally online. Manually created requisitions can be traced to their author. The conversion of requisitions to purchase orders, and eventually to a delivery being tested by the lab, all show up when Bryan looks at the stock requirements list.

He also remembers Ted saying that managing approved vendors has become simpler. The corporate purchasing organization can enter customer masters and work with the quality management group on quality information records. Ted's group at the plant can also enter customers for the limited areas they managed at the plant level. All in all, Purchasing seems pleased by the system.

Bryan turns back to his computer and continues the process of converting planned orders with a satisfaction he hadn't felt for a while. He realizes that the world isn't a perfect place, but his little slice of it has recently improved. That is something to be happy about.

The Assessment

The Production Planning arena of Electro Tech offers several "opportunities for improvement." The use of a truly integrated system allows for the flow of information that is essential in running a business efficiently. The complete picture of production, maintenance, and purchasing demands can now be considered in plant scheduling activities.

If you step back and examine the work processes and system tools involved in this case study, you can note the following:

- Production now has the necessary information available to them to move out of a fire-fighting mode and into a planning mode.
- The CSRs no longer have to make repeated calls to the Production Planning staff. The Stock Requirements List allows Production, Customer Service, and Purchasing personnel to view and, based on security, process items on the list.

- Maintenance activities are visible online.
- Purchasing activities are integrated with plant scheduling.
- A real-time system is the link between departments word-of-mouth.
- Changes to the schedule are no longer based on gut reactions but are sensitive to changes in sales demand.

Purchasing and Goods Receipt

CHAPTER 16

A Day-in-the-life of Purchasing and Goods Receipt

Having examined customer service, production scheduling, and maintenance activities at Electro Tech, turn your attention to purchasing activities. All companies, no matter how large or small, must deal with purchasing activities. Whether it is purchasing materials or services, proper management of purchasing activities is one of the first areas companies turn to when cash flow gets tight. This chapter takes a closer look at these activities to understand the problems and opportunities present at Electro Tech, Inc.

While there are those who try to make a career out of trips to the mall, for many people, purchasing goods and services is a job. This function is often stereotyped as the person who gets free lunches and tickets to local sporting events. Close examination of this job function presents so much more.

The purchasing organization at Electro Tech is somewhat splintered. A corporate group is located in the Cincinnati head office, but each plant is responsible for purchasing its own goods and services. For high-volume, big-dollar items, the corporate office specifies the allowed vendors. For localized, special items, the plant's Purchasing department handles the vendors. While this sometimes provides flexibility, it just as often creates overhead in administrative records for the various smaller vendors.

Understanding the Purchasing Department

Ted Goldfield has been in Purchasing for 30 years. He has designed every system that the Purchasing department has ever used, and all the forms, too. Ted and his staff spend most of their time interpreting the production schedules that come from Bryan Luther's group and using a "fudge factor" to determine when and how much material to buy. Inventory reports are usually walked over from the production area every Monday morning.

The receiving reports come from the receiving docks twice a day and are compared to the Hot List. Ted designed the Hot List five years ago to expedite those requirements that arrived absolutely too late to fulfill. The Hot List, considered a huge success when originally designed, is the main reason that Ted is currently running the department.

Among the reports that Ted designed and utilized is the Premium Inventory report. This report identifies to Ted's buyers what materials in inventory were purchased at a premium for rush situations that never really happened. This excess inventory is to be worked off or disposed of gradually so that the accountants won't report the losses all at once. This avoids attention from management and a review of his department's current buying and expediting activities.

The Players

The following is a list of the employees involved in the Electro Tech customer service example:

- Ted Goldfield—Purchasing department
- Bryan Luther—Plant Production Scheduler
- Dave Jackson—Area Supervisor Manufacturing Line 4

■ Marge Houlihan—Plant Manager

■ Irving Mayer—Maintenance Manager

■ Laurie Stewart—Warehouse and Ship Dock Manager

■ Cindy Kendall—Buyer

■ Tom Norr—Maintenance Supervisor

■ Lester Elkins—Incoming Inspection Lab Manager

The Situation

Returning from lunch with a vendor at around 1:30 p.m., Ted picks up his phone to hear that familiar stuttered dial tone indicating there are messages in his voice mailbox. Ted dials-in to discover that he has five new messages he needs to listen to. There is a message from his wife, two from vendors trying to schedule appointments, and one each from Dave Jackson and Irving Mayer. Both of these messages seem to have an urgency about them, but in different ways. Dave is looking for components he needs at the manufacturing line. Irving is looking for information about a belt that came up missing during maintenance activities over the weekend. Irving says that he has been summoned to a meeting with the plant manager and he's sure the missing belt will be a topic of discussion.

Ted has already heard rumblings about the missing belt, so this voicemail doesn't surprise him. Ted also knows that he has to proceed carefully with the current situation. While he does need to find out the story on the missing belt, that problem is history at this point. However, Dave Jackson is looking for material for the manufacturing line today. Irving will have to wait. Ted knows he can't afford to be associated with shutting down the manufacturing line after the problems with the missing belt.

The Problem

Ted pages Dave and in moments is talking to him on the phone. Dave explains that he knows a shipment of logic chips was delivered late Thursday of the previous week. He continues by saying that he needs the chips at the manufacturing line but so far they have not been delivered to his department. He also tells Ted that he walked down to the dock, and the shipment of chips was nowhere to be found. Dave says he tried to find Laurie Stewart to ask her about the shipment, but was unable to locate her. Ted agrees to do what he can to track down the shipment when Dave mentions that he has to attend a 2:30 p.m. meeting with Irving Mayer, Bryan Luther, and Marge Houlihan.

As a starting point, Ted goes to his receiver file for the previous Thursday. Dave was correct. A shipment of logic chips arrived late Thursday from A.L.K. Chip Technology. Ted knows this means that the hunt is on. He picks up the phone to try and locate Laurie Stewart. Laurie has returned to the dock from her daily after-lunch trip to the lab and office area.

"Warehouse, this is Laurie," she says.

Ted explains the problem with the missing chips and how the manufacturing line needs them immediately. Laurie seems to remember the shipment and asks Ted to hold while she checks her paperwork. Ted waits patiently as he hears papers shuffling over the phone. After a moment, Laurie returns with a simple explanation. "Ted, those chips were moved to the quarantine area," Laurie explains. She tells him that the lab sampled the shipment and asked that they be held until testing was complete. The lab analyst had talked about an issue with the supplier.

In a case where the lab asks that material be held up, standard operating procedure is to move the material to the quarantine area. There, the lab uses a sticker system to control the status of the material. Five different labels are used:

First is the *Quarantine* sticker. This sticker means the material is to be isolated for in-depth testing. This status is generally used for complaint material.

Second is the *On-hold* sticker. This sticker is normally used for new goods receipts and means a concern is being investigated.

The third sticker is *Under test*. This sticker represents normal goods receipts testing.

The fourth is the *Rejected* sticker, indicating material should be returned or scrapped.

The fifth and final sticker is *Released*, indicating that testing is complete and the material is approved for use.

Laurie tells Ted that the material is in the quarantine area and marked with an *On-hold* sticker. Ted is relieved to hear that the chips are still on site, but knows all is not well if the lab has asked that the material be held. He thanks Laurie for her help and says he will get in touch with the lab. Slowly but surely the picture is starting to come together.

Just as Ted hangs up the phone, Cindy Kendall, a buyer who reports to Ted, appears at his door. Cindy was stopped by Tom Norr in the hall and asked about a missing belt. Cindy explains that Tom is the supervisor who claims to have filled out the handwritten requisition for the belt. Tom claims that the requisition was put in Purchasing's mailbox on Tuesday of last week. Cindy says she does not remember seeing the requisition, but thinks another buyer might have processed it, even though she typically handles maintenance purchase requisitions.

Ted asks Cindy to check with the other buyers. He knows that it is unlikely that someone else processed the requisition, but knows it needs to be checked out. He also knows that it is unlikely that Cindy would have forgotten processing the requisition. The plant practice is that all maintenance parts requisitions go to Cindy. She then looks up any approved supplier from the published corporate list. If no corporate supplier is specified, she looks up local suppliers in a card file kept in the purchasing offices. After an appropriate supplier has been determined, she enters the requisition into the purchasing computer system and prints the purchase order. The Purchasing department still uses a dot matrix printer because the forms are two-part carbons. They need the impact printer to make the carbon work.

Cindy agrees to look into it further and goes off in search of the missing requisition. Ted has to refocus on what he was doing before Cindy came in. He thinks for a moment and remembers the missing logic chips and the lab. Again, he picks up the phone and dials.

The Solution

The Incoming Inspection Lab is a separate facility from the lab that tests manufactured parts. This is partially due to the added administrative burden of maintaining vendor certifications. Lester Elkins runs the lab. Lester is a Certified Quality Auditor and long-term employee of Electro Tech. He is deliberate in everything he does, which is often confused with stubbornness. Lester believes that he has to make sure every component that enters the facility is up to standard. He takes a no-defects approach to quality.

After three rings, Ted hears Lester's voice at the other end of the phone. "Hi, Lester. Ted Goldfield here. How are things going?" Ted asks. Lester, deliberate in his answers to such questions, responds by asking Ted what problem had him calling. Lester knows that Ted never calls just to make small talk. Ted obliges Lester and cuts to the chase. "Lester, there is a shipment of logic chips that came in last Thursday from A.L.K. Chip Technology. Your lab has them on hold, and the manufacturing line is screaming for them. They're part of a blanket purchase order placed against a certified vendor. So what's the problem?" Ted inquires.

Lester pauses as in deep thought and then asks Ted to hold on for a minute while he looks up the material in question. After a moment, Lester returns and says, "Yeah, you're right. We have them on hold." Lester explains that the shipment was part of the vendor certification process. Once a year, certified vendors are spot-checked on a shipment. As luck would have it, A.L.K. was due for its annual inspection.

Ted knows this is a good news, bad news situation. It means that there is probably nothing wrong with the chips, but it also means he is at the mercy of the lab. Almost afraid to hear the answer, Ted asks when he might expect to have the material released. Again Lester pauses and then gives Ted the best possible news he could have hoped for. Lester tells Ted that the chips have already been tested and are fine. While this is good news, it leaves Ted confused. "Lester," Ted says, "I just got off the phone with Laurie Stewart, and she claims the material is still on hold." Lester explains that Laurie is probably correct. Even though testing is complete, it is unlikely the inspector has made his way down to the dock to switch the labels from *On-hold* to *Released.*

Ted knows that he is caught in the middle. He asks if Lester can call Laurie and tell her it is okay to move the material from the quarantine area to the Manufacturing department. To that question, Lester makes it perfectly clear that the material can be moved only after the labels have been switched. Ted, of course, moves to the obvious question, "When can the labels be changed?"

Ted is patient while Lester explains that his inspectors have more things to do than run back and forth between the dock and the lab. He explains that no testing would be completed if they ran to the dock every five minutes. Normal procedure is to go to the dock during the last hour of the shift and make appropriate label changes at that time. Ted's persistence pays off, however. One last time, he asks Lester how he can get the material released so production won't shut down. Lester agrees to have the inspector go to the dock, this one time, to change the labels. He assures Ted that the material can be moved in about a half an hour.

This is a small victory for the Purchasing department, but Ted knows that when he tells Dave Jackson that the material will be there soon, he will score a win in manufacturing's eyes. He decides to wait 20 minutes or so before calling Dave. That way, the material will show up almost immediately after he makes the call.

With that crisis averted and Cindy chasing the missing requisition, Ted turns his attentions to his daily activities. Every afternoon, he has to sign all the purchase orders his department generates. The two-part carbon printouts are collected and put on his desk for approval. This is a security measure so that no one buyer can purchase materials or services without proper approval. This, of course, means that Ted needs to review and sign approximately 60 or 70 purchase orders a day. Making matters worse is the fact that three separate purchase orders might be written to the same vendor in a given day. The computer system has no way of cross-referencing open purchase orders. The approval process quickly becomes an exercise in penmanship. There is no review process, but rather a sign-off process. At one time, Ted had even purchased a signature stamp, but the carbon did not carry through on the stamp.

As Ted is finishing the purchase orders, Cindy Kendall reappears at his door, this time holding a purchase requisition. Cindy tells Ted that she has found the requisition on another buyer's desk. Apparently, the requisition had been misrouted when it came into the department. The other buyer had recognized that the requisition should have gone to Cindy and set it aside with the intent of passing it on to her. Unfortunately, the requisition got buried on the other buyer's desk and never made it to Cindy.

Ted is happy to hear the requisition was found, but is dissatisfied by the problem that occurred. He knows that he is going to take a few lumps from Irving and Marge on this one. Frustrated, he starts to snap at Cindy but quickly stops, realizing he would be shooting the messenger. He thanks Cindy and asks her to leave the requisition with him. He tells her he will take care of it from here and that she should direct Tom Norr his way if he comes looking for the missing requisition again.

At this point, almost 40 minutes have passed since Ted spoke with Lester Elkins. He picks up the phone and calls Dave Jackson's number. Dave is just returning from his meeting with Marge, Irving, and Bryan. Ted tells Dave that he has tracked down the missing chips and that they should be showing up in Dave's department any minute. Dave tells Ted that they are being delivered at that very moment. He thanks Ted for the good work.

As Ted hangs up the phone, he realizes that he has broken even for the day. He's managed to look good over the missing chips but is responsible for the added maintenance down time due to the missing motor belt. He decides to wait out the call from Irving. He is certain Irving will come find him, but figures there is no reason to push the subject. If asked, he can explain what happened to the missing requisition. If luck is on his side, no one will remember to ask.

At around 4:30 p.m., Ted looks in his mailbox and finds a revised schedule. Bryan Luther has distributed the modified schedule, and Ted needs to make sure the required components are available. He picks up his latest inventory report, which includes some updates from some cycle count checks. He starts comparing the inventory levels to the new schedule. Several of the components are low, and Ted knows that he will have to make sure the items are on order. Tired from the afternoon's struggles, he decides to leave that for the next morning.

The Assessment

The purchasing function is an intricate part of the supply chain. Without the necessary base materials or components, manufacturing cannot function. The importance of this relationship is often misunderstood until lack of raw materials causes a shutdown situation. The case study demonstrates how purchasing touches both manufacturing and maintenance. SAP R/3 provides several opportunities for improvement over Electro Tech's current operating situation.

If you examine the work processes and system tools involved in this case study, the following problems present themselves:

- Control of approved vendors is fragmented and managed manually.
- Manual purchase requisitions can be lost, causing delays in material receipts.
- Division of responsibility with a manual purchasing system can cause errors.
- Goods receipts and quality management activities are not integrated.
- Manual management of inventory occurs with a *label* system.
- Deliveries are managed manually using the Hot List.
- MRP demands are passed from scheduling to purchasing via paper reports.

Making the Move from Purchasing Past to SAP R/3

Purchasing is an activity with which all companies are familiar. The system of purchase requisitions becoming purchase orders becoming goods receipts has been played out many times over. This only scratches the surface of a typical company's purchasing needs. Long-term contracts, approved vendors, and interaction with production planning activities all have to be considered in today's business world. SAP handles these issues and more.

Understanding Procurement

The procurement function within an organization manages the purchase of goods and services utilized by the company. Everything from the most expensive electronic components to pencils are purchased items. The purchase of services, such as janitorial services or sub-contracted work such as custom machining, all must be managed through a procurement process.

With SAP, a highly functional purchasing system can be developed. Using Material Requirements Planning (MRP) techniques to feed the process, SAP supports a full range of source determinations. Once the supply source is known, purchase requisitions, requests for quotes, contracts, scheduling agreements, purchase orders, delivery schedules, goods receipts, and invoice verification are all linked in a common process.

The integration of the R/3 system links procurement, accounting, production planning, quality management, and inventory management into a common thread of business practices. The Materials Management module, one of SAP's most dynamic modules, allows for differentiation of procurement situations such as purchase for stock, purchase for consumption, and one-time purchases. Proper planning and focus are required to implement procurement with SAP's MM module.

The Scope

When Electro Tech examines its corporate structure and begins defining its hierarchy in SAP terms, the procurement team will need to decide whether to have centralized or decentralized purchasing. Electro Tech can opt for central purchasing (with one purchasing organization responsible for all plants), or distributed purchasing (with many purchasing organizations, each responsible for different plants).

One advantage that Electro Tech will realize by having one purchasing organization is having greater negotiating power for prices and terms of delivery with the vendor, due to greater purchase volumes. A central purchasing department can negotiate high-level contracts for all plants to use to meet their requirements. A high-level, centrally agreed-on contract will more likely allow for the negotiation of better conditions than an individual plant could negotiate on its own.

Other advantages of having a centralized purchasing organization include the standardization of business practices and easier visibility of what Electro Tech, as a whole, is spending for materials and services. Currently, Electro Tech has problems with varying and, in some cases, conflicting procurement procedures between plants and in determining total dollars spent on items obtained at multiple plants.

The advantages of a central purchasing organization need to be considered in relation to the advantages decentralized or distributed purchasing departments give the company. Namely, keeping the purchasing distributed at the plant level enables Electro Tech to control the scope of individual buyers a little easier. In addition, keeping buyers distributed at the plants keeps them a little more responsive to immediate plant needs. Each buyer can see, feel, and taste the needs of the those individuals who need the materials and services.

The Basic Team Definition

One of the biggest selling points of the SAP R/3 system is that it is comprised of many modules (more or less divided by functional area) which are fully integrated with one another—allowing all the departments within a company to access and maintain the same data. The fact that SAP is so highly integrated virtually mandates that the Business Process Simulation (BPS) teams not only communicate decisions among each other effectively but are also, to a certain degree, cross-functional.

To Electro Tech, Inc., this means that although its procurement BPS teams will be comprised mainly of purchasing-type folks, it should also ensure that it includes representation (even if only on an as-needed basis) from other functional areas such as Controlling, Finance, Sales and Distribution, Materials Management, Production, and Quality Management. Representation from each of these areas in the procurement BPSs will ensure a smooth purchasing process.

In terms of how many procurement BPSs should be set up, it depends on the size of the overall project implementation team, what the time frame for the implementation is, how many "bells and whistles" are desired, and what kind of a methodology is being used. Electro Tech will need to decide whether it will have one all-encompassing procurement BPS or many BPSs, divided by area, such as Vendor Master, Requisitions, Purchase Orders, Long Term Contracts, Request for Quote, and so on.

Business Process Simulation

Make the assumption that Electro Tech has made the decision to have multiple procurement BPSs as follows:

- Purchasing Organization BPS   Responsible for defining how the Electro Tech Purchasing organization would be structured in the new business and system environment

- Material Master BPS (not actually a purchasing BPS but very relevant to purchasing activities/processes)   Responsible for defining the process by which Material Master records will be created and maintained

- Vendor Master BPS   Responsible for defining the process by which Vendor Master records will be created and maintained

- Purchasing Master Data BPS   Responsible for defining the process by which purchasing information records, source lists, and quota arrangements will be created and maintained

■ Requisitions BPS   Responsible for defining the process by which requisitions will be created, released, and converted into purchase orders

■ Purchase Orders BPS   Responsible for defining the process by which purchase orders will be created, released, and tracked

■ Long Term Contracts BPS   Responsible for defining the process by which contracts are created, released, and maintained

■ Request for Quotes BPS   Responsible for defining the process by which quotes are created, and vendors are chosen

■ Goods Receipt BPS   Responsible for defining the process by which materials are received at the dock, including links to the inspection process

Now analyze how each of these BPSs will approach decision making within their areas of responsibility and how SAP R/3 will make their process more efficient.

Level 1: Enterprisewide

As you have already seen in Chapters 9, "Making the Move from Customer Service Past to SAP R/3," and 13, "Making the Move from Production Planning Past to SAP R/3," the BPS process starts at the highest level and works down to detailed processes. In this way the discovery of business processes is handled at all levels.

The Level 1 flow diagram depicts the business from a strategic standpoint but with a little more detail (see Figure 17.1). The processes being addressed in the SAP implementation are considered. If, at some time in the future, the organization expanded horizontally in its implementation, this would most likely be displayed within the Level 1 process flow.

FIG. 17.1

An example of a Level 1 process flow.

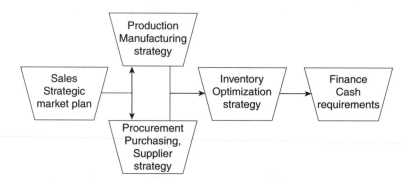

Level 2: Inter-Function Process Flows

The inputs for Production Planning or Plant Maintenance to Purchasing are specified in the Level 2 flow. In effect, the broad integration points between the various modules are identified and the overall Procurement process is identified.

The Electro Tech Level 2 process would likely depict links to Production Planning, represented by demand, and links to Financial management, represented by invoice handling (see Figure 17.2).

FIG. 17.2
An example of Level 2 process flow.

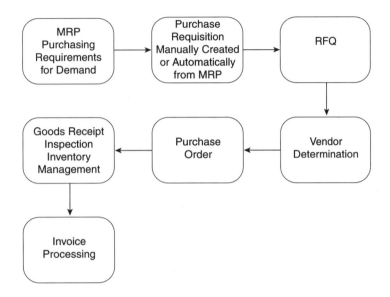

Level 3: Intra-Function Process Flows

Within each specific department, such as Procurement, process flows are derived representing departmental workings. This mapping identifies all functions within a sub-organization of your company.

As an example, a Level 3 process flow for Electro Tech's Purchasing department would likely depict the receipt of demand data and its processing to determine allowable sources, price, creation of necessary purchasing documents, and delivery schedule (see Figure 17.3).

Level 4: Transactions

For each action described within the applicable Level 3 process flow, the actual transactions to be performed are presented. In other words, the daily work task associated with performing each step of a Level 3 becomes a Level 4 flow. An example of a Level 4 flow diagram in the procurement process might be the handling of a purchase order (see Figure 17.4).

Level 1 and Level 2 process flows are largely determined at a middle- to upper-management level. In this way, the desired high-level operating strategies for the entire enterprise are specified. These strategies serve as guidelines for the derivation of the necessary Level 3 and Level 4 process flows. The real meat of the BPS process occurs in the derivation of the Level 3 and Level 4 flows. It is here that the actual business transactions are defined and the links between them are specified.

FIG. 17.3

An example of a Level 3 process flow.

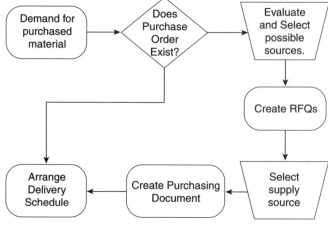

FIG. 17.4

An example of a Level 4 process flow.

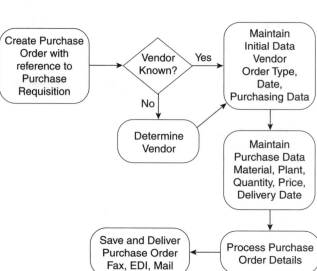

Because of the large number of issues at hand, proper documentation becomes an increasingly important element of the BPS process. Prior to the initiation of Level 3 activities, the creation of a suitable BPS workbook can prove to be an enormous subsequent time saver. Through the use of such a workbook, the intended scope and direction of the BPS sessions can be better controlled. In essence, the workbook serves as a BPS roadmap. However, the workbook itself is to be considered a living document, subject to modification as necessary.

Hopefully, modification to a BPS workbook will consist of additions of detail rather than gross changes. This issue deserves some additional consideration. When properly established, the entire business process can be examined through the combination of many BPS workbooks. For example, Procurement processes are described in one workbook. Production Planning processes are described in another workbook. Integration points between the two areas are identified in both workbooks. In this way, each area's internal processes can be defined, along with the necessary integration points. This method provides a tool by which gaps in the overall process are identified.

Through the definition of scope, selection of an empowered cross-functional BPS team, and the documentation of the process flows and BPS handbooks, the implementation can be properly steered. The existing Electro Tech processes are generally sound but complicated by an over-dependence on personal interactions and suffer from a lack of integration of systems. It is the objective of the BPS process to bridge this gap.

Purchasing Organization

The first decision to be made involves the definition of the Electro Tech purchasing organization. What organizational configuration allows Electro Tech to maximize the benefits that can be derived from the new environment?

Some of the advantages and drawbacks of centralized and distributed purchasing organizations have been discussed previously. The Purchasing Organization BPS considered these benefits and drawbacks, how the new SAP system could be enabled under each configuration, and the resulting business process changes that would be required under each. After weighing the information, the team decided on a compromise of sorts.

The Purchasing organization was centralized within the system but the buyers remained distributed at each plant. This enabled Electro Tech to standardize their business processes and data records while allowing the buyers to remain focused on requirements specific to a particular plant. The centralized data would allow the buyers to see how other plants addressed certain issues and leverage agreements between multiple plants for favorable pricing conditions. It also allowed Electro Tech to easily track the purchasing history across the entire organization while giving the flexibility to track at the plant or even buyer level. Keeping the people in the same physical locations not only allowed them to react quickly to specific plant requirements but also eliminated the costs and personal implications of asking buyers to pack up and move to a different city.

This decision to centralize the data but keep the buyers distributed was made knowing that it would affect every subsequent procurement BPS. Therefore, much care and thought went into the decision. You will see throughout the procurement example how this decision affects the other decisions made in subsequent BPSs.

Material Master

In Electro Tech's current environment, its Material Master information is maintained on several different systems. Its productive (or direct) materials—those materials which are components of the products they produce—are maintained on one system; its nonproductive (or indirect) materials—those materials not components of products, such as operating supplies, tools, and packaging material—are each maintained in a separate system.

Electro Tech currently uses an intelligent numbering system for the materials it produces, which will ideally represent the product line, product type, and application of the product it represents. In reality, however, Electro Tech has so many exceptions to this intelligent numbering system and so many errors in material number creation that the actual purpose of the intelligent numbering system is oftentimes defeated. Electro Tech will also sometimes use a customer's material number for material it produces.

For its purchased productive materials, Electro Tech uses the vendor's part number as its own material number. This means that if it procures the same material (same fit, form, function part) from three different vendors, Electro Tech will have three different master records in the system. This poses a further problem for the procurement people, in that they need to know which materials can be "substituted" for each other—when the requirement is for Material A from Vendor A, but Vendor A can't supply it, the purchasing person must know that Material B from Vendor B is really the same material.

For Electro Tech's nonproductive materials, it has a combination of system assigned numbers, unintelligent numbers, and the vendor part number for the material. Some of the vendor part numbers fall within the range of the unintelligent material numbers to cause yet more confusion.

So Electro Tech's Material Master BPS must decide how material numbering will happen in SAP R/3 and how the existing material numbers will be converted to SAP. This is no small task because many of Electro Tech's employees have been working with the current process for many years, are comfortable with the numbers and process as they are, and fear a change of something so basic as material numbering.

The Material Master BPS team decides to convert all existing productive materials numbers as they are, with the exception of the purchased productive material numbers, which they decide will be *cleaned*. By cleaned, they mean that all the same fit, form, and function materials will be identified and converted over as one Material Master record. This will cause the Bill of Material BPS to also have to clean their records, but it will make the procurement process more efficient and thus alleviate shortages caused by unknown "substitute" materials in the long run. It will also reduce the number of expedites and rush orders that result when shortages occur.

The team decides to convert over all existing nonproductive material numbers using a system-assigned, unintelligent material number. They will ensure that the old material number will be referenced in the SAP material record in a field designed specifically for old material numbers from legacy systems. This will allow employees to search for the material by its old number but will ensure that the conversion will go smoothly by eliminating the chance that duplicate material numbers will be created. Again, they will clean any vendor material numbers that exist by bringing over only one record for the same fit, form, and function materials.

Regarding the creation of new material numbers in SAP, the team decided that productive and nonproductive material types would each have one internally assigned number range and no external number range. This will ensure that only the system can assign material numbers and alleviate the need to maintain an intelligent numbering system, which never really worked anyway.

The decision to eliminate vendor material numbers from the system raised more than a few eyebrows at Electro Tech, and the concern was legitimate. How is a purchasing agent supposed to order a material from a vendor if the agent only knows the Electro Tech material number, which is of no use to the vendor? This issue was raised to the Purchasing Master Data BPS for resolution.

The Material Master BPS will need input from the procurement BPSs in order to determine the use of the purchasing fields in the Material Master record. The Material Master BPS meets with all the procurement BPSs and explains the functionality of the purchasing fields of the Material Master, mostly contained in the Purchasing view but some of which are in the MRP views. They ensure that the procurement BPSs understand that the decision to use, and any valid entries for, these purchasing-related fields is up to them, and that they must communicate any Material Master-related decisions back to the Material Master team.

Vendor Master

Electro Tech had several problems to address in the Vendor Master BPS. First and foremost was a terminology issue. Electro Tech liked to refer to companies and individuals from whom they procured materials and services as suppliers, not vendors. More than once a vendor was referred to as "someone who sold hotdogs on the street corner." As trivial as it may sound, this small terminology difference needed to be addressed and everyone involved in the procurement functions had to be aware of the change. This held true not only for the word "vendor" but many other terms as well.

When Electro Tech began to examine its current vendor database, it found that it was examining many vendor databases. Several plants used systems from different companies to track the vendor information. But that was not all the vendor information that could be found. Outside the typical information held on vendors—address, contact name and number, payment terms, and the like—the Vendor Master BPS team found that spreadsheets, documents, and other mini-databases had been created to track what the team referred to as *peripheral information*. There was a spreadsheet maintained in the Quality department, for example, that held information about the vendor audit dates, scores, and comments. Other documents tracked additional contacts, preferred freight carriers and rates, and other various business information. These were usually maintained on an individual computer and published to interested individuals periodically, either weekly or monthly. This often meant that data being used to make important procurement decisions was inaccurate. Audits had been completed or contacts had changed and decisions were made without knowing this information. The Vendor Master BPS team decided this needed to be changed.

Because multiple databases were used to track Vendor Master data, much of the data very quickly became duplicated and inconsistent. The same vendor would have different contact information, payment terms, delivery lead times, and other information within the different systems. It became impossible to determine which information was accurate. Furthermore, the same vendor could be listed multiple times within the same system. Because one of the purchasing systems did not allow multiple payment terms for separate purchase orders with a single vendor, the purchasing staff was relegated to creating a new Vendor Master record any time a different payment term was negotiated for a purchase order.

All these symptoms led to the same diagnosis: the Vendor Master data would need to be maintained centrally to minimize redundancy and inconsistencies. In addition, the Vendor Master would have to track all the information that was now being maintained not only in the various purchasing databases, but also the peripheral spreadsheets and documents. This would ensure that everyone was accessing the same information when making important business decisions.

To ensure the accuracy of the data, each buyer was responsible for maintaining vendor information when they became aware of changes. Since the buyers were often the only individuals, or at least the first, to learn of changes, it was decided that they should enter that information in the system. Because SAP tracked all changes to the Vendor Master record, the old and new values, and who made the changes, auditing the buyers would be an easy task. Of course mistakes would be made, the BPS team knew. SAP's tracking capability allowed those mistakes to be caught and corrected quickly. The buyers could subsequently be trained to avoid making those same mistakes in the future.

You've briefly looked at some of the problems the Vendor Master BPS team saw in the current system and how they planned to address them. Now you'll briefly see how the SAP system enabled these changes. You will stay at a very high level at this time, as the details will be discussed in depth later in the book.

The SAP Vendor Master was configured to use unintelligent numbers as the key identifier. This solved several problems. First, the current systems used intelligent numbers based on the vendor name and address. As vendors changed their names or moved, however, this intelligent number scheme lost its value. Further, since several vendors had multiple Vendor Masters in the current Electro Tech systems, this allowed these Vendor Masters to be forged into one master record in SAP. The old vendor numbers would be loaded into the Vendor Master for existing vendors only as a reference for finding the new vendor number.

Because considerable peripheral data was to be included on the Vendor Master, the BPS team decided to use the SAP classification system to identify additional information that needed to be tracked. The classification system was designed so only information that was directly relevant to a specific vendor would be maintained. There was no use in maintaining audit information on vendors from whom Electro Tech only bought office supplies, for example.

Certain fields on the Vendor Master record were designated as mandatory. This meant that when creating a new vendor or maintaining an existing vendor, appropriate values would have to be maintained in the Vendor Master record. Certain address, telephone number, payment terms, and currency used for payment fields, for example, were set as mandatory in the SAP system.

The remaining fields on the Vendor Master record were reviewed in detail for their relevance at Electro Tech. In the end, it was decided that all the fields would be available for data entry, even though some may not be used immediately. This would allow Electro Tech to quickly react to changes in its business that would require it to maintain data that was not currently relevant.

After the decisions were made on what the Vendor Master would look like and who would maintain the information, very specific audit practices were put in place to ensure the data was accurate. Prior to the vendors being copied from the existing systems to the SAP system, a team was formed to "clean up" the current data. Obsolete vendors were deleted from the current systems, values were checked for consistency between multiple vendor records, and field values were checked for accuracy. This same team was then responsible for checking and correcting all the new vendor records created after the data load into SAP. A separate audit team was formed to periodically check new vendors that would be created in SAP to make sure all information was maintained properly. This team met weekly immediately following the switch to SAP, and eventually moved to monthly meetings after the users had more experience with the SAP system.

These decisions helped Electro Tech standardize its Vendor Master records, react quickly to changes in the vendor's organization, and ensure accuracy in the vendor data. All of those qualities enabled the purchasing organization at Electro Tech to make informed decisions when procuring materials and services for the company.

Purchasing Master Data BPS

The Purchasing Master Data BPS is responsible for addressing purchasing information records, source lists, and quota arrangements for Electro Tech. Currently Electro Tech does not have this functionality, so the team must decide whether or not to use these applications, based on the potential for improvement in their current procurement activities by using them.

SAP's purchasing info record is a source of information about a specific material from a specific vendor. It contains the vendor-specific information for a material, including the current vendor price, pricing conditions, under and over delivery tolerances, planned delivery time, material origin, vendor material number, and the order unit (if this differs from the base unit of measure). This information will default in from both the Material Master record and the Vendor Master record, but may be overridden. Each vendor who supplies a particular material will have an info record for the material, and, when a purchase order is created for the material/vendor combination, the data contained in the info record will default into the purchase order. Since the info record is plant-specific, each plant must define its own information. For example, perhaps Electro Tech's Cincinnati plant prefers to order a certain material by the pallet, whereas the Indiana plant prefers to order it by the box. This offers much flexibility to the plants. The BPS decides that info records will be used, and each plant will be responsible for maintaining its own.

The Material Master BPS is informed about the possibility of recording the vendor material number in the info record, which will enable purchasing agents to reference the vendor material number when placing orders.

SAP's source list is a record that defines the preferred or allowed supply source for a material. It allows vendors to be effective for certain periods of time, permanently fixed, or permanently blocked. This feature will allow Electro Tech to determine, per plant, who the valid sources of supply for a material are. The Purchasing Data BPS sees many benefits to this functionality. Because it will ensure that materials will not be ordered mistakenly from an incorrect vendor, it helps the purchasing agent determine the valid supply source for a given time and is also used in the automatic selection of vendors for purchase orders. Because the existence of source lists provides so much value, the team decides to make source lists required for all procured productive material. They inform the Material Master BPS to add this requirement to the Material Master record's purchasing data.

Quota arrangements are records that allow the determination of a supply source based on quotas. If quota arrangements are used, the total requirement of a material will be automatically apportioned over a period of time among the different valid sources of supply. The team sees great potential for improvement in their current process by using quota arrangements since they have certain material requirements that cannot be filled by a single vendor. Currently the purchasing agent must manually determine whether or not a vendor has been "maxed out" and then choose an alternate supplier. By setting a quota arrangement among the valid vendors, the system itself will be able to determine which vendor will get the order and, thus, avoid over-ordering from any single supplier for a given material.

The Purchasing Master BPS also informed the Material Master BPS of their intention to use the source list and quota arrangement indicators on the Purchasing view of the Material Master record.

Requisitions

The Requisitions BPS was chartered to examine all requests for the purchase of material created at Electro Tech. These included requisitions from the production area that came as a result of MRP runs and the paper requisition forms that could be filled out by any employee at Electro Tech. The team's goals were to minimize the time spent creating and reviewing requisitions and to improve the purchasing lot sizes in order to minimize procurement costs.

First, examine how Electro Tech generated requisitions prior to their SAP implementation. The requisitions that came from the production area were actually a simple combination of the production schedules and inventory reports. These reports were sent to Purchasing weekly. For each material on the production schedule, an Electro Tech employee had to compare the material required for production with the available inventory and expected receipts. For any material that needed to be purchased, a requisition for an appropriate amount was created in the Purchasing System. The appropriate amount was determined manually by using certain "fudge factors" defined in the purchasing procedures. This was a terribly time-consuming process that required five full-time employees.

Manual requisitions were even more of a mess. Any request for the purchase of material or services not generated by MRP was written on pre-printed requisition forms. There were four different forms being used by different departments within Electro Tech. These forms then were routed through company mail to the appropriate individuals for approval. A signature on the requisition form indicated approval. Since certain requisitions could require as many as three different signatures, the routing of the requisition for approval could take as many as 7 to 10 business days, assuming no one was on vacation or away from his or her office for any time. When the requisition was finally approved, it was routed to the appropriate buyer through the company mail. The buyer verified the approval signatures and checked for available stock in one of Electro Tech's storage locations before actually entering the requisition in the Purchasing System.

As you can see, both procedures were extremely time-consuming and prone to error. Any mistake in comparing the inventory levels with the production requirements, applying the "fudge factor," or the routing of requisitions for approval could lead to material shortages. In fact, this was a common problem at Electro Tech, as can be seen by the earlier example of the missing motor belt.

Without going into too much detail, take a look at how the Requisitions BPS team was able to greatly improve the requisition process through SAP. First look at material requirements for production. By implementing SAP's Production Planning module, Electro Tech enabled the computer system to automatically create requisitions for production material. In fact, by maintaining the appropriate data on the Material Master record, the SAP system not only compared the production requirements with the inventory levels, it also applied the appropriate "fudge factor" to ensure the material was being ordered in economical lot sizes. This meant that the production schedule could immediately be converted to purchase requisitions for the correct quantity. Thus, the five individuals who previously did this work were reassigned to focus on materials that showed as being late. They essentially worked on the Electro Tech *Hot List* to ensure production would not be delayed by a lack of materials.

For the manual requisition process for non-productive materials, the team decided that all employees of Electro Tech should be able to enter requisitions in the system. This meant the elimination of paper forms and the inherent problems they caused. The SAP requisitions could not be lost, for instance. In addition, the requisition team interviewed all the departments of Electro Tech and was able to define an approval process that met everyone's needs. This approval process was entered into SAP as a series of release strategies. No longer would requisitions be routed through the mail for approval. Instead, the system automatically routed the requisitions to the appropriate individuals for approval based on the requisition dollar value, plant, and department being charged. After each approval was entered on the requisition, the next level of authorization immediately had access to the document. This cut the approval time from an average of 8.3 days to 1.7 days at Electro Tech.

Two other aspects about the new requisition process proved especially beneficial. The fact that the document was entered in the system one time by the original requester minimized data-entry time. Also, the document history maintained by SAP allowed any user to see who had or hadn't approved his or her requisition, whether the material had been ordered yet, and whether anyone had changed anything in the requisition.

All of these changes helped minimize the time spent creating and reviewing material and service requisitions, as well as the cost of mistakes. Material and services could be ordered more promptly and less expensively.

Request for Quotes

The Request for Quotes (RFQ) BPS team focused on how Electro Tech sent Request for Quotation notices to vendors and subsequently entered the vendor's quote. Because the RFQ process was not entirely troublesome for Electro Tech and the volume of RFQs did not approach the volume of requisitions or purchase orders, the BPS team decided to concentrate on automating the process rather than re-engineering the process tremendously. Also, since the RFQ BPS was the first to address a process that involved sending documents to vendors, this team made many of the decisions on how information transfer would occur with vendors.

Start by taking a look at the RFQ process at Electro Tech. Electro Tech policy states that material or service requisitions should be bid to at least three vendors if no purchase order exists and the total order value is greater than $50,000. Enforcement of this policy had been lax the last few years, and management more-or-less left it up to the buyers to use their best judgment. The end result was that buyers often conducted informal RFQs for large orders but rarely entered the RFQ and resulting quotations formally in the Purchasing System. When a buyer decided that a formal RFQ was warranted, the document was typed into one of the Purchasing Systems and printed out. Multiple copies were made and were mailed or faxed to the appropriate vendors. One copy was stapled to the requisition and filed in the buyer's filing cabinet. As quotations were received from the vendors, the quoted price was entered on the RFQ in the Purchasing System. That was the only information that was entered. A copy of the quotation was also stapled to the packet with the requisition and RFQ. After all quotations were received, the buyer made a decision about which vendor to write the purchase order with. This choice was entered on the RFQ in the Purchasing System.

After examining the process, the RFQ team decided to focus on automating as much of the process as possible and enforcing the policy that was currently being ignored. Using SAP's functionality, the team was able to make the RFQ process capture more data and be much easier. The RFQ was designed to be created easily off the requisition. That meant any data, text, or conditions entered on the requisition could be copied to the RFQ with just a few keystrokes. The team also focused on the information that should be maintained with the vendor quotes. In addition to basic price, price break levels, and delivery lead times, other data could be maintained on the quote. This meant that all information could be stored within the SAP system, and the previous method of stapling the documents together to maintain a history was no longer necessary. The vendor quotes were also fully integrated with some of the purchasing master data previously discussed. The Purchasing Info record, for example, could be automatically created and maintained with the information in the vendor quote. Another benefit of SAP was the quote due-date tracking capability. Tracking quotation due dates was previously done manually by each buyer. SAP tracked all due dates for all buyers and standard reports informed everyone when a quote was past due.

In order to enforce the written policy, the RFQ team passed a requirement on to the Purchase Orders team. They asked that a separate level be placed in the approval process of purchase orders that checked only that the appropriate RFQs and quotes had been maintained. Thus, any purchase order for an amount greater than $50,000 would automatically trigger a release strategy that included an individual whose sole purpose was to verify that the RFQ policy had been followed.

Probably the greatest challenge that faced the RFQ team was defining how Electro Tech would interact with its vendors in the new world-class environment. Whereas phone calls, mail, and faxes had been the only choices for communication, the RFQ team began to look at options such as Electronic Data Interchange (EDI), autofax, and allowing vendors to actually dial in to access the Electro Tech SAP system. Eventually, the RFQ team recommended that a separate cross-functional team be created to decide these issues because other BPS teams were also looking at how to interact with Electro Tech vendors. The RFQ team did recommend that a combination of all communication techniques would probably be most beneficial because of the diverse technical capabilities and volume of each vendor.

Purchase Orders—Long Term Contracts and Spot Buys

Electro Tech had all kinds of purchase orders, both long-term agreements and spot buys, floating around. Purchase orders could be created in each Purchasing System, in addition to special terms and conditions that would be typed in a word processor because they didn't fit in the purchase order. Because of the confusion and difficulty in tracking these purchase orders across multiple systems, there were often multiple purchase orders open with the same vendor, many times even for the same materials or services.

The Purchase Orders BPS team at Electro Tech first noticed some terminological differences between what Electo Tech and SAP called purchase orders. At Electro Tech, any contract for the purchase of materials or services was called a purchase order. In SAP, a purchase order specifies the exact quantity and date(s) when the material is to be delivered or the services performed. For long-term agreements that specify only a validity period and maximum or estimated quantity, SAP requires that you create an outline agreement. There are two types of outline agreements in SAP—contracts and scheduling agreements. The only discernible difference between the two is that scheduling agreements allow you to attach a delivery schedule directly to them, whereas contracts require a release order to be generated for actual delivery.

Part
IV

Ch
17

Using SAP's purchase order, contract, and scheduling agreement functionality, Electro Tech easily moved its existing purchase orders into the correct SAP document. The SAP document included plenty of room for the terms and conditions to be entered as text or condition records. This eliminated the need to use a word processor for these items. Just moving all these documents to SAP was a great benefit to Electro Tech. It allowed much easier tracking of purchase orders, resulting in far fewer orders being written because instances of multiple purchase orders for the same vendor were greatly reduced. In addition, SAP enabled easy reporting on open purchase orders, past-due deliveries, and long-term agreements whose validity end date was approaching. This last item helped inform the buyers when a new agreement would need to be initiated before the old one was invalid, and was a great help in ensuring that materials and services could be ordered promptly when needed.

In addition to the centralized maintenance, tracking, and reporting of purchase orders, the Electro Tech team implemented additional SAP functionality. First, a very basic release strategy (approval process) was defined to ensure that all purchase orders met Electro Tech policy and to accommodate the request of the RFQ BPS team. Second, scheduling agreements were configured along with source lists in the system to allow MRP to automatically generate delivery schedule lines to the vendor for items with long-term agreements and single source of replenishment. This eliminated the need for buyers to spend their time generating purchase orders on those production materials. All of this functionality enabled Electro Tech to be much more efficient in their handling of purchase orders.

Goods Receipt for Purchase Order

Electro Tech's Goods Receipt (GR) BPS is responsible for improving its current goods receipt process for deliveries from vendors that are the result of purchase orders initiated by the Purchasing department. When the team looked at the current process, it realized that standard SAP functionality would improve the existing process merely because of the high level of integration SAP provides.

For example, in Electro Tech's current system, the receiver not only enters the purchase order number, he or she also enters each of the goods receipt materials manually, including the quantity. Due to data-entry errors that result from manual entry, there are often inaccurate inventory balances, which usually get fixed either by the cycle counter or by a warehouse employee who notices discrepancies when he goes to pick material. Needless to say, these inaccuracies more often than not result in panic for production planners and rush orders being created by the Purchasing department.

Furthermore, because there is a lag time between the physical goods receipt and the electronic goods receipt, planners regularly leave urgent messages for the Purchasing department regarding material that is actually already in-house. This ties up the purchasers who must hunt down material either on the dock or in Quality Inspection. Also, since Electro Tech's current MRP system does not incorporate the processing time after physical goods receipt, which includes inspection activities and transfer times, into the total lead time for the material, there is usually much tension between the production manager and the quality personnel regarding the availability of the material.

The GR BPS discovers that the goods receipt procedure in SAP will alleviate many of these problems. First, the system will automatically propose the open line items and open order quantities of the purchase order when the receiver enters the purchase order number into the system. Because the material numbers and quantities are proposed, there is less need for manual entry, and thus fewer data-entry errors result. Also, because of tolerance limits that can be set up for material in the Material Master, the purchasing information record, or even ultimately the purchase order itself, if the receiver does need to change the proposed quantity, he or she will be alerted via a warning or error message if the changed quantity is outside of the acceptable under- or over-delivery tolerances for the material.

Second, the team realizes that in SAP, unlike in their current system, even if a material must be quality inspected upon receipt, the stock overview will still show the material as being in-house. The material will appear in a Quality Inspection inventory *bucket*, where it will remain until the material passes inspection and is transferred from the Quality Inspection bucket to the unrestricted use bucket by the inspector. (More information regarding stock overview and different stock statuses will be discussed later in this book.) The fact that SAP's inventory management and inspection activities are so integrated will alleviate the need for Ted, the purchasing manager, to have to physically track down material to determine which label the quality inspection team has placed on the shipment. Also, Dave, or any other production managers, will be able to see real-time in the system that a material is in Quality Inspection—no more need for Quality Inspection labels that are manually changed only during the last hour of the shift!

In order to further alleviate the time crunch between the physical goods receipt and material availability, the GR team investigates the functionality of goods receipt processing time in the Material Master. The GR process time is the number of days required after physical goods receipt of a material before it is available for use; this time can include inspection time, material transfer time, and so on. MRP adds this processing time to the vendor's lead time to create a total lead time; thus, when the system does backwards scheduling, it starts with the requirements date and then schedules backwards, using the total lead time to determine the release date of the purchase requisition. This feature will further reduce tension between production and inspection because inspection time will have been adequately planned for when the release date of the requisition is calculated—Lester will have plenty of time to perform his inspection and release the material for use before it is even required by production. This total lead time will also lighten the purchasing group's load because they will no longer have to add "fudge factors" to determine when to order materials. And best of all, since SAP's MRP system automatically calculates release dates, production will never pass demands from scheduling to purchasing via paper reports.

The GR BPS informed the Material Master BPS of their decision to use the GR processing field in the Purchasing view of the Material Master. The GR BPS also informed Quality Management that they needed to provide inspection times for materials subject to Quality Inspection so that the GR processing field could be accurately calculated.

Next, the GR BPS realizes that SAP's missing parts check will allow Ted to do away with his infamous *Hot List*. The reason the Hot List was needed was to help expedite materials immediately after their arrival. With SAP's missing parts check, a manual comparison of the hot list to the receiving reports will be replaced with a mail message to the MRP controller of any goods receipts of *missing* parts. A material is flagged as missing in SAP when the requirement for it exceeds the available quantity. When the goods receipt is posted for the missing part, the responsible MRP controller receives a mail message notifying him of its arrival—so the next time hot parts are delivered, Dave will be notified in real-time.

Other Purchasing Functionality and Processes

There was some additional purchasing functionality available in SAP that Electro Tech decided to delay implementing. Specifically, Electro Tech saw value in SAP's vendor evaluation and External Service Management functionality but decided, for time and resource reasons, that they should be re-examined after the initial implementation and users had some experience with SAP.

Vendor evaluation, something Electro Tech didn't do formally, would allow Electro Tech to define standard criteria that every vendor would be measured against. Scores for these criteria could be automatically maintained by SAP or manually entered by the user for more subjective matters. Procedures could be predefined and vendors would be automatically scored in areas such as late deliveries, quality problems, and price fluctuation. More subjective scoring could include such things as technical capabilities and flexibility. In fact, up to 99 criteria, each with up to 99 sub-criteria, could be configured. In addition, each criteria and sub-criteria could be weighted to meet Electro Tech's requirements.

The External Service Management functionality in SAP would allow Electro Tech to maintain Service Master records, write special purchase orders specifically for services, and enter and approve services as performed by vendors. The Service Master is similar to the Material Master in that a master record is maintained to track all purchases of the service. Service Masters for items such as systems consulting, lawn care, or painting, for example, would allow Electro Tech to track purchases of these items across multiple purchase orders. The process of purchasing services using the External Service Management functionality also differs from the process used to procure materials. Essentially, purchase orders can be written with multilevel outlines of the services to be performed, and limits can be placed on individual service costs in addition to overall purchase order limits. Following the entry of the service, a Service Entry Sheet is created and Service Acceptance is maintained in the system rather than a Goods Receipt document being created. Only after a Service Entry Sheet had been entered and the service had been accepted would the system allow payment. This allowed for greater control over the services being performed.

SAP Business Navigator

As discussed in Chapters 9 and 13, to steer the definition of business processes, SAP provides the Business Navigator. In SAP R/3 V3.0, the Business Navigator is essentially a graphical depiction of the decision logic tree reflected in the base SAP.

The Navigator serves as a training aid to help companies grasp a more physical understanding of the logic and transactions within SAP. The Navigator eventually serves to guide the configuration of the system to better suit the company's needs. Used in conjunction with the Level 1 to 4 process flows, the Navigator then can be used as a flexible business strategy modeling tool. By examining the many decision and action steps depicted by the Navigator, the company is forced to map out desired business practices in great detail. Such detail is necessary if subsequent configuration of the system's response is to be accomplished correctly and efficiently.

Keep in mind that the SAP Business Navigator is a tool not a solution, and it is unlikely that it is immediately suitable to a specific organization. Therefore, the Navigator may be modified as necessary to reflect the company's desired decision logic. Again, SAP configuration-related tools are intended to allow the system to support the company's desired operating modes. They follow the company's desired structure. They do not impose a structure upon the company.

Implementation Guide (IMG)

The Implementation Guide (IMG) is an SAP tool that is provided to ease the actual act of system configuration. In effect, the IMG is nothing more than a graphical front end to the configuration tables. Versions of SAP prior to 3.0 did not require the use of the IMG. Versions 3.0 and above use this tool to simplify configuration. It is organized by hierarchical business functions and allows the company to drill-down to the configuration settings of specific transactions.

The IMG allows the company to select, or even create, desired configuration options that will direct the system's response. The IMG does not necessarily assist the company with process definition decisions, but rather provides the method by which existing process definition decisions may be enabled within the system.

Procurement as an Element of the Whole Business

It seems simple enough, without inputs to a process there are no outputs. However, without adequate controls on the inputs, the expected output can be unpredictable. In a procurement process, these controls may be cost controls, quality controls, supplier controls, or material definition controls. SAP delivers a system capable of providing all the necessary tools to manage these issues for any business.

When implemented, in conjunction with the FI, CO, PP, SD, and QM modules, the purchasing functionality of the MM module of SAP shines. It allows for detailed controls while providing ease of use. As a result, your business as a whole will benefit. ●

Part

IV

Ch

17

Purchasing Functionality with SAP R/3

Materials management is the control of the materials a company utilizes. Think about what that means for a minute. Materials have to be purchased. This can require the processing of several documents such as requisitions, purchase orders, or contracts. The material has to be stored. Inventory equates to dollars and cents, so it has to be managed from the time the raw material comes in to the time the finished product goes out the door. The conditions the material is stored in, whether refrigeration or a rack system is necessary, and the quality of the material in inventory are all parts of materials management.

This chapter looks at purchasing, inventory management, and quality management functions within SAP R/3. The integration of these elements with other SAP modules provides a well thought out business process.

Understanding Materials Management

The Electro Tech manufacturing process is a complex assembly system. Materials are purchased, processed through the plant, and converted into various finished and semi-finished products, which are hopefully sold for a profit. This doesn't sound too difficult when put in such simple terms, but the typical manufacturing process requires elaborate planning and cost management, combined with deliberate execution, to achieve the desired profit.

Embedded in these processes is the materials management function. Starting with the purchasing function, you will look at how SAP automates and simplifies the management of materials. You will see how specific costs are tied to specific movements and why understanding and controlling your inventory makes a company more profitable.

Purchasing and MRP

Planning for procurement follows the same process as planning for production. Using MPS and MRP functionality in the system, a list of requirements for procurement is generated in addition to the planned orders generated for production. Requirements for procurement can initially take one of three forms: planned orders, purchase requisitions, or schedule lines.

Planned Orders

Planned orders have already been discussed in detail in Chapter 14, "Production Planning and Execution Functionality with SAP R/3." As was described, planned orders can then be converted into production orders for items to be produced in-house. These same planned orders could alternately be converted into purchase requisitions for items to be procured from an external vendor or separate plant.

The MRP run creates planned orders for all materials that are to be produced in-house, as well as for all materials that may be produced in-house or procured from an external source. This distinction is made within the Procurement Type field in the Material Master record. The planned orders can then be modified as required before being converted to either production orders or purchase requisitions. To convert the planned order, go to menu path:

Environment > Convert from the Stock Requirements List or MRP list. The SAP system will then copy the information from the planned order and create the new document.

Purchase Requisitions

You have already seen how production orders function within SAP and your business. Now take a brief look at purchase requisitions. Requisitions define the need for materials or services that are to be procured from outside the company. It is an internal document that authorizes the Purchasing department to procure materials or services in specified quantities within specified time periods. Much like production orders, however, purchase requisitions are driven by demand. To understand how these documents fill demand and feed the manufacturing process, you will examine how requisitions fit within the scheduling process.

As previously stated, the MRP run will create three different procurement documents: planned orders, purchase requisitions, and schedule lines. The planned orders can then be converted into either production orders, for those items to be produced in-house, or purchase requisitions, for those items to be procured from an external vendor or plant. All of these elements can be viewed via the Stock Requirements List as is seen in Figure 18.1.

FIG. 18.1
Stock Requirement List showing purchase requisition.

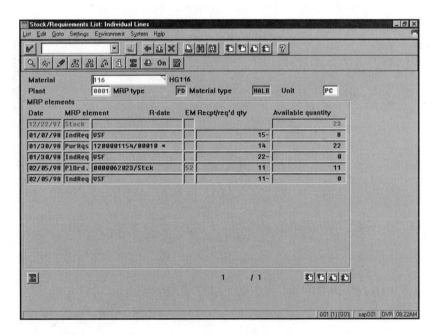

The requisitions hold much the same data as the planned orders do. Primarily, the requisition identifies the material, quantity to be procured, and several date values. The dates maintained on the requisition include the planned date (date the material requirement exists), delivery date (date the material is to be received), and release date (date the procurement process is to be initiated to ensure timely delivery). The quantities and dates are calculated by the system from information contained in master data. Similar to planned orders, the requisition is either firmed or unfirmed. The scheduling run typically creates unfirmed purchase requisitions. However, once a change has been manually entered in the requisition or the procurement process has begun (an RFQ or PO has been created), the requisition is then firmed. Firmed requisitions will not be adjusted by future scheduling runs.

These requisitions, generated directly by MRP or through the conversion of planned orders, are identical to those requisitions created manually through direct data entry. Sources of supply (vendors or other plants) can be assigned to the requisition item, the requisition item may be subject to an approval process (release strategy), and the requisition may be converted to either a request for quote, purchase order, or long-term agreement with the source.

Schedule Lines

The final document, which can be created as the result of a scheduling run, is a schedule line for an item. This occurs when a long-term agreement has been formed with a source of supply, and the MRP run is simply scheduling a release against that agreement. A delivery schedule can simply be released to the vendor as required, rather than having to deal with separate requisitions and purchase orders for each item delivery. These schedule lines then appear on the stock requirements list, as represented in Figure 18.2.

FIG. 18.2

Stock requirement list showing schedule lines.

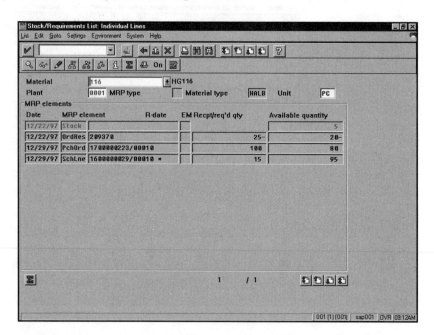

To enable the automatic generation of schedule lines by the scheduling run, several items must first be maintained in the SAP system. First, a valid Material Master and Vendor Master must be maintained. If the item is being procured from another plant rather than a vendor, the plant must be created in the SAP system. These requirements are held true for requisitions as well. In addition to the Material Master and Vendor Master, a scheduling agreement and source list must be maintained in SAP for schedule lines to be generated automatically by the schedule line. If the requirement is to be split using particular logic, a quota arrangement is required as well.

Scheduling agreements are types of outline agreements within SAP. Think of them as types of long-term contracts. The scheduling agreement, seen in Figure 18.3, details an agreement with a vendor to procure a target quantity of specific material(s) over a defined time period with an agreed-upon price. Attached to each item of the scheduling agreement is a delivery schedule that actually details when the material is to be delivered. Of course there may be multiple delivery dates on the delivery schedule. This delivery schedule can either be maintained manually or populated automatically by MRP. The latter is what you are interested in at this time.

FIG. 18.3

Scheduling agreement item overview.

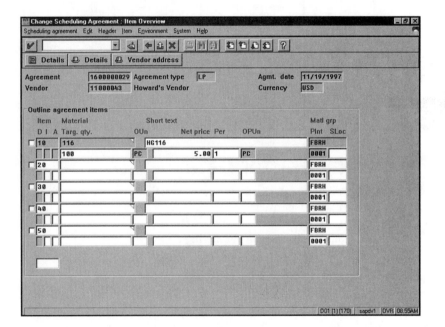

In order for the scheduling agreement to be automatically populated by MRP, a source list must be maintained for that material. The source list (see Figure 18.4) details which vendors or plants a particular material can be procured from over a given time period. For the scheduling run to automatically generate schedule lines, a source list record must be maintained that includes the scheduling agreement number. In addition, the MRP field located at the far right of the source list record must contain a 2. This tells the system that this source list record is relevant to MRP, and that schedule lines should be generated automatically.

If the procurement requirements are to be split using fixed percentages or if the lot size is too large, a quota arrangement can be maintained to automate this splitting process.

Part

IV

Ch

18

FIG. 18.4

Source list detail with one item including scheduling agreement and MRP field with value of 2.

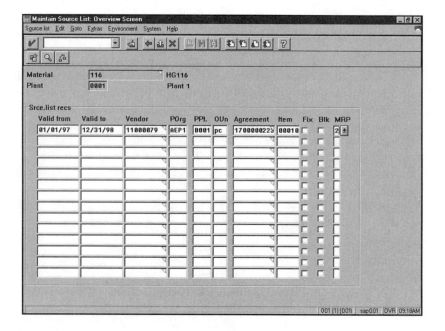

Purchasing Master Data

Before talking about the purchasing transactions, you should briefly cover some of the purchasing master data available in SAP. This includes purchasing information records, source lists, and quota arrangements. Each holds slightly different information, but each is very powerful in minimizing manual purchasing tasks.

Purchasing Information Record

The purchasing information record, commonly referred to as the *info* record, contains information about a specific material-vendor relationship. Pricing conditions and planned delivery time, for example, are maintained on the info record. These are specific to a specific material or service as procured from a specific vendor, rather than the more general prices and lead times that can be found in the Material Master or Vendor Master records.

The purchasing information record can be created manually or automatically from quotation information. Further, the pricing conditions in the info record can be automatically adjusted to reflect the latest purchase orders. To create an info record manually, follow this menu path:

> **Menu:** Logistics > Materials Management > Purchasing > Master Data > Info Record > Create
>
> **Transaction Code:** ME11

On the initial screen (see Figure 18.5), enter the vendor number, material number, purchasing organization, and plant. If the info record number range is set up for external numbering, enter the info record number. Otherwise, leave the Info Record field blank. Press Enter to proceed to the next screen.

FIG. 18.5
The purchasing info record initial screen.

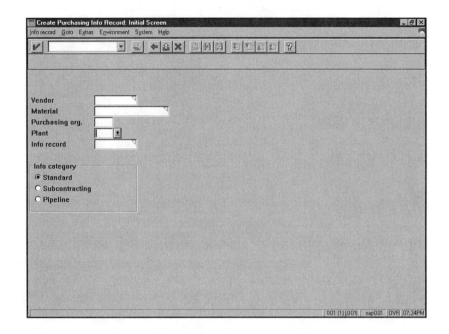

Enter the appropriate data within the info record data screens. Use the menu paths and buttons to move between the general data, purchasing organization data 1, purchasing organization data 2, conditions, and text screens. The general data needed for creation of a purchasing info record can be seen in Figure 18.6.

When you're finished entering data into the info record, click the Save icon.

Source List

The source list identifies valid vendors for a specific material. The source list can be created manually or maintained automatically from valid info records. To create a source list manually, follow this menu path:

> **Menu Path:** Logistics > Materials Management > Purchasing > Master Data > Source list > Maintain
>
> **Transaction Code:** ME01

On the initial screen (see Figure 18.7), enter the material number and plant for which that the source list is valid. Press Enter to proceed to the next screen.

FIG. 18.6

The general data screen for the purchasing info record.

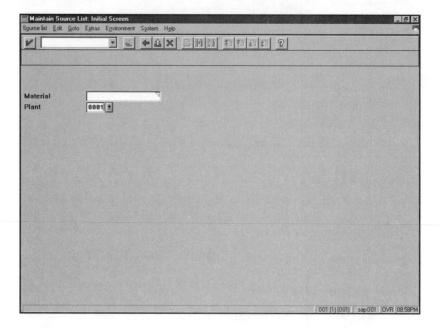

Each row in the source list represents a separate source of supply for the material. In the screen pictured in Figure 18.8, you initially identify the validity period (Valid From and Valid To) and purchasing organization (POrg) for which the record is valid. Next identify the source of supply as either a Vendor or another plant (PPl.) within the company. The order unit of measure (OUn) will default from the Material Master record. If the source is based on an outline agreement (contract or scheduling agreement), enter the Agreement number and Item number as well. The source list also allows the source to be fixed as a primary source (Fix) or blocked (Blk) for a particular time period. The MRP field allows you to specify whether the source list is to be considered in sourcing decisions made by the MRP run.

FIG. 18.8

The source list overview screen.

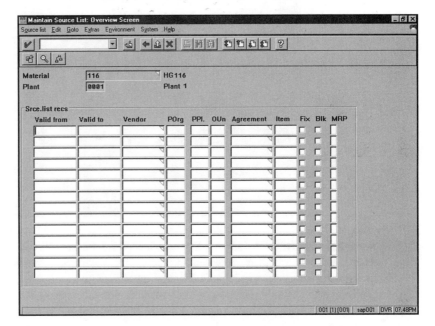

The source list can have multiple records for different validity periods or different sources. The dates on these records can overlap if desired. After you are finished entering data into the source list, click the Save icon.

Quota Arrangement

The quota arrangement allows a purchasing organization to set rules for the allocation of purchases for a particular material. Use the quota arrangement to specify that a given material is to be purchased 20 percent of the time from vendor A, 30 percent of the time from vendor B, and 50 percent of the time from vendor C, for example. Although many more detailed parameters such as minimum lot sizes and minimum splitting quantities can be entered in the quota arrangement, this simple allocation is the heart of the quota arrangement. To create a quota arrangement, follow this menu path:

> **Menu Path:** Logistics > Materials Management > Purchasing > Master Data > Quota arrangement > Maintain
>
> **Transaction Code:** MEQ1

On the initial screen (see Figure 18.9), enter the material number and plant that the quota arrangement is valid for. Press Enter to proceed to the next screen.

FIG. 18.9

The initial screen for the quota arrangement.

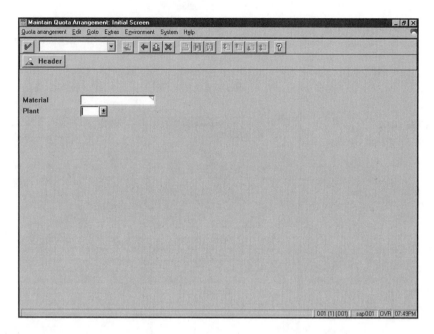

On the Maintain Quota Arrangement: Overview of Arr. Periods screen (see Figure 18.10), enter the date the quota arrangement is valid to. The Valid From date will default as the date the quota arrangement was created. The minimum quantity for splitting quota (Min. Qty Splitting) field is used to identify at what quantity an order should be split. For example, if 100 is entered in this field, only orders for a quantity greater than 100 will be split using the quota arrangement. This is an optional field. After you've entered the appropriate values on this field, click the Item button to proceed.

Each quota arrangement item (see Figure 18.11) has several pieces of information that can be maintained. The mandatory items are the procurement type (P), Vendor or plant (PPl.) from which the material is being procured, and the Quota, which is the percentage of time to procure from this source. Other fields allow you to specify minimum and maximum lot sizes, rounding profiles, and a base quantity to be used for this procurement source. When finished entering data into the items, click the Save icon.

Purchasing Transactions

Now that you have looked at the purchasing master data, you can look at the daily or transactional data. Transactional data changes and is dealt with on a daily, weekly, or possibly hourly basis. It is real-life transactions that must occur to keep the business running.

FIG. 18.10

The Maintain Quota Arrangement: Overview of Arr. Periods screen.

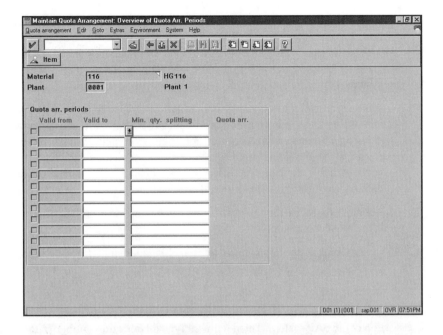

FIG. 18.11

The next quota arrangement item overview screen.

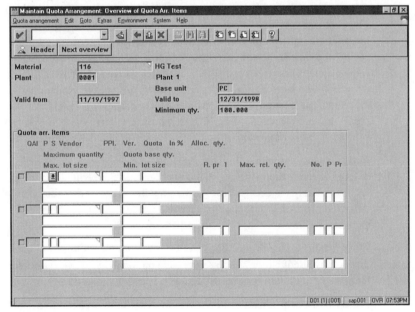

Purchase Requisitions

A purchase requisition is the document in SAP that identifies the need for a material or service. It is an internal document that is not used outside the company. A requisition may be subject to a very elaborate approval process, denoted in the SAP system by a release strategy. A requisition can be created through several methods in SAP, both directly and indirectly. Indirectly, the requisition can be created by the MRP run, from networks in the Project Systems module, or via Plant Maintenance orders. Directly, an individual may manually enter a requisition into the system. The SAP system tracks how the requisition was created.

After a requisition has been created, it may be subject to an approval process. The flexible approval process, known in SAP as the *release strategy*, allows a company to define a set of rules dictating who must approve requisitions before the material or service can be purchased. The release strategy is based on field values in the requisition and dictates what processing can occur with the requisition at different levels of approval. Multiple release strategies can be defined, each with multiple levels of approval.

Although there are multiple paths that can be used to access purchase requisition creation, this is the most common path:

> **Menu Path:** Logistics > Materials Management > Purchasing > Requisition > Create
>
> **Transaction Code:** ME51

From the Create Purchase Requisition: Initial Screen, seen in Figure 18.12, enter the document type being created. The list of available document types is configurable during the implementation of the SAP system. The document type dictates the number range to be used for the requisition number, as well as the status of each field as mandatory, optional, display, or suppressed. The standard SAP document type for purchase requisitions is NB. If an external number range is used for requisitions, meaning the user defines the requisition number, enter the appropriate requisition number in the Purchase Requisition field. If the system is internally assigning requisition numbers, leave the Purchase Requisition field blank. If the system is to try to determine the source for this purchase, click the Source determination field on. This tells the system to examine purchasing master data such as purchasing info records, outline agreements, source lists, and quota arrangements to determine from which vendor the material or service is to be purchased.

The fields located within the Default Data for Items block are optional at this point. Any values entered in these fields will copy into each item of the requisition. For example, if a requisition for several items is being written with each item required at the same plant, it makes sense to enter the plant code at this time. This will prevent you from having to enter the plant code on each line item.

When creating a new requisition, you may copy information from an existing requisition through the Requisition > Copy reference option. This serves simply to minimize data entry time, as the link between the requisitions is not maintained.

Press Enter or the click the Item overview button to proceed to the next screen.

The Purchase Requisition: Item Overview screen seen in Figure 18.13 shows a concise list of information about the items requested on the requisition. Look briefly at each field. The Item field shows the item number of the requisition. The first item is item 10, the second is item 20, and so on. SAP requisitions can contain up to 9999 items if the item numbers step by multiples of 10. The system will default the correct value in this field.

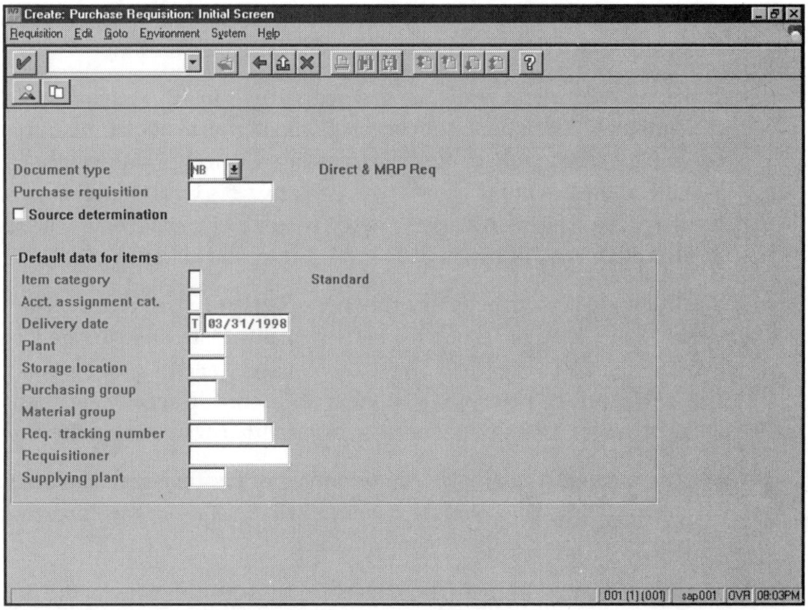

FIG. 18.12
The Create Purchase Requisition: Initial Screen.

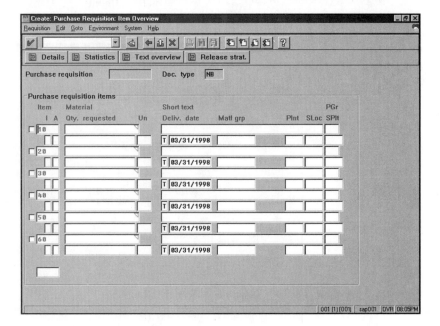

FIG. 18.13
The next Create Purchase Requisition: Item Overview screen.

One of the next two fields, Material and Short Text, is mandatory. If the material being requested has a Material Master record in SAP, enter the material number in the system. If not, a short text description of what is being requested is required. If a material number is entered, the short text description will copy from the Material Master record. The purchasing group,

PGr field, is used to identify which purchasing group is responsible for this purchase. In many companies, each buyer has his or her own purchasing group.

The item category, I field, is used to specify whether the requested item is a standard material, material for consignment, subcontracting material, third-party purchase, stock transfer between plants, or purchase of a service using SAP's external service management functionality. The account assignment category, A field, dictates what financial accounts will be charged for the purchase. This field is used to specify whether a cost center, asset account, or project is to be charged for the material.

The other fields dictate the quantity (Qty. Requested), unit of measure (Un), delivery date (Deliv. Date), material group (Matl Grp), plant (Plnt), and storage location (SLoc) for the requested material or service. The unit of measure and material group will default from the Material Master record if a material number is entered. The SPlt field, supplying plant, is used if the material is actually being requested from another plant within the company.

You can maintain the overview information for multiple items before proceeding to the detailed item information. Once you have entered all the appropriate information on the Item Overview screen, press Enter or the Details button.

Much of the detail from the Item Overview screen will copy to the item details screen (see Figure 18.14). Start by noting that the title of the screen dictates the requisition item being displayed. Several important fields are located on the item detail screen.

FIG. 18.14

The purchase requisition item details screen.

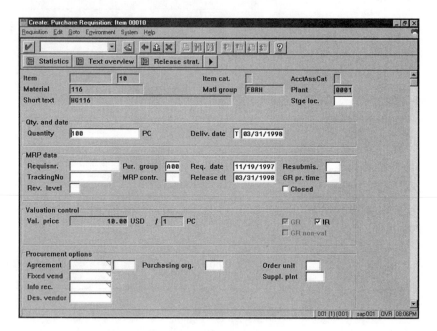

The delivery date (Deliv. Date) shows when the material or service should be delivered, the requisition date (Req. Date) shows when the requisition was created, and the release date

(Release Dt) tells the buyer the date when the ordering process should be initiated in order to receive the materials or service on time.

In the Procurement Options block, the requestor can enter an outline agreement number (Agreement), Fixed Vendor (Fixed Vend), or info record (Info Rec.) if the vendor that the material or service should be purchased from is known. If no outline agreement or info record exists, enter a desired vendor (Des. Vendor) for the purchase.

The additional information of the item detail screen includes the name of the requisitioner (Requisnr.) and an appropriate tracking number for the item (TrackingNo). Other fields include the estimated valuation price of the material (Val. Price), the MRP controller (MRP Contr.), number of dates before the requisition is resubmitted to the Purchasing department (Resubmis.), the time required to process the goods receipt when the material is delivered (GR Pr. Time), and whether a goods receipt and invoice receipt is expected (GR, IR, and GR Non-Val). Finally, any special vendor promotion number can be maintained in the requisition.

When finished entering values of this screen, press Enter to validate and continue to further screens.

Depending on your entry in the account assignment field on the Item Overview screen, the system may ask for the accounts to be charged for the purchase (see Figure 18.15). Enter the proper account information. This may include a general ledger account number, asset account number, cost center, or project number.

FIG. 18.15
The purchase requisition account assignment pop-up window.

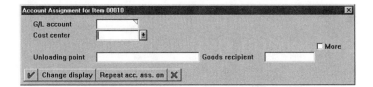

There are several other screens of information about the requisition.

The text overview screen allows you to enter multiple text items. During implementation, you can configure the text items that are available and whether to copy the subsequent documents or not. For each of the text items, a long text area is available to enter more information than will fit in the fields as shown.

The release strategy shows what approvals the requisition item will need before it can be converted to a request for quote or purchase order.

The statistics screen shows important information about the requisition such as who created the document, when it was created, release indicator, processing status, and RFQ or purchase order number if one has been created. The information on the screen is tracked automatically by the system and cannot be changed.

After the requisition is finished, click the Save icon. This will generate a requisition number (if internal number assignment is used).

After the requisition is saved, it is available for the release strategy if enabled. If no release strategy is enabled, the requisition is ready to be converted into an RFQ, outline agreement, or purchase order. The requisition will immediately show up list displays, which the buyers use to determine what needs to be processed. In short, it is immediately ready to be processed.

RFQ/Quotation

If no source of supply exists for a requested item, it may be necessary to send requests for quotes (RFQ) to various vendors. To access the RFQ screen, follow this menu path:

> **Menu Path:** Logistics > Materials Management > Purchasing > RFQ/Quotation > RFQ > Create

> **Transaction Code:** ME41

Notice the initial screen displayed in Figure 18.16 looks very similar to the requisition initial screen. In fact, all purchasing documents contain a similar set of screens, each with a similar format and set of data. The typical screens include an Initial screen, Item Overview, Item Details, Header Details, Header and Item Texts, Pricing Conditions, and Statistics screens. Only on the requisition is no header data maintained.

FIG. 18.16

The RFQ initial screen.

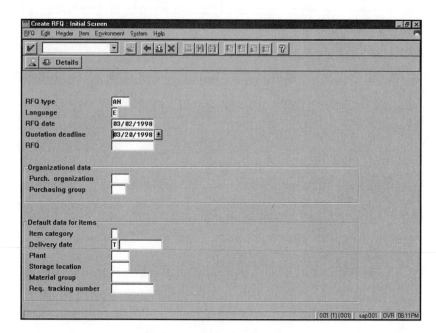

The RFQ type is similar to the requisition document type. It controls the number range and fields available for data entry in the RFQ. The RFQ Date is the date the RFQ is being written. The Quotation Deadline is the date that the vendor's responses to the RFQ are due in. If external numbers are used for the RFQ's, enter the RFQ number in the RFQ field. If the system is assigning the RFQ number, leave the RFQ field blank.

In the Organizational Data block, enter the purchasing organization (Purch. Organization) and Purchasing Group the RFQ is valid for. In the Default Data for Items block, enter any values that should copy for all items of the RFQ. This area is very similar to that on the Requisition initial screen.

The RFQ can be created by referencing one of three documents: a Requisition, another RFQ, or an outline agreement (contract or scheduling agreement). This minimizes data entry and, in the case of the Requisition, links the two documents. Therefore, anyone can go into the requisition and see that it has been sent out for quote. To create the RFQ with reference to one of these documents, go to the menu option RFQ > Create w. Reference. Enter the appropriate document number in the pop-up window that appears.

If the RFQ is not being created with reference to another document, press Enter to proceed after entering the appropriate values on the initial screen.

On this screen (see Figure 18.17), enter the Material number or Short Text description, material group (Matl Grp), RFQ quantity, order unit of measure (OUn), delivery date (Deliv. Date), plant (Plnt), and storage location (SLoc) for each of the items.

FIG. 18.17

The RFQ item overview screen.

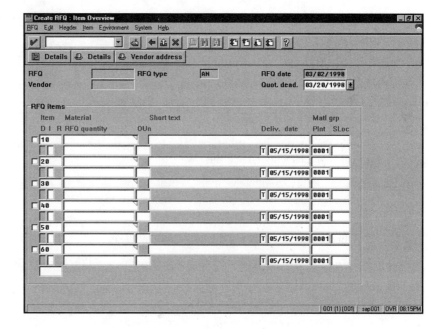

Next, use the buttons and menu paths to proceed to the following screens in order to maintain all appropriate information: the item details, the header details, item texts, and header texts.

If a delivery schedule needs to be entered for any item rather than a single delivery date, go to menu path: Item > Delivery Schedule.

At the RFQ item delivery schedule screen seen in Figure 18.18, enter the appropriate delivery dates (Deliv. Date) and scheduled quantity (Scheduled Qty.) on each date. When finished, press the Overview button to return to the item overview screen. From the item overview screen, press the Vendor address button to choose the vendor(s) this RFQ should be sent to.

FIG. 18.18

The RFQ item delivery schedule screen.

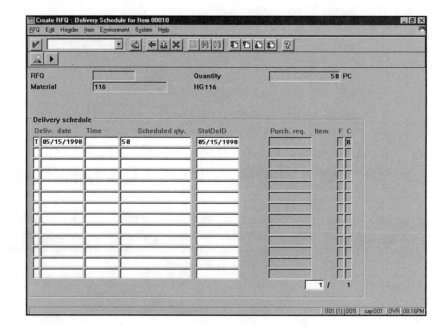

Enter the Vendor number and press Enter to populate the screen. When you are satisfied that this is the correct vendor, click the Save icon.

To send the RFQ to multiple vendors, repeat the previous steps. After you have created RFQ for each of the vendors desired, click the Exit arrow to exit the RFQ.

The vendor's response to the RFQ is maintained as a quotation in SAP. To enter a quotation, follow this menu path to get to the quotation initial screen.

> **Menu Path:** Logistics > Materials Management > Purchasing > RFQ/Quotation > Quotation > Maintain
>
> **Transaction Code:** ME47

Enter the RFQ number and press Enter to proceed.

Notice that the information from the RFQ has copied into the quotation. On the item overview screen (see Figure 18.19), only the net price (Net Pr. in USD) is missing. Enter the vendor's quoted price.

FIG. 18.19

The quotation item overview screen.

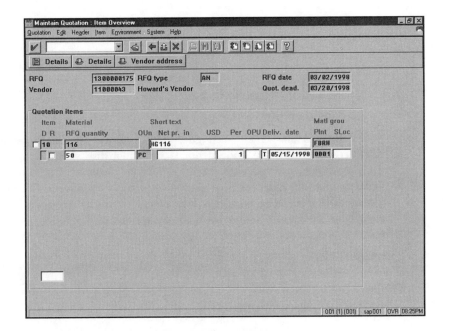

Use the menu paths and buttons to proceed to the item details, item delivery schedule, pricing conditions, item texts, header details, and header texts screens to maintain any further information that may be appropriate. Information such as the vendor material number, rejection indicator, additional price breaks or charges, and whether the info record should be updated are all available on those screens.

When finished entering the desired information on the quotation, click the Save icon.

Outline Agreements

An outline agreement in SAP is a long-term contract with a vendor for the procurement of materials or services. It is often referred to as a *blanket order*. An outline agreement requires that the buyer dictates the validity period and either an estimated quantity or value for the agreement. The exact date(s) and quantities of the materials or services to be delivered is not required.

There are two types of outline agreements in SAP: contracts and scheduling agreements. Further, there are two types of contracts: quantity contracts and value contracts. The difference between contracts and scheduling agreements is that contracts require a release order for delivery, whereas a single delivery schedule can be attached to the scheduling agreement to reflect all expected deliveries. Each release order is actually a separate purchase order as created in SAP.

Since the fields are extremely similar on the contract and the scheduling agreement, you will focus solely on the details of the scheduling agreement. To create a scheduling agreement, follow this menu path:

Menu Path: Logistics > Materials Management > Purchasing > Outline Agreement > Scheduling Agreement > Create

Transaction Code: ME31

Notice that the initial screen (see Figure 18.20) looks very similar to the requisition and RFQ initial screens. The Vendor code identifies the vendor with whom the agreement is being written. The Agreement Type, similar to the requisition document type and RFQ type, controls the number range and fields available for data entry in the agreement. The Agreement Date is the date the agreement is being written. If externally assigned numbers are used for the agreement, enter the agreement number in the Agreement field. If the system is assigning the agreement number, leave the Agreement field blank.

FIG. 18.20

The scheduling agreement initial screen.

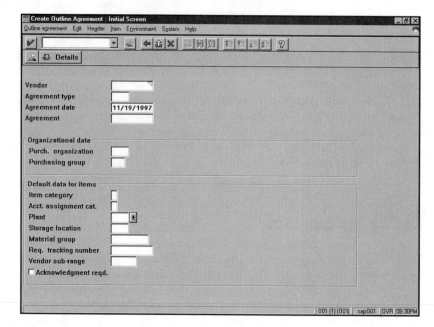

In the Organizational Data block, enter the purchasing organization (Purch. Organization) and Purchasing Group for whom the agreement is valid. In the Default Data for Items block, enter any values that should copy for all items of the agreement. This area is very similar to that on the requisition and RFQ initial screens.

The agreement can be created by referencing either another agreement or an RFQ. This minimizes data entry and, in the case of the RFQ, links the two documents. To create the agreement with reference to one of these documents, go to the menu option Outline Agreement > Create w. Reference. Enter the appropriate document number in the pop-up window that appears.

If the agreement is not being created with reference to another document, press the Header details button to proceed after entering the appropriate values on the initial screen.

Validity data, Terms of Delivery and Payment, and Reference data are all available on the header details screen (see Figure 18.21). Maintain the appropriate values in each of the fields. After entering the appropriate values on this screen, click the Overview button to proceed to the item overview screen.

FIG. 18.21
The scheduling agreement header details screen.

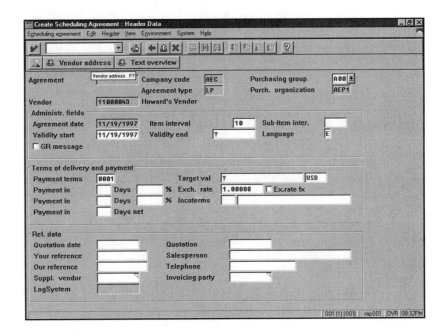

The Create Scheduling Agreement: Item Overview screen, shown in Figure 18.22, is similar to both the requisition and RFQ item overview screens. On this screen, enter the Material number or Short Text description, material group (Matl Grp), target quantity (Targ. Qty.), order unit of measure (OUn), Net Price, plant (Plnt), and storage location (SLoc) for each of the items. Also, enter any item categories (I) or account assignment categories (A) that may be appropriate for the items.

Depending on your entry in the Account Assignment field on the item overview screen, the system may present a pop-up window asking for the accounts to be charged for the purchase. Enter the proper account information. This may include a general ledger account number, asset account number, cost center, or project number.

Next, use the buttons and menu paths to proceed to the following screens in order to maintain all appropriate information in the agreement: the Item Details, Item Additional Data, Item Texts, and Header Texts.

When finished maintaining the appropriate data on each of the screens, click the Save icon.

Part
IV

Ch
18

FIG. 18.22

The Create Scheduling Agreement: Item Overview screen.

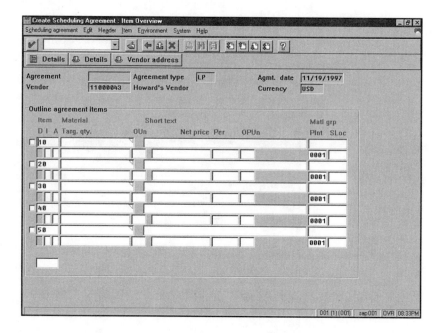

In the case of a scheduling agreement, a delivery schedule can be directly attached to the scheduling agreement. This delivery schedule can be automatically populated via the MRP run if the proper parameter is maintained in the source list or generated manually. To generate the delivery schedule manually, follow this menu path to get to the scheduling agreement delivery schedule initial screen (see Figure 18.23).

> **Menu Path:** Logistics > Materials Management > Purchasing > Outline Agreement > Scheduling Agreement > Follow-on Functions > Sch. Agmt. Schedule
>
> **Transaction Code:** ME38

Enter the scheduling Agreement number and press Enter to move to the item overview screen seen in Figure 18.24.

Select the item for which you want to maintain a delivery schedule and press the Deliv. Schedule button.

Enter the appropriate delivery date(s), delivery times, and scheduled delivery quantities. When finished entering data in the delivery schedule, click the Save folder.

Purchase Orders

The SAP system requires that the exact quantity and delivery date(s) be identified on the purchase order. The purchase order can have multiple items, and each item can have multiple delivery dates.

FIG. 18.23
The scheduling
agreement delivery
schedule initial screen.

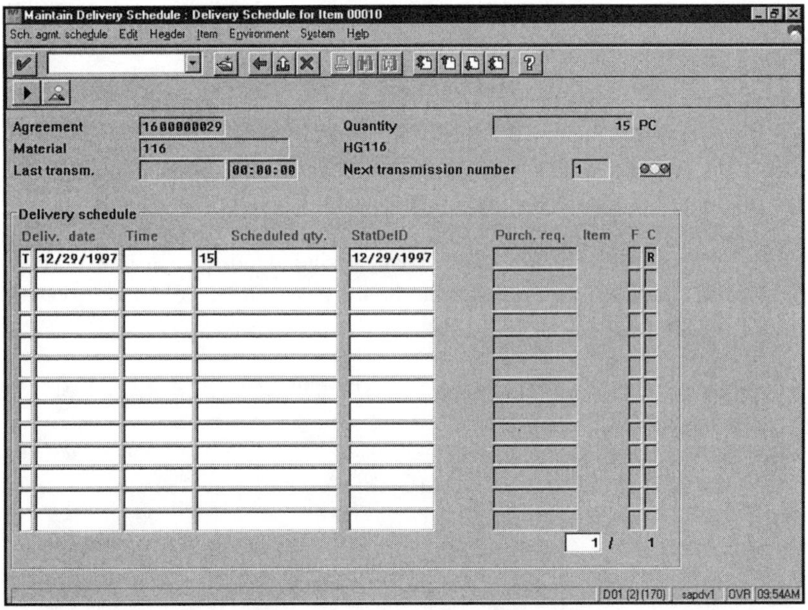

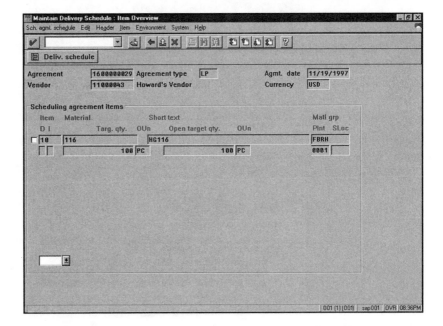

FIG. 18.24
The Maintain Delivery
Schedule: Item
Overview screen.

There are several ways to create purchase orders in SAP. They can either be created manually or by processing outstanding requisitions. You will look at manually creating purchase orders. To create a purchase order, follow this menu path:

Menu Path: Logistics > Materials Management > Purchasing > Purchase Order > Create > Vendor Known

Transaction Code: ME21

Notice that the initial screen seen in Figure 18.25 looks very similar to the requisition, RFQ, and outline agreement initial screens. The Vendor code identifies the vendor for whom the purchase order is being written. The Order Type controls the number range and fields available for data entry in the purchase order. The Purchase Order Date is the date the purchase order is being written. If externally assigned numbers are used for the purchase order, enter the purchase order number in the Purchase Order field. If the system is assigning the agreement number, leave the Purchase Order field blank.

FIG. 18.25

The Create Purchase Order: Initial Screen.

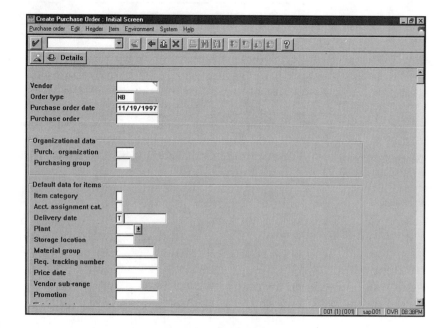

In the Organizational Data Block, enter the purchasing organization (Purch. Organization) and Purchasing Group the purchase order is valid for. In the Default Data for Items block, enter any values that should copy for all items of the purchase order. This area is very similar to that on the requisition, RFQ, and outline agreement initial screens.

The purchase order can be created by referencing another purchase order, requisition, RFQ, or contract. This minimizes data entry and links the documents. A purchase order created with reference to a contract is also known as a release order against a contract. To create the agreement with reference to one of these documents, go to the menu option Purchase order > Create w. Reference. Enter the appropriate document number in the pop-up window that appears.

If the purchase order is not being created with reference to another document, press Enter to proceed after entering the appropriate values on the initial screen.

The purchase order item overview screen shown in Figure 18.26 is similar to that on the other purchasing documents. On this screen, enter the Material number or Short Text description, material group (Matl Grp), PO Quantity, order unit of measure (OUn), Net price, delivery date (Deliv. Date), plant (Plnt), and storage location (SLoc) for each of the items. Also, enter any item categories (I) or account assignment categories (A) that may be appropriate for the items.

FIG. 18.26

The Create Purchase Order: Item Overview screen.

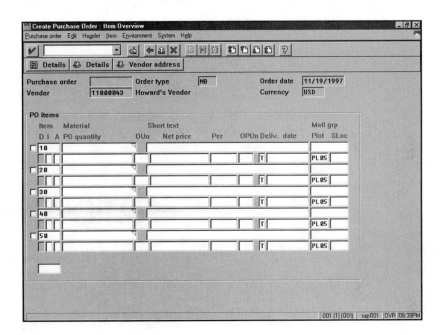

Depending on your entry in the account assignment field on the item overview screen, the system may present a pop-up window asking for the accounts to be charged for the purchase. Enter the proper account information. This may include a general ledger account number, asset account number, cost center, or project number.

Next, use the buttons and menu paths to proceed to the following screens in order to maintain all appropriate information in the purchase order: the Item Details, Item Delivery Schedule, Item Texts, Header Details and Header Texts.

When finished entering the appropriate data on each of the screens, click the Save icon.

Goods Receipt

The goods receipt transaction causes an increase in stock. The system uses the purchase order number as the basis for the goods receipt. The order number enables receiving to verify that the delivery actually corresponds to the order. The system will propose data from the order, such as the material number and quantity, simplifying the data entry at the time of the goods receipt and eliminating data entry errors.

When performing a goods receipt, the stock can be received into a number of destinations, depending on the circumstances of the goods receipt. If the material is purchased for a particular department and is to be used upon receipt (order items with account assignments), it will be expensed to that department upon receipt. If the material is purchased for stock, a storage location must be specified. The storage location can be specified in the purchase order and will then be proposed by the system, or it can be specified at the time of the goods receipt. If the material is purchased for stock and requires quality inspection, the system will receive the material into stock in quality inspection. If the material does not require quality inspection, the system will propose receipt into unrestricted-use stock for the storage location specified on the purchase order. The user also has the ability to receive the material into blocked stock or *GR blocked stock*. The GR blocked stock category allows you to acknowledge receipt of the material, however the goods are not yet part of valuated stock and therefore no accounting document is created.

The goods receipt transaction can be accessed via the following menu path.

Menu Path: Logistics > Materials Management > Inventory Management > Goods Movement > Goods Receipt > For Purchase Order > PO Number Known

Transaction Code: MB01

Once at the initial screen, pictured in Figure 18.27, the user should select the movement type and input the purchase order number. The movement type can be selected through the menu path or entered directly. If the entire quantity is destined for stock or for consumption, the user should select: Movement Type > PO to Warehouse (movement type 101). The goods could also be received into GR blocked stock as described previously by selecting the menu path: Movement Type > PO to Blocked Stock (movement type 103). When you enter the goods receipt, you can indicate to print a Goods Receipt/ Issue slip. Assume that the goods will be received into stock and the first Movement Type menu path is selected. After specifying the PO number and the movement type, the user should click the green check mark button. This will take you to the screen in Figure 18.28.

This screen displays the items on the purchase order. The user can change the receipt quantity if different from the PO quantity and has the ability to change the storage location on this screen. The DCI field on this screen is the delivery completed indicator. If set, this indicates that no further goods receipts are expected with respect to this order item. This indicator is set automatically if the delivery is within the under/over delivery tolerances. The Stock Type field indicates which of the following stock categories the quantity will be posted: unrestricted-use stock, stock in quality inspection, or blocked stock.

The user has the ability to change the stock type at the time of the goods receipt.

After verifying the data, click on the Post button to post the goods receipt. A message will display at the bottom of the screen specifying the material document number that was created and posted.

At this time, displaying the stock overview for the material, as explained in Chapter 10, "Sales and Distribution Functionality with SAP R/3," will show the increase in stock in the corresponding stock category.

FIG. 18.27

The Goods Receipt for Purchase Order: Initial Screen.

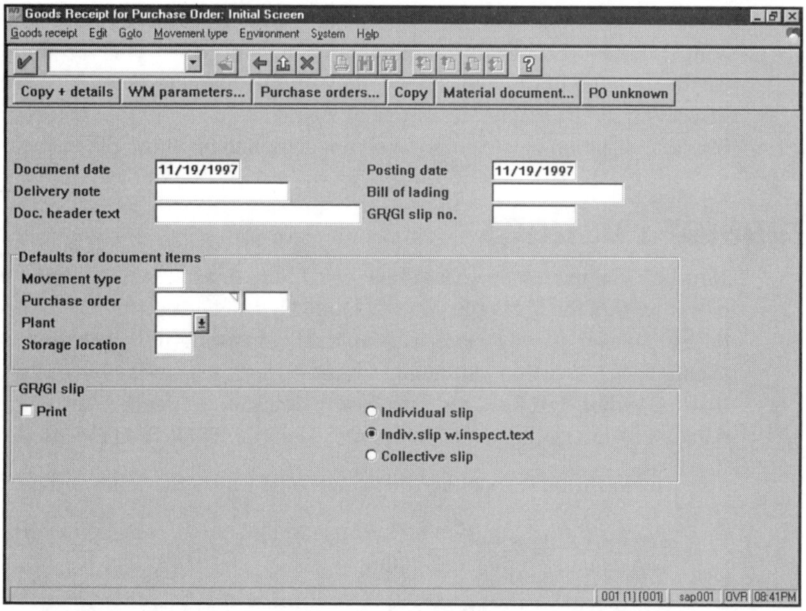

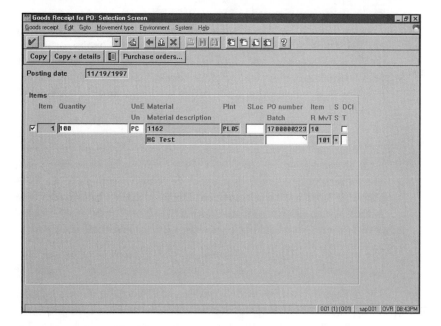

FIG. 18.28

The Goods Receipt for PO: Selection Screen.

A material document is created when you post the goods receipt. This document serves as proof of the goods movement. Associated with the material document, an accounting document is created. The accounting document contains information regarding the accounts that were posted to when the goods receipt was completed. When the goods receipt is posted, the system automatically updates the G/L accounts by the value of the goods receipt, as explained in the "Automatic Account Determination" section, later in this chapter. Additional updates are also carried out in other modules depending on the characteristics of the receipt. For example, an inspection lot in Quality Management would be created if the material required inspection, vender evaluation data needed to be updated, and planning file entries were created in MRP.

Transfer Postings

Now that you have seen an example of a goods receipt, take a look at another type of inventory movement. In this example you will look at a transfer posting. More specifically, you will demonstrate how to move a material from quality inspection to unrestricted stock. This corresponds to the situation outlined in Chapter 16, "A Day-in-the-life of Purchasing and Goods Receipt," when Ted from the Purchasing department needed Lester from the Incoming Inspection Lab to switch the labels on the material from *On-hold* to *Released*.

To perform a transfer posting the user should utilize the following menu path.

> **Menu Path:** Logistics > Materials Management > Inventory Management > Goods Movement > Transfer Posting
>
> **Transaction Code:** MB1B

The initial screen pictured in Figure 18.29 is used to process a transfer posting. This screen contains data that will be copied to the material document and accounting document if one is created. The screen is separated into three sections. The top section of the screen contains data that is stored at the header level of the document. The Document Date and Posting Date fields are located in this section of the screen. Both dates default to the current date but can be modified by the user. Other fields in this section include the Material Slip, Doc. Header Text, and GR/GI Slip No.

The middle portion of the screen contains data fields used as defaults for the document items. Different data fields will be required depending on the goods movement being performed. The fields in this section are Movement Type, Plant, Storage Location, and Special Stock indicator. The movement type identifies the specific goods movement being performed and was explained in detail in an earlier section. The Plant is the plant where the material is located and the Storage Location is a location within the plant. The Special Stock indicator will not be used in this example, but could be used if the material is special stock such as vendor consignment.

The last section of the screen contains a check box to allow the user to print a slip documenting the goods movement and radio buttons to select which output format is desired.

The most important data entered on this screen are the movement type and plant. The plant is necessary because the system needs to know where the goods movement is taking place. The movement type will determine what the next screen will look like and will also play an important part in automatic account determination. The movement type can be entered via one of three methods. The first method is to type in the movement type if it is known. Many users select this option once they are familiar with the system and know the different movement types. A second option is to select a movement type by using the pull-down menu for movement type. The third option is to use a menu path to select the correct movement type.

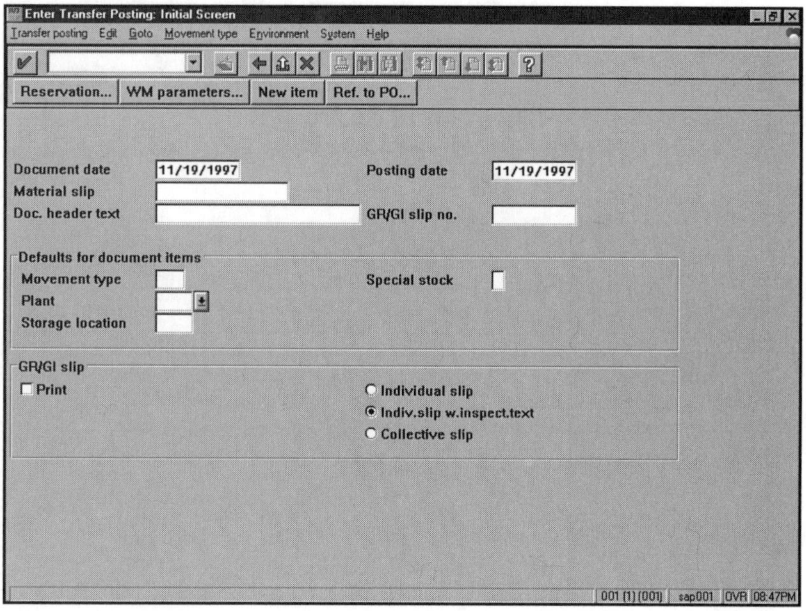

FIG. 18.29

The Enter Transfer Posting: Initial Screen.

In this example, use the third option to select the movement type. Remember that you are going to perform a transfer posting to move a material from quality inspection to unrestricted stock. To select the movement type for this transfer posting use the following menu path:

Menu Path: Movement Type > Transfer Posting > Stock to Stock > QI to Unrestricted.

The system will propose movement type 321 (Transfer posting quality inspection to unrestricted) in the Movement Type field. A warning message will appear at the bottom of the screen to check your input. The user should enter a plant in the Plant field and click the green check mark button to continue on to the next screen.

The Enter Transfer Posting: New Items screen (see Figure 18.30) will allow the user to enter specific data, such as the material number and quantity. The movement type selected on the previous screen (321) is displayed near the top of the screen and may not be modified. The next field on the screen is the Receiving Storage Location (Recv. SLoc.). This would be used in the case of a storage location-to-storage location move. In this example, assume that the material is not being physically moved so this field will be left blank.

The main portion of this screen is for item data. Item data includes the material being moved, quantity, storage location, and plant. Notice the plant entered on the previous screen was copied to this screen. At this time, the user should enter the material being moved and the quantity. If the exact material number is not known, the user can use a matchcode to locate the number.

FIG. 18.30

The Enter Transfer
Posting: New Items
screen.

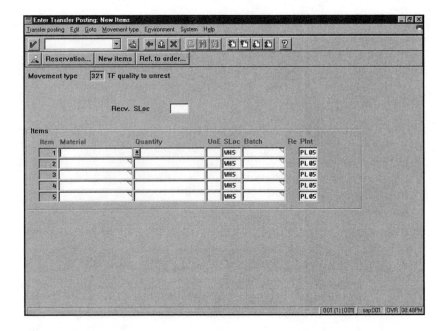

The Quantity and Storage Location (Sloc) fields are also required on this screen. Type in a quantity and storage location and click the green check mark Enter key. If the user enters a quantity greater than the amount in the entered storage location, the system will display an error message stating that there is a deficit of storage location stock of *xxx* pieces. The user should check the entry to ensure he or she has entered the correct material and quantity. He or she can also check the stock overview for the material to view the stock levels currently in the system. The stock overview was described in detail in Chapter 10.

If no errors are displayed the user should click the Post button to save the document. A message will be displayed at the bottom of the screen stating Document *XXXXXXXXX* posted. This number is the material document number. Because this transaction has no affect on accounting, an accounting document was not created. The result of this transaction is that unrestricted stock of the material will be increased and quality inspection stock will be decreased. This information can be viewed on the stock overview screen.

Quality Management

The quality management process in SAP uses a three-step approach. The first step is planning. SAP's QM module allows for a wide range and flexible application of planning. The second step is execution. This is the actual inspection of material, results, recording, and dispositioning of material. The final step is improvement. The many reporting mechanisms and somewhat limited SPC capabilities within SAP allow for these improvement activities. All together, these three elements make up the Quality Management Life Cycle (see Figure 18.31).

FIG. 18.31
The Quality Management Life Cycle.

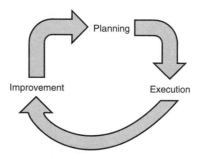

Inspection at the time of goods receipt is a typical use of these features within SAP. An inspection plan can be designed for each material. The receipt of material can trigger the automatic creation of an inspection lot that is used to collect inspection results and provide a mechanism for executing a usage decision. The quality info record allows for monitoring of vendor performance against quality standards. These three elements represent the quality cycle for procurement activities.

Quality Planning

Within the quality planning structure of SAP there are six components or master data elements that must be considered for goods receipt inspection. These components are typical of any quality system used by industry today with an emphasis on inspection. The six components are

- Master inspection characteristics
- Catalogs
- Inspection plans
- Quality info records

The first four components feed into the inspection plan. All together these components contribute to a well-orchestrated quality system.

Master Inspection Characteristic   In any quality control/assurance system, materials are reviewed for adherence to a set of standards. Whether this is a physical inspection as simple as a visual review or a complex chemical analysis, SAP's *master inspection characteristic* feature can be used to define the inspected feature. In simple terms, a master inspection characteristic is the attribute of the material that needs to be inspected. The master inspection characteristic also serves as a reusable template allowing standardization of inspection practices.

For example, in the Chapter 16 Electro Tech discussion, a shipment of logic chips was on hold for testing. The testing requirements for those chips would be outlined through an inspection plan within SAP. The plan would define all necessary attributes or "characteristics" that needed to be tested. These attributes would be defined as master inspection characteristics within SAP, allowing the same characteristic to reused in different inspection plans.

To create a master inspection characteristic, use the following menu path:

> **Menu Path:** Logistics > Quality Management > Quality Planning > Basic Data > Insp. Characteristic > Create
>
> **Transaction Code:** QS21

The screen that appears (see Figure 18.32) requires the entry of a name of the Master Insp. Charac., the Plant in which the characteristic is to be available, and a Valid From date.

FIG. 18.32

The Create Master Inspection Characteristic: Initial Screen.

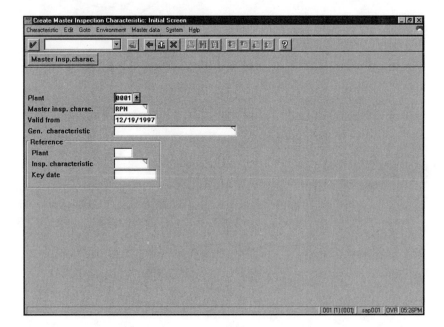

The Create Master Inspection Characteristic: Master Data screen, seen in Figure 18.33, will appear. This screen is used to define the elements that make up the master inspection characteristic. First specify whether the characteristic is a Quantitative or Qualitative. This can be done by selecting the appropriate check box or by entering a Preset Indicator that fits one of the two characteristic types.

The Status controls how the master inspection characteristic can be used. The choices range for Not Released to Archived. The Short Text is a description of the master inspection characteristic. This text might include a test name such as "Hardness." Search Field allows for quick look-up of master inspection characteristics with common application. Each company should define its own use of Search Field.

Once these items have been filled in, press the Enter key and the Edit Characteristic Control Indicators box will appear (see Figures 18.34 and 18.35). The content of this box varies depending on whether a quantitative or qualitative characteristic was chosen. The control indicators define how each characteristic behaves. They include elements like whether a quantitative characteristic has an upper tolerance, lower tolerance, or both; whether a sampling procedure is used; and whether results will be recorded as summarized, individual, or fit to a class. The control indicators also define if the characteristic is required or optional and whether additional documentation is required.

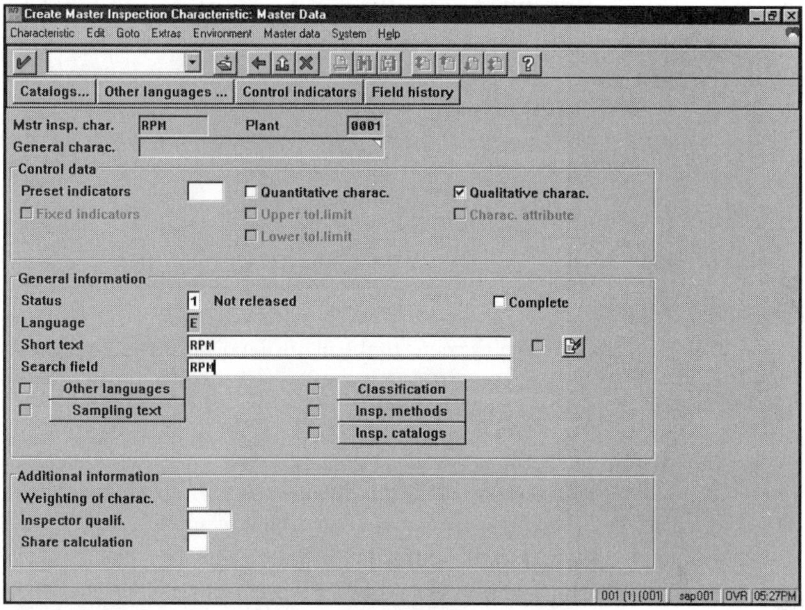

FIG. 18.33
Create Master Inspection Characteristic: Master Data screen.

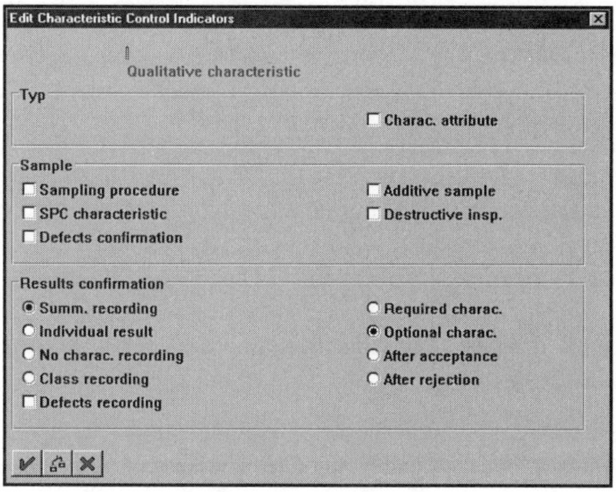

FIG. 18.34
First control indicators pop-up window.

Part
IV

Ch
18

FIG. 18.35
Second control
indicators pop-up
window.

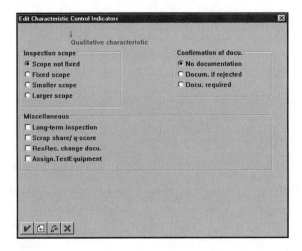

There are two different screens to the control indicators. Fill out the first screen as appropriate for the characteristic you are defining and press Enter to move to the second screen. Complete the second screen and press Enter again.

The screen will return to the Create Master Inspection Characteristic: Master Data screen. There are several buttons in the middle of the screen that control links to the master inspection characteristic. If you specified a qualitative characteristic, you should click the Insp. Catalogs button. This allows you to define a selected set, which is a listing of allowable results for the qualitative characteristic. Selected sets will be discussed later in this chapter. The remaining buttons link inspection methods and sampling text to the master inspection characteristic.

Once the master inspection characteristic has been defined to your satisfaction and you are certain that it performs the way you want it to, click the Complete check box. This allows changes to the master inspection characteristic to be controlled through versions.

Catalogs When recording results for a qualitative characteristic, it is often useful to standardize the possible answers for the characteristic. On a characteristic that asks for a color rating, the appropriate answers might be yellow, orange, pink, and red. If no control is applied to the expected answer, an inspector might give a rating of magenta. This creates two problems. First, is the rating of magenta good or bad? Since it is not one of the expected answers, it could be difficult to determine acceptability. The second problem occurs when doing problem solving based on the recorded results. If standardization of answers is not mandatory, analyzing the data could be difficult.

SAP handles this problem through the definition of catalogs. Simply put, catalogs are groupings of allowable answers. They can be used for a variety of purposes such as qualitative characteristics, defect or cause code reporting, even activity definition for corrective action or plant maintenance activities.

For use with qualitative characteristics, there are four steps to set up catalogs. The first step is to define a code group. A code group is the highest level of catalogs and defines a group of common answers. If you were defining a code group for the color characteristic previously mentioned, you might name the code group, Colors. The second step would be to define group codes. This terminology is sometimes confusing at first, but a group code is simply one of many allowable answers. For the group Colors, you might define the group codes Black, Blue, Purple, Gray, Red, Orange, Yellow, Pink, and White.

The next step of the process is defining a selected set. A selected set is a sub-set of a code group. Much like the code group, you must first define the selected set and then define the codes that go into the selected set. Extending the color example one step further, you might define a selected set of Light Colors that contains the codes Yellow, Orange, Pink, and Red as represented in Figure 18.36. This selected set can then be linked to a master inspection characteristic to limit the possible answers that could be recorded.

FIG. 18.36
Graphic relationship of catalogs: code groups versus selected sets.

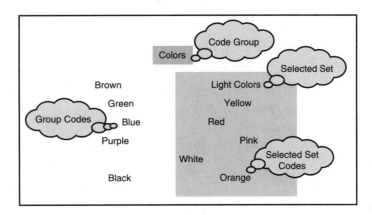

Walking through this process, the first step is creating a code group. To create a code group follow the menu path:

> **Menu Path:** Logistics > Quality Management > Quality Planning > Basic Data > Catalog > Code Groups > Maintain Individual
>
> **Transaction Code:** QS43

On the initial screen, you must specify a Catalog type and the name of the Code group you wish to create. If you were creating a catalog for a qualitative characteristic for color ratings you would select Catalog Type 1 = Characteristic Attributes, enter a name like **COLOR**, and then press Enter.

On the following screen, specify the language, a short text description of the group and a status (Created, Released, Marked for Deletion). Save the code group.

To maintain group codes (add a code to the group):

> **Menu Path:** Logistics > Quality Management > Quality Planning > Basic Data > Catalog > Group Codes > Maintain
>
> **Transaction Code:** QS44

On the initial screen, you must specify a Catalog type, Language, and the name of the Code group you wish to edit. Press Enter. On the following screen, specify a code to identify each and a short text for each code. In the color example discussed here, you might enter **C01 = Black**, **C02 = Blue**, **C03 = Purple**... Once all codes have been entered, save the code group.

To create a selected set:

> **Menu Path:** Logistics > Quality Management > Quality Planning > Basic Data > Catalog > Selected Sets > Maintain Individual
>
> **Transaction Code:** QS53

On the initial screen, you must specify a Catalog type, Plant, and the name of the Selected set you wish to create. If you were creating a selected set for a qualitative characteristic for color ratings you would select Catalog Type 1 = Characteristic Attributes, enter a name like **LTCOLORS**, and then press Enter.

On the following screen, specify a short text description of the selected set and a status (Created, Released, Marked for Deletion). Save the selected set.

To maintain selected set codes (add codes from a code group to a selected set):

> **Menu Path:** Logistics > Quality Management > Quality Planning > Basic Data > Catalog > Selected Sets Codes > Maintain
>
> **Transaction Code:** QS54

On the initial screen, you must specify a Catalog type, Plant, Language, and the name of the Selected set you wish to edit. Press Enter. On the following screen, click the Code Groups button and The Display Code Group Index: Initial Screen will appear. Leave the wildcard defaults in place and press the Index overview button.

A list of all available code groups appears. Scroll to the code group from which you want to select items. Highlight each individual code you wish to have in the selected set by clicking the item and selecting the Select/Deselect button. Once all appropriate codes have been selected, click the Copy button. The screen returns to the initial view with the selected codes copied into the selected set. For each code, specify a valuation of Accept or Reject and a defect class for the Reject codes. Save the selected set.

Once these four steps have been completed, the selected set can be linked to a master inspection characteristic.

Inspection Plans   The quality emphasis that dominated industry in the 1980s highlighted the need for suppliers who provide materials that conform to agreed upon requirements. Structure was added to the inspection of incoming goods while, at the same time, auditing and certification of suppliers grew. SAP provides for the ability to automatically determine if inspection is necessary when a goods receipt is posted. By using a combination of an inspection plan with a sampling plan and quality info records that tie the material and vendor together, varying techniques of monitoring the incoming goods can be utilized.

In SAP, an inspection plan is a list of tasks that are to be carried out at the time of goods receipt. This "task list" can have master inspection characteristics linked to it, or plan specific characteristics can be defined. When a goods receipt is posted for the material, an inspection lot is created that contains an interactive copy of the inspection plan. The lot is interactive because it is used to record test results, update vendor performance information, and allow for a usage decision on the receipt. Dependent on the results of testing, the usage decision allows for material to be accepted to unrestricted stock, returned to the vendor, scrapped, placed in a blocked status, placed in reserves stock, or consumed as a sample.

N O T E Before automatic creation of an inspection lot can occur, the corresponding inspection type must be defined in the Quality Management view of the Material Master. By defining inspection types at the Material Master level, SAP allows for different materials to have different levels of inspection. Inspection can occur as a result of a goods receipt, during production, due to an inventory receipt from production, as a result of a planned shipment, and so on. ▩

In the Electro Tech example, a shipment of logic chips had been received and was being held because of quality inspection. A sticker system had been employed to manage the state of the inventory. Through SAP, the status of the inventory is managed via the usage decision.

To create an inspection plan, follow the path:

Menu Path: Logistics > Quality Management > Quality Planning > Inspection Planning > Task lists > Inspection Plan > Create

Transaction Code: QP01

On the Create Inspection Plan: Initial Screen, seen in Figure 18.37, provide the Material, Plant, and Key Date. You can optionally provide the Group to provide a link between common materials. Press Enter to create the plan.

The header details screen will appear (see Figure 18.38). This screen controls the usage of the plan and the status. Usage relates to whether the plan should be used at time of goods receipt, during production, or at goods issue. The Status controls how the plan can be used. The plan can be in a created state, released for costing, released for use with an order, released for costing, and used with an order.

Once the required information has been supplied at the header level, the Operation Overview can be displayed (see Figure 18.39). The Operation Overview allows for definition of a list of task steps. 9999 inspection characteristics can be placed behind each operation. To add an operation, enter the Work center (Work Ctr) and Control Key (CtrK) and a text Description of the operation.

Once the operation is completed, an inspection characteristic can be added by selecting the check box in front of the operation and clicking the Insp.characs button.

FIG. 18.37

The Create Inspection Plan: Initial Screen.

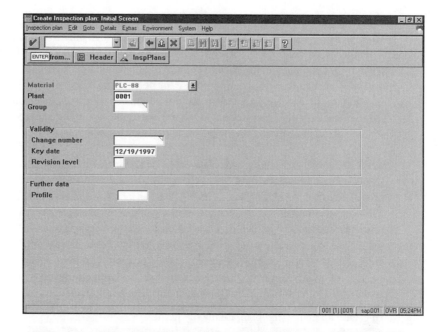

FIG. 18.38

The Create Inspection Plan: Header Details screen.

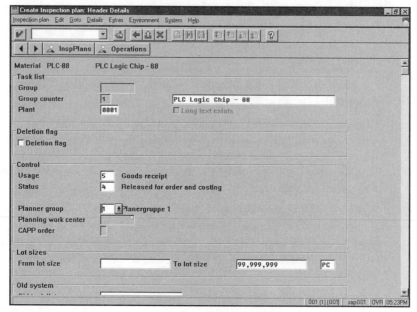

N O T E The control key and text description for an operation can default in from the work center if desired. In the work center definition, provide a default control key and a standard text key. These items will default in after the work center is added to the inspection plan's operation listing and the Enter key is pressed. ▪

FIG. 18.39

The Inspection Plan Create: Operation Overview screen.

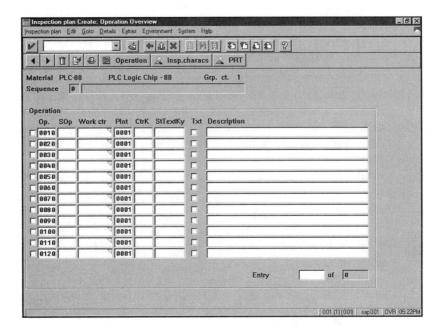

At the characteristic overview screen pictured in Figure 18.40, enter the name of the master inspection characteristic you want to link to the operation. Press Enter and confirm the master inspection characteristic, the inspection method, and supply a sampling procedure if necessary. Repeat the process to add as many characteristics as necessary. Save the inspection plan.

FIG. 18.40

The Create Inspection Plan: Characteristic Overview screen.

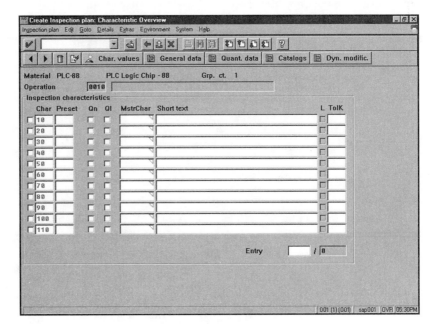

Part

IV

Ch

18

Once a released inspection plan is defined and all other master data requirements are in place (such as the goods receipt inspection type in the material master), the inspection plan will be automatically pulled at the time of goods receipt. The inspection lot will be created and used to control the quality status of the receipt.

Quality Info Records   Many companies have chosen to limit the number of vendors that are allowed to supply a given material. These vendors are often scrutinized on their performance to standards and then approved as a certified supplier. This may mean they perform source inspections, they may be required to maintain a certain quality system, or they may have to maintain a certain level of performance against incoming inspections. If they fail to meet these standards, they may be temporarily or permanently halted from supplying product.

With SAP, performance to quality standards is managed via a quality info record. The quality info record ties a material and a vendor together. Working in conjunction with the Quality Management view of the Material Master, the Q-info record can define requirements the vendor must comply with, and provide a means of blocking that vendor should its performance fail to meet standards.

To create a Q-info record, use the path:

> **Menu Path:** Logistics > Quality Management > Quality Planning > Procurement > Q-info Record > Create
>
> **Transaction Code:** QI01

At the initial Create Q-info Record screen, seen in Figure 18.41, enter the Material, Vendor, and Plant. If Material Masters are managed via revisions, enter the appropriate Revision Level. If you wish to create the Q-info record based on an existing example, enter the necessary information in the Copy Model section. Press Enter to continue.

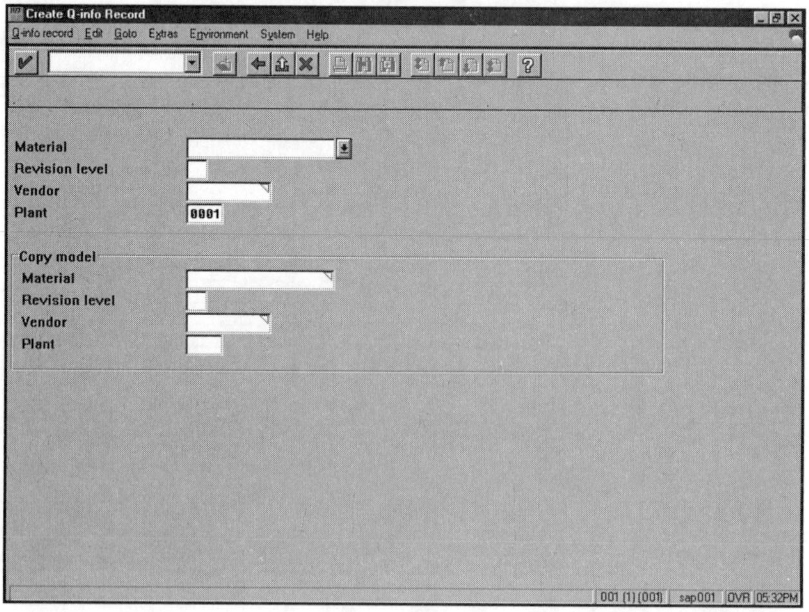

FIG. 18.41
The Create Q-info
Record initial screen.

The overview screen that appears (see Figure 18.42) requires the entry of a Release Until date. This date defines the time period that the combination of material and vendor is valid. Often this date is used to monitor annual review requirements. Through the overview screen you can also maintain the Vendor's QM System the Release Quantity and any Block Function settings. The block function allows the quality management staff to block a vendor from a variety of activities such as source determination, purchase requisitions, purchase orders, or even a total block.

FIG. 18.42
The Create Q-info Record overview screen.

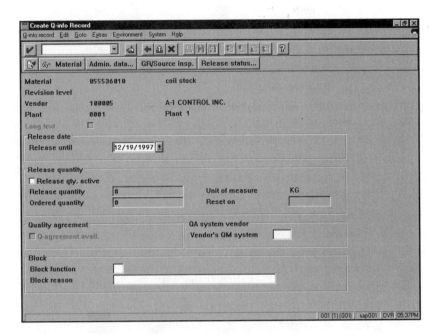

The Q-info record also allows for management of source inspections. A source inspection is conducted with the assistance of the vendor, normally with the attendance of the receiving company or by a third party agency. By clicking the GR/Source Insp. button, you can define if only a incoming inspection, only a source inspection, or both are to be conducted.

Other QM Master Data You have now been introduced to many of the QM related features that SAP provides. These objects are basic building blocks. There are several other lesser-used but equally important types of QM master data. The inspection plan tells you what to test. In the real world you must also know how to test and how many to test. These issues are handled by the inspection method and dynamic modification capabilities of SAP.

Dynamic Modification

Another common development of the quality push of the 1980s was the move from fixed sample sizes to inspection based on quality sampling plans that take into account the current quality performance level. A vendor that has repeatedly demonstrated superior performance requires less monitoring than one with reoccurring quality problems.

To handle this, SAP has a multilevel design approach utilizing sampling schemes, sampling plans, and dynamic modification rules. During the goods receipt process, this allows for a varying sample size to the extreme of skipping inspection of certain receipts by changing the stage of the inspection from normal to tighten or reduced, based on the vendor's quality level.

Sampling Scheme A sampling scheme is a table that outlines sample size based on lot size. It also defines the acceptance criteria by means of an Acceptance and Rejection number.

To create a sampling scheme use the path:

> **Menu Path:** Logistics > Quality Management > Quality Planning > Basic Data > Dynamic Modification > Sampling Scheme > Create
>
> **Transaction Code:** QDP1

Sampling Procedure The sampling procedure uses the sampling scheme to calculate the required sample size. It also determines how valuation of results recording will occur. The acceptability of the material can be determined manually, based on an entered code, attributive or variable. Each characteristic of the inspection plan can carry a different sampling procedure. The control indicators of the master inspection characteristic determine if a sampling plan will be used.

To create a sampling procedure, use the path:

> **Menu Path:** Logistics > Quality Management > Quality Planning > Basic Data > Dynamic Modification > Sampling Procedure > Create
>
> **Transaction Code:** QDV1

Dynamic Modification The ability for inspection to adjust to changing quality performance is handled via a dynamic modification rule within SAP. These rules allow for varying levels of inspection severity. Typically, the stages of normal, tightened, reduced, and skipped are used. As results are recorded and valuated as accepted or rejected, the quality level for the material/vendor is updated. The dynamic modification rule looks at this quality level to determine if a stage change should occur.

The dynamic modification rule can be stored at the header level of the inspection plan or at the characteristic level. To create a dynamic modification rule, follow the path:

> **Menu Path:** Logistics > Quality Management > Quality Planning > Basic Data > Dynamic Modification > Dynamic Modifcn rule > Create
>
> **Transaction Code:** QDR1

Inspection Methods

Inspection of a material, whether at very cursory level or at a very detailed level, is normally conducted by guidelines laid out in an inspection method. This method describes how a specific attribute or characteristic is to be inspected.

This functionality within SAP is still somewhat weak. Basically, a reference to a method is defined but actually constructing and maintaining the method within SAP is difficult. The text editor does not have the capabilities of most word processors on the market today, so it is more commonly accepted to build a reference to an externally maintained test method, thus allowing a link to be made between the master inspection characteristic and the inspection method.

To create an inspection method, use the path:

> **Menu Path:** Logistics > Quality Management > Quality Planning > Basic Data > Inspection Method > Create
>
> **Transaction Code:** QS31

Incoming Inspection

Once all the master data necessary to complete an incoming inspection has been established, an inspection lot will be automatically created when a goods receipt is posted for a quality relevant material. The inspection lot is the depository of information related to inspection activities. The results of testing are recorded in the inspection lot, and, in some cases, the status of the inventory is controlled via the inspection lot.

Goods movements often trigger the creation of an inspection lot. Goods receipts, goods issues, and transfer postings within a storage location can be used to create inspection lots automatically. When a goods receipt is posted, SAP checks the Material Master to see if the appropriate inspection type has been activated. If it has, the system then looks for a valid, released inspection plan. If both of these requirements are met and the Q-info record does not block goods receipt inspection, an inspection lot will be created.

Results Recording   The inspection lot will contain inspection operations and inspection characteristics as defined by the inspection plan. To record the results of testing, follow the menu path:

> **Menu Path:** Logistics > Quality Management > Quality Inspection > Results > For Operation > Record
>
> **Transaction Code:** QE01

Enter the Inspection Lot, Operation, and Processing Mode to call up the inspection lot. If the inspection lot number is not known, you can look it up using the Find Insp. Lot button. This button allows for searches based on the purchasing document number, material number, vendor, or a variety of other criteria. Once the necessary inspection lot information has been provided, press Enter to continue.

A listing of characteristics for the operation will be displayed. Select the check box(es) for the characteristics you wish to process and click the Choose button. Enter the data based on the characteristic type. The screen appearance differs depending on whether the characteristic is qualitative or quantitative and whether individual, summarized, or class data recording was called for in the inspection characteristic's control indicators. When all results have been recorded for a given characteristic, valuate and close the characteristic using the provided buttons. Save the data when all the characteristics have been adequately fulfilled. Repeat this process for all necessary operations in the inspection lot.

Usage Decision   The final step of the goods receipt inspection process is posting the stock status changes through the usage decision. Normally, if incoming inspection is to be performed, the stock is posted to QI (quality inspection) stock at the time of goods receipt. Once inspection is complete, the stock will be moved from QI stock to unrestricted stock. If problems were noted during inspection, the stock can be moved to blocked stock or returned to the vendor through the usage decision function.

To perform a usage decision, follow the menu path:

> **Menu Path:** Logistics > Quality Management > Quality Inspection > Insp.lot Processing > Usage Decision > Record

> **Transaction Code:** QA11

Enter the Inspection lot number or look it up using the Find Insp. Lot button. Press Enter to continue. The Record Usage Decision: Characteristic Overview screen will appear. At the bottom of the screen you can select a UD code (usage decision code). This code affects the vendor rating and seals the data record. Before saving the usage decision, click the Stock for Inspection Lot button.

The Record Usage Decision: Stock screen (see Figure 18.43) allows for movement of the stock from QI to seven other stock categories. Enter the appropriate quantity for each stock category and specify the appropriate storage location where allowed. Depending on which categories are selected, additional data may need to be supplied. Save the usage decision to post the stock transfers and seal the data record.

FIG. 18.43

The Record Usage Decision: Stock screen.

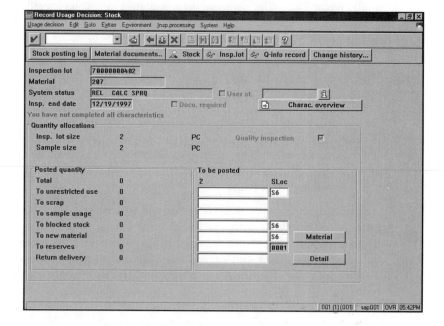

Once this transaction has been completed, the inventory is now under inventory and possibly warehouse management control. It is important to note that prior to the usage decision, the only way a stock status change can occur is through the usage decision transaction.

Inventory Management

The next section will discuss SAP functionality contained in two of the sub-modules of the Materials Management module: Inventory Management and Physical Inventory. The Inventory Management sub-module has two major functions: *inventory tracking* and *inventory movements*. Inventory tracking involves monitoring the stock levels and status of materials in various locations. Inventory movements are any events that cause a change in stock, such as changes to inventory levels or stock status. Examples of inventory movements are goods receipts, goods issues, and transfer postings.

Inventory Movements

How inventory movements affect other areas in SAP will be described in greater detail later in this section. The last part of this section will address the Physical Inventory submodule. The main purpose of this submodule is to validate the accuracy of the inventory data in the system against actual counts of the material contained in the plant. Any differences in the counts will be handled in this area.

> **N O T E** Details about inventory tracking are outlined in Chapter 10 in the "Stock Overview List" section, and will not be covered in this chapter. ▩

Part IV

Ch 18

Inventory movements can be divided into four major categories: goods receipts, goods issues, stock transfers, and transfer postings. A brief description of each of the categories and examples of when they are used is outlined here.

- *Goods receipt* is a goods movement used to receive material. This will usually lead to an increase in warehouse stock. However, in some cases the material may be purchased for consumption and will not increase inventory levels. A common example of a goods receipt movement is when goods are received from a vendor or from production. Other examples of goods receipts in SAP include customer returns and initial entry of stock into the system.

- *Goods issue* is a goods movement to withdraw material from stock. This will lead to a reduction in stock levels. A common example of a goods issue is to issue raw material to production for use in the manufacture of another material. Other examples of goods issues in SAP include goods issue to scrap, consumption to a cost center, and goods issue to a delivery to send a finished good to a customer.

- *Stock transfer* is the movement of material between locations. Examples of stock transfers include storage location-to-storage location movements and plant-to-plant movements.

- *Transfer posting* is an inventory movement that changes the stock type or stock category of a material. This movement may or may not involve a physical movement of the material. Common examples of transfer postings include: moving material from QI status to unrestricted status, moving material from unrestricted status to blocked status, and transferring consignment inventory into the company's own stock.

Each of these movements is assigned a specific *movement type*. A movement type is a three-digit number used to identify a specific goods movement. Examples of movement types include

101—Goods receipt for a purchase order

221—Goods issue to a production order

301—Plant-to-plant transfer

Movement types control which fields are displayed during entry of data into the system for an inventory movement. Movement types also play a key role in automatic account determination, which will be covered later.

Every movement in the SAP system results in the creation of a material document. Data included on the material document includes material, quantity, plant, storage location, and movement type. Material documents are evidence that a move occurred and can be used by management to review historical material movements.

Certain inventory movements also affect accounting. Performing these movements will lead to the creation of an accounting document in addition to the material document. The accounting document identifies which general ledger accounts are debited and credited and the amount of each debit and credit. Which general ledger accounts are debited and credited for each movement is controlled by automatic account determination, which will be covered in the next section.

An example of a movement that creates both a material document and an accounting document is a goods receipt for a purchase order. Accounting is affected because inventory increases when the goods are received. In addition, accounts payable will increase because you now owe the vendor money for the delivered materials. A storage location-to-storage location movement is an example of a movement that does not result in the creation of an accounting document. This is true because there has been no change in the total value of the inventory at the plant caused by this move.

N O T E   Although not covered in this section, it should be noted that the SAP system includes reversal movement types for most movement types to allow users to back out of erroneous transactions.

Automatic Account Determination

As noted, automatic account determination controls which general ledger accounts are posted when a specific movement is performed. Automatic account determination allows someone to perform a movement transaction in SAP without having to know which general ledger accounts need to be debited and credited. For example, someone working on the receiving dock does not have to know to debit the raw material inventory account and credit the vendor's accounts payable account when a shipment of raw materials is received at the dock. In addition to simplifying the process of updating the general ledger accounts when a movement takes place, this also serves as a control mechanism to ensure accounts are posted correctly.

Automatic account determination is set up via the IMG in configuration. The combination of a number of different pieces of data determines which accounts are posted. Movement types and material types are two of the key factors used in automatic account determination. For example, you would not want a goods issue to scrap to post the same accounts as a goods issue to a production order. Although they may both credit the same general ledger account, the account being debited will differ. Following the same logic, you can see that different material types will need to be posted to different accounts. For example, a goods receipt of packaging material will not hit the same accounts as a goods receipt for raw materials.

A number of other factors are involved in automatic account determination, but they will not be covered in this book. The previous description should provide the general concepts required allowing you to understand that inventory movements in Materials Management are integrated with Financial Accounting in SAP.

It should be noted that this particular section of the IMG must be configured correctly to ensure that the financial records of the company are correct. It is important that the person or persons in charge of configuring automatic account determination has a strong understanding of the business process being performed and the general ledger accounts being posted. In many cases, it is a good idea to have more than one person work on this configuration due to the importance of getting it right or, more accurately, the cost of completing it incorrectly. A good combination is someone with a materials management background that is familiar with the goods movement teamed with someone from the financial accounting team that understands the general ledger and the implications of debiting or crediting the wrong account.

Part
IV
Ch
18

After reading this section, it should be obvious that inventory movement is a piece of the Materials Management module that is integrated with many other modules. There is integration with Financial Accounting to ensure that the proper accounts are posted. There is integration with Production Planning when raw materials are issued to production. Issuing a finished good for delivery to a customer is an integration point with the Sales and Distribution module. These are only a few examples of the many integration points between Materials Management and other SAP modules related to goods movements.

Physical Inventory

This chapter has looked at a variety of movements and statuses that impact inventory within an organization. Often companies try to minimize, if not eliminate, inventory. Few, if any, have ever succeeded in totally eliminating inventory, but many have achieved an optimal level. The first step in controlling inventory is understanding it. Inventory is money. Just as you wouldn't allow stacks of dollar bills to be mismanaged or lost, neither should you allow inventory to be lost or mismanaged.

Unfortunately, the many necessary movements of inventory within a company often lead to errors. Material may be damaged, miscounted, misplaced, or simply never acknowledged when received or consumed. This is where SAP is helpful. Inventory movements are one of the fundamental building blocks for many SAP business transactions. Movements tie to financials, as well as basic purchasing, production, quality management, and distribution activities. Still errors do occur.

The Electro Tech company, like every company, must carry out a physical inventory of its stock at least once a year to balance its inventory. SAP supports the following procedures, which can be implemented to accomplish physical inventory: periodic inventory, continuous inventory, inventory sampling, and cycle counting. Periodic inventory, sometimes called *Annual Inventory*, is a procedure where all stocks of the company are counted on a specific date. Every material must be counted, and therefore all materials must be blocked from movement. This type of inventory normally requires a lot of labor hours and could require a plant shut down.

Inventory sampling involves randomly selecting stocks to be counted on a specific date. This method assumes the sample is representative of the other stocks, and if the variation between the count and the book inventory balance is small, it is assumed that deviations from the book inventory are so small that they can be neglected. Continuous inventory is a procedure whereby stocks are counted continuously during the year. Each material is counted at least once during the year.

Some companies feel that certain stock should be counted more often than other stocks, based on selection criteria. In those cases, SAP supports cycle counting in which inventory is counted at regular intervals within the year. The number of intervals per year depends on the cycle counting indicator for the material. Because of the high-dollar nature of its inventory, Electro Tech utilizes the cycle counting method of monitoring inventory.

Cycle Counting

Cycle counting allows high-usage or high-dollar parts to be counted more often. In this section you will learn how to perform a cycle count in the SAP system. Begin by following the menu path:

> **Menu Path:** Logistics > Materials Management > Physical Inventory > Special Procedures > Cycle Counting > Create Physical Inventory Document
>
> **Transaction Code:** MICN

This is the initial screen (see Figure 18.44) in the transaction to create physical inventory documents for cycle counting. The user should enter the Plant, Storage Location, and Planned Count Date From information. The material number or range of numbers can also be specified to cycle count particular materials if desired. Other parameters can be specified to narrow the cycle count to specific material. The user also has the option to sort the documents by storage bin description or material group if desired.

After the this data has be specified, select Program > Execute from the menu path or select the Execute button.

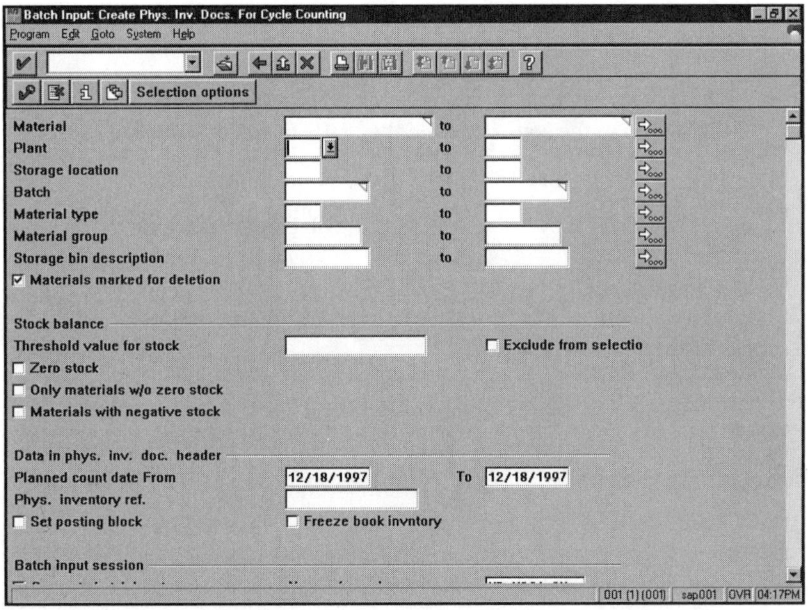

FIG. 18.44

The Batch Input: Create Phys. Inv. Docs. For Cycle Counting screen.

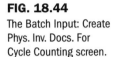

The next screen (Figure 18.45) displays the output list of materials due for cycle counting based on the criteria specified in the previous screen.

FIG. 18.45

Batch Input: Create Phys. Inv. Docs. For Cycle Counting— screen 2.

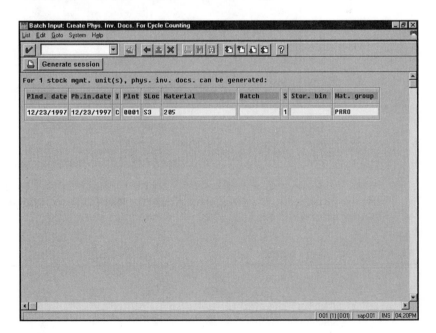

The user should select Edit > Generate Session or click the Generate Session button to generate the batch input session.

The system will display the message "BTCI session MB_MI01_CN created" at the bottom of the screen in the status bar and then take the user to the next screen.

This screen (Figure 18.46) shows the same display of materials for cycle counting as in screen 2, however the menu options and pushbutton have changed. The input session has been created and is ready to process.

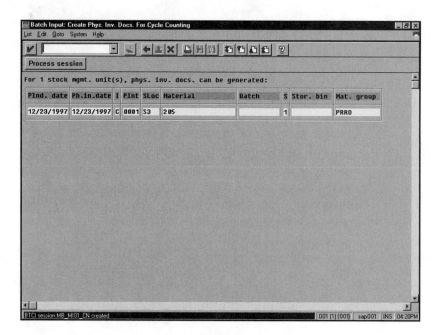

FIG. 18.46

Batch Input: Create Phys. Inv. Docs. For Cycle Counting— screen 3.

The user should select the Process Session button, which will take you directly to Batch Input: Session Overview.

This screen (Figure 18.47) displays the specific batch input session created for the cycle count.

Select the session to be processed by placing the cursor on the session line and choosing Session > Process Session from the menu path or clicking the Process Session button. This will bring up the Process Session.

This is a pop-up window of options the user can choose when processing the batch input session (see Figure 18.48).

The user has the following options:

- Process in foreground.
- Display errors only.
- Process in the Background. This will allow the terminal to be available for input again as soon as the session has been transferred to the background processing system.

FIG. 18.47
Batch Input: Session
Overview.

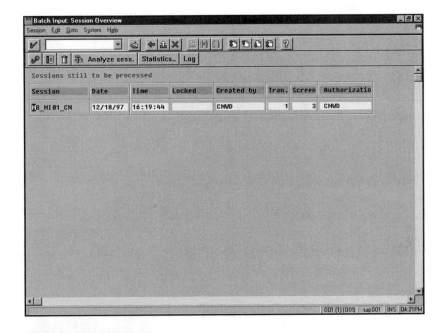

FIG. 18.48
Process Session
MB_MI01_CN pop-up
window.

Select Background Destination to create and print the inventory documents in the background.

After the physical inventory counts are taken and the count has been recorded on the inventory document, the user should enter the count via the following transaction menu:

Menu Path: Logistics > Materials Management > Physical Inventory > Inventory Count > Enter

Transaction Code: MI04

This is the initial screen (see Figure 18.49) to enter an inventory count result with reference to a physical inventory document. Enter the physical inventory document number. Also enter the fiscal year to which the document relates and the count date if different than the current date defaulted. A percentage variance between the quantity of stock counted and book inventory can also be specified, above which the system is to issue a warning message on entry of count results. This is done only if you want to be notified of large inventory differences.

FIG. 18.49

Batch Input: Enter Inventory Count: Initial Screen.

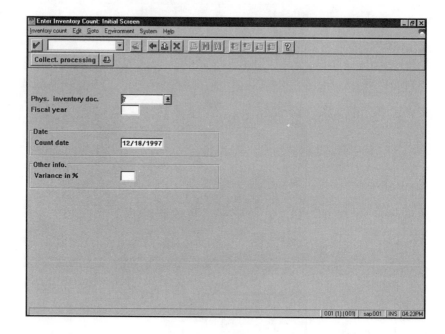

Press the Enter key to proceed.

Enter the counted quantity on the screen seen in Figure 18.50, and then click the Post button. The count is now entered into the system.

The user can display the differences between the counted quantity and the book quantity from the main Physical Inventory screen, menu path: Differences > Print. This list can be used to determine which materials for which you would like to initiate a recount. Once all counts are complete, the differences must be posted in the system. The following transaction will post the differences.

> **Menu Path:** Logistics > Materials Management > Physical Inventory > Difference > Post
>
> **Transaction Code:** MI07

Enter the physical inventory document on the screen shown in Figure 18.51 and press Enter. The material, difference quantity, and difference amount will be displayed. Click the Post button to post the differences in the system. Posting the differences will update the stock quantities and post the value of the difference to the proper general ledger accounts via automatic account determination.

FIG. 18.50

Batch Input: Enter Inventory Count xxxxxx: Collect.Processing.

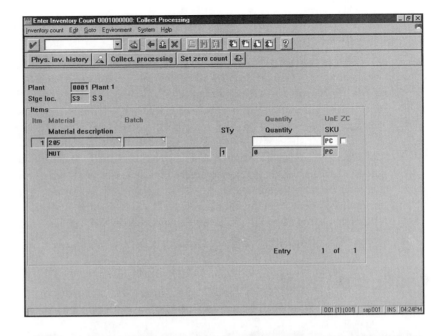

FIG. 18.51

Post Inv. Differences: Initial Screen.

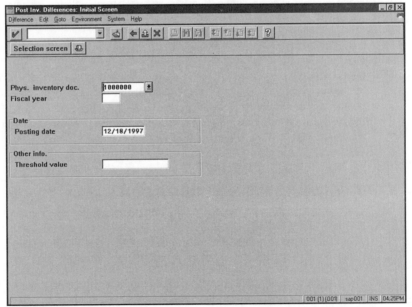

In this section the focus has been on Inventory Management. More specifically inventory movements and physical inventory were discussed. These items were described in detail and instructions for performing specific transactions were outlined. The work processes covered in this section include: performing a goods receipt for a purchase order, performing a transfer posting to move stock from quality inspection to unrestricted, and performing a cycle count for a material.

The Inventory Management sub-module of the Materials Management modules is integrated with many other modules in SAP. The Financial Accounting module is directly affected when goods movements that create accounting documents and post general ledger accounts are performed. Although it was not covered in this section, many goods movements also create costing documents used by the Controlling module. The Material Management and Sales and Distribution modules are integrated because all issues for deliveries to customers are goods movements to satisfy a customer order created in Sales and Distribution. Production Planning and Materials Management are integrated because goods movements are used to issue goods to production and receive goods created in production into inventory. These are only a few examples of the integration between Materials Management and other SAP modules, but it shows that a transaction performed in one module in SAP can have far reaching effects in many other SAP modules.

Accounts Payable

This chapter has taken a close look at the business transactions involved in purchasing and inventory management. The final piece of the purchasing process is payment. There is no free lunch, as the old saying goes. In business terms this final step is the management of accounts payable.

The accounts payable system is the accounting structure for vendors. Within SAP, accounts payable is deeply integrated in the purchasing system where items like deliveries and invoices are recorded for each vendor. Each of these transactions within SAP creates a material document that automatically posts a corresponding FI record. This means that an accounts payable posting automatically updates the general ledger. Dependent on the different transactions involved, various general ledger accounts are updated. Various reporting functions allow for the monitoring of open items and the creation of a variety of accounting reports like a balance list.

Posting Accounts Payable Documents

Prior to processing postings within SAP, the appropriate master data must be set-up. Elements like the Vendor Master, Material Master, and General Ledger must be properly established. The set-up of these master data elements has been discussed in Chapter 6, "Data Types in SAP R/3."

The accounts payable system within SAP utilizes a document methodology. This means that for a posting to occur, a zero balance must exist between the credit and the debit. Additionally, all necessary document data must be provided. These items include amount, account number, and posting date, to name a few. If all the necessary information is not available at the desired posting time, only a preliminary posting can occur, or in other words, the document is parked.

There are a couple of document types that can be posted through the accounts payable system in SAP. These are

- Invoice
- Credit memo

Take a quick look at processing these two documents types.

Invoices   To enter and post a vendor invoice using SAP, follow the menu path:

> **Menu Path:** Accounting > Financial Accounting > Accounts Payable > Document Entry
> > Invoice
>
> **Transaction Code:** F-43

Enter the necessary header information such as company code, document date, posting date, document type, and possibly currency. Once the header data has been completed, line items can be added. The individual line items will require information such as the vendor account number and the posting key. Once the document information has been properly supplied, including any line item detail information, follow the menu path Document > Post to complete the transaction. The system will update both the vendor account balance and the general ledger account balance.

Credit Memo   To enter and post a credit memo using SAP, follow the menu path:

> **Menu Path:** Accounting > Financial Accounting > Accounts Payable > Document Entry
> > Credit Memo
>
> **Transaction Code:** F-41

Enter the necessary header information such as document type, posting key, and the vendor account number. Once the header data has been completed, line items can be added. Enter the vendor line item and complete the entry by debiting the sales or revenue account. Once the document information has been properly supplied, post the document.

Payment

SAP comes equipped with a payment program designed for processing both domestic and foreign payments to both vendors and customers. It creates payment documents that are fed to a media program designed to print checks. SAP is delivered with most standard payment methods already defined in configuration.

The process of conducting a payment occurs in three steps. The payment program processes any open item and determines if it should be listed on a payment proposal. Once the proposal is created, the program can make payment by posting the appropriate documents and structuring the data for check printing. Finally, the checks, or as SAP terms them, the print forms, are output.

This completes the purchasing loop from demand to payment. As you can see, the functionality within SAP is very powerful. As always, this power with SAP comes from the impressive integration the system provides.

Purchasing Department with SAP R/3

Looking at the purchasing organization at Electro Tech, you see an organization that is somewhat splintered. There is a corporate group in the Cincinnati head office, but each plant is responsible for purchasing its owns goods and services. For high-volume, big-dollar items, the corporate office specifies the allowed vendors. For localized special items, the plants' Purchasing departments handle the vendors. While this sometimes provides flexibility, it just as often creates overhead in administrative records for the various smaller vendors. Unlike the production-planning group, the purchasing organization did not choose to redesign their organizational structure. They did, however, adapt the job functions to those suggested by SAP.

Manual systems are now integrated—not only to the other planning functions of the organization, but also among the corporate headquarters and the plants. Paper systems have been replaced by SAP.

Understanding the Purchasing Department with SAP R/3

In Chapter 16, "A Day-in-the-life of Purchasing and Goods Receipt," you met Ted Goldfield, who has been in Purchasing for Electro Tech for 30 years. He designed every system that the Purchasing department ever used and was a big part of the BPS team that put in SAP for Purchasing. Many of the things SAP offered pleased Ted, but there were those things that concerned him—the visibility of inventory that had been overpurchased, for one thing.

Ted had also designed most of the forms that the Purchasing department used before SAP. There was no question in his mind that handling these forms online was much better, but he did miss seeing his forms being used. All things considered, though, he was a big supporter.

The Players

The following is a list of the employees involved in the Electro Tech purchasing example:

- Ted Goldfield—Purchasing Manager
- Cindy Kendall—Buyer
- Bryan Luther—Plant MRP Controller
- Lester Elkins—Quality Inspection Supervisor
- Tom Norr—Maintenance Supervisor

The Situation

Ted and his staff used to spend most of their time interpreting the production schedules and inventory reports to determine how much material to buy. With SAP, this is no longer necessary. The MRP runs that are produced by Bryan Luther and the other MRP controllers create purchase requisitions that can be converted to purchase orders.

Likewise, finding the right vendor was a hassle. Making sure they were on the approved list from corporate, or that the quality management group had not rejected them, was difficult. Paper and problems were plentiful until SAP came along.

SAP's Approach

On this particular morning, Ted starts his day early with a cup of coffee and a copy of the local paper. As he sits in his office, he sees the members of the Purchasing department filter in. He has learned to enjoy these occasional moments. It wasn't so long ago that as soon as he walked through the door he was faced with some emergency. From time to time he still is, but as he sips on his coffee, he can't help but think how things have gradually improved since SAP went live.

At first it was difficult getting used to working online. Everyone in the Purchasing department was used to working with paper requisitions, paper purchase orders, and printed reports. SAP enables them to create requisitions and orders online from their reports. There were those who resisted this transition, but eventually everyone was won over. Now, instead of chasing problems, Ted actually gets to manage his department and buyer staff.

One of the buyers that has quickly accepted the new system and its online approach is Cindy Kendall. Reacting to an MRP run that had occurred over the weekend, she begins to work through a list of materials for which she is responsible. She calls up the stock requirements list for each material to see if there are planned orders that need to be converted to purchase requisitions. This is only necessary for items that can be manufactured in-house or purchased. The items that are purchased are automatically converted to purchase requisitions or schedule lines. This process makes life simpler, but Cindy is aware that a great deal of planning had to be done to make it possible.

The BPS process for Purchasing involved both Cindy and Ted. They worked with buyers from their corporate office to define the purchasing organization and the responsibilities of its employees. The definition of suppliers through Vendor Masters, Purchasing Info Records, and Source Lists allows corporate purchasing to control from what companies materials can be bought. Ted, as the manager of the small plant purchasing group, was also given the security rights to maintain these master data records. This allows the plant to define vendors for small-dollar items that corporate does not need to control.

The purchasing BPS process also involved Bryan Luther, Lester Elkins, and Tom Norr. Bryan's group creates the schedules that pass requirements to the purchasing organization. Lester Elkins's incoming inspection laboratory has to monitor incoming shipments so that goods receipt inspection plans are defined. His staff also defines the Quality Info Records that monitor the quality status of a vendor. For maintenance, many of their purchases are for spare parts and tools. Tom Norr helps establish minimum inventory levels and reorder points for spares and works with purchasing on requisitions for tools. SAP helps by creating purchase requisitions from maintenance orders.

From the Purchasing department's point of view, a complex process that is impacted by many different groups was made clearer and, at the same time, organized by SAP's capabilities. After

Cindy converts planned orders into purchase requisitions, she can use the requisitions as a reference to create a purchase order. In fact, a purchase requisition, a request for quote (RFQ), or a contract can be referenced to create a purchase order. Once the purchase order is created, it can be passed to the customer by printing and mailing it, faxing it, or EDI.

Paper requisitions are no longer lost. The controls on where items can be purchased have been improved. Requirements from the Production Planning and Maintenance departments are better managed. Simply put, SAP has made Ted and Cindy's jobs easier.

Ted has also found that he chases fewer problems with deliveries. He and his staff still have to manage delays from the suppliers, but the Purchasing Info Records allow them to see which vendors have on-time delivery problems. When the material hits Electro Tech's dock, it is easy to track in the system. The receiving dock, the quarantine area, and the shop floor supply area are all defined as a storage locations in SAP. This allows Ted to look at inventory through the stock overview and see if material is being held. The sticker system used by the incoming inspection lab is no longer utilized either.

Goods receipts are automatically posted to inspection stock and an inspection lot is created to manage the material while it is under test. Lester Elkins and his lab personnel now control the flow of this stock through the system. Once a lot has been inspected, the usage decision allows them to post the material to unrestricted stock without leaving the confines of the lab, and without stickers.

Through the use of the Quality Info Records, Lester is able to specify whether a source inspection, a goods receipt inspection, or both should occur. By tying the vendor's quality system to the requirements for the material, screening can occur on which suppliers can provide materials. Here again, SAP has made managing the complex requirements of purchasing quality control easier.

As Ted gets into the flow of his workday, he does think of how things have changed, and how they didn't change. When he first heard about SAP and its great capabilities, he and many others thought that jobs might be eliminated. He thought that if all Electro Tech's processes could be linked and seen online, fewer firefighting activities would occur, meaning the required staff would decrease. During the BPS process, however, he began to realize that what SAP does is take a company out of the reactionary mode and into a planning mode. By planning materials, vendors, and business practices thoroughly in advance, the number of crises did decrease, but the employee count did not. Accurate, detailed planning and maintenance of the corresponding master data takes a fair amount of resources. It is better to front-load those resources, though, rather than back-load them to chase problems that have already occurred.

Electro Tech has even realized improvements in its payment practices with SAP. Financial transactions are triggered through inventory movements, such as goods receipts. This has helped link payments to receipts.

For Electro Tech's Purchasing department, the integration between production planning, maintenance, quality management, financial, and the procurement activities has been successful. Ted thinks to himself that you can't beat a cup of coffee, a newspaper, and a successful day's work.

The Assessment

The purchasing arena demonstrates the integration of SAP as well as any area.

- Control of approved vendors is managed through SAP with both corporate and plant personnel involvement.

- Purchase requisitions, schedule lines, and purchase orders are created electronically, either as a result of an MRP run or manually.

- Goods receipt and quality management activities are integrated. The status of goods receipts is managed online.

- MRP demands are passed from scheduling to purchasing via paper reports.

- The system allows review of MRP results by product group, MRP controller, vendor, production line, and class. This allows for an organized division of work for the buyers.

- Deliveries are managed online, eliminating the need for a *Hot List* printed report.

- Tight integration among Purchasing, Production, Quality Management, and Accounting improves the overall business.

Financial and Other Metrics

CHAPTER 20

A Day-in-the-life of the Accounting Department

In this chapter

Whether a company is a one-man shop or a global organization with thousands of employees, certain measurements must be taken to analyze company performance. It has been said, "If you can't measure it, you can't improve it," and, "It's only practice until you start counting." Many of these measurements or *metrics* are financial measurements, so a quick and accurate analysis is important.

Another old saying goes, "Figures don't lie, but liars figure." This suggests that data is only as good as the analysis conducted on it. The truth is that many things affect the collection and analysis of data. In the quest to improve the profitability of a company, however, the case of data availability and logical presentation of that data is important. This is where SAP excels.

SAP is designed so that real-time transactional data required to operate the company is modeled by the financial organization. These transactions generate real-time updating to the detail and General Ledgers within SAP. This concept—from the perspective of an accounting organization—is revolutionary. In a world that is attempting to reduce the cycle time of all operations, relying on batch updates of the financial implications of these operating cycles is both inadequate and counter-productive. SAP has linked the generation of activity with the generation of financial metrics to assist evaluating the economics of that activity.

Understanding Financial Metrics

John Jeffery Donaldson, or J.J. as his friends and coworkers call him, is a long-term employee and accounting manager at Electro Tech. He was one of the first college recruits with an Accounting degree hired by Electro Tech for its management-training program. J.J. helped design many of the current legacy systems in the organization. Over the years, he was often called on to work on financial packages that were selected to replace the existing legacy systems.

The latest combination of financial packages operating at Electro Tech includes the basics: General Ledger, Accounts Payable and Receivable, and Fixed Assets. The remainder of the Accounting department's information requirements are supported by home-designed and programmed solutions built by personnel in the Information Systems (IS) department.

J.J. is considered an expert at Electro Tech's accounting systems because he knows how each one was designed and how all of Electro Tech's non-financial systems interface with the accounting systems.

The Players

The following is a list of the employees involved in the Electro Tech accounting example:

- John Jeffery "J.J." Donaldson—Accounting Manager
- Tim Warren—Asset Accountant
- Sheila Graham—Accounts Receivables
- Horace Brock—Production Analysis
- Frank Brewer—Quality Control Analyst
- Tim Dalton—Budgeting Supervisor

The Situation

In financial operations for many companies—Electro Tech included—accountants are dependent on non-financial systems to generate appropriate (if not accurate) journal entries. Into the 1990s, it was typical for companies to rely on legacy systems to perform multiple tasks, report on operations, support other departments' reporting, and support the company's financial accounting operations. Because of this, companies have adapted their approach to performance and analysis in order to optimize their performance with the systems provided to support this activity.

Most systems are designed or acquired for specialized and singular use. Because of budget constraints and, in many cases, limited availability of functionality, the IS departments of corporations spend significant time determining how to achieve the broadest objectives from these limited-use systems.

Customer Service support systems are used for inventory control. General ledgers are used for project control. Production reporting systems are used for MRP or cost accounting. It is the job of the MIS department and other various departments to develop solutions to their own internal requirements by using as many of theses systems in combination as necessary. It is the requirement of the MIS department to transfer the data between the systems as effectively as possible. It is the responsibility of the users to reconcile the systems or persevere in order to use whatever information is provided to them as reasonably as possible.

What is needed is a truly integrated system, without redundancy, that would not require the MIS department to get in the middle of the operation to transfer data, information, and knowledge between organizations. What is needed is the concept that SAP operates under—full, real-time, transactional integration between business functions.

The Problem

J.J.'s current problem centers around a new companywide report writer that the IS department installed over a year ago. It was installed to overcome some significant reporting issues. The Accounting department's primary responsibility is to generate budgets, departmental performance reports, and the company's standard financial reporting package—income statement, balance sheet, and cash flow. There is little time for the staff to analyze or research other information.

At their regular management meetings, the operations managers find it more and more difficult to answer senior management's operations performance questions. Additionally, operations management is hiring a more sophisticated management team. This new generation of manufacturing or marketing employees know something about computers and feel that they want to analyze their own operations, and not let this be done by those *ivory tower* accountants who don't understand the operations anyway.

Therefore, the MIS group purchased this new reporting system with funding from Operations. The system is designed to allow users to use English language commands rather than highly formatted computer jargon in order to produce reports from the company's systems.

As J.J. sees the problem, non-accounting people generate reports on performance without the usual disinterested objectivity that accountants provide. Also, without a deep knowledge of how the data is developed in the system, the reports are not completely accurate, nor can these reports be reconciled back to the financial reports that J.J.'s boss, the controller, is required to produce for the senior management team.

Here is the dilemma. In order to analyze information in a time frame that can resolve problems, the normal information generators—the accountants—are too busy. However, the people that need the analysis and are closest to the problems that need to be solved are not sophisticated enough to generate objective reports.

Often, J.J. and the other accountants are called on by management to re-analyze the reports generated by operations to insure that they are accurate and appropriate.

It is two days before the month-end closing at Electro Tech. Reports are coming in from overseas. J.J.'s team has to consolidate these reports. It is always a problem because the Asian operations close on the fifteenth of the month in order to send their reports to the U.S. in time for the month-end closing. Normally, Asian operations sends results for a 30 day period, but sometimes, in the interest of time, the report represents different periods. It is only at year-end that the information coincides—and this is because U.S. operations don't close year-end until February.

In the U.S., most of the accountants are busy reconciling the various accounts in the general ledger. These accounts are reconciled at least once a quarter to insure that they never get far out of balance. The asset accountants are reconciling their fixed asset accounts and determining the appropriate depreciation charges to be sent to the management accountants in order to close the divisional books.

The MIS organization is beginning to perform its end-of-month routine. All the non-financial business systems are being closed, and the information is being run through the various home-grown reporting systems to generate the necessary financial information for reporting inventory, sales, cost of sales, production variances, and so on. These operations have to be complete by the first work day of the new month if the schedule for closing is to be met.

J.J.'s staff has expanded over the years as the requirements for closing grew. It is recognized that J.J. has 2 or 3 more people than he needs for the non-closing time of the month, but, because closing occurs 12 times per year for periods of 15–18 workdays, that only leaves about one week for him to be "overstaffed," and he desperately needs those people to catch up on the work that can't be performed due to closing requirements.

After J.J.'s staff completes its reporting—and this is usually one day before senior management requires it—he has the responsibility of determining what information in the reports will get the most concern from management. Once identified, J.J. will spend the evening and tomorrow morning chasing down the appropriate people who know something about the information so he can write additional notes for senior management.

J.J. has a template that he uses for this analysis because there is always a repeating condition that had to be explained. "Sales were down this month due to… and this caused Electro Tech to be 20% below budget…"or, "…introduction of a new line of products caused unfavorable production variances as… and this caused Electro Tech to spend 15% more than budget."

It always seems to J.J. that his management knows more about what he is writing than he does. Sometimes, with the new report writer, J.J. gets comments from the senior management team that questions the accuracy of the balance sheet or income statement. Questions like, " J.J., Mark Smith from Production reported that inventory was down and inventory turnover was better than prior months. However, your financial reports show that inventory is higher and sales is somewhat lower. How can Mark report one thing and you another? Please check YOUR work and get back to us ASAP."

While these requests come in, J.J. still has the responsibility of orchestrating the timing for closing each of the individual financial software packages that contribute information to the financial closing. Each of J.J.'s professional accountants is responsible for a different package.

Tim Warren, the Asset Accountant, spends his time working between the Accounts Payable System and the Asset Management System to insure that they are in balance. In addition to that responsibility, he has to insure that the company's Capital Project System and the home-grown maintenance reporting system provide the necessary information required to keep the Asset system up-to-date and verifiable for the regular audits that Tim has to endure. Tim pub-lishes a monthly closing schedule for his operations and coordinates the results with J.J. so that the accounting closing is as efficient as possible.

Sheila Graham is responsible for reconciling the Sales and Receivables Systems and reports inventory balances from the *Customer Service Inventory system*, another homegrown system. Sheila and her staff spend a significant amount of time tracking down shipments made between plants in order to reconcile in-process transactions and accruals. She also has to make sure that all shipments are properly recorded and that her inventory reports are consistent with the sales reports and the production reports generated by Horace Brock.

Sheila's problems are the easiest of any of the accountants' to resolve. The sales reporting system is scrutinized by management everyday. Unlike most of the other systems that the Accounting department uses, this system is cleansed by operations BEFORE the accountants received the reports. This doesn't mean that they are accurate. However, it does mean that all sales that should be reported are in the report.

The inventory system that Sheila has to reconcile is not part of the sales system. Therefore, after the MIS department transfers the information between the systems and reconciles incon-sistent reporting, Sheila and her staff have to correct all other errors. The journal entries that Sheila makes to correct the inventory balances are primarily made to reduce negative inven-tory on some products to zero or positive inventory.

Horace Brock and his staff have the responsibility of analyzing the *Production Reporting system*, another homegrown system. Horace's responsibility includes reconciling the Accounts Payable System for raw material in production and inventory, the Payroll for production employees, and the Personnel systems to insure that the reports accurately reflected the payroll benefits. Horace's staff is also responsible for validating the Plant Operations Production, Raw Material Purchasing, and Variance Reporting systems.

With all the other reports he has to deal with, early on Wednesday morning J.J. receives a call from Frank Brewer. J.J. and Frank are friends, although they rarely socialized outside the walls of Electro Tech. Accounting and Quality Control are both controlling departments for the company but, as far back as either J.J. or Frank can remember, there has never been a time when their organizations were invited to the same meetings. Even with this little contact, Frank and J.J. have become confidants. "J.J. this is Frank, I need some help associating cost with scrap rates on Production Line 6," says Frank.

Much like the Accounting department, Quality Control has certain reports they have to provide to upper management on a monthly basis. Production also has to generate monthly reports. The problem is that now that a variety of people can produce reports using the new report writer, there seem to be three versions of the same data. Production claims that scrap is down so costs are down, and Frank wants to see the data for himself.

While J.J. knows that Frank is probably correct, the company's cost collection system makes it difficult to pinpoint the cost of scrap and rework. While the production schedule calls out a specific quantity of parts to be manufactured, this doesn't necessarily guide the production line. If there aren't enough components available to make the requested quantity, production makes as many as they can. On the other hand, if it is convenient to make more than what is scheduled, production does so. Intermixed in all of this is rework. If bad parts are discovered from a previous production run, it is not uncommon for these parts to be reworked during a new manufacturing run. These parts incur added labor costs, and these costs often are not properly recorded.

"Frank, I'd like to help you, but we are in the middle of the month-end closing right now. You know they've cut my staff lately and have asked me to reduce overtime as well so that we can make budget," says J.J. "The Accounting department is so deep into putting together the 'Book' that it will be a few more days. Can it wait?" The tone of J.J.'s statement makes it clear that he is not a fan of the staffing cuts or the reports that he is required to produce with his limited staff.

Frank has been through this before and knows he has limited options—he can try to analyze the accounting information himself or he can wait a few days.

"J.J., the problem I have is that we are looking to sell a large order to a new customer and we think that, with your numbers, we may be pricing too low. On the other hand, if we raise the price to cover your cost information, we're afraid we could lose the customer. Marketing just told me this morning that they don't trust the numbers and they are in paralysis until they decide what costs are correct. I wish I had more time, but I'm afraid that I will have to analyze your information, and I have no understanding of what your people do. HELP!"

"Listen, Frank," J.J. says as politely as possible, "this happens whenever Marketing decides to do something. They wait until the last minute and expect us to perform cartwheels to deliver the information. I know it is critical. I know we need new customers. I also know that if this were more important to them, we would have a system to perform this activity more accurately and in a more timely fashion, but management doesn't feel the need to spend the money. I also know that I have no choice but to get something to you as quickly as possible. Will tomorrow be OK?"

"Listen J.J., that's great. If you can get me the actual cost by tomorrow, I can compare it to what manufacturing is saying so that we can make the best possible decision. Tomorrow by noon, no later? Please?" asks Frank. "By noon, look, I gotta run," J.J. replies.

It is only morning, thinks J.J.; he can call home and say he is going to sleep at the office in order to get the "Book" out and complete Frank's request by tomorrow. Without seeing what Production reports as the cost of the products in question, J.J. feels that he is in some jeopardy reporting his information, but he also knows that Marketing knows what they were going to do and only want the appropriate information to support their plan of action.

The Solution

Reconciling these systems in order to provide financial integrity to the reports is a full-time job. Over the past several years, Horace, J.J., and plant management have had regular meetings in order to develop enough integrity out of these systems from production personnel. When Horace first started to improve these systems, he got significant resistance from production because, as they said it, "Our first responsibility is to make the product, and we barely have enough resources available to do that effectively. If you want us to report the information accurately for Accounting, you're going to have to put some of your people in the production plants or train our people to give you what you want."

After years of working together, the plant has finally started to report information accurately enough to eliminate most of the correcting entries that Horace's group has to make. At last count, in order to close the production accounting operation monthly, Horace only has to correct 20% of the transactions.

In addition, Horace initiated a monthly cycle count procedure to insure that some of the inventory is reported correctly for balance sheet purposes. The inventory adjustments that accounting make had finally been reduced to 5% of the inventory value per month. This was too high by a factor of 10 for Horace, but significantly reduced from two years ago when every entry was wrong and all of the inventory was corrected significantly during the semi-annual physical inventories.

To deal with Frank Brewer's requirements for the monthly Quality Control reports, J.J. has to take inventory of the information that he needs:

- The Production Reporting System—Where the actual production information (what was made, how much material and time was used, and how much was produced) is kept.
- The Bill of Material System—Where the assembly bill is kept so J.J. can determine how much product should have been made and how long it should have taken to make it.
- The Variance Reporting System—Where a monthly calculation of the difference between production and production standards are booked for the month. There is no production variance by job currently available.
- Indirect Cost Reporting System—Where the cost of production, other than direct materials, is charged to the product. This system is used primarily to determine inventory costs. Each month, one variance is booked by plant for each indirect cost (labor, benefits, operating expenses, other fixed costs).
- The Payroll and Purchasing System—In order to determine what costs are charged to production

J.J. is familiar with analyzing requests like the one that Frank has made. He knows just where to go to get the information. J.J. also knows that there is no way that he or anyone else can provide accurate, definitive information to assess Frank's request. In addition, he knows that nobody can refute his calculations. (At one time, J.J. would submit his information rounded to the nearest dollar. However, management was appalled and requested more detailed analysis from him. He now submits all analysis to precisely 4 decimals, however accurate.)

J.J. completes his analysis in an Excel spreadsheet and submits the answer to Frank on time. He never hears another word about the analysis and never hears that the analysis generated some level of activity either to perpetuate what was being done on the #6 Production line or to eliminate waste there.

Tim Dalton has been the Electro Tech budget supervisor for the last five years. He and his staff of three are responsible for preparing the plans for the company's annual budget and supervising its completion. In addition to this responsibility, Tim is responsible for coordinating the three quarterly pro-forma forecasting activities and generating the five-year financial forecast. Tim is an accomplished spreadsheet user, as is his entire staff.

Tim has often wondered why everything his department generates is on Excel while nobody in any other department uses his spreadsheets for anything. Tim's organization is responsible for collecting the information for budgeting from each organization.

In an attempt to control the total budget, budgeting activity for the succeeding year starts at Electro Tech during the summer. Tim sends reports to all managers summarizing their current expenses and the company guidelines for the next years' expenses. The spreadsheet that Tim sends has room for each manager to enter, by type of expense, how much they expect to spend.

Later in the summer, Tim sends out additional spreadsheets to the appropriate managers asking for sales quantity, revenue expectations, inventory levels, production requirements, and manpower needs.

Later, Tim sends out requests for Capital budgeting requests.

By autumn, all of the reports have been returned and Tim and his organization use the information to develop detailed budgets for the senior management committee. In early November, Tim submits his detailed budget and summary reports to the management committee. Within three weeks, the committee returns the information—with corrections—to Tim. Prior to Christmas, Tim's busiest time, he corrects the details to support the requirements of management and distributes these final reports to the operations managers for their review and understanding. Only in the rarest situations do these budgets get changed after the management committee approves them.

Upon completion of Tim's exercise, he submits all of his reports to J.J.'s department so they can enter the spending budgets into the general ledger. All of the other supporting activity required of the operating departments (changes in bill of material, purchased material delivered pricing, capital projects identification, and so on) are performed separately from the financial operations and generally are not available to J.J. or Tim except on an as-needed basis.

J.J. develops the pro-forma balance sheet and income statement preparation. He also generates the business unit income statements. It is these statements that actual results will be compared to throughout the year to assess Electro Tech's business performance.

The Assessment

As you follow the operations at Electro Tech, you see how much effort they spend just to get information to a point where they can act on it appropriately. Looking at the problem points, you see:

- Lack of integration in the data collection systems makes information difficult to obtain and analyze.
- The company metrics are determined by what can be derived from antiquated systems rather than business needs.
- Accurate pricing is impossible because cost collection is inaccurate.
- Production variances cannot be explained due to the poor understanding of the variances.
- Budgeting is doomed to failure since real costs are not understood.

CHAPTER 21

Making the Move from Accounting Past to SAP R/3

In this chapter

How to define and maintain a scope related to the implementation of the financial measurement processes

How breaking the entire business process into five levels helps build a clearer definition of required activities

The content of the financial section of the SAP R/3 Implementation Guide

The SAP R/3 Business Navigator and how it aids in defining business processes

Throughout this book, you have gained an understanding of the problems Electro Tech has experienced in its attempt to gather timely and useful data that successfully provides to management an accurate assessment of the organization's success in achieving its desired objectives. Every enterprise struggles with developing the optimal set of performance measurements. However, regardless of the metrics chosen, any company can employ a process that effectively implements their chosen metrics.

As presented in Chapters 9, 13 and 17, the core fundamentals of the implementation process require a thorough analysis of the company's current business processes. Next, any re-engineering needed should be performed. Then, specific activities should be mapped to the specific SAP R/3 functions. Finally, document all process and procedural changes, make required adjustments that result in efficient and streamlined processes, and obtain agreement on the new operating practices. Consistent with the approach of this book, this chapter is based upon actual application experiences of the Business Process Simulation (BPS).

Understanding Finance and Controlling

Leading a company from a life without SAP to the SAP promised land demands a hard look at the metrics that define success for the enterprise. Before starting any SAP R/3 implementation, it is advisable to define the metrics by which the organization will be judged. This allows the system to be configured properly and provides a steady objective with tangible results.

The purpose of any business is to make money and yet the metrics managers are judged by often have little to do with profit or loss. Up time on a machine or idle time by an operator often take precedence over making money. Many companies get so wrapped up in whether a machine is running that they fail to look at whether the machine is making salable parts. Supervisors often think that if a floor operator is not busy every second of the day, they are loosing money. This misconception often leads to the manufacture of unneeded parts, increasing inventory and thus costs. Establishing proper metrics before entering the Enterprise Re-engineering Process (ERP) can help ease the change process and make implementing SAP R/3 simpler.

Within the finance and controlling arena, the transition from pre-SAP to post-SAP often requires several procedural and culture changes. Typically, both executive management as well as middle management believe their existing framework of financial and performance measures does not provide the information necessary to determine the proper course of management actions. In fact, if asked, most of those in a managerial capacity would tell you that they maintain and rely upon their own "scorecard" of specific measures relevant to their involvement in the business. They pay little attention to the "official" scorecard (such as the standard financial reports issued by Accounting) as they have lost faith in its usefulness.

Usually, the majority of the information provided is developed or compiled by accountants, and at best, the information may reveal comparisons of actual performance with established goals. However, it does not tell the story of what events drove the results. Management must then request that their analysts research what happened, and unfortunately, by the time an analyst determines the cause, it's often too late to take corrective action.

The Scope

The fundamentals of scope management were discussed in great detail in Chapters 9, 13 and 17. The theory of controlling both the validity and time frame of the project is essential to understand. As it relates to the implementation of the financial business processes, scope management is critical. The scope of the implementation project must be defined so that all resources involved focus their effort on tasks that result in successful implementation of those processes agreed to be "in-scope." It is very easy for an implementation to fall behind schedule or become over budget when scope is not relentlessly managed. During an implementation, as the team members learn about SAP, they become exposed to new capabilities not available in their legacy system's environment. Likewise, they become enchanted with learning about business practices employed by other companies (as told by outside consultants). As the team becomes exposed to new ways of doing business, they may devote some efforts toward implementing new capabilities or other processes that are "nice to have" items. While it is important for an organization to strive for continuous improvement through the constant examination and validation of its business processes, some limits must be established. Otherwise, the critical business requirements identified in the project justification may never be implemented.

Accordingly, early on in the project, the finance transformation team must identify those critical business requirements to be addressed by the implementation. For example, if Electro Tech does not send dunning notices to customers with past due credit balances, then the dunning process would be identified as out of scope. This decision would require a commitment by all team members to limit their efforts and decisions toward those identified in the scope document. Periodically throughout the project, scope may need to be reevaluated. However, until the all transformation teams and project sponsors agree to scope changes, no efforts outside of the agreed scope should be allowed.

The Basic Team Definition

Within the financial realm there will likely be several BPS teams. This is necessary due to the diverse elements involved in the finances of a business. One team may look at how to set up and control the General Ledger, while another deals with the cost accounting structure of the company. In the case of finance, teams could include the areas of General Ledger, external regulatory financial reporting, internal management reporting, cost control analysts, cash management, credit, accounts payable, budgeting and forecasting, product cost, customer invoicing, payroll, fixed asset managers, and inventory to name the major points.

The breakdown of these subjects helps define the skill sets of potential BPS team members. A strong client representation must form the core of the BPS team. While various types of consultants are frequently involved, it is the client representatives who must claim the process decisions made as their own.

Beyond the specific teams needed for development of the companies accounting structure with SAP, the financial organization must take on an added burden. The inclusion of accounting staff on BPS teams with financial implications can prove invaluable.

Part
V

Ch
21

Teams, such as Shop Floor Execution, that touch on the collection of actual hours and material costs and sale's review of the billing process *both* have financial implications. While the individuals involved in these tasks may think they know the easiest or best way to conduct these business tasks, they may not understand the full financial effects of their decisions.

It is true that in order to achieve success throughout the BPS process, client involvement should consist of a small number of individuals who are able to provide full representation of the functional areas involved. However, to accurately structure the business process, the dollars and cents of the business must be considered. While it would be nice to have full-time accounting representation on each team, it is probably unrealistic to expect such resources. J.J. Donaldson, who you met in Chapter 20, might make a good team member on many of the BPS teams. In the Electro Tech BPS process, he served as a team leader for several of the financial teams and also acted as part-time consultant to a few others. Keep teams small so decisions can be made, but be certain to address all underlying issues.

Selection of suitable people to the BPS team has a lot to do with reducing the number of people required. More than anything else, the ability of those individuals selected to make decisions is key. Few things in the SAP implementation process are more frustrating than to place together experienced, knowledgeable client representatives only to find that they are unwilling to commit to process decisions within their own areas of expertise. It is possible that an occasional poor decision will be harmful to the overall BPS process. It is a certainty that indecision will always be harmful.

In order to gain and maintain support from upper management on the decisions made by the BPS team, the team members must possess excellent communication skills. If they are unable to communicate the merit of their decisions to their superiors, the ability to make decisions will be lost. In most cases, upper management representatives are mainly interested in the overall strategy to be applied, the risk incurred by the switch to a new strategy, and the benefits expected from it. BPS team members must be able to represent their decisions within these boundaries. At the same time, those same BPS team members will often be called upon to describe the detailed business transactions to individuals at a more operational level.

Business Process Simulation

The financial BPS process provides a forum by which a structured view of current accounting techniques, desired practices, and a transition from one to the other can occur. This focus may be applied at all levels of the accounting processes beginning with a broad, overall view and working down to the actual, individual transactions necessary to conduct business. Perhaps more importantly, the numerous integration points between everyday business activities and financial requirements may be itemized and controlled. A process whereby the structure is derived in four distinct levels has proven to successful in this analyzing a large organization.

Level 1: Enterprisewide

The overall SAP implementation is viewed from an enterprisewide vantage point. Relationships between separate business requirements are depicted. In the case of the example firm Electro Tech, the Level 1 flow would depict the overall business functions of the firm but with little detail (see Figure 21.1).

FIG. 21.1
A Level 1 process flow
for Electro Tech.

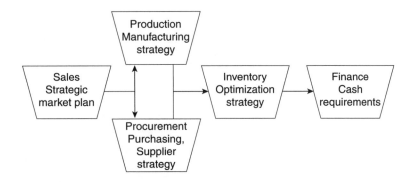

Level 2: Inter-Function Process Flows

Within a company, the relationships between the business functions are depicted in Level 2 flows. For example, the link between Purchasing and Accounting in terms of accounts payable are specified (see Figure 21.2).

FIG. 21.2
A Level 2 process flow
for the financial BPS
team.

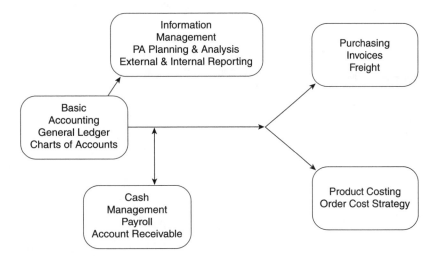

Level 3: Intra-Function Process Flows

Within each specific accounting function, such as cost accounting or asset management, the Level 3 process flows are derived. As an example, a Level 3 process flow for Electro Tech's Accounting department might depict the steps required to conduct a month end closing (see Figure 21.3).

Level 4: Transactions

For each action described within the applicable Level 3 process flow, the actual transactions to be performed are presented as can be seen in Figure 21.4.

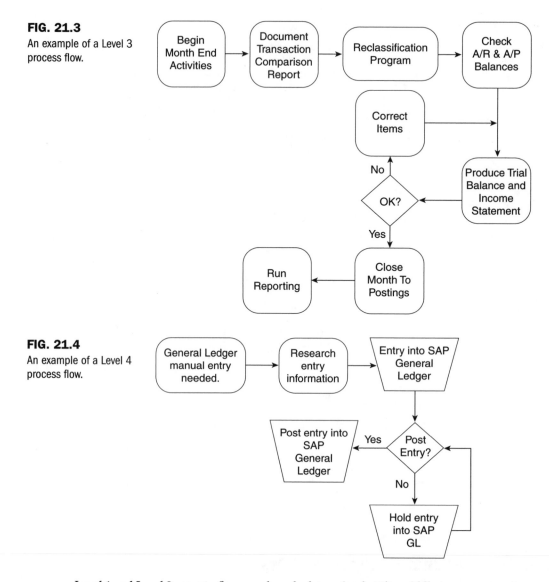

FIG. 21.3

An example of a Level 3 process flow.

FIG. 21.4

An example of a Level 4 process flow.

Level 1 and Level 2 process flows are largely determined at the middle to upper management level. In this way, the desired high-level operating strategies for the entire enterprise are specified. These strategies serve as guidelines for the derivation of the necessary Level 3 and Level 4 process flows. The real meat of the BPS process occurs in the derivation of the Level 3 and Level 4 flows. It is here where the actual business transactions are defined and the links between them are specified.

Because of the large number of issues at hand, record keeping becomes an increasingly important element of the BPS process. Prior to the initiation of Level 3 activities, the creation of a suitable BPS workbook can prove to be an enormous subsequent time saver. Through the use of such a workbook, the intended scope and direction of the BPS sessions can be better controlled. In essence, the workbook serves as a BPS roadmap. However, the workbook itself is to be considered a living document, subject to modification as necessary.

Hopefully, modification to a BPS workbook will consist of additions of detail rather than gross changes. This issue deserves some additional consideration. When properly established, the entire business process can be examined through the combination of many BPS workbooks.

In order for the BPS to offer the complete documentation of the new process design, any system-enabled processes must be documented. Specifically, if the detailed process flow references the performance of an SAP transaction, documentation must be completed in the form of a *script* or instruction explaining how to execute the transaction. This script should explain what steps a user would follow in the system to successfully perform the transaction. If specific requirements or procedures existed in relationship to the transaction, those too would need to be documented. For example, internal accounting control policies may require some segregation of duties with regard to the calculation of standard costs (from the product cost rollup) and the actual revaluation of inventory that results from the changes in the standards since the last calculation.

In addition to documentation of the as-is process, the to-be process, and required detail, the BPS should also address the following areas.

- *Resolution of any issues which arose out of the new process.* For example, prior to the implementation of SAP, Electro Tech's inventory accounting system may not have been able to track an operating supplies inventory. For this reason a company may have, for simplicity, recorded an expense upon receiving such items from a vendor. However, the implementation of both FI and MM would allow the inventory items to be monitored and accounted for upon the actual consumption of the items (as opposed to upon receipt from the vendor). This would mean that in the new environment, the receipt of these items would result in an increase in inventory on the balance sheet, as opposed to an immediate recognition of expense. Such a change in accounting treatment may need to be documented and reviewed with the appropriate parties like the company's internal and external auditors, the corporate treasury or tax departments, as well as director of accounting policy and procedure.

- *Documentation of specific system configuration considerations.* For example, a position paper may be needed to document the decision of how to configure the system with regard to the timing of recognition financial statement variances from standard cost related to the production of a product. The system will allow variances to be recognized periodically, even if the production cycle is not complete for the order. In this case the system compares actual expenditures to a variable target cost estimate based upon the production activities completed. Alternatively, the system can be configured to only recognize financial statement variances from standard cost upon full completion of the production cycle. In this case the variance would be based upon a comparison of the actual costs incurred versus the standard cost of the materials produced. The position paper should explain the configuration decision made, the alternatives considered, and a discussion of how the decision made best fits with the designed processes and company objectives.

■ *Policy and procedures.* In order for the new processes to be enabled, certain policies and procedures may need to be implemented. Any new or modified policies and procedures need to be documented as part of the BPS process.

■ *System start-up/data conversion issues.* From a technical standpoint, certain old system data must be mapped to new system data. For example, the BPS should outline how the General Ledger account data will be loaded from the old system.

■ *Other technical requirements.* Any technical issues that impact the implementation of the process must be addressed in the BPS. For example, the specific sequence of events to be performed at month-end to insure that all cost allocations are performed must be documented.

Financial Management

As obvious as it seems, it is not uncommon for employees to lose sight of the fact that a business exists to make money. The greatest challenge that faces the Finance BPS team is one of educating the participants from the Production, Procurement, and Sales and Distribution organizations on what required financial controlling objectives must be met.

Next, and equally important, the financial team must seed an education in those fundamentals that ensures optimal management of the core business processes. For example, what information is needed for a manufacturing manager to perform effectively? How does meeting a manufacturing schedule on time translate to an increased bottom line? In short, it is important for the financial manager to gain an understanding of those non-financial performance objectives that directly or indirectly have a bearing on the financial well being and performance of the organization.

For non-financial reporting, SAP R/3 provides several ad-hoc reporting mechanisms that can include financial links. The Logistic Information System (LIS) includes Sales and Distribution, Purchasing, Quality, Production, Inventory, and Plant Maintenance reporting mechanisms. The Human Resources information system allows for quick and accurate analysis of personnel. Of course, the Financial information system allows analysis of General Ledger, Accounts Payable, and Accounts Receivable.

In a typical implementation, the Finance BPS process should offer a means to develop formal documentation of existing business processes, and related policies and procedures. These simulations also act as the vehicle to identify those critical business requirements related to the specific business process under evaluation. Once the requirements are documented, the team can develop updated business processes that reflect the business requirements as identified by the members of the cross-functional, transformation team. For example, in a manufacturing organization, a company would need to work through the manner in which the accounting process should occur for events and transactions related to the production of a product. The output of the BPS should include documentation of the old process as well as the new process to be enabled. The new process design should be documented at multiple levels of detail. These various levels of design serve different purposes and different players in the transformation process. For example, the chief financial officer of the organization may need to understand only how the cost accounting process integrates within the production process.

However, the cost accounting manager would want to understand the detail process design that illustrates every touch-point involving each detail accounting transaction that comprises the high-level process. For example, in SAP's product costing area there are a number of details and simple transactional steps required to perform a product cost rollup (a high-level process).

SAP Business Navigator

To assist in process definition, SAP provides the Business Navigator. In SAP R/3 V3.0 the Business Navigator is essentially a graphical depiction of the decision logic tree reflected in the base SAP configuration.

The Navigator is often used as an initial training aid to help clients grasp a more physical understanding of the logic and transactions within SAP. The effectiveness of the Navigator becomes increasingly apparent as the client discovers the need to configure the system to better suit its needs. The Navigator can then be used for its intended purpose, as a flexible business strategy modeling tool. By examining the many decision and action steps depicted by the Navigator, the client is forced to map out desired business practices in great detail. Such detail is necessary if subsequent configuration of the system's response is to be accomplished correctly and efficiently.

Often times, the Business Navigator is ignored or forgotten during the implementation process. Once clients become involved in the definition of their own processes, it is easy to become buried in detail and forget that a structured model exists. This is unfortunate because the Navigator's purpose is to provide a decision-making path such that total confusion and information overload is avoided for the client.

As in the case of configuration, it is extremely unlikely that the initial decision tree depicted in the SAP Business Navigator is immediately suitable to a specific organization. This is assumed. Therefore, the Navigator may be modified as necessary to reflect the client's desired decision logic. Again, SAP configuration-related tools are intended to allow the system to support the client's desired operating modes. They follow the client's desired structure. They do not impose a structure upon the client.

Implementation Guide (IMG)

The Implementation Guide (IMG) is an SAP tool that lists all the necessary settings for implementing SAP R/3, while helping control and document the implementation process. In effect, the IMG is nothing more than a graphical front-end to the configuration tables (see Figure 21.5). It is organized in a hierarchy of business functions and allows the client to quickly drill-down to the configuration settings of specific transactions.

The IMG allows the client to configure the system's options, which will direct the system's response when transacting business. This is not to say that the IMG assists the client in making process definition decisions but rather provides the method by which existing decisions may be defined to the system.

FIG. 21.5

The SAP R/3 IMG.

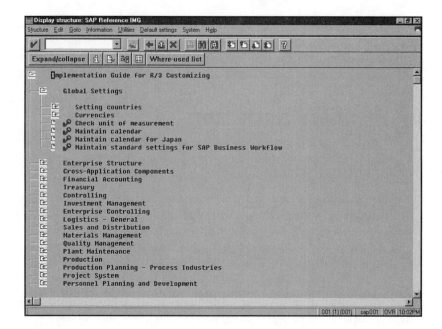

The configuration of the system from a financial viewpoint is broken down in the same manner that SAP has divided its financial modules. In the global settings, elements such as currencies, exchange rates, and the financial calendar must be defined. From a division of purpose point of view, the IMG has broken the accounting role into the parts of financial accounting, treasury, controlling, investment management, and enterprise controlling.

The financial accounting section of the IMG deals with the General Ledger, Accounts Receivable, and Accounts Payable, Consolidation, Asset Accounting, and the Special Purpose Ledger. The treasury section of the IMG includes cash management and budgeting. Controlling in the IMG includes product costing, overhead cost, and profitability analysis.

Configuration is the key to SAP's flexibility and power. Much of the integration that SAP delivers centers on the financial structure of the organization. The financial configuration lays the groundwork from which many other elements grow.

Running the Business

The purpose of a business is to make money, as has been noted. As obvious as this seems, many managers and supervisors forget this when caught up in the everyday hassle of the job. This is why the integration of SAP R/3 is so very important. With SAP, information is available at any time, from any terminal (assuming proper security clearance). If these reports reflect standardized metrics and these metrics include the necessary dollars and cents, informed decisions are made. Informed decisions tend to be good decisions.

Remember the discussion between J.J. Donaldson and Frank Brewer in Chapter 20 about scrap rates? Frank Brewer felt that only part of the story was being told. Through the use of the information systems in SAP, Frank could have researched the problem. If this is a company defined metric, a standardized method of looking at the data should exist. SAP allows for complete analysis of the problem because the financial and production information is in the same integrated system.

The financial structure and reporting, as well as the basics of the varying information systems are examined in the Chapter 22, "Finance and Reporting Functionality with SAP R/3." As stated repeatedly in this book, both the how and the why are discussed. Keep in mind that businesses do not exist to provide information, but without information, businesses do not exist. ●

Finance and Reporting Functionality with SAP R/3

At the heart of any business is the purpose of making money. Whether the business sells a material or a service (unless it is a not-for-profit organization), its goal is to realize a profit. This should not suggest, however, that any company that makes money is a strong company. The proper management of funds can play just as an important a role in a company's success. This is the role accounting typically plays in an organization.

This chapter looks at the role that accounting plays in the management of internal and external accounts using SAP R/3. The breakdown and the integration of the various accounting elements with other SAP modules are examined here. You will also examine how this integration plays a role in various reporting mechanisms available in SAP.

Understanding the Business of Making Money

A company's financial organization is typically divided into external and internal organizational units. The external organizational units represent legal corporate entities. They are a roll-up or grouping of financial data that must be reported to regulatory agencies for external investor or tax purposes. The balance sheet, profit and loss, and cash flow statements are reflections of these legal entity structures. The internal organizational units are typically grouped according to how the company wishes to analyze its business. Many companies refer to these internal groupings as departments. The SAP Financial Accounting module primarily concerns itself with structuring a company according to the external reporting requirements of the company.

Each legal entity is represented in SAP by a company code. All financial postings into SAP must contain a company code. The information systems capabilities of SAP allow for reporting all financial data based on company code. A single enterprisewide implementation of SAP will contain a company code for every legal entity recognized by the enterprise. The company code is the smallest organizational unit in SAP for which a balance sheet and profit and loss statement can be produced. The financial results of company codes can be consolidated into a company in SAP. A company can contain one or many company codes. This consolidation will be performed in the Legal Consolidation sub-module of SAP.

The Financial Accounting module of SAP contains the following sub-modules: General Ledger, Accounts Receivable, Accounts Payable, Legal Consolidation, Treasury, and Special Purpose Ledger. The six sub-modules are fully integrated and exchange data with the other SAP modules (MM and SD) so that a transaction does not have to be entered more than once. All transactions entered into SAP must post to the Chart of Accounts, which resides in the General Ledger (G/L) module. Each transaction will receive a unique document number. Transactions can originate in SD (sales order), MM (receipt of material), or other modules of SAP. If the transaction has a financial statement impact, the dollar amounts will be posted to Financial Accounting.

The Accounts Receivable and Accounts Payable sub-modules are updated based on transactions posted to Customer and Vendor Master records, respectively. The integration of SAP allows the user to view the sales-related data by examining the invoice posted to the Customer Master record in Accounts Receivable. Customer transactions are posted to the Chart of

Accounts via reconciliation accounts. Reconciliation accounts are actual accounts within the Chart of Accounts that are linked to the to Customer or Vendor Master records. Thus, a posting to the customer actually triggers an automatic posting to the reconciliation account linked to the customer in the Customer Master record.

The Legal Consolidation sub-module will allow the user to consolidate the financial results of all of their company codes. Legal Consolidation requires that a new Chart of Accounts be created that will roll up the postings from the Charts of Accounts used with all of the company codes in the enterprise. A user can perform typical month/year-end consolidation activities, such as elimination of inter-company profits, using the standard functionality offered by SAP Legal Consolidation.

The SAP Treasury System offers the tools to perform detailed cash flow analysis, budgeting, and forecasting activities. The user can determine actual present cash flow and predict future cash flows based on data residing in the SAP Financial Accounting module. This information, coupled with real-time market data and the ability to perform what-if analyses on hypothetical financial instrument portfolios, gives the corporate treasurer an integrated system providing the information necessary to maximize the enterprise's return on cash.

The SAP Special Purpose Ledger provides a database where the user can collect data stored within any module in SAP. The Special Purpose Ledger will provide summary information from the modules chosen at a level of detail determined by the user. Unique reporting requirements may require that data be combined and summarized from different modules within the SAP system. This data can then be sorted into usable reports via the SAP Report Painter or Report Writer tools.

Financial Data

Links to financials have been included in discussions of various business transactions throughout this book. This is due to the fact that SAP springs from financial roots. It is also because the ultimate goal of a business is to make money. If a company doesn't make money, it doesn't stay in business long.

The advantage of having an integrated system, such as SAP, is that financial data that has been questionable before now becomes reliable. The integration of the SAP system links business transactions, like purchasing a belt for a motor, confirming a production operation, or posting goods issue for a shipment to the corresponding financial transactions.

Once all of the configuration and master data for FI is established, transactions can be posted in FI. Transactions in FI include G/L account postings, incoming/outgoing payment, invoicing, and reversals. These postings record the real-world transactions into the system to facilitate reporting.

G/L Account Posting   A G/L account posting is used to record financial transactions that are not reflected through integration from other modules. For instance, while sales orders will make the appropriate G/L postings automatically, an entry to record interest would be done through a manual posting.

To enter a G/L account posting into SAP use the following menu path:

> **Menu Path:** Accounting > Financial Accounting > General Ledger > Document Entry > G/L Account Posting
>
> **Transaction Code:** F-02

This initial screen (see Figure 22.1) requires posting and document date, company code, and document type. The document type provides further identification to the transaction. It can, for instance, identify a vendor payment from a customer payment. It also controls portions of the transaction entry.

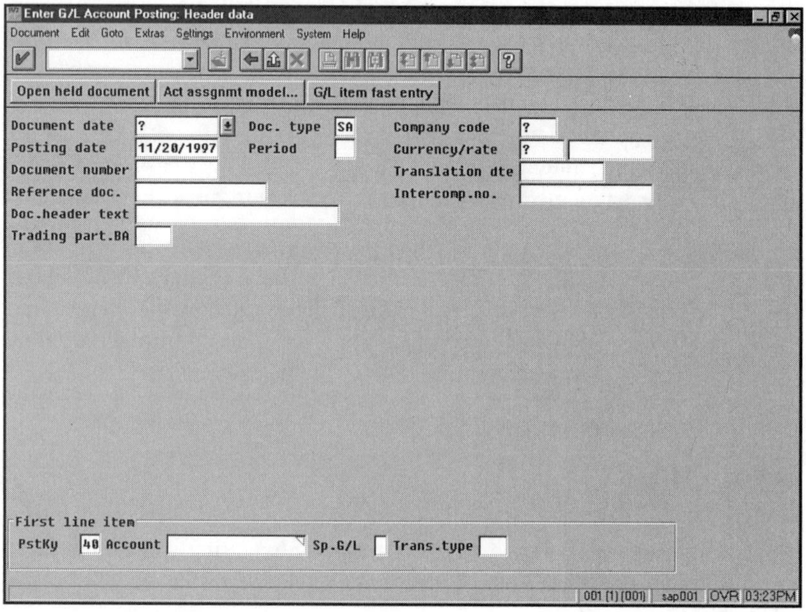

FIG. 22.1

Enter G/L Account Posting: Header Data screen.

Additionally, identify a posting key and account to be charged. The account could represent a G/L account, vendor, customer, material, or asset. The posting key determines the type of account and the debit/credit indicator.

The account/posting key combination determines the screen layout for the additional entry fields from the field status variant on the account master data, as discussed in Chapter 6, "Data Types in SAP R/3." Additional information may be required to post to the account—cost center, text, or business area as seen in Figure 22.2.

SAP validates each field for completeness and accuracy. In order to get to the next screen, all the data must be correct on the current one. Additionally, SAP verifies that the entry is in balance before it will allow the document to be posted. When the entry is complete and accurate, clicking the File Folder button will post (save) the document.

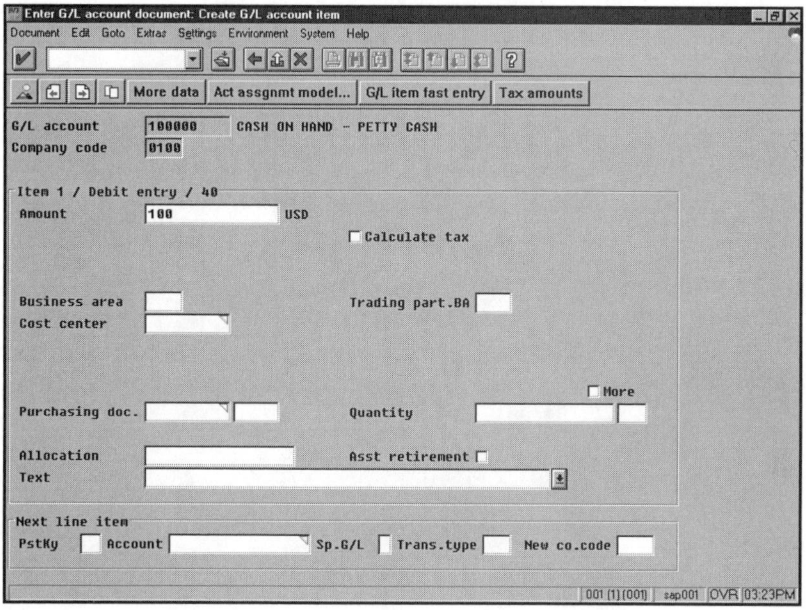

FIG. 22.2
Enter G/L Account
Document: Create G/L
Account Item screen.

Post Outgoing/Incoming Payments   For posting of outgoing/incoming payments that are not processed through automated integration of the payment program and cash application, entries must be manually posted to clear the appropriate customer and vendor balances.

To enter a manual outgoing payment into SAP use the following menu path:

> **Menu Path:** Accounting > Financial Accounting > Accounts Payable> Document Entry > Outgoing Payment > Post
>
> **Transaction Code:** F-53

The initial screen (See Figure 22.3) requires data to identify the posting and document date, document type, and company code, just like the G/L Account Posting screen. This screen additionally requires the G/L account representing the bank from which the payment is made. The vendor account also is required to identify which account to clear.

The system should then return the open items on the vendor identified on the first screen, as seen in Figure 22.4. Select the item(s) that should be cleared against the payment. The total of the selected items should equal the total of the amount of the check. If it does not, the difference, if allowed, would be settled to a tolerance account. This posting will clear the line items selected while processing open items.

To enter a manual incoming payment into SAP use the following menu path:

> **Menu Path:** Accounting > Financial Accounting > Accounts Receivable > Document Entry> Incoming Payment
>
> **Transaction Code:** F-28

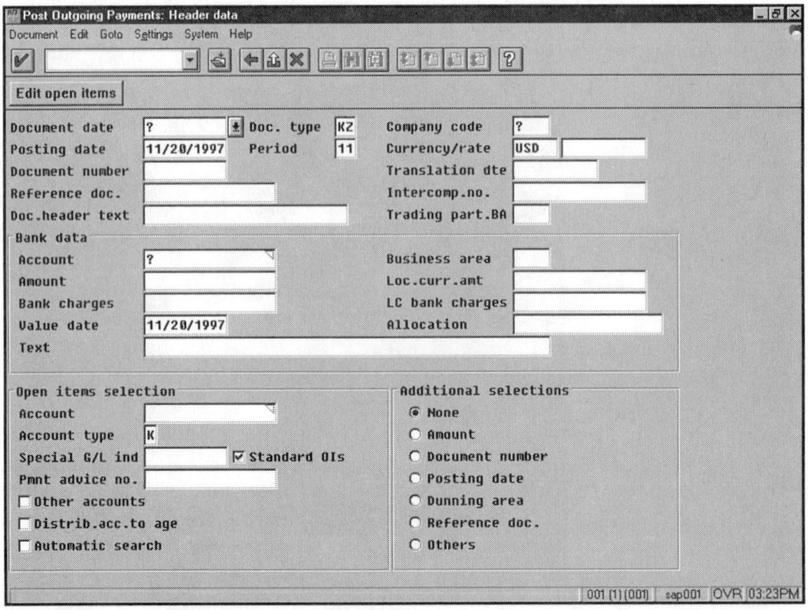

FIG. 22.3

Post Outgoing Payments: Header Data screen.

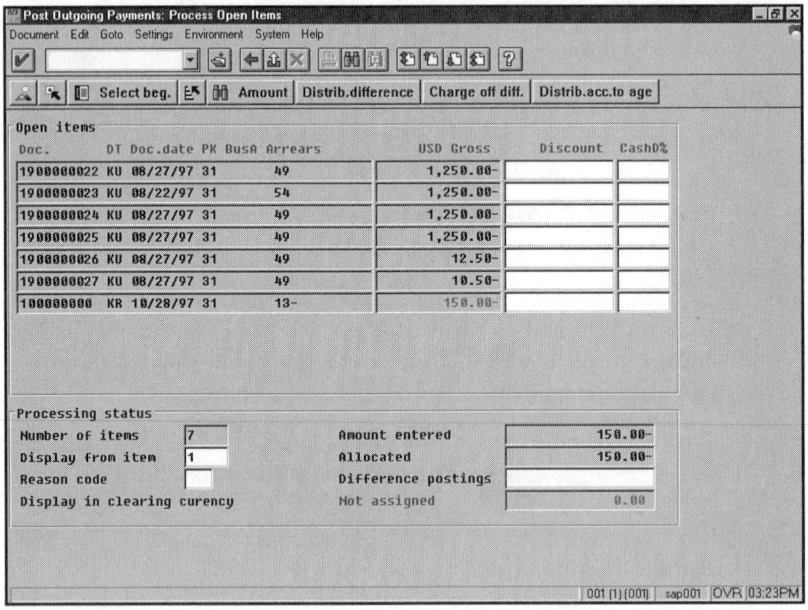

FIG. 22.4

Post Outgoing Payments: Process Open Items screen.

The initial screen (see Figure 22.5) requires data to identify the posting and document date, document type, and company code, just like the G/L Account Posting screen. This screen additionally requires the G/L account representing the bank that receives the payment. The customer account also is required to identify which account to clear.

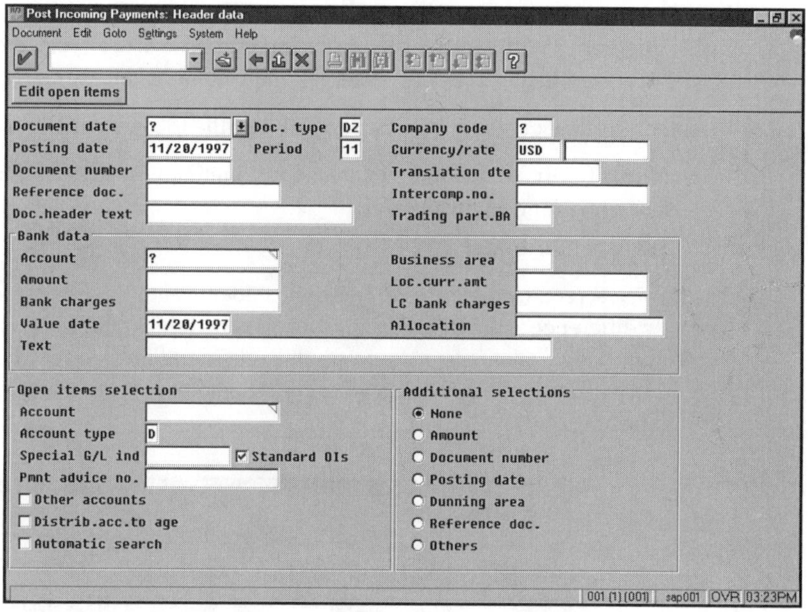

FIG. 22.5

Post Incoming
Payments: Header Data
screen.

The system should then return the open items on the customer identified on the first screen, as seen in Figure 22.6. Select the item(s) that should be cleared against the payment. The total of the selected items should equal the total of the amount of the check. If it does not, the difference, if allowed, would be settled to a tolerance account. This posting will clear the line items selected while processing open items.

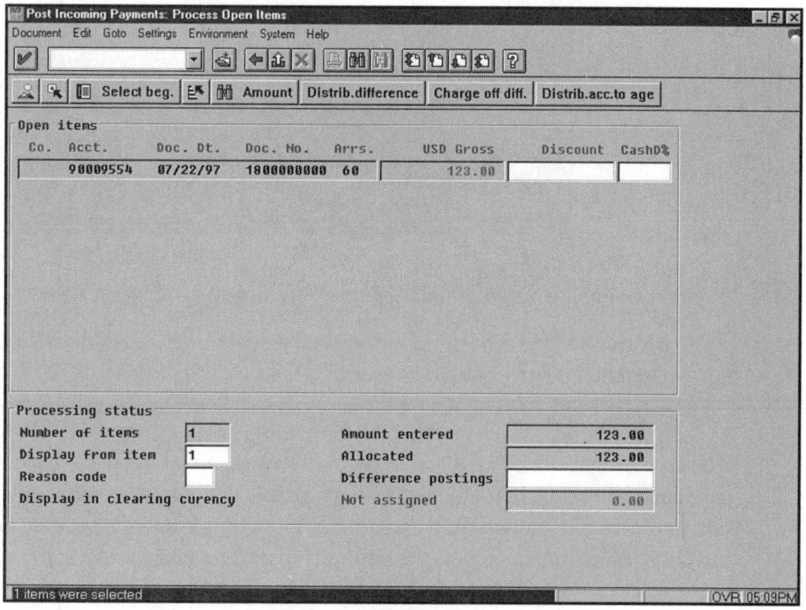

FIG. 22.6

Post Incoming
Payments: Process
Open Items screen.

Invoicing For posting of outgoing/incoming invoices that are not processed through automated integration of the sales order cycle and purchase order cycle, entries must be manually posted to record the appropriate customer and vendor balances.

To enter a manual outgoing invoice into SAP use the following menu path:

> **Menu Path:** Accounting > Financial Accounting > Accounts Receivable > Document Entry> Invoice
>
> **Transaction Code:** F-22

The invoice screen (see Figure 22.7) is almost identical to the G/L Account Posting screen. The only difference is the default values for the document type and posting key fields. Depending on the configuration, they could default to customer invoice-specific document types and posting keys. All of the same fields are required and the processing is the same as in a G/L account posting.

FIG. 22.7

Enter Customer Invoice: Header Data screen.

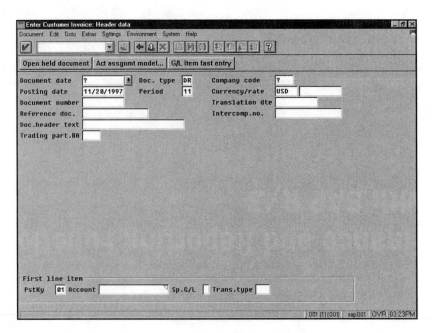

To enter a manual outgoing invoice into SAP use the following menu path:

> **Menu Path:** Accounting > Financial Accounting > Accounts Payable > Document Entry > Invoice
>
> **Transaction Code:** F-43

The invoice screen (see Figure 22.8) is almost identical to the G/L Account Posting screen. The only difference is the default values for the document type and posting key fields. Depending on the configuration, they could default to vendor invoice-specific document type and posting keys. All of the same fields are required and the processing is the same as in a G/L account posting.

FIG. 22.8
Enter Vendor Invoice:
Header Data screen.

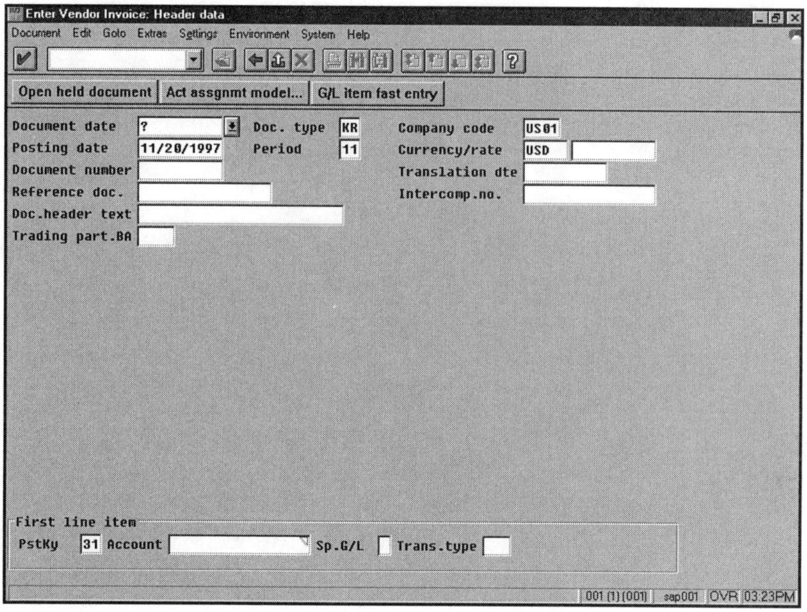

Reversals   Reversals will post a document with all of the same company and account information and dollar values with opposite signs as the original values. So for each debit entry on an original document, there would be a corresponding credit entry with the same account information on the reversal document. Since documents cannot be deleted, this allows a user to back out the financial effect of an entry.

To make a reversal entry, the user must know the document number, company code, and fiscal year of the original entry.

To post a reversal into SAP use the following menu path:

> **Menu Path:** Accounting > Financial Accounting > General Ledger OR Accounts Receivable OR Accounts Payable > Document > Reverse > Reverse Ondivid. Docs
>
> **Transaction Code:** FB08

After entering the document number, company code, and fiscal year on the screen seen in Figure 22.9, clicking the Display Document button will bring up the document. This allows the user to verify that he or she has chosen the correct document. Clicking the Save button from the Reverse Document: Header Data screen will create a document that is the reverse of the document identified.

Cost Center Accounting

As is the case with SAP's other modules, Cost Center Accounting's (CO-CCA) processing is driven by its master data. The master data governs the posting, planning, allocation, and subsequent reporting that occurs in CO. Once the CO-CCA master data is established, CO functionality can be used to facilitate the allocation of actual costs within a controlling area. These actual costs and revenues are posted to CO from the other SAP modules.

FIG. 22.9
Reverse Document:
Header Data screen.

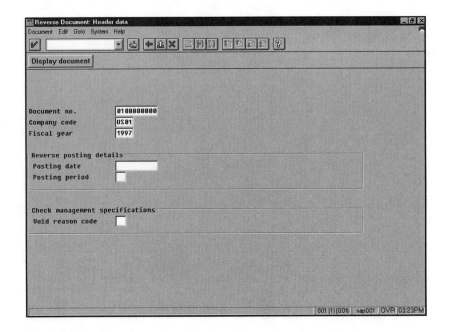

In this section, you will review the major types of CO-CCA master data and discuss the various tools available to assist in the allocation of costs within a company's organization.

Cost Elements and Cost Element Groups   Cost elements are used in cost center accounting to identify the nature of the expense or revenue of controlling transactions. There are two types of cost elements in SAP, primary and secondary. Primary cost elements correspond directly to the profit and loss General Ledger accounts configured in the Financial Accounting module. In order to create primary cost elements, a corresponding FI profit and loss G/L account must first exist. On the other hand, secondary cost elements are strictly used for processing internal to CO; no corresponding FI G/L account exists.

To create cost elements, use one of the following menu paths:

> **Menu Path:** Accounting > Controlling > Cost Centers > Master Data > Cost Elements > Create Primary
>
> **Transaction Code:** KA01

For the following menu path, the Create Primary Cost Element: Request screen will appear (see Figure 22.10):

> **Menu Path:** Accounting > Controlling > Cost Centers > Master Data > Cost Elements > Create Secondary
>
> **Transaction Code:** KA06

For the following menu path the Create Secondary Cost Element: Request screen will appear, as shown in Figure 22.11:

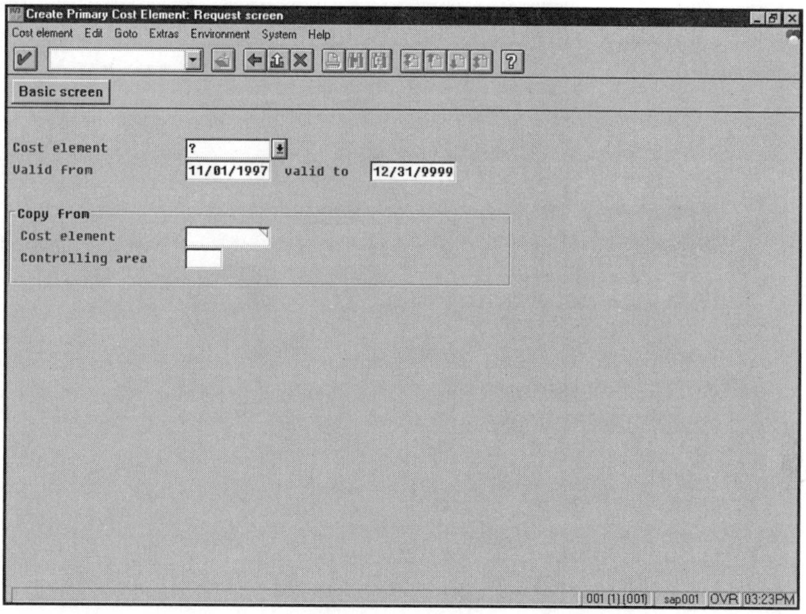

FIG. 22.10

Create Primary Cost Element: Request screen.

FIG. 22.11

Create Secondary Cost Element: Request screen.

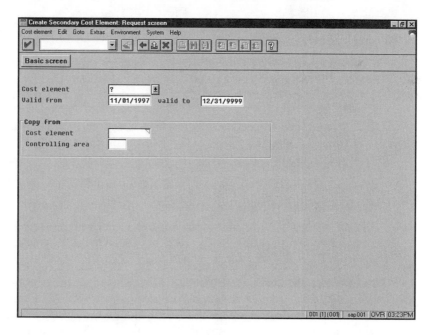

Input the cost element number to be created, as well as the Valid From and Valid To periods for the cost element. To ease cost element master data creation, reference can be made to an existing primary or secondary cost element. Select the Basic Screen button to access the Create Primary (or Secondary) Cost Element: Basic screen (see Figure 22.12).

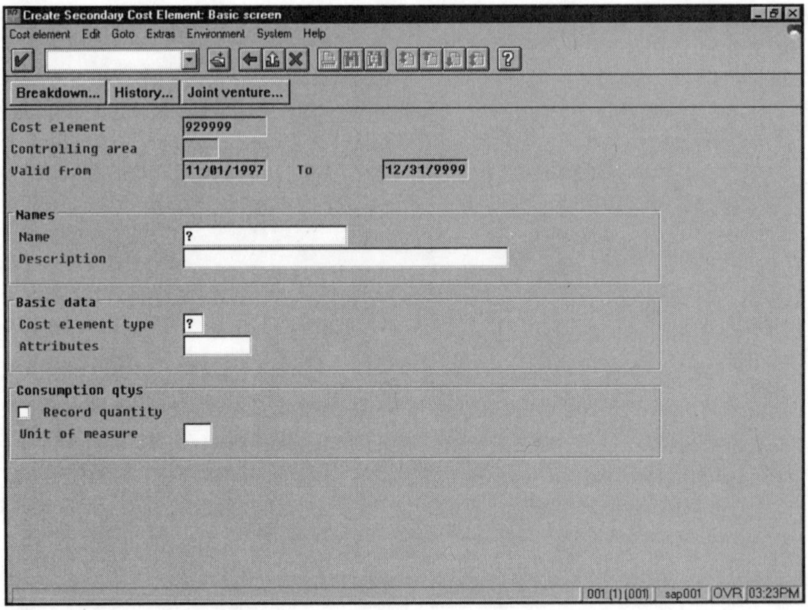

FIG. 22.12

Create Secondary Cost Element: Basic screen.

Complete the required and optional fields as necessary. Select the Save button to save the new cost element.

If a user wants to report on groups of cost elements or wants to reference a group of cost elements in CO allocations, cost element groups can be created.

To create cost element groups, use the following menu path:

> **Menu Path:** Accounting > Controlling > Cost Centers > Master Data > Cost Element Group > Create
>
> **Transaction Code:** KAH1

After specifying the appropriate cost element group name on the screen seen in Figure 22.13, select the Execute button.

Input an appropriate description for the Cost Element Group and select the Maintain Values button on the screen pictured in Figure 22.14 to input the cost elements to include in the group.

Cost Centers and Cost Center Groups Cost centers represent the lowest level of cost responsibility within an organization and are incorporated within a company's organizational structure, referred to as the *Standard Hierarchy*. Cost center hierarchies are used to group cost centers according to area of responsibility, decision making, and control to facilitate overhead cost management.

To create cost centers, use the following menu path:

Menu Path: Accounting > Controlling > Cost Centers > Master Data > Cost Center > Create

Transaction Code: KS01

FIG. 22.13

Create Cost Element Group: Initial screen.

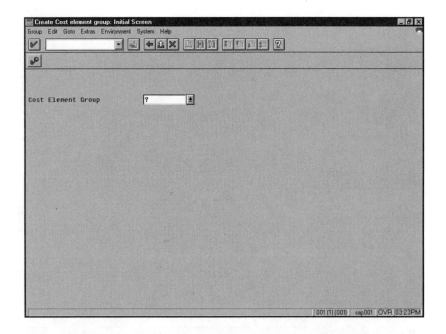

FIG. 22.14

Create Cost Element Group: Structure screen.

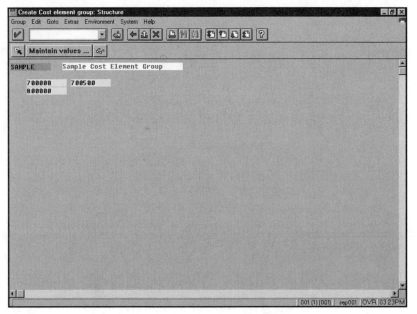

Input the cost center number to be created, as well as the Valid From and Valid To periods for the cost center (see Figure 22.15). To ease cost center master data creation, reference can be made to an existing cost center. Select the Basic Screen button to access the Create Cost Center: Basic screen (see Figure 22.16).

FIG. 22.15

Create Cost Center: Request screen.

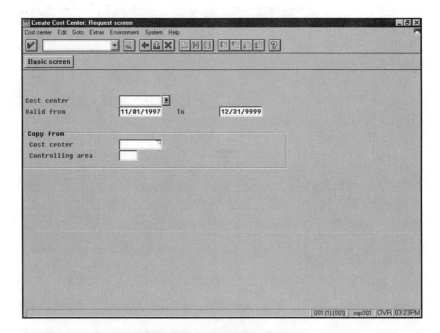

FIG. 22.16

Create Cost Center: Basic screen.

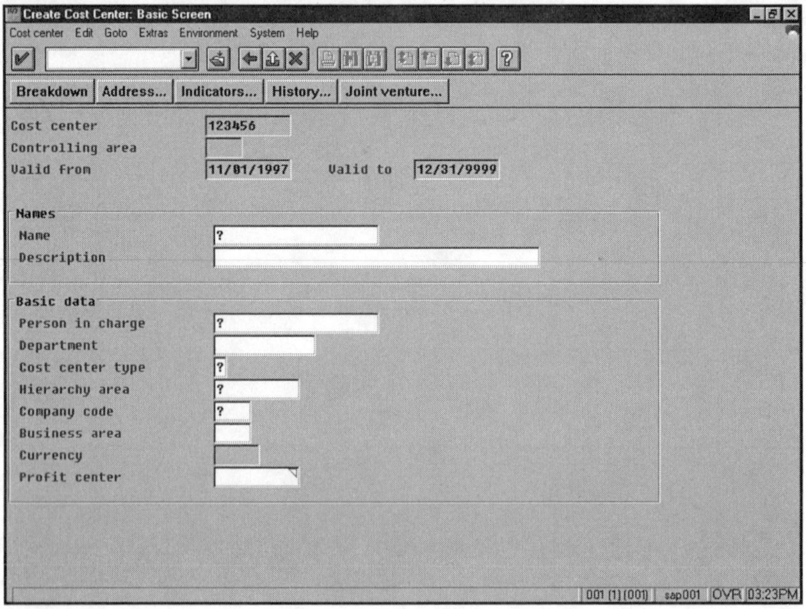

Part

V

Ch

22

Complete the required and optional fields as necessary. Select the Save button to save the new cost center.

In addition to a cost center's inclusion in the Standard Hierarchy, cost center groups can be created to facilitate cost center reporting, planning, and periodic allocations.

To create cost center groups, use the following menu path:

> **Menu Path:** Accounting > Controlling > Cost Centers > Master Data > Cost Center Group > Create
>
> **Transaction Code:** KSH1

After specifying the appropriate cost center group name on the screen pictured in Figure 22.17, select the Execute button.

FIG. 22.17
Create Cost Center Group: Initial screen.

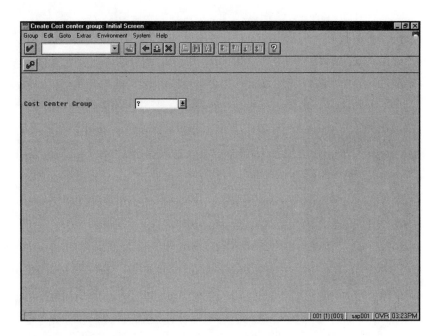

Input an appropriate description for the cost center group on the screen pictured in Figure 22.18 and select the Maintain Values button to input the cost centers to include in the group.

Activity Types and Activity Type Groups   One of the numerous cost allocation tools available in the CO module is the activity allocation, which allocate costs based upon quantities consumed for a particular good or service produced by an organizational unit of a company. Activity types are used in SAP to represent these goods and services. Secondary cost elements are assigned to each activity type so that any costs allocated using an activity allocation posting is recorded using the specified secondary cost element.

FIG. 22.18

Create Cost Center
Group: Structure screen.

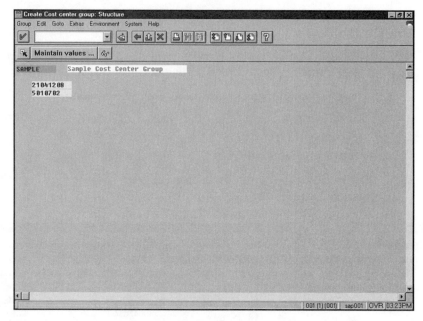

For example, a maintenance cost center may want to charge costs to all users of its services based upon the hours worked for a particular cost object. In this instance, an activity type relating to maintenance hours would be created. On a periodic basis, hours of consumption of this activity type would be recorded to allocate costs from the maintenance cost center to the cost object utilizing the cost center's services. To create an activity type, use the following menu path:

> **Menu Path:** Accounting > Controlling > Cost Centers > Master Data > Activity Type > Create
>
> **Transaction Code:** KL01

Input the activity type number to be created as well as the Valid From and Valid To periods for the activity type (see Figure 22.19). To ease activity type master data creation, reference can be made to an existing activity type. Select the Basic Screen button to access the Create Activity Type: Basic screen (see Figure 22.20).

Complete the required and optional fields as necessary. Select the Save button to save the new activity type.

To assist in reporting on activity types, activity type groups can be created. To create activity type groups, use the following menu path:

> **Menu Path:** Accounting > Controlling > Cost Centers > Master Data > Activity Type Group > Create
>
> **Transaction Code:** KLH1

FIG. 22.19
Create Activity Type:
Request screen.

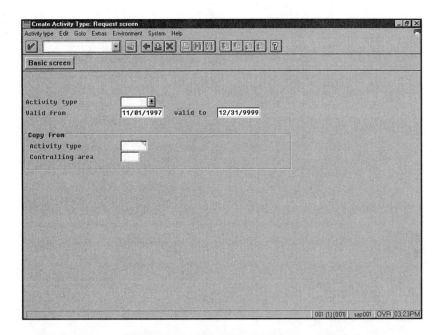

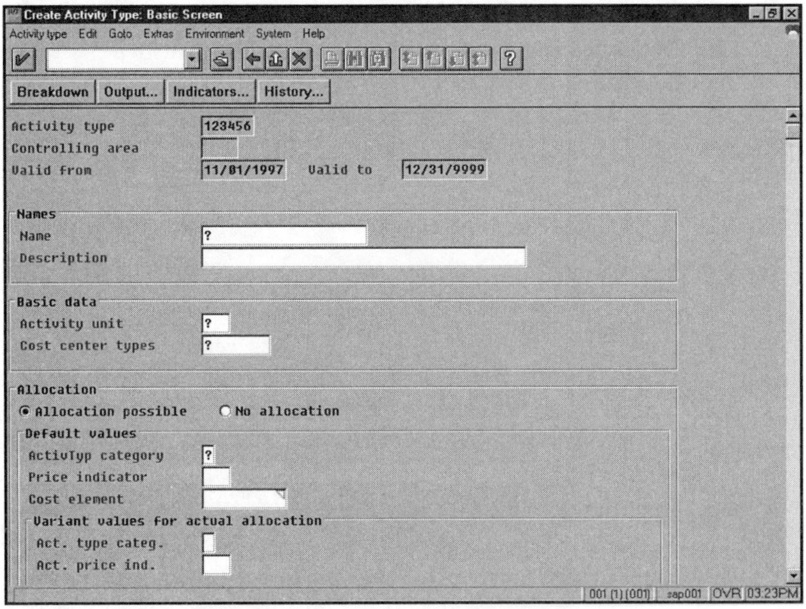

FIG. 22.20
Create Activity Type:
Basic screen.

After specifying the appropriate Activity Type Group name on the screen seen in Figure 22.21, select the Execute button.

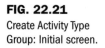

FIG. 22.21
Create Activity Type
Group: Initial screen.

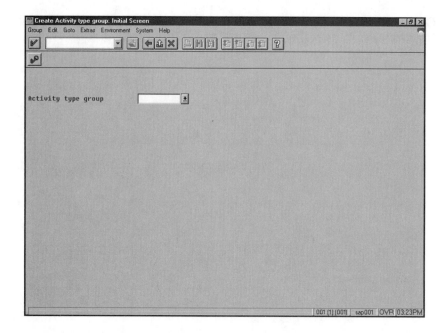

Input an appropriate description for the activity type group on the screen pictured in Figure 22.22 and select the Maintain Values to input the activity types to include in the group.

FIG. 22.22
Create Activity Type
Group: Structure screen.

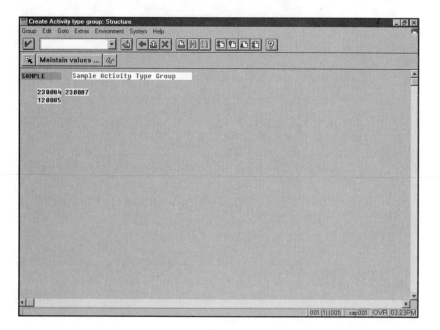

Statistical Key Figures and Statistical Key Figure Groups   Statistical key figures (SKF) can be used as the basis of CO periodic allocations. For instance, a Human Resources cost center may want to allocate its costs to all the cost centers within an organization, based upon the number of employees in each cost center. In this situation, an SKF could be created that would represent head count. Values would then be recorded for this SKF for each cost center in the company. This SKF, and its associated values for each cost center, would be used as the basis (known as a *tracing factor* in SAP) in a periodic allocation.

To create a statistical key figure, use the following menu path:

> **Menu Path:** Accounting > Controlling > Cost Centers > Master Data > Stat Key Figures > Create

> **Transaction Code:** KK01

Input the statistical key figure number to be created as seen in Figure 22.23. To ease statistical, key figure, master data creation, reference can be made to an existing statistical key figure. Select the Basic Screen button to access the Create Statistical Key Figure: Basic screen (see Figure 22.24).

FIG. 22.23

Create Statistical Key Figure: Request screen.

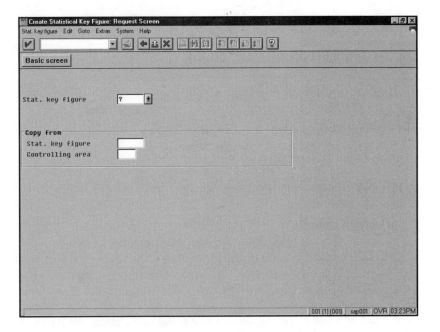

Complete the required and optional fields as necessary. Select the Save button to save the new statistical key figure.

To assist in reporting on statistical key figures, statistical key figure groups can be created. To create statistical key figure groups, use the following menu path:

Menu Path: Accounting > Controlling > Cost Centers > Master Data > Statistical KF Group > Create

Transaction Code: KBH1

FIG. 22.24

Create Statistical Key Figure: Basic screen.

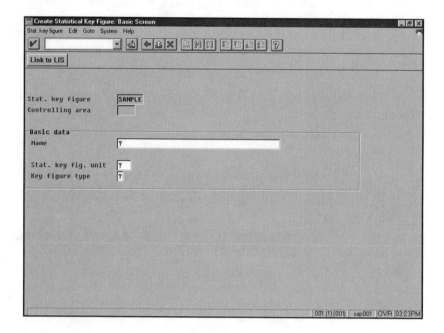

After specifying the appropriate Statistical Key Figure Group name on the screen pictured in Figure 22.25, select the Execute button.

Figure 22.26 pictures the screen where you will input an appropriate description for the statistical key figure group and select Maintain Values to input the statistical key figures to include in the group.

Activity Allocations   Activity allocation postings can be used to allocate costs between CO cost objects based upon the measured consumption of a particular activity type. Activity allocations consist of a sending cost object, an activity type, a consumption quantity of the activity type, and a receiving cost object. Activity allocation postings are posted to the secondary cost element specified on the activity type, master data record. Prior to the posting of an activity allocation, a price must be associated with the sending cost center and the activity type combination. These prices can be set using actual costs, planned costs, or a planned rate.

To post an activity allocation posting, use the following menu path:

Menu Path: Accounting > Controlling > Cost Centers > Actual Postings > Activity Allocation > Enter

Transaction Code: KB21

FIG. 22.25

Create Statistical Key Figure Group: Initial screen.

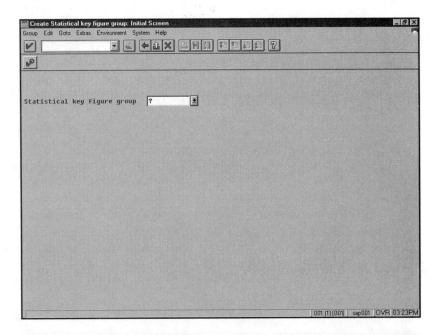

FIG. 22.26

Create Statistical Key Figure Group: Structure screen.

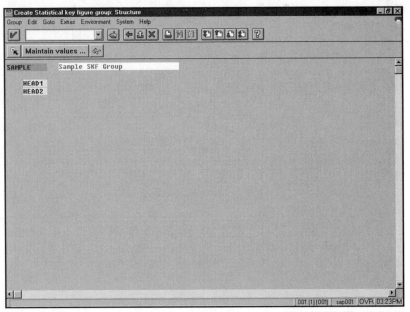

On the screen pictured in Figure 22.27, input the appropriate Document Date, Posting Date, and Screen Variant (depending on the type of receiving cost objects) for the activity allocation posting. Select List Screen to input the activity allocation posting details (see Figure 22.28).

FIG. 22.27
Activity Allocation Enter:
Initial screen.

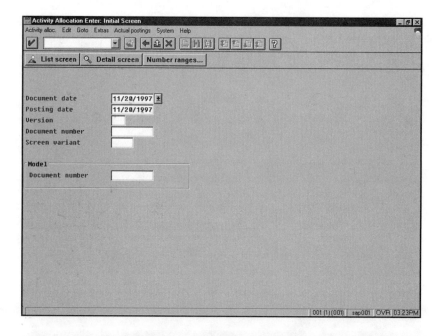

FIG. 22.28
Activity Allocation Enter:
List screen.

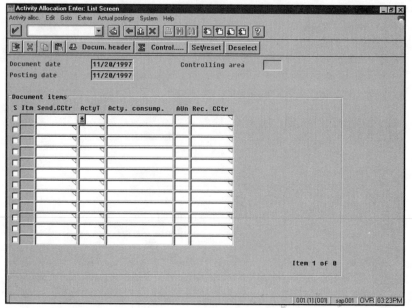

During data entry, SAP validates the sending and receiving cost objects, as well as the activity type. Once all line items for the activity allocation have been entered, select Post to complete the activity allocation.

Statistical Key Figures Postings In order for SKF to be used as tracing factors in periodic allocations, values must be posted for the necessary cost object-statistical key figure combinations. These values can then be used as the basis for an allocation from one CO cost object to another.

To complete a SKF posting, use the following menu path:

> **Menu Path:** Accounting > Controlling > Cost Centers > Stat. Key Figures > Enter
>
> **Transaction Code:** KB31

On the screen shown in Figure 22.29, input the appropriate Document Date, Posting Date, and Screen Variant (depending on the receiving cost objects) for the SKF posting. Select the List Screen button to input the SKF posting details (see Figure 22.30).

FIG. 22.29
Statistical Key Figures
Enter: Initial screen.

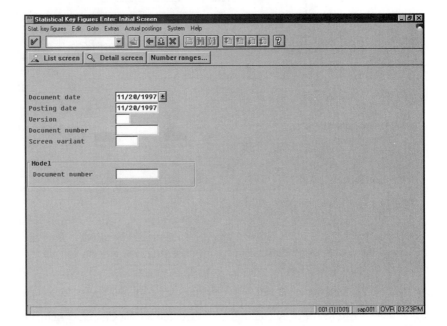

During data entry, SAP validates the cost objects and the statistical key figure. After all line items for the SKF posting have been entered, select Post to complete the posting.

Periodic Repostings, Distributions, and Assessments In addition to the use of activity allocations, costs can be allocated between sending and receiving cost objects using one of CO's periodic allocations. Both periodic repostings and distributions allocate costs while retaining the primary cost element of the sending cost object; however, distributions only allow cost centers as sending cost objects while periodic repostings allow all cost objects to serve as senders in the allocation. On the other hand, assessments allocate costs utilizing secondary cost elements, but like distributions, only cost centers are allowed as sending cost objects. When organizations are deciding which of these periodic allocation tools to utilize, consideration should be given to the types of senders as well as the level of necessary detail posted from the periodic allocation.

FIG. 22.30

Statistical Key Figures Enter: List screen.

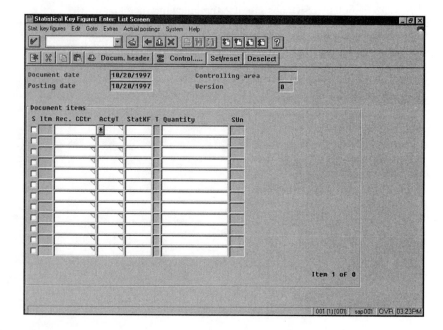

In order to execute a periodic allocation, cycles and segments must first be created. A cycle is simply a group of allocation segments that can be executed at one time. Segments contain the details (such as sending cost objects, receiving cost objects and allocation basis) of each allocation to be performed.

To create periodic allocation cycles and segments, use the following menu path:

> **Menu Path:** Accounting > Controlling > Cost Centers > Actual Postings > Period-end Closing > Periodic Repostings > Extras > Cycle > Create

On the screen pictured in Figure 22.31, input the name of the cycle to be created and the starting date for the periodic reposting cycle. To ease in data entry, reference can be made to an existing periodic reposting cycle. Click the Proceed button to access the Create Cycle for Actual Periodic Repostings: Header Data screen (see Figure 22.32).

Specify an appropriate description for the cycle and designate an ending date. Also, complete the indicators and field groups as necessary. To attach segments to the allocation cycle, select the Attach Segment button.

FIG. 22.31

Create Cycle for Actual Periodic Repostings: Initial screen.

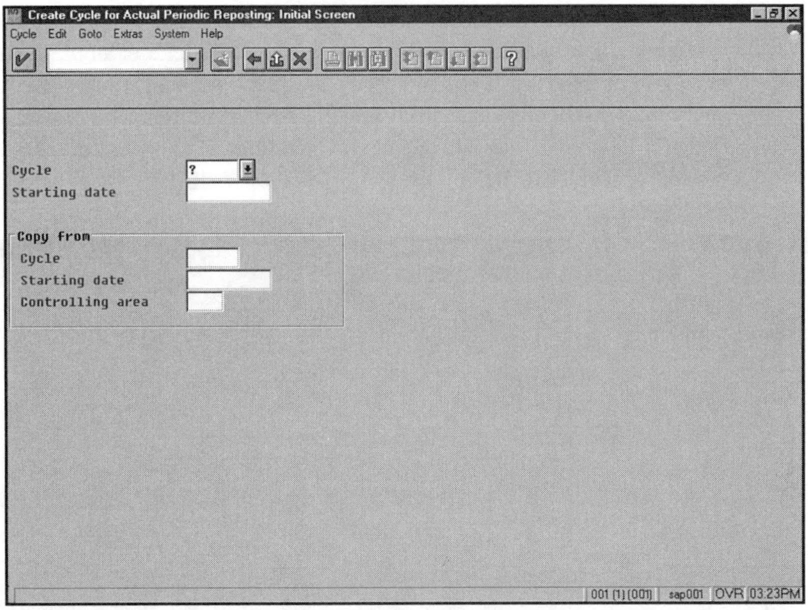

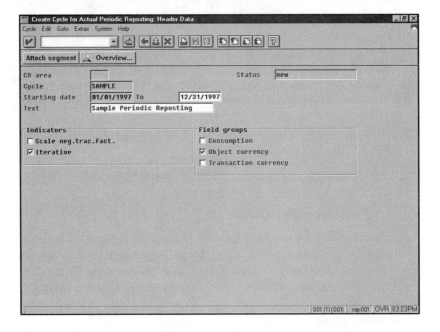

FIG. 22.32

Create Cycle for Actual Periodic Reposting: Header Data screen.

On the screen seen in Figure 22.33, enter a name and description for the allocation cycle's segment. Additionally, specify the sender value rule to be used, the portion to be allocated, and the type of costs (actual versus planned) to allocate. In the Tracing Factor rule field, identify the basis that should be used to allocate the costs to the receiver objects. In other words, the tracing factor rule identifies whether costs should be allocated from the sending objects to the receiving objects based on variable portions (an SKF, for example), fixed amounts, fixed percentages, or fixed portions. To specify the exact tracing factor values to use once a tracing factor rule is specified, select the Tracing Factors button. The Allocation Characteristics portion of this screen is used to specify the sending cost objects and cost elements and the receiving cost object for the allocation.

FIG. 22.33

Create Cycle for Actual Periodic Reposting: Segment screen.

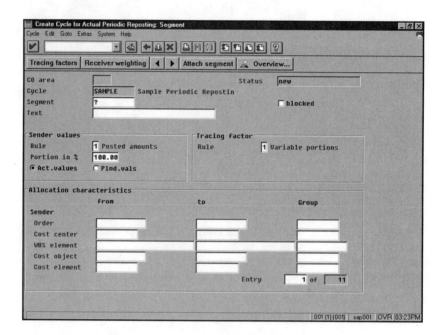

Click the Save button to save the segment, or click the Attach Segment button to create an additional segment within the cycle.

> **Menu Path:** Accounting > Controlling > Cost Centers > Actual Postings > Period-end Closing > Distribution > Extras > Cycle > Create
>
> **Transaction Code:** KSV1

On the screen pictured in Figure 22.34, input the name of the cycle to be created and the starting date for the distribution cycle. To ease in data entry, reference can be made to an existing distribution cycle. Click Enter to access the Create Actual Distribution Cycle: Header Data screen (see Figure 22.35).

Specify an appropriate description for the cycle and designate an ending date. Also, complete the indicators and field groups as necessary. To attach segments to the allocation cycle, select the Attach Segment button.

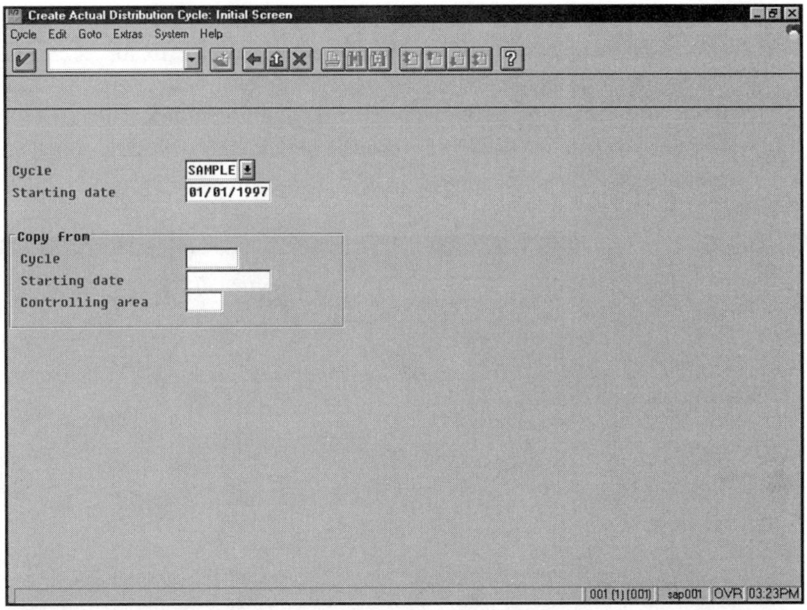

FIG. 22.34
Create Actual
Distribution Cycle:
Initial screen.

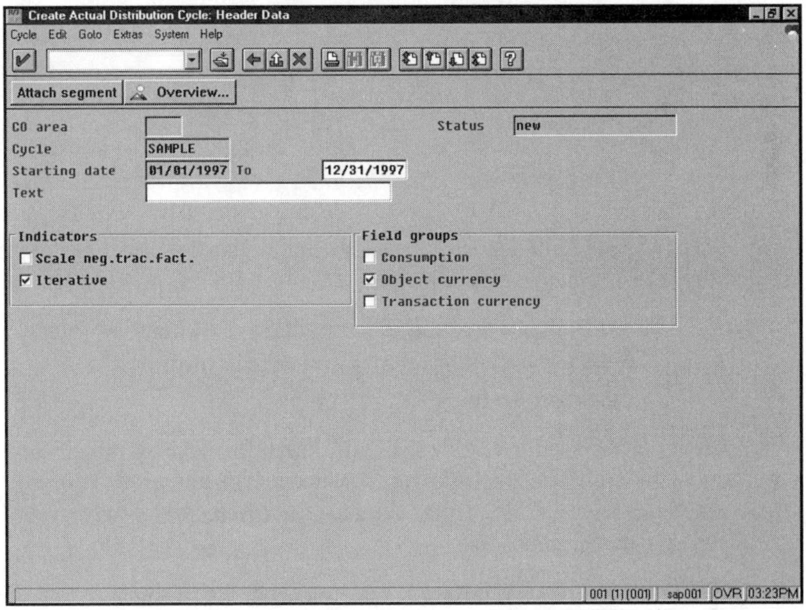

FIG. 22.35
Create Actual
Distribution Cycle:
Header Data screen.

On the screen seen in Figure 22.36, enter a name and description for the allocation cycle's segment. Additionally, specify the sender value rule to be used, the portion to be allocated, and the type of costs (actual versus planned) to allocate. In the Tracing Factor Rule field, identify the basis that should be used to allocate the costs to the receiver objects. In other words, the tracing factor rule identifies whether costs should be allocated from the sending cost centers to the receiving objects based on variable portions (an SKF, for example), fixed amounts, fixed percentages, or fixed portions. To specify the exact tracing factor values to use once a tracing factor rule is specified, select the Tracing Factors button. The Allocation Characteristics portion of this screen is used to specify the sending cost centers, cost elements, and the receiving cost object for the allocation.

FIG. 22.36

Create Actual Distribution Cycle: Segment screen.

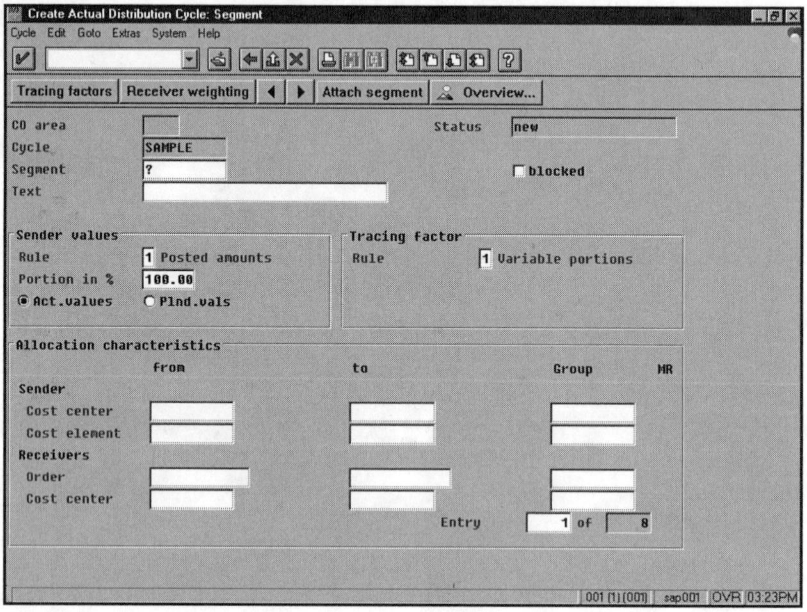

Click the Save button to save the segment, or click the Attach Segment button to create an additional segment within the cycle.

> **Menu Path:** Accounting > Controlling > Cost Centers > Actual Postings > Period-end Closing > Assessment > Extras > Cycle > Create
>
> **Transaction Code:** KSU1

On the screen pictured in Figure 22.37, input the name of the cycle to be created and the starting date for the assessment cycle. To ease in data entry, reference can be made to an existing assessment cycle. Press Enter to access the Create Actual Assessment Cycle: Header Data screen (see Figure 22.38).

Specify an appropriate description for the cycle and designate an ending date. Also, complete the indicators and field groups as necessary. To attach segments to the allocation cycle, select the Attach Segment button.

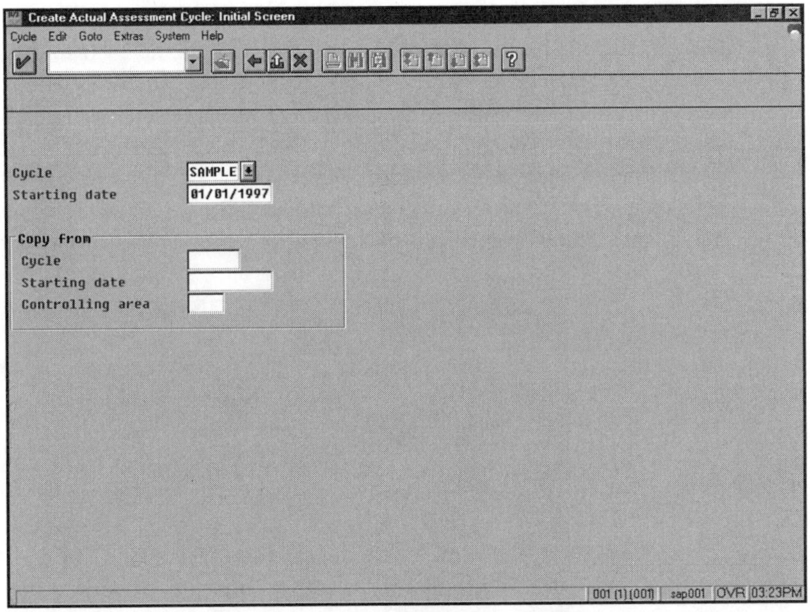

FIG. 22.37

Create Actual
Assessment Cycle:
Initial screen.

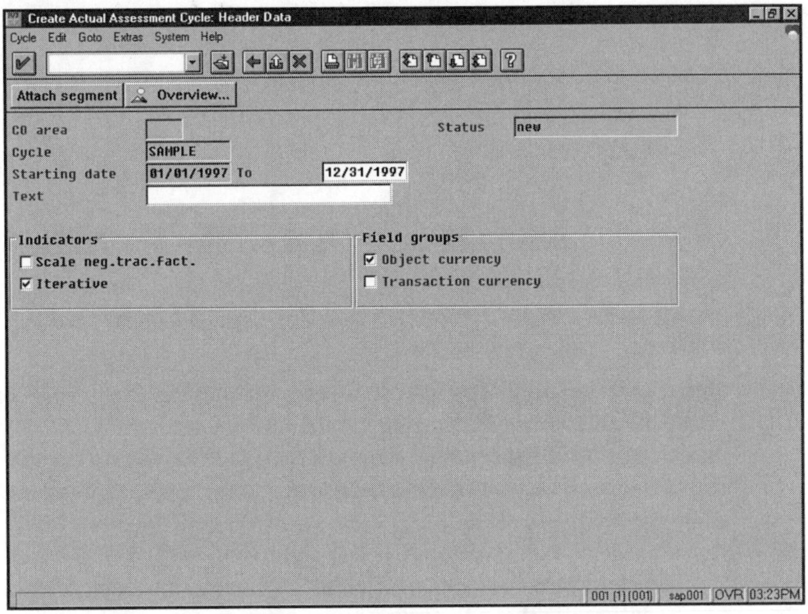

FIG. 22.38

Create Actual
Assessment Cycle:
Header Data screen.

On the screen seen in Figure 22.39, enter a name and description for the allocation cycle's segment. Since assessment allocations assign costs using secondary cost elements, the appropriate secondary cost element to be used with the assessment allocation posting should be specified on this screen. Additionally, specify the sender value rule to be used, the portion to be allocated, and the type of costs (actual versus planned) to allocate. In the Tracing Factor Rule field, identify the basis that should be used to allocate the costs to the receiver objects. In other words, the tracing factor rule identifies whether costs should be allocated from the sending cost centers to the receiving objects based on variable portions (an SKF, for example), fixed amounts, fixed percentages, or fixed portions. To specify the exact tracing factor values to use once a tracing factor rule is specified, select the Tracing Factors button. The Allocation Characteristics portion of this screen is used to specify the sending cost centers, cost elements, and the receiving cost object for the allocation.

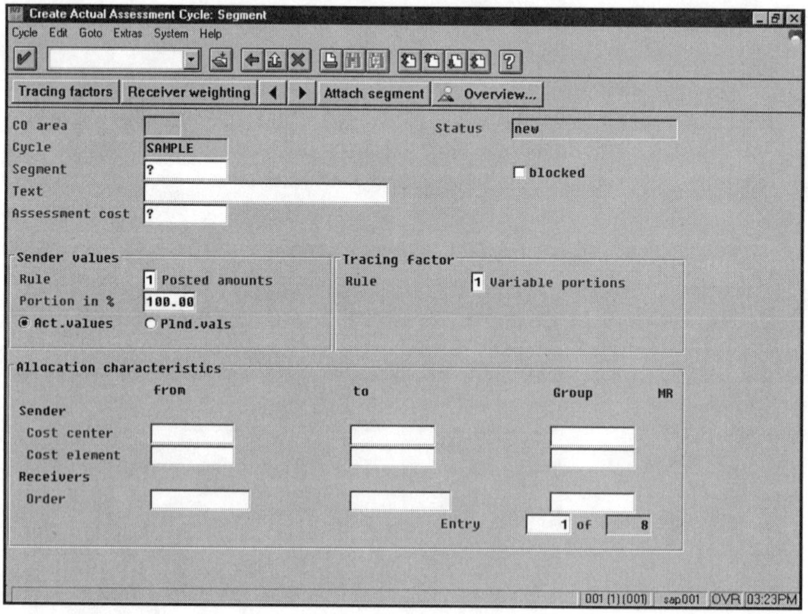

FIG. 22.39

Create Actual Assessment Cycle: Segment screen.

Click the Save button to save the segment, or click the Attach Segment button to create an additional segment within the cycle.

Once the periodic allocation cycles are created, these cycles must be executed each period to create the appropriate CO postings. It should be noted the periodic allocation cycle can only be executed once during a period. If a cycle is executed again during a period, SAP will reverse all the CO postings made by the previous execution of the periodic allocation cycle.

To execute a periodic allocation cycle, use the following menu path:

Menu Path: Accounting > Controlling > Cost Centers > Actual Postings > Period-end Closing > Periodic Reposting

Transaction Code: KSW5

Menu Path: Accounting > Controlling > Cost Centers > Actual Postings > Period-end Closing > Distribution

Transaction Code: KSV5

Menu Path: Accounting > Controlling > Cost Centers > Actual Postings > Period-end Closing > Assessment

Transaction Code: KSU5

On the screen shown in Figure 22.40, specify the period and fiscal year for which the periodic allocation cycle should be executed. Additionally, specify the cycle name(s) to execute, as well as the processing options. Select the Execute button to invoke the execution of the periodic allocation cycle(s) specified.

FIG. 22.40

Execute Actual Assessment: Initial screen.

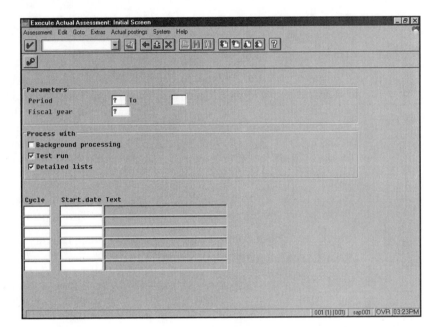

Special Purpose Ledger

Each of the SAP modules provides standard reports that will meet most companies' reporting requirements. However, to accommodate customers whose reporting requirements go beyond SAP's standard reports, SAP offers the Special Purpose Ledger. The Special Purpose Ledger allows users to define the data from the other SAP modules that they need to report on, configure the system to post that data into the Special Purpose Ledger, summarize that data at a level of detail they desire, and report on the data using the flexible Report Painter or Report Writer tools.

Many companies use the Special Purpose Ledger to produce their United States Generally Accepted Accounting Principles (GAAP)-compliant financial statements. Due to the nature of the SAP Chart of Accounts and Cost Center relationship, it is more efficient to produce a GAAP-compliant profit and loss statement out of the SAP Special Purpose Ledger. This section will discuss how to use the Special Purpose Ledger to produce a GAAP-compliant profit and loss statement.

Special Purpose Ledgers and Tables　Table Groups need to be defined within the Special Purpose Ledger to store your financial postings. The Table Group will contain the dimensions that you will need to use for your financial reporting.

The user must assign dimensions or fields to the Table Groups that specify what data will be posted and maintained in the table. Examples of dimensions that could be assigned to the tables would be Company Code, Local Currency, Quantity, Fiscal Year, and so on. This table acts as the database for all postings that will impact your financial reporting.

You can create the table by going to configuration (transaction code SPRO), and in the Financial Accounting section of the IMG use the path:

> **Menu Path:** Special Purpose Ledger > Basic Settings > Tables > Definition > Define Table Group.
>
> **Transaction Code:** GCIN

Special Purpose Ledgers are created that determine the fields to capture from each SAP transaction. These ledgers determine the types of transactions to be posted into the Special Purpose Ledger and the data that will be taken from the transaction. The Special Purpose Ledgers are tied to the Table Groups previously defined that act as databases to store the data collected in the Special Purpose Ledgers. Within Special Purpose Ledger configuration, the user will determine which company codes can post transactions into the Special Purpose Ledger and from which modules the data will come.

The Special Purpose Ledger is created by going to configuration (transaction code SPRO), and in the Financial Accounting section of the IMG use the following path:

> **Menu Path:** Basic Settings > Master Data > Maintain Ledgers > Create Ledger.
>
> **Transaction Code:** GCL1

Functional Area　Functional areas are created to properly group expense postings for GAAP reporting purposes. Functional areas are necessary to structure the financial accounting postings to meet the requirements of cost-of-sales accounting. The functional area for a transaction is derived based on substitution rules, which must be defined during configuration of the system. The most common field used in the substitution rules to determine the functional area is cost center type. All cost centers are linked to a cost center type, which is then associated with a functional area. For example, cost center 123 captures expenses related to administrative operations. This cost center is linked to cost center type A which is the Administration cost center type. Within functional area configuration, the user has specified that when a posting is made to cost center type A, the system should substitute functional area Administration into the transaction. Thus, when a financial transaction is executed that posts to this particular cost center, the system will automatically assign functional area Administration to the dollar amount of the posting.

The functional area can be determined based on the initial posting into SAP Financial Accounting, either through the cost center assignment associated with the primary cost element of the transaction or by being entered manually into the transaction. The functional area can also be determined based on secondary postings internal to the Controlling module of SAP. These postings have no effect on the accounting values in the Financial Accounting module; they do not post to General Ledger accounts. However, if this internal Controlling transaction posted dollar amounts to a cost center of a different cost center type than the original posting, the dollar amounts of the secondary posting must be reposted into Financial Accounting in order to be assigned to the correct functional area. The reposting into Financial Accounting is done via the Reconciliation Ledger.

Starting from transaction code SPRO in SAP, the menu path to configure the functional is

> **Menu Path:** Enterprise Structure > Definition > Financial Accounting > Maintain Functional Area
>
> **Transaction Code:** OKBD

Reconciliation Ledger   The Reconciliation Ledger must be activated for the Controlling Area in which Financial Accounting/Controlling reconciliation's will need to occur. Cost flows occurring in Controlling (secondary postings) but not originating in Financial Accounting, can be maintained and properly reconciled with postings in Financial Accounting. For example, a primary cost element is posted to Financial Accounting and subsequently posted to a cost center in Controlling. Within Controlling, the posting is split into two cost centers via secondary cost allocations. The two cost centers represent different cost center types and, thus, different functional areas. The Reconciliation Ledger will create the necessary postings to be made back into Financial Accounting, which will allow the secondary posting in Controlling to be assigned to the correct functional area.

The Reconciliation Ledger allows for an audit trail from the original document in FI to the secondary cost allocation in CO. Theoretically, internal and external reporting will never be out of balance. The Reconciliation Ledger is typically run at month-end subsequent to any internal allocations of expense performed in Controlling.

Starting from transaction code SPRO, the configuration menu path to activate the Reconciliation Ledger is

> **Menu Path:** Controlling > Overhead Cost Controlling > Cost and Revenue Element Accounting > Reconciliation Ledger > Activate Reconciliation Ledger
>
> **Transaction Code:** KALA

Reports   Define the templates for your GAAP-compliant financial statements via the Report Writer or Report Painter. The first step is to create a library in which to store the report structures. The library must be linked to the table group created within the Special Purpose Ledger. This allows the library ZAE to pull data elements from the assigned table group only. When creating the library, you assign characteristics, key figures, and predefined columns to the library. The data elements defined at the library level are the only data elements that can be included when creating reports residing in the library.

The library can be created via the following menu path:

> **Menu Path:** Accounting > Financial Accounting > Special Purpose Ledger > Tools > Report Painter > Report Writer > Library > Create
>
> **Transaction Code:** GR21

All reports created in SAP must belong to a report group. The report group will be linked to the library, and more than one report group can be assigned to a single library. In order to run reports, the report group that contains the report must be generated. By generating the report group, you pull all of the data necessary to populate the rows and columns of the reports that comprise the report group.

The report group can be created via the following menu path:

Menu Path: Accounting > Financial Accounting > Special Purpose Ledger > Tools > Report Painter > Report Writer > Report Group > Create

Transaction Code: GR51

The Profit and Loss statement structure is configured using the Report Painter. The Report Painter allows the user to assign combinations of characteristics to rows and columns of a report in order to structure the information in a desirable format. The Report Painter provides a graphical presentation of the rows and columns to facilitate report creation. The user does not need to create sets prior to configuring reports with the Report Painter. SAP has standard report layouts which are useful when starting the configuration of the Report Painter reports.

Each row and column in the report is called an *element*. To define the element, the user will position the cursor on the element and choose characteristics that he or she wants to use in defining the row or column of the report. In order to configure the Profit and Loss statement, combinations of General Ledger accounts and functional areas must be used. The functional areas are used to properly reflect the expense amounts on the Profit and Loss statement. If an element is defined with only the General Ledger account, the actual amount posted to the account will be used to comprise the balance of the line item on the report.

The Report Painter can be accessed via the following menu path:

Menu Path: Accounting > Financial Accounting > Special Purpose Ledger > Tools > Report Painter > Report Writer > Report > Create > Report Painter

Transaction Code: GRR1

One of the advantages to reporting in SAP is the drill-down capability of the online reports. The Special Purpose Ledger allows the user to create reports that store detail underneath reports. This is done when creating the Report Group. The Report Interface button will allow the user to configure reports that provide drill-down to the transaction level from the reports created from Report Painter.

Treasury

The SAP Treasury module contains three main sub-modules: Cash Management, Treasury Management, and Market Risk Management. The three sub-modules integrate to provide a fully functioning treasury system from the actual trading of financial instruments to accounting for managing your financial instrument portfolio. When integrated with the General Ledger, financial transactions entered into the Treasury Management module will immediately update Cash Management and be available in the General Ledger. This provides for better decision making, and allows users to forecast and analyze their cash position with the most up-to-date data.

Cash Management The SAP Cash Management module monitors your daily inflows and outflows of cash to produce a daily cash position and a longer-term liquidity forecast. The daily cash position is determined by polling bank accounts for cash that will clear on both the receivable and disbursement side, and memo records manually entered into the Cash Management system. The daily cash position is often used to determine the borrowing or investment needs of a corporation on a daily basis. The liquidity position is a forecast of cash requirements out into the future. SAP will forecast cash based on the investment maturity of financial instruments, anticipated receivables based on historical cash receipt data, anticipated disbursements based on vendor payment terms, and memo records for planned disbursements or receivables. The liquidity position is most often used to monitor the cash requirements of a corporation into the future (from one week to six months).

Planned cash flows are entered into the SAP Cash Management system via memo records. A memo record impacts Cash Management but has no impact on the SAP General Ledger. The user must specify the company code, planning type, planning group, and date when the cash flow is to be realized. Memo records are also entered with an expiration date. Thus, the user can enter a memo record with an expiration date of the day the amount was entered. This would then impact the cash position for that day and would expire that evening.

Key master data used with Cash Management includes the planning type, planning level, planning source, and planning group. Planning types are only used when entering memo records. The planning type is used like a field status group with General Ledger accounts. It will determine a number range for transactions, the fields that are mandatory, optional, or suppressed when entering the transaction, and the dates during which the transaction will affect the cash position or the liquidity forecast. Planning levels are used to determine the source or use of cash. For example, a planning level of A can be used to identify memo records that are impacting the cash position. The planning level is used to facilitate the analysis of the cash position and the liquidity forecast. The planning source will identify whether the transaction came from an SAP subledger or as a result of polling the bank accounts. Customer and Vendor Master records are allocated to planning groups. The planning group is used to categorize certain types of vendors and customers and to aid in the analysis of the liquidity position. Typical planning groups could be domestic vendor, foreign customer, and affiliated customer.

The Cash Management module also has the functionality to forecast medium- to long-term cash developments. This is done via the Cash Budget Management menu items. Cash Budget Management allows the user to create a budget of planned revenues and expenditures and evaluate the actual results compared to the budget. The user can create budgeted cash flows by period. This allows for longer term analysis of cash surpluses and shortages.

Every transaction posted into SAP Financial Accounting will impact Cash Budget Management. This is done via commitment items. There are three different types of commitment items: revenue items, expenditure items, and inventory items. The user will plan and create budgets at the commitment item level. Each General Ledger account in Financial Accounting will then be assigned to a commitment item. Thus, when the General Ledger account in Financial Accounting is posted to, the amount will automatically update Cash Budget Management.

To facilitate analysis, the commitment items are arranged in hierarchies in Cash Budget Management. The hierarchy allows users to view their budgets to see actual results in multiple formats.

Treasury Management   The Treasury Management module is designed to handle financial instrument transactions and manage financial instrument positions. The Treasury Management module will perform the front office trading functions to the back office and accounting for the financial instrument transaction. All transactions in the Treasury Management module will automatically update the cash position in Cash Management and the SAP General Ledger. The General Ledger is updated via the account assignment reference functionality. Account assignment reference defines the posting details for each financial instrument transaction within the SAP Treasury Management module.

Currencies, reference interest rates, and business partners are some of the master data used in SAP Treasury Management. The exchange ratios for currencies is maintained in a table for exchange rate translation in SAP. Currency rates can be assigned to rate types which will flag the rates as beginning- or end-of-month rates. The reference interest rate is the base interest rate on the open market used as a benchmark when fixing interest rates for financial instrument transactions. The business partner concept is similar to the customer in Accounts Receivable or the vendor in Accounts Payable. A business partner can be a borrower, a bank, or a trustee. Most transactions in Treasury Management involve a business partner. When a new business partner is used, a business partner master record must be created.

Treasury Management allows for an automatic data feed from a service such as Reuters or Telerate to update interest rates, security prices, and foreign exchange rates. This data feed will populate SAP tables in the Treasury Management module.

The Treasury Management module contains five separate sub-modules: Foreign Exchange, Money Market, Derivatives, Securities, and Loans. The five sections are created in order to handle the different types of financial instrument transactions.

The Foreign Exchange sub-module handles the transactions related to foreign exchange swaps and spot transactions. Each purchase/sales transaction of foreign currency must involve a business partner and must include foreign exchange rates, which can be populated via a rate table in SAP. The Foreign Exchange sub-module allows users to analyze their global exposure to foreign currency, facilitates hedging decisions, and allows for foreign currency valuation.

The Money Market sub-module is used to account for commercial paper, fixed-term deposits, and deposits at notice transactions. Money market transactions are created as contracts and include the type of financial instrument (product type), the currency, and the business partner. Confirmations can be created automatically to be sent to the applicable business partner. SAP will automatically post all interest accruals and maturity information into Cash Management and Financial Accounting. The reporting structure will allow for a listing of all money market financial instruments and a payment schedule to analyze cash flow as a result of the money market transactions.

The Derivatives sub-module will handle derivative transactions such as swaps and options. Derivative transactions always contain the product type you wish to buy or sell, the transaction currency, and the business partner. For options, an option price calculator exists to determine the option premium. Interest rate transactions, such as Caps and Floors, are part of the standard functionality. The interest rates are adjusted based on defined reference interest rates on certain dates. The reporting structure will allow for a journal showing a history of derivative transactions, a payment schedule to analyze cash flow, an interest rate adjustment schedule, and a maturity schedule for option transactions.

The Securities sub-module accounts for stock and bond transactions. A transaction entered into the Securities sub-module will contain the company code, security account, price, the stock exchange in which the transaction was executed, CUSIP # if required, and business partner. The security account indicates the physical location where the securities are going to be held. SAP will perform a valuation on the financial instruments within the Securities module, when required by the user, to reflect the change in the market price or foreign exchange rates. SAP will automatically create the journal entries to accrue for interest based on the interest calculation period associated with the financial instrument.

The Loans sub-module will handle mortgage loans, policy loans, bank loans, and employee loans. A loan transaction can be initially entered into the system as an application. A note can be made as to the type of collateral that is being offered as part of the loan. When the loan is posted into Financial Accounting, an abbreviated payment program session is run that allows for disbursement to be made to the business partner of the transaction. Correspondence can be automatically generated that can be sent to the business partner confirming the parameters of the loan. SAP will automatically accrue interest. The reporting functionality will provide for a portfolio listing of all loans, a statement of security deposits, a report of loan commitments, overdue items report, and other standard reports.

Market Risk Management   The Market Risk Management sub-module is used to evaluate currency and interest rate exposure within your actual and fictitious financial instrument portfolios. The user can create hypothetical financial portfolios using fictitious financial transactions to simulate different market scenarios. It can be used as a decision-making tool to determine risk thresholds as a result of what-if analysis scenarios. The user can create interest rate yield curves based on multiple currencies and reference interest rates.

Integration   The SAP Treasury System integrates real-time into the SAP Financial Accounting module. All transactions executed in the system that impact cash will automatically update the cash position in Cash Management. The treasurer will use the Cash Management module to poll bank accounts, analyze maturities on investments, and to enter planned receipts or disbursements of cash. This information will form the daily cash position. Based on this information, the treasurer will determine if the company is in a borrowing or investing position. An analysis of the liquidity forecast will give a longer term view of cash requirements.

The treasurer can establish target values for liquidity and risk thresholds in Market Risk Management. Based on the cash position and liquidity forecast, the treasurer can enter hypothetical transactions into Market Risk Management and analyze the effects on the company's currency and interest rate exposure. The treasurer will have access to recent market data via the data feed from Telerate or Reuters. A thorough analysis of trading options in Market Risk Management allows the treasurer to determine the appropriate trading transactions to pursue.

As the trades are executed, the data is input into the SAP Treasury System modules based on the product type of the financial instrument. Upon entering the transaction, confirmation letters can be generated, the payment program updated, and the transaction automatically posted to Financial Accounting and Cash Management. The SAP Financial Accounting module will determine the accrual schedule for interest payments and reflect the cash impact of maturity in Cash Management.

Profitability Analysis

Profitability Analysis (PA) is one of the key components to financial reporting in SAP. It allows a company to examine the profitability of a number of different key indexes. It is a highly flexible tool that allows the user to determine for which segments of an organization profitability is to be measured. PA is part of the Controlling module and therefore considered internal reporting. SAP likes to represent PA as a multi-dimensional cube allowing clients to slice-and-dice profitability from a number of different vantage points.

The basic structure within PA is the Operating Concern. Most companies measure profitability consistently across the organization, and therefore require only one Operating Concern. Only dramatic differences in this measurement would require more than one operating concern. There are two different types of PA: costing-based and account-based.

Both types allow users to configure the *characteristics* of the company for which they want to measure profitability. Seventeen of these characteristics come standard when the Operating Concern is generated. They include such structures as product, customer, profit center, company code, and plant. An additional 30 characteristics may be defined and used in PA. These may include characteristics pulled from nine standard SAP tables. They are fields that are found on sales tables, customer tables, and material tables. For example, some corporations may desire profitability by material group. Material group would then be activated as a characteristic in PA. Every time that a material in that material group is sold, the profitability is recorded. Derived characteristics are another type of characteristic. They are created by using other characteristics to define them. For example, a company may divide up the U.S. into regions based on geographic locations. A region called Southwest could be defined by deriving data from all of the plants within the region. Now the profitability of the region Southwest is available. A company should spend a large amount of time to determine how it wants to measure profitability. This will translate into how the necessary characteristics to be generated. Close integration should exist during this activity because it is imperative to know what fields will be available from the material tables, the customer tables, and the sales tables.

Account-based PA simply allows the analysis of these characteristics by the accounts defined in the General Ledger. This type of PA is rarely implemented because most of the analysis that can be performed with account-based PA is overlapping in other modules, such as FI, PCA, and SD. Most companies implement costing-based PA. It allows companies to define Value Fields, which are the dollars, quantities, or what they want to measure the profitability of. It often allows a more detailed look at internal profitability. Costing-based PA also enables a company to create internal profit and loss statements for different segments of the corporation. It sounds a little like costing-based PA is similar to Business Areas in that sense, which is true. However, PA allows much greater flexibility and does not use General Ledger accounts. Some value fields can be pulled from existing SAP tables. However, most companies will need to create the fields from scratch. Again, a lot of time should be spent developing these value field requirements. An in-depth knowledge of the company's internal financial policies, as well as an understanding of the cost modules team's decisions, are important tools for successfully defining the value fields.

Configuration and Functionality   PA is a standalone database that can only be updated if transactions are mapped to value fields. After all value fields and characteristics have been generated for the Operating Concern, the rest of the configuration time is spent determining how these fields get populated. Data can flow into PA in only a limited number of ways. These are sales orders, billing documents, production order variances, projects, internal orders, cost center assessments, financial postings, and material movements. Correct configuration will ensure that all transactions in the system that have a financial impact will filter into PA. Each time one of these transactions is made, one record is written to the PA line item database. Each of these line items contains all of the relevant characteristics and all of the value fields mapped during the transaction.

Both sales documents and billing documents post to PA in a similar manner. When sales orders are transferred to PA, estimates of revenues and cost of sales are transferred to PA. When the actual orders are billed, the actual revenues and cost of sales are transferred to PA. The configuration of the sales order and billing document transfer to PA primarily replicates the functionality of both SD pricing and product costing. The entire pricing procedure must be reconfigured in PA to reflect how sales has configured it, including condition tables, condition types, and costing sheets. The product costing also references the product cost estimate and can actually provide PA with the cost components versus the total standard cost. Thus, both revenue and cost of sales are transferred to PA via valuation in PA. This valuation does not simply transfer values on the billing and sales documents; it creates logic to mimic the sales and costing functionality. This transfer alone allows contribution margin to be computed for every characteristic on the billing document.

Production order variances, projects, internal orders, and financial postings all use a similar vehicle to post to PA, the settlement structure. Settlement structures define which cost elements are to be posted to PA and to which value fields the dollars will be posted. After the finished goods value has been delivered from a production order, variances remain. These variances are posted both to FI and PA based on the Production Order Settlement Structure. Certain month-end financial transactions should be posted to profitability segments such as bad debt. Typically these accounts are posted to a value field called Bad Debt to a particular profitability segment. (Be sure that these accounts have profitability segment as mandatory in the field status variant for the account.) Projects can even settle out revenue as well as costs to PA. Internal orders can be used for a variety of reasons at a company. Each company should determine the appropriateness of settling to PA. Thus, all settlements are transferred into profitability analysis.

Cost Center Assessment allows below-the-line costs to be transferred to PA. These typically include costs like marketing and administration and can be allocated to any level of profitability in PA. Recent notes on OSS indicate that it is now possible to transfer material price differences to PA as well.

Now that all financial transactions have been transferred to PA, reports can be created. Unfortunately, PA only comes with a few standard reports; most clients must create their own. PA utilizes a specialized version of Report Painter to create reports. Each posting to PA has created a line item populated with the relevant value fields and characteristics. The Report Painter is then used to create an endless amount of reports, which can include profitability by customer or product, sales by state, or full profit and loss statements by product line. PA is a versatile tool that allows a corporation to define how it wants to report internal financial results. Sophisticated users of PA can use the planning tool to allow the integrated planning of profitability across modules including Sales, SOP, and Finance.

Profit Center Accounting

Profit Center Accounting (PCA) offers a fairly limited view of the organization on the revenue and expense side but can be a great tool to get balance sheet items by product line and provide a structure to utilize in PA. PCA is technically a part of the Special Purpose Ledger and basically allows both expense and revenue accounts to be posted to profit centers.

Profit centers are assigned to a number of structures in SAP so that, when financial transactions affect these objects, the revenue and costs are simultaneously posted to PCA. These objects are material masters, sales orders, production orders, and internal orders. In this respect, revenues and expenses are posted via accounts to the profit center ledger as transactions take place. The profit centers themselves are organized in a hierarchy that allows viewing of the entire internal reporting structure all the way to the top. This hierarchy can then be recreated in PA via derivation. Thus, even though the profit center reporting itself is not that strong, the presence of the structure and the means to populate it are key for reporting in PA.

At the end of the period, balance sheet items can also be transferred to PCA. Assets, Receivables, Payables, Inventory, and WIP can all be configured for transportation to PA. This provides a company with an internal structure for reporting all balance sheet items. Certain standard reports are delivered with the system. However, most clients will still need to create their own reports via Report Writer. PCA is still a powerful tool within SAP but mainly so when utilized in conjunction with PA.

Periodic Closing of Accounting Records

Throughout this book, the point has been emphasized that, as an integrated system, SAP is deeply rooted in financial accountability. This book has attempted to illustrate the concept that SAP simultaneously posts the financial effect of each and every business transaction from the Logistics module including Sales and Distribution, Production Planning, Materials Management, Quality Management, and so on. This online/real-time transaction recording ensures better integrity of the accounting ledgers. Secondly, it provides business managers more timely information regarding the financial impact of business events. This, in turn, allows for quicker and more responsive decision making by management.

As mentioned, the integrated nature of SAP ensures that it records the direct financial effect of any business transaction—as it happens. This ensures that the financial accounts are kept in balance at all times. However, in keeping with generally accepted accounting principles (in the United States, this is commonly referred to as GAAP), the accounting books and records must be *closed* periodically to provide information to the various stakeholders of the organization. This is commonly termed the *fiscal period*. Most companies maintain 12 or 13 fiscal periods within a fiscal year. While the happenings of a business do not cease at the end of an operating period, the basic nature of business dictates that each enterprise report on its results. Internal management desires information to ensure that the goals of the organization are being met. Tax and regulatory bodies (for publicly traded companies, the United States Securities and Exchange Commission) also require certain financial information. Likewise, creditors and investors demand information to ensure the security of their financial capital entrusted to the organization.

The *closing* of the financial books of an organization is just one of the steps that occurs during the periodic accounting cycle. These stages of the process include

1. Planning and budgeting the expected financial impact of the anticipated business events expected to occur in the upcoming period.

2. Posting the financial documents associated with actual specific business events as they occur during the period (such as the increase in finished goods inventory associated with the completion of manufacture of a product or the cost of goods sold related to the shipments of goods to a customers).

3. Recognition of periodic accounting adjustments to ensure that the financial statements properly reflect the organization's financial performance and position for the current period. Accountants, working within the public sector in the United States, are generally required to record these postings as part of the "accrual accounting" method that requires the recognition of revenues when earned and expenses when incurred. For example, at month-end, accrued wage expenses must be recorded.

4. Closing the financial books to allow the preparation of financial statements related to the period.

5. Issuance of financial statements, including those for regulatory, tax reporting, internal management analysis, and other requirements. External reporting requirements may differ based on whether the financial close is for one specific period or for a fiscal quarter.

6. Opening the subsequent period and reversing any temporary accounting adjustments made during the *close* for purposes of proper financial statement reporting.

Items 3 through 6 are directly related to period-end close. This book has already explained the *how to* in SAP completely for items 3 and 5 and partially for item 6. The posting of an accrual (item 3) can be accomplished through the creation of a General Ledger document. Similarly, reversing documents (item 6) in SAP is quite straightforward. Generation of financial statements (item 5) has been addressed at a high level in the discussion of Special Purpose Ledger, Profitability Analysis, and the Financial Accounting modules' Information System. That leaves an explanation of the various processes required in SAP to successfully close the books (item 4) as well as to *open* the next period.

Closing in SAP

This section will address the SAP processes necessary to effectively perform a close at month-end and year-end. These two intervals have been chosen since most companies do not prepare GAAP basis statements at any intervals less than monthly. As you have seen earlier, the financial accounting books are always in balance in SAP. Similarly, the Controlling module provides up-to-the minute cost performance information. However, the mere existence of a balanced ledger is not sufficient to prepare financial statements for GAAP purposes. Likewise, the cost accounting information provided by SAP only presents a complete report on cost trends and performance, if the cost drivers and activities are based on direct, full absorption. In other words, if the company's methods are based upon the application of overhead costs in a batch process, then any mid-month review of cost accounting does not reflect full absorption and, hence, would likely be useful but not complete. Usually, a company that applies overhead costs in batch is willing to accept this compromise. In any event, SAP is capable of performing these batch allocations as frequently as needed. The only limitations are the system performance capabilities of the actual hardware used to operate the system.

Monthly Closing Process

Each month, certain processes must be performed in order to close in SAP. This section discusses the general requirements for each of the major areas within the following accounting modules and sub-modules of SAP:

- Accounts Receivable and Accounts Payable
- Financial Accounting
- Special Purpose Ledger
- Controlling
  - Cost Center Accounting
  - Internal Orders
  - Production Orders
  - Profitability Analysis

Accounts Receivable and Accounts Payable

In order to ensure that the month-end balance sheet reflects the proper accounts receivable as well as accounts payable, you should perform the Goods Receipt/Invoice Receipt (GR/IR) clearing process. As discussed earlier in this book, the GR/IR account contains credit balances for those goods received from vendors but not yet invoiced. It also includes debit balances for invoices received from vendors for goods that have not yet been received. In the case in which the goods receipt follows the processing of an invoice, the two offsetting posting items in the GR/IR account will not have cleared. The GR/IR clearing program analyzes each uncleared item in GR/IR and calculates the net financial balance for GR/IR. Next, a batch program makes the entries needed to a specified target account to ensure that payables and receivables are properly stated. Since these reclassifications are only needed for the purpose of preparing the balance sheet, they are automatically reversed on the date manually entered by the user on the input screen of the program. The clearing process program is executed by performing the following menu path:

> **Menu path:** Accounting > Financial Accounting > Accounts Payable > Periodic Processing > Closing > Restructure > Clear Goods/Inv. Rec.

Enter the general selection information requested on this screen, and proceed to the next screen. Here, the processing can be restricted to only certain criteria, such as a particular account.

Financial Accounting—General Prerequisites

As is standard procedure per GAAP, certain basic accounting transactions must be completed before generating the financial statements. For example, all Sales and Distribution module transactions must be complete, including the processing of billing documents/invoices as well as the post goods issue transactions.

Similarly, all Asset Management entries for depreciation expense should be entered. Essentially, any transaction relating to the period that has not yet been processed should be.

Special Purpose Ledger—Prerequisites

The section on the Accounting Information System explained how to create and generate reports for external financial reporting from the Special Purpose Ledger module. However, a prerequisite to complete before generating the reports involves the Reconciliation Ledger. The Reconciliation Ledger is used to maintain the proper classification of expenses that pass to the Controlling module and change character. For example, salary expenses on the General Ledger may be posted in CO to an administrative cost center. In this case, this cost would be classified as an administrative expense on the external income statement. But if this cost were reallocated within the Controlling module to a selling cost center, it would need to change its classification. The Special Purpose Ledger allows the user to create functional areas for capturing expenditures. When an expense is allocated from one functional area to another, it crosses functional areas. The Reconciliation Ledger in SAP tracks each of these occurrences. Therefore, the Reconciliation Ledger program needs to be run prior to generating any Special Purpose Ledger reports. This is executed by performing the following menu path:

> **Menu:** Accounting > Controlling > Cost and Revenue Element Acctg > Actual Postings > Reconciliation with CO-FI

From this point, enter the company code, the period, and the year. Select the desired indicators for a Test Run, Background Processing, or Detailed List (for output purposes), and then click the Execute icon. The amounts that crossed functional areas during the period will be captured within a General Ledger account specified within the configuration. This General Ledger account is assigned to all of the applicable line items in the company's profit and loss statement, in combination with the functional area. By reposting the allocations of expense amounts, which occurred within the Controlling module, back into the Financial Accounting module (by running the Reconciliation Ledger) the expense amounts have been properly stated for external reporting purposes.

Controlling—Closing Processes

Closing in the CO module can vary depending upon the organization's cost accounting framework. It is critical that all parties involved understand cost flow and accordingly perform all required allocations, absorption, settlements, and so on, in the specific order desired. For example, some organizations allocate overhead costs to production orders via a month-end process (as opposed to the activity rate including overhead). In this instance, the sequence of the CO module allocations must ensure that the overhead surcharge application occurs prior to the calculation and subsequent settlement of work-in-process and variances of production orders. Otherwise, unabsorbed standard cost variances will remain in the production orders at month-end. The closing process in the CO module may require some or all of the following transactions to be complete.

Cost Center Accounting   Any external business/accounting transactions that result in a posting to a primary cost element must be complete.

Any transaction-based cost allocations that occur as a result of business transactions, including

- Internal activity allocations such as those in connection with production order completion confirmation
- Reposting of costs

Periodic cost allocations including

- Assessments
- Distributions
- Reposting of costs
- Internal activity allocations
- Determination of cost center variance

Internal Orders   Application of Overhead via

- Cost Center Assessment (transaction covered earlier in this chapter)
- Overhead/Surcharge Application using a costing sheet in SAP that links the following:

   Calculation base upon which overhead is applied (for example, labor overhead may be based on the cost element for direct labor)

   Rate of overhead (expressed as a percentage of the base)

   Cost object to be credited when the internal order is debited:

   Menu path: Accounting > Controlling > Internal Orders > Actual Postings > Period Closing > Overhead > Collective Processing (Note: for a single order, Individual Processing can be selected)

Enter the current period, year, and order group to process. Then select Proceed to calculate and apply overhead to the internal orders.

■ Settlement of Internal Order Costs to internal and external receivers:

Menu path: Accounting > Controlling > Internal Orders > Actual Postings > Period Closing > Periodic Allocations > Settlement > Order (Note: For multiple orders, "Order Group" may be selected instead)

Production Orders   Application of Overhead via

■ Cost Center Assessment (transaction covered earlier in this chapter)

■ Overhead/Surcharge Application using a costing sheet (see discussion of internal orders)

Calculation of Work-In-Process (WIP) costs to be capitalized in inventory. WIP is generally calculated for all applicable orders that are released and not yet completely delivered. In either case, SAP records the amount of WIP on special secondary cost elements called *results analysis cost elements*. These elements are only used in the Results Analysis tables of SAP; they are not used in the rest of the Controlling module. The month, in which an order reaches full/complete delivery status, is when the WIP balance is canceled. The menu path to perform this transaction is as follows:

Menu: Accounting > Controlling > Product Cost Acctg > Order-related Prod. > Period-end Closing > Work in Process > Collective Processing > Calculate

Enter the controlling area, the year, the period, and the specific results analysis version that is desired. Select desired indicators for processing in the background (usually recommended), Test Run, Display Orders with Errors, and whether the log of the calculation run should be saved. Then click the Execute button.

Based on the method desired, SAP allows WIP to be calculated based on

■ Actual costs (total cumulative actual costs recorded on the object, less any costs absorbed or credited for deliveries to stock from the order)

■ Planned costs (based upon the standard costs for the operations confirmed cumulatively)

Calculation of Order Variances. For those orders desired, SAP can calculate variances incurred during the completion of the order. This is executed by performing the following menu path:

Menu: Accounting > Controlling > Product Cost Acctg > Order-related Prod. > Period-end Closing > Variances > Collective Processing > Next

Enter the plant, the year, and the period. Select desired indicators for processing in the background (usually recommended), Test Run, Display Orders with Errors, and whether the log of the calculation run should be saved. Then click the Execute button. The system performs the calculation using one of two methods:

- Cumulative variances can be calculated at the month-end in which the order reaches either the complete delivery status or the technically complete status. These variances represent the difference between the cumulative actual costs less the costs absorbed for "deliveries to stock" from the order.

- Periodic variances can be calculated in any month in which a delivery occurs. The planned costs for each operation (as per the standard cost estimate) are considered. In effect, the WIP calculated under the "plan cost" method is subtracted from the actual costs incurred.

Order Settlement. SAP settles costs in the order based on the settlement rule of the order. In the case of a production order, the normal settlement receiver is the material. If the variances indicator has been set for the order, the variances are settled to the Profitability Analysis module. When this occurs, any calculated unfavorable variances are credited (debited in the case of a favorable variance) from the order. The offsetting entry for this posting is made to a price difference account in Financial Accounting. The menu path for order settlement is as follows:

> **Menu:** Logistics > Production > Production Control > Period End Closing > Settlement > Collective Processing

Enter the period, year, order type (for example, PP01), and settlement type. Then click the Execute button.

Profitability Analysis   The month-end processing related to Profitability Analysis relates to settlements, assessments, activity allocations, and direct adjustments to PA. Any settlements of internal orders, production orders, or projects that have profitability segments as valid receivers will settle costs to PA as part of their normal settlement sequence. There is no extra processing for the transactions to post in PA. If there are any special cost center assessments desired to allocate to PA, they can be run once all other cost allocations that might affect those specific cost centers have been completed. Similarly, any special activity allocations to PA can be performed at month-end. Once all the closing activities prior to reporting are complete, the PA reporting activities can begin. At this point any needed adjustments to transactions can be made directly in PA. This is not recommended unless the correction of a source transaction would require large volumes of repostings, corrections, reversals, and so on.

Year-End Closing Process

The only significant differences related to the year-end closing as compared to month-end closing relate to balance carry forward, technical settings to open the subsequent year, and ensuring that the Accounting document number ranges are active. The latter two items are handled in configuration, or customizing preferably, and need not be discussed in this book. However, balance carry forward is important.

When a new accounting year is opened, the balances from the previous year are not automatically carried forward. A process for this purpose exists in SAP, and it acts to carry forward balances as follows:

1. Customer Accounts Receivable balances from year-end are carried forward to the opening balance of the new year.

2. Vendor Accounts Payable balances from year-end are carried forward to the opening balance of the new year.

3. Other Balance Sheet Accounts from year-end are carried forward to the opening balance of the new year.

4. Profit and Loss Accounts from year-end are carried forward to the Retained Earnings Account(s) established in the organizations chart of accounts. This account must also be identified within the closing steps of the SAP Implementation Guide.

5. The balance carry forward program can be run multiple times in order to capture the accounting effects of all transactions related to the particular fiscal year.

No special year-end manual closing entries are required to close the traditional income summary to retained earnings:

Menu: Accounting > Financial Accounting > General Ledger > Periodic Processing > Carry Forward > Bal. Carry Forward.

Next select Program > Execute, and the balances will be carried forward. Like other programs in SAP, the indicators for Test Run are available.

Closing Conclusions

Periodic closing of the financials is a straightforward process in SAP. There is some degree of planning required to ensure success. Good communication and a clear understanding of the timing and sequence of events is essential. However, closing in SAP as compared to traditional legacy systems is more efficient in many respects. Gone is the need to summarize, close, and post the effect to the General Ledger of the detail subsidiary ledgers maintained by accountants. The closing process in SAP certainly presents finance departments an opportunity to reallocate resources. With the elimination of many of the tedious bookkeeping tasks, financial managers can devote more efforts to the other purposes of accounting—providing timely information that assists reaching decisions that continually improve business performance.

Other Metrics Via Information Systems

In addition to the Accounting Information System described in the previous section, SAP also has a Logistics Information System and Human Resources Information System to view other data in SAP. The Logistics Information System is used to create various reports containing data maintained in the Logistics modules in SAP. The Logistics Information System is further broken down into the following sub-systems: Inventory Management, Purchasing, Sales and Distribution, Production, Plant Maintenance, and Quality Management.

Sales Information System

In addition to the integration with the MM and FI modules the Sales and Distribution business processes of Order Entry, Shipping and Invoicing can also transfer data to the Logistics Information System (LIS). The Logistics Information System is actually made up of a number of subsystems, each referred to as an *Information System*. The areas of Inventory Management, Purchasing, Production, and Sales each have their own unique reporting structure within SAP.

The Sales Information System (SIS) allows for online reporting of key figures (such as items ordered, dollars billed, and so on) to be presented according to pre-defined characteristics (customer, material, time period, and so on) using a standard pull-down menu technique. The reasons to use SIS, or any SAP-supplied information system versus standard database reporting, are many.

Most importantly, retrieving and manipulating data from the SIS system is not database-intensive. By defining the key figures, as well as the characteristics, before any transactions take place in the system allows SAP to continually create the needed values and sort them in the desired manner in a real-time manner. When the user accesses analysis reports, SAP retrieves a handful of values and does not have to labor through each and every transaction record creating the desired figures and using valuable processing time.

The definition of the key figures and characteristics is done through a menu-driven, point-and-click manner. Experience in ABAP programming is not necessary to establish or use of the SIS system. The basis of storing the key figures and characteristics is done through the creation of an Information Structure. Each Information Structure is made up of the key figures to be tracked, the characteristics these figures should be stored for, and the timing of the data storage. It may prove beneficial to the enterprise to store certain information for each order entered and other types of data for each invoice created.

Lastly, the SIS system is equipped with strong internal graphical capabilities. All of the Information Structure data can be easily represented in text format or in one of many graphical means. Through the use of pull-down menus, the user has the choice of representing data in many 2D or 3D formats, changing the colors, or even editing the report headings. In short, through the use of SAP's standard SIS graphics capabilities, any user can create quality presentations of any of the Sales and Distribution transactional values.

Standard Analysis   SIS comes delivered with a number of pre-defined Information Structures. If the proper controls have been set in the master files and in configuration, data can be viewed at any time via the menu path:

> **Menu Path:** Logistics > Sales/distribution > Sales Info System > Standard Analyses
>
> **Transaction code:** MCT0

All it takes to collect the data designated in these Information Structures is to ensure that the Statistics fields are entered into the proper master data files and in the proper configuration items. Entries must be made in each of the following:

- Item Category
- Sales Document Type
- Customer Master
- Material Master

In order for data to be stored according to any Information Structure, transactional data must be entered into the system. Switching on the proper controls or generating a new structure via Flexible Analysis (see the next section) does not access data from past transactions. For this reason, it is important that the enterprise decide on the data to be tracked during the project development phase so that the SIS controls and Information Structures can be activated before live data is entered.

A number of report selections can be made from the menu path Standard Analyses, such as

- Customer
- Material
- Sales Organization
- Shipping point
- Sales employee
- Sales office
- Variant configuration

Choosing any of the report selections will present a selection menu to the user. Based on the characteristics defined in the Information Structure, users may be able to define their requested data by customer number, material number, date of transaction, sales area, and shipping point. Entering this defining criteria, or not, and pressing Execute or F8 will access the data stored and present it to the user in a text format.

All of the standard Information Structures have been created in a drill-down format. This means that the data shown onscreen can be sorted according to any of the characteristics defined and not just the one shown on the report. Using the Switch Drill-Down button or the View menu, all of the key figures displayed can be resorted. Each Standard Analysis Information Structure has a standard drill-down defined. By double-clicking any of the characteristics displayed on the text report, the next level of drill-down will be displayed. For example, if the key figure Invoices Sales is being displayed by Sold To Party, double-clicking a single Sold To Party will list the same key figure according to month.

Via the menu path Goto > Graphics, the user will be asked to choose which key figure(s) he or she wants to see displayed graphically. If more than one figure is chosen, the 3D options of the SIS can be used. Three main screens are used in SIS graphics: the 2D view, the 3D view, and the Overview, which is a combination of both. Via the menu path Options >, all of these views can be altered. Colors can be changed as well as the report type. A number of other presentation options exist as well.

Flexible Analysis Because not every company has the same reporting needs, SAP does not attempt to provide every report contingency in the Standard Analysis Information Structures. Via the menu path

> **Menu Path:** Logistics > Sales/distribution > Sales Info System > Flexible Analyses > Evaluation Structure > Create
>
> **Transaction Code:** MCS7

new Information Structures, referred to under Flexible Analysis as Evaluation Structures, can be created. A great many characteristics and key figures appear on selection lists in this transaction. In order to run a data report off of an Evaluation Structure, an Evaluation must be created and linked to the Evaluation Structure. This Evaluation creates the data selection screen for the report. To do this, follow the menu path:

> **Menu Path:** Flexible Analyses > Evaluation > Create
>
> **Transaction Code:** MCSA

All of the graphical and drill-down features present in Standard Analysis are also available when using Flexible Analysis reports.

Early Warning System The early warning system for the Sales and Distribution module is similar in characteristic to the other SAP Logistics modules. Like standard and flexible online reporting, early warning reporting also utilizes characteristics and key values to display useful information to the user. In addition to the basic data, users can specify the following requirements:

- Threshold Value—For example, display all customers (characteristic value) with sales orders larger than $25,000

- Trend Analysis—For example, display all customers with positive trend in quantity ordered

- Planned Versus Actual Comparison—For example, display the customers with sales realization less than 50%

The requirements can also be designed into exception groups for more complex analysis. A relatively simple example would be the identification of small customers (sales of less than $10,000) with positive sales trends. This information may be used to target fast-growing customers for an aggressive marketing campaign.

There are three ways to use the early warning system:

- Standard Analysis—Reports will highlight the pertinent data using different colors (for example, sales over $25,000 can be displayed in red).

- Exception Analysis—Reports will only display data that satisfy the requirements (for example, only sales over $25,000 will be displayed).

- Periodic Analysis—The system can be set up to check for exceptions on a periodic basis (daily, weekly, or monthly) without a user's prompt or request. In addition to basic scheduling of data check, exceptions can also be prompted by an event. For example, all sales order transactions can be checked every time for sales larger than $25,000. A report or email can be triggered for both checks so that the appropriate action can be taken.

To create an exception, use the following menu path:

> **Menu Path:** Early Warning System > Exception > Create
>
> **Transaction Code:** MC/Q

The exception has to be applied to an information structure. Specify this in the Information Structure field in the initial screen.

Shop Floor Information System

Within the Logistics Information System (LIS) lies the Shop Floor Information System. Similar to other components of the LIS, the Shop Floor Information System serves to provide meaningful output and summarization of the operational data contained within the system. As indicated by the name, the Shop Floor Information System (SFIS) is primarily focused on the data pertaining to production activities.

Firms implementing the PP module of SAP typically have a wide variety of production operations that function concurrently and are greatly interdependent on each other. While MRP serves to generate a production plan that encompasses all of the pertinent factors, it does little to illustrate the status of plan out on the shop floor. This crucial functionality is provided more directly via the SFIS.

Providing the information necessary for the desired SFIS evaluations are what are referred to as Information Structures. These Information Structures are essentially data files constantly updated from data collection in the operative system. These structures are then accessed as necessary in order to consolidate data into a desired format. Data contained within the Information Structures is based largely on production orders. Production orders with a wide variety of statuses such as created, released, partially confirmed, fully confirmed, technically completed, flagged for deletion, and so on, can be evaluated as desired.

The SFIS provides the status information necessary to support improved production decision making. In fact, the SFIS compliments the MRP functionality by allowing direct comparisons between planned and actual results. This serves to close the loop of the planning process by providing status information back to scheduling personnel who can then make subsequent decisions regarding the production plan itself.

In the case of Electro Tech, it is apparent that this type of reporting is completely absent from the management of the production processes. Without timely feedback regarding the actual status of the Production department, Bryan Luther is deriving a production schedule largely based on demand data and optimal standard processing times. The actual status of production operations is largely unavailable to him because of the lack of a systemized data reporting system and because of the Production department's reluctance to take the time to report its actual (and often poor) conformance to schedule. Without this information, Bryan is perpetually in a mode of deriving a schedule that is unlikely to be followed and then chasing information regarding the plant's actual results. In effect, his daily activities more closely resemble that of firefighting than scheduling.

The Shop Floor Information System may be accessed via

> **Menu Path:** Logistics > Logist. Controlling > Shop Floor Info System
>
> **Transaction Code:** MCP0

Analysis   There exist several modes of output generation within the SFIS. Three commonly used tools are a standard analysis, flexible analysis, and the early warning system. Each allows a concise view of production status information.

As implied by its name, the standard analysis provides data evaluations which are common to a wide variety of production environments. The format is somewhat pre-set but still allows for specific evaluation of desired data via drill-down capabilities.

A standard analysis is initiated via the following menu path:

> **Menu Path:** Logistics > Logist. Controlling > Shop Floor Info System > Standard Analyses
>
> **Transaction Code:** MCP0

The flexible analysis capability allows much greater tailoring of the way that data is consolidated and presented. It is intended to allow production reporting in a manner meaningful to a specific application but perhaps not generally utilized throughout a wide variety of production environments.

A flexible analysis is initiated via the following menu path:

> **Menu Path:** Logistics > Logist. Controlling > Shop Floor Info System > Flexible Analyses
>
> **Transaction Code:** MCP0

A capability known as the early warning system exists along with the reporting methods already described. However, the early warning system functions in such a way that the user may be automatically advised of specific conditions existing within the production operations. The early warning system provides the capability to pre-define specific data conditions and then announce the presence of these conditions to the user whenever they occur. For example, when a production plan is constructed to accommodate a forecast demand of 1000 units, but sales orders subsequently entered total a value far above this amount, a comparison performed within the early warning system could alert the scheduling areas of the upcoming shortage situation.

Establishing parameters to be evaluated by the early warning system are performed via the following initial menu path:

> **Menu Path:** Logistics > Logist. Controlling > Shop Floor Info System > Early Warning System
>
> **Transaction Code:** MCP0

Production Order Info System Somewhat separate from the Shop Floor Information System, but of similar functionality, is the Production Order Info System (POIS). Through the use of the POIS, a wide variety of evaluations of production orders can be easily performed.

Entrance into the POIS is typically accomplished via the following menu path:

> **Menu Path:** Logistics > Production > Production Control > Control > Information Systems > OrderInfoSystem > Object Overview
>
> **Transaction Code:** CO26

The data entry screen in Figure 22.41 will result.

FIG. 22.41

Data entry screen for Production Order Information System: Initial screen.

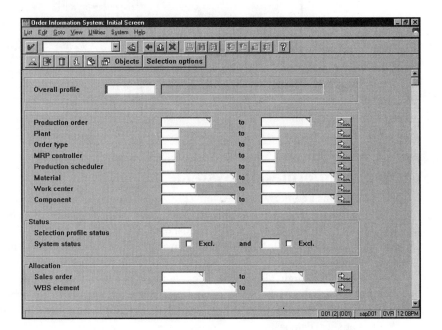

As depicted, a wide variety of search criteria can be specified as necessary to limit the report to the desired information. In fact, most users of this system need to spend some time experimenting with the data entry in order to derive the concise reports they desire. After a small amount of familiarization, however, the tremendous reporting capabilities of this system quickly become apparent. The reports generated may be as broad or specific as desired by the user. In either case, the reports can be generated quickly.

As an example, examine the output in Figure 22.42. This report was quickly generated to depict all of the production orders that were generated by a specific set of MRP Controllers.

In addition to listing the orders themselves along with their overall respective status, the report is active and allows the user to drill-down through each individual order as desired to review elements of greater detail. In the example shown here, one order within the report has been exploded to provide detailed information regarding the operations and components contained within it.

FIG. 22.42

A report depicting all production orders that were generated by a specific set of MRP Controllers.

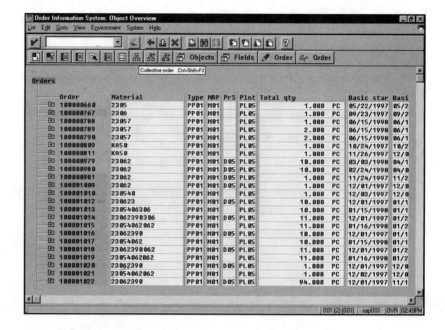

Purchasing Information System

The Purchasing Information System (PIS) is the component of the LIS that deals specifically with purchasing statistics within SAP. Each purchasing-relevant transaction that is posted in SAP results in an update of the statistical database, or Information Structure, used by the PIS for its analyses. Purchasing-relevant transactions include a change to a purchase order, the creation of a scheduling agreement, a goods receipt for a purchase order, an invoice receipt, and so on. Although it is possible to configure which item and document types within purchasing affect updates of the information structures, only standard analyses with standard configuration will be discussed here. Again, the basis of the standard analyses is the data contained in the statistical database.

To access the purchasing information system menu, go to

Menu Path: Information Systems > Logistics > Purchasing

Transaction Code: MCE9

From the Information System for Purchasing menu, there are several menu choices that constitute the main criteria by which you can access information, including Material, Vendor, Material Group, Purchasing Group, and Purchasing Documents. The nature of the inquiry will dictate which of the criteria is appropriate. For example, if you would like to know which materials in what quantities have been ordered from a particular vendor (or for a range of vendors or for all vendors), the Vendor criteria would be fitting. If you would like to know the frequency of purchase orders for each purchasing group, the Purchasing Group criterion is suitable.

Regardless of which standard analysis you choose, you are able to view both the initial and drill-down lists of statistics, as in the other Information Systems. The initial list is the result of the selection criteria, and includes the particular characteristic value and other significant information. The drill-down provides further details of a specific characteristic value. There are different types of drill-down, depending on the analysis. There is also the option to view the result graphically for an overview of a standard analysis.

Look at a few of the standard purchasing analyses.

Purchasing Values   The Purchasing Values analysis is available for the Material, Vendor, Material Group, and Purchasing Group main criteria. As its name implies, the function of the analysis is to determine the purchasing values. To view the purchasing values by material, go to the menu:

>   **Menu Path:** Information Systems > Logistics > Purchasing Material > Purchasing Values
>   **Transaction Code:** MC$G

At the selection screen, it is possible to define selection criteria to narrow the scope of the analysis: the selection parameters include Purchasing Organization, Material, and Plant. It is also possible to define the months to be analyzed. Once the selection parameters are input, click the Execute button to begin the tally. The initial list shows the Order Value, the Goods Receipt Value, the Invoice Value, the Purchase Order Price, and the Invoice Price per material. A drill-down by material will show the breakdown of the initial list by vendor and then by month.

When you run the analysis by vendor, it is possible to enter selection criteria for Purchasing Organization, Vendor Country, Vendor, and Plant. The initial list displays the Order Value, the Goods Receipt Value, and the Invoice Value. A drill-down by vendor shows the breakdown by material and then by month.

>   **Menu Path:** Information Systems > Logistics > Purchasing Vendor > Purchasing Values
>   **Transaction Code:** MC$4

Similar displays result when the Purchasing Value analysis is run by the other main criteria.

Purchasing Quantities   The Purchasing Quantities analysis contains essentially the same information as the Purchasing Value analysis; only it is in terms of quantity and not value. The Purchasing Quantities analysis is available by Material and Material Group.

On Time Delivery   The function of the On Time Delivery analysis is to calculate the number of deliveries that deviate from their due date, and how many days they vary from the due date based on a preconfigured deviation range grid. It is possible in customizing to set four variances ranges (per Purchasing Organization), for example 10 days early, 5 days early, 5 days late, and 10 days late. The implied fifth range is any delivery that is received more than 10 days after its due date. With this configuration, the system will tally deliveries according to the following intervals:

>   Interval 1: x days to 10 days early
>   Interval 2: 9 days to 5 days early
>   Interval 3: 4 days early to 5 days late

Interval 4: 6 days late to 10 days late

Interval 5: 11 days late and later

N O T E The fifth interval is implied and not actually configured in the grid.

To view the on-time deliveries by material, from the Information System for Purchasing menu go to

Menu Path: Material > On-time Delivery

Transaction Code: MC$K

The input parameters include Purchasing Organization, Material, Plant, and Month to analyze. The initial display shows the number of deliveries per material for each of the variance intervals. It is then possible to drill-down per material to the vendor, and then month. You can also run this analysis by Vendor and Material Group.

Quantity Reliability The Quantity Reliability analysis is similar to the On Time Delivery analysis but calculates, as its name suggests, the number of order items delivered (both purchase order and scheduling agreement items) that deviate from their order quantities and by what percentage they vary based on yet another preconfigured deviation grid. This grid, however, contains four intervals of variance percentages; the analysis will tally the number of order items that vary from their order quantities based on percent intervals. The Quantity Reliability analysis is available by Material, Vendor, and Material Group.

Inventory Management Information System

The Inventory Management sub-module of the Logistics Information System is also known as the Inventory Information System. Three reports from the Inventory Management sub-module will be described in this section. The first report will be a plant stock report. The second report will be a slow-moving inventory report. The third report will be a receipts/issues report by storage location.

The following SAP menu path will take the user to the Inventory Information System:

Menu Path: Information Systems > Logistics > Inventory Management

Transaction Code: MCC2

The first report you will learn about is the plant stock report. This report can be used to view information relating to materials stored at a specific plant. To access this report use the following SAP menu path from the Inventory Information System screen:

Menu Path: Plant > Stock

Transaction Code: MC.1

This will take the user to the Plant Analysis: Stock: Selection screen shown in Figure 22.43.

FIG. 22.43

Plant Analysis Stock: Selection screen.

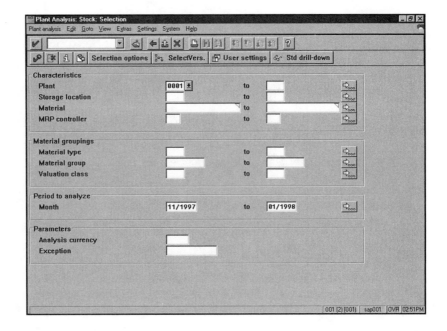

This screen is used to input the selection criteria for the report. This screen is divided into four sections. The first section is labeled Characteristics and contains the following fields: Plant, Storage Location, Material, and MRP Controller. Data can be entered in one or more of these fields to narrow down the selection criteria and limit the results of the report. For the purpose of this example, enter a Plant and Storage Location by using the pull-down list.

The second section is labeled Material Groupings and contains the following selection fields: Material Type, Material Group, and Valuation Class. These fields are used when someone is only interested in viewing data for a specific material type such as all raw materials. In this example, use material type HALB to limit the report to only semi-finished goods.

The third section of the screen is labeled Period to Analyze and contains the Month field. A date range should be entered in the Month field to limit the output of the report. Enter a date range that includes three months, for example, 08/1997 through 11/1997.

The fourth section of the screen is labeled Parameters and contains the following fields: Analysis Currency and Exception. The Analysis Currency field is used if the results are desired in a specific currency. The Exception field is used if specific exception criteria has been set up in advance and the user would like to search for that exception. These fields will be left blank in this example.

After entering the desired selection criteria, click Execute to run the report. A report similar to the one in Figure 22.44 will be displayed.

FIG. 22.44

Plant Analysis: Stock: Initial List screen.

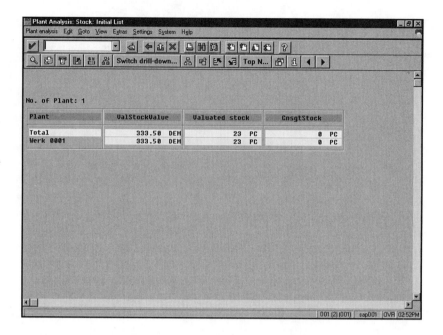

This screen displays a report with four columns and two rows. The first row is a totals row, while the second row contains data for the specific plant entered as selection criteria for the report. The first column on the report identifies the plant. On your report there is only one plant, but this column could contain more plants if more than one was entered on the selection screen. The second column is the value of valuated stock, which contains the value of all the stock in the plant in U.S. dollars. If another currency is specified on the selection screen, this value will be shown in that currency. The third column is valuated stock, and it displays how much material is at the plant. The last column is the quantity of consignment stock at the plant.

This report can be used by plant managers to determine the dollar value of inventory stored in their plant in a specific time period. It can also be used by a controller or someone else in the Accounting department who may be interested in how much inventory is stored at a specific plant. Companies are very sensitive about inventory levels these days because money tied up in inventory is money that cannot be used somewhere else in the company.

The user has a number of options for drilling-down on the data displayed on the report or for viewing the data in a different manner. By selecting a plant and clicking the Choose button, the report will be changed to display the data at the storage location level if one or more storage locations was entered on the selection screen. The user can also drill-down one more level and view the specific materials in the plant/storage location combination. It should be noted that although the numbers will change as the user drills-down, the column titles will remain the same. Figure 22.45 shows the same report as the last figure, drilled-down to the material level.

FIG. 22.45

Plant Analysis: Stock: Drill-Down screen.

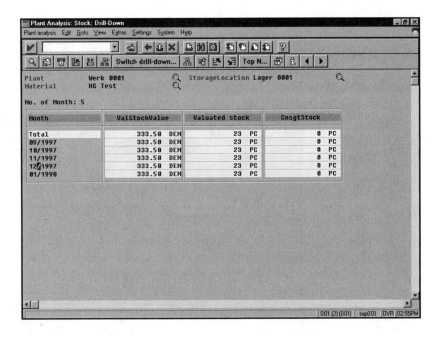

Another option the user has is to click the Switch Drill-Down button to change the drill-down displayed on the screen. The user has the option of drilling-down by the following fields: Business area, Division, MRP controller, MRP type, Material, Material group, Material type, Plant, Storage location, Valuation class, or Month.

It should also be noted that the user has the option of viewing this report in graphic form. To view the report in graphic form, the user should click the Graphics button. A SAP Business Graphics pop-up window will be displayed with the report in graphic form. The user has the option to view the report in 2D or 3D, and to modify other options to change the way the report looks. Graphics is only mentioned to let the user know that the option is available. No screenshots of graphic reports have been included in this section.

Storage Location Receipts and Issues Analysis   The last report described in this section is an analysis of goods receipts and goods issues by storage locations. This analysis allows you to view data of goods receipts and goods issues summarized at the following levels: Business area, Division, MRP controller, MRP type, Material, Material group, Material type, Plant, Valuation class, or Month. The report can be based on a particular plant, storage location, material, or time frame by entering the appropriate selection criteria on the initial screen. Execute the analysis via the following menu path:

   Menu Path: Information Systems > Logistics > Inventory Management > Storage Location > Receipts/issues

   Transaction Code: MC.6

Based on the criteria entered on the initial screen, seen in Figure 22.46, the total value of goods received and issued for valuated stock will be displayed for each storage location, as well as the total number of material movements resulting in a change in stock within the storage location (see Figure 22.47). To obtain the amount of goods received and issued by Business area, Division, MRP controller, MRP type, Material, Material group, Material type, Plant, Valuation class or Month, click the Switch Drill-Down button, select the desired option, and click the green check button.

FIG. 22.46

An initial screen for the analysis of goods movement transaction by storage location.

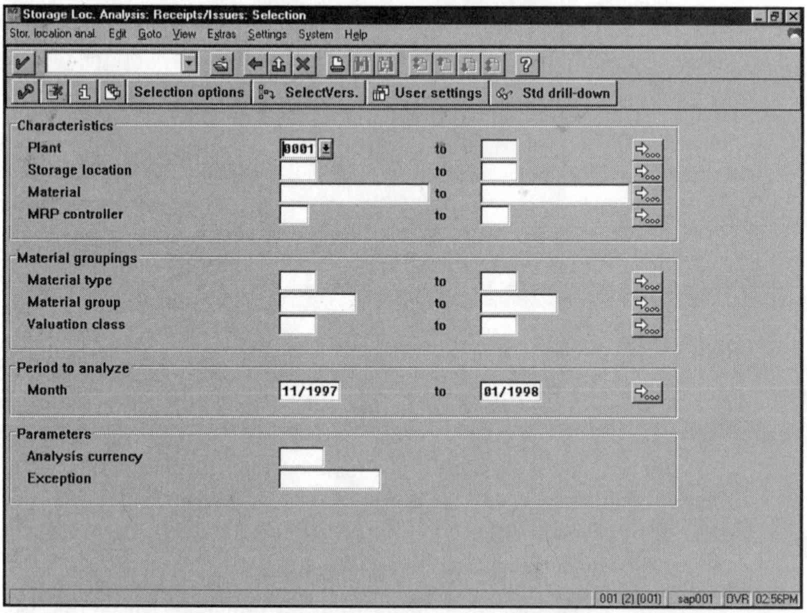

FIG. 22.47

Analysis of goods movement transaction by storage location.

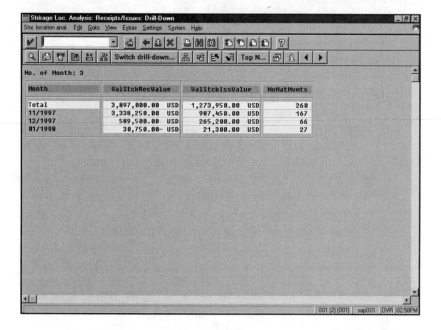

Another feature allows for the display of the report to be sorted according to ascending or descending value of goods receipts, goods issues, or goods movements within the drill-down option selected. To utilize the function, click in the valuated goods receipts, valuated goods issues, or number of goods movements column, depending on how the report is to be sorted, and click the button for Sort Ascending Order or Sort Descending Order.

Furthermore, the top contributors to the total number of goods movements, value of stocks for goods receipts, or value of stocks resulting from goods issues can be displayed by selecting the appropriate column of the report and clicking the Top N button. On the following pop-up window, enter a number on which the display of top contributors will be based and click the Continue button. The report will then display the top contributors for the column selected.

Slow-Moving Items Report   The second report described in this section is the slow-moving items report. SAP defines slow-moving items as materials that have little to no consumption over a specified period of time. The slow-moving items report enables you to identify materials that are not being used. This report can be used to determine which stocks are a potential for removal from inventory. The report can be executed via the following menu path:

> **Menu Path:** Information Systems > Logistics > Inventory Management > Material > Document Evaluations > Slow-moving Items
>
> **Transaction Code:** MC46

This analysis can be executed per Plant, Purchasing organization, Sales organization, or Cumulative for all plants (see Figure 22.48). For this demonstration, run the analysis for a particular plant. The user should click the radio button for Plants and specify the plant to be analyzed. Enter the number of days for which the consumption values should be examined in the Period: Last Consumption field. Other selection criteria can be specified to narrow the analysis, such as material numbers, ABC indicator, or MRP controller. Also, the scope of the list can be narrowed by specifying the number of days until last consumption or specifying a certain number of materials to display. After selection criteria has been specified, click Execute to display the report as the example in the next screen print shows.

The screen, as shown in Figure 22.49, will show the results of the analysis based on the criteria specified in the previous screen. The report lists the material number, description, and the number of days since the last consumption. The number of days since last consumption will equal the analysis period if the material has not been consumed during the entire period. More information can be displayed on this screen by clicking the Double Line or Triple Line button. Double line displays the current stock and the date corresponding to the days since consumption. Triple line displays the MRP controller, MRP type, ABC indicator for the material, Material group, Material type, and the Purchasing group.

Many other reports can be created using the Inventory Information System. The three reports selected and described in the previous section were meant to provide an introduction to the functionality available in this area of the Logistics Information System.

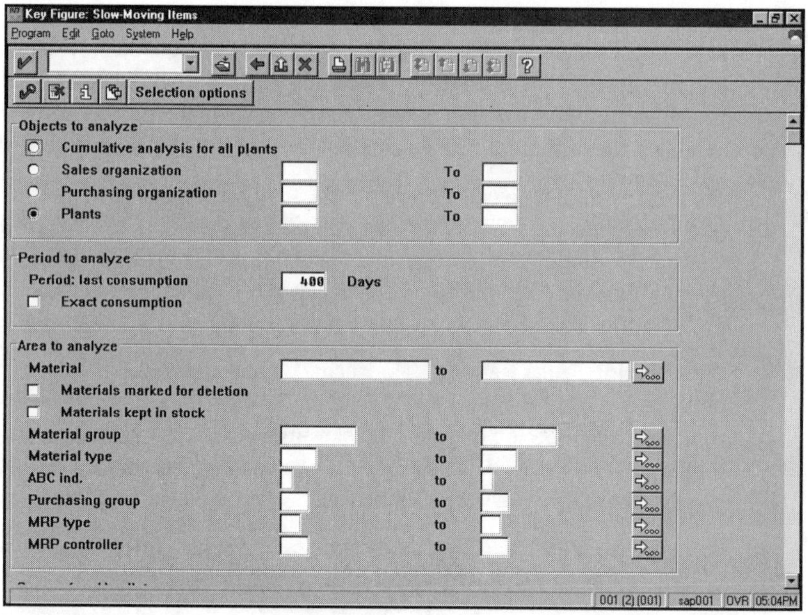

FIG. 22.48

Key Figure: Slow-Moving
Items screen.

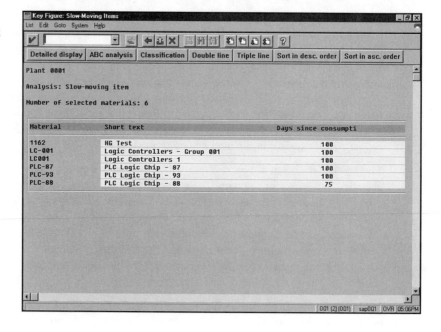

FIG. 22.49

Key Figure: Slow-Moving
Items screen.

Human Resource Information System (HRIS)

The SAP Human Resource Information System allows the end user to run reports off of a graphical representation of the Organizational Structure built in Personnel Planning and Development. The type of authorization given to a user will determine the type of reports he or she will be able to access.

Using the HRIS system, the SAP system fills in the reporting selection criteria for the user when running the report from the normal report request window; the user must fill in all the detail criteria for the desired report.

The user has the freedom to run reports from the Personnel Administration sub-module to the Personnel Planning and Development sub-module, without having to navigate from one sub-module to the other.

To use the HRIS system, the user, using the match code function, will select the highest organizational unit in the reporting structure. A graphical representation of the client's organizational structure will appear using SAP R/3's structural graphics interface. The user can now do one-stop shopping by selecting a particular organizational unit within the structure to conduct employee reporting.

The SAP standard report selection covers a broad range of topics from the Personnel Administration sub-module, such as employee birth date reports, work schedule reports, absences/attendances, and base employee information, without having to specify employee numbers. The Personnel Planning and Development sub-module can provide reports on qualification/requirements, EEO reports, and position descriptions. Many more reports can be developed, depending on the clients requirements, and these reports can be added to the report request box when using structural graphics.

After becoming familiar with the data stored in the SAP system, the user should take some time to explore the various Information Systems to learn about the wide variety of available reports. Many reports that the user thinks need to be custom-written may actually be available in the Information Systems. ●

CHAPTER 23

Accounting Department with SAP R/3

In this chapter

How Financial has become integrated with the metrics used to run the organization

The financial operations of Electro Tech, using SAP R/3

The reporting benefits of SAP R/3

SAP R/3 is built on a strong financial foundation. The integration of the Accounting modules to the Sales and Distribution, Production Planning, Materials Management, and other modules makes R/3 the impressive tool that it is. Data is captured consistently, at least from a systems standpoint. The integration assures that once the system has been configured to satisfy a given business, the dollars and cents of every business transaction are accounted for properly. In this way, SAP has revolutionized financial management for businesses. It is designed so that real-time transactional data that is required to operate the company is modeled by the financial organization so that these transactions generate real-time updating to the detail and General Ledgers within SAP.

Understanding Financial Metrics with SAP R/3

J. J. Donaldson, the Accounting Manager at Electro Tech, has been very satisfied with SAP R/3 since it went live. Even though J.J. helped design many of the legacy systems the organization had used prior to SAP, he could see the advantages of an integrated system. He was part of the BPS team that helped design the accounting functionality put in place with SAP. Besides the accounting team, he and his staff participated in many of the other BPS teams. Even with the additional burden it put on his staff during the BPS implementation process, he is pleased that it happened.

The integration SAP provides means that everyday business activities, like goods receipts, goods issues, confirmation of production work, scrapping of material by QC, and even material movements within the organization, all are captured as financial transactions. For the first time in his career, J.J. believes that the data his staff now works with accurately represents the finances of Electro Tech. It has been an eye-opening experience.

The Players

The following is a list of the employees involved in the Electro Tech financial example:

- John Jeffery "J.J." Donaldson—Accounting Manager
- Tim Warren—Asset Accountant
- Sheila Graham—Accounts Receivable
- Horace Brock—Production Analysis

The Situation

Many companies, Electro Tech included, rely on their accounting staff to provide financial reports that guide the business. In the past, accountants were dependent upon non-financial systems to guide the manual updating of financial journal entries. Because of this companies had adapted their approach to performance and analysis in order to optimize their performance with the systems provided to support this activity. With SAP, this dependency became a function of the integrated system. No longer are systems for a specialized or singular use.

J.J. remembers too clearly how the IS department tried to build links, and his staff had to take down information from Customer Service, Manufacturing, and Purchasing. Now any information they might need is available through the system. SAP is the integrated system Electro Tech needed—full, real-time, transactional integration between business functions.

SAP's Approach

Even with the new integrated system, the primary responsibility of the Accounting department is to generate budgets, departmental performance reports, and the company's standard financial report package—Income Statement, Balance Sheet, and Cash Flow. This is no minor task, with or without SAP. The beauty of the new system is the accuracy of the data. There is still the need to track down discrepancies and missing data, but these are most typically due to human error. Inevitably, data problems are the result of incomplete or missing data entries. Fortunately, the ease with which problems are tracked down is greatly improved with SAP.

Besides the normal monthly financial reports, the company still needs many operational reports that contain financial data. J.J. had been frustrated with the company-wide report writer that the IS department had provided with the legacy systems. He is much more satisfied with the information systems provided by SAP. During the BPS process, he helped scope out a number of reports the Operations managers could use during their regular management meetings. This helped provide a common approach to departmental reporting.

Since the data comes from a common system, in a common format, metrics can truly be compared and used to measure performance. When Operations managers analyze their data, a more consistent picture is presented. For a short time there were those who downloaded the data to a spreadsheet and tried to manipulate it to the position they wanted supported, but, since their managers were able to confirm the data online, a few managers have been embarrassed by this practice. J.J.'s pet peeve of non-accounting people generating reports on their department's performance, without the usual disinterested objectivity that accountants bring, is eased by the use of R/3.

SAP also allows the Accounting staff to become more involved in these reporting mechanisms. Since many of the managers had not taken a truly financial approach to their reporting before, they needed Accounting's help to understand all that was available to them in SAP. Again, fortunately, the integration of data within SAP allows the Accounting staff to more quickly collect and analyze data. The job function has not changed, but suddenly the tools are available to make the job more functional. No longer are J.J. and the other accountants called on by management to re-analyze reports generated by Operations to insure that the reports are accurate and appropriate.

As J.J. sits at his desk two days before the month-end closing at Electro Tech, there seems to be a reassuring businesslike feeling in the air. Month-end closing no longer means exhaustingly long nights. Instead it represents what closing operations should include, the true accounting functions of periodic accrual/deferral of expenditures and revenues, recording and evaluating payables and receivables, creating the balance sheet and the profit and loss statement, and documenting the posting data.

The SAP system provides reports for many of the operations involved in preparing the balance sheet and profit and loss statement. To check the balance of payables and receivables, Electro

Tech uses special reports to generate balance confirmations based on the company's standard methods. Obtaining a list of open items, such as vendors with debit balances and customers with credit balances, is simple. The system even provides for the handling of valuation of balance sheets and open items in foreign currencies.

The desired layout for the balance sheet and profit and loss statement was determined during the BPS process. A structure was set up with the G/L accounts assigned to the individual items contained in the balance sheet and profit and loss statement. Electro Tech is even able to define multiple balance sheet/profit and loss structures. This means that at month-end it is easy to print a consistent and accurate balance sheet and profit and loss statement.

Ultimately, Electro Tech compares planned data and actual transactional data. With SAP, they are able to create planning versions based on planning data and make planned versus actual comparisons. J.J.'s group is actually able to create a budgeted balance sheet that contains both the actual values and planned values with calculated differences. The analysis can be limited to a given month or a given quarter to produce the reports needed.

J.J. recognizes that Electro Tech still has problems to overcome, but at least now they have believable data to help resolve the problems. His staff is happier, too. Tim Warren, the Asset Accountant, no longer spends days working between the Accounts Payable System and the Asset Management System to insure that they are in balance. Sheila Graham's responsibility for reconciling the inventory balances with sales is much simpler with SAP. Horace Brock and his staff can reconcile accounts payable for raw material in production and inventory much more quickly.

All in all, the data generated by business activities within Electro Tech and analyzed by Accounting now seems more worthwhile. J.J. and his staff can feel good about the job they are doing and actually seem to have time to do it. Now, when they are faced with a question of why two pieces of data don't match, they don't automatically assume it's because the data is bad or some manager had altered it to his or her favor. J.J. thinks to himself how fun and rewarding it is to know the business has improved because of the work he and his staff do with SAP as a tool.

The Assessment

Electro Tech realized an improved informational flow with SAP, while achieving a decrease in the amount of effort needed just to get information to a point where the company can act appropriately. Looking at the advantages gained, you see:

- ■ Integration in the data collection systems makes information easier to obtain and analyze.
- ■ The company metrics are determined from business needs rather than the limitations of antiquated systems.
- ■ Accurate pricing is possible because cost collection represents true business practices.
- ■ Production variances can now be explained due to the improved understanding of the variances.
- ■ Budgeting more accurately represents real cost since it is now based on believable data.

SAP Advantages

Electro Tech with SAP R/3

Every company wants to realize the great American dream of making it big-time. In today's world, companies are judged on the awards they have won and how strong their stock is. At the same time, keeping pace with the competition has become harder and harder. The world has gotten smaller through overnight mail, faxes, email, and, yes, the Internet. The technological wonders have taken the normal business pace to a sprint. A common theme heard in industry today centers around keeping a competitive advantage through technology. This is easier said than done.

SAP has realized this dream in 25 short years. They are one of the largest computer software companies in the world. Even more impressive is the fact that they have helped over 6,000 companies in 40 different countries worldwide keep pace. All of this is because of one simple value that SAP has held true through the years; better control of information allows a company to make the most of changes in the marketplace. This leads to increased revenues, profits, and growth opportunities. A tighter control of information leads to a stronger company.

Electro Tech Looking Back

The management of Electro Tech formed a theory before implementing SAP. Their theory was that change is inevitable, so you can either control it or go along for the ride. If you decide just to take the ride, eventually you will fall off. Today's marketplace doesn't stop and wait for a company to change. It simply passes it by if it doesn't change.

In many ways this was a difficult concept for Electro Tech to grasp. It had been a leader in the electronic components and factory automation products industry for many years. It was hard for Electro Tech to believe that anyone could understand its business as well as it did. It was a company based on technology, so becoming antiquated in their ways seemed impossible to them.

As Electro Tech began to understand the source of many of its difficulties, it realized the root of the problem lay in an old issue, lack of communication. It wasn't dealing with the typical communication problem of not talking to each other though. In fact, talking seemed to be in abundance. Phone call after phone call had customer service representatives talking to production schedulers. Production schedulers were constantly talking to department mangers and maintenance supervisors. Purchasing was calling quality control and they all wanted to know where accounting was coming up with those crazy numbers. No, there was definitely not a lack of communication.

The communication problem Electro Tech faced went much deeper than just not talking. The problem was that when the employees talked, the data being discussed was more often than not out-dated or just plain inaccurate. Real-time integration was nonexistent. Even with superior products and a long history in the market, Electro Tech was losing its competitive advantage. Customers were tired of delayed shipments and missed requirements.

The Players

The following is a list of the employees involved in moving Electro Tech from the past to the present with SAP:

■ Marge Houlihan—Plant Manager

■ Bob Peters—Customer Service Representative

■ Bryan Luther—MRP Controller

■ Irving Mayer—Maintenance Manager

■ Ted Goldfield—Purchasing Manager

■ Laurie Stewart—Warehouse and Ship Dock Manager

The Situation

The realization that information flow was at the root of their problems led Electro Tech's employees on a search for a better way to manage business data. They looked at several enterprise software solutions and even strongly considered building their own solution in-house. The selection of SAP came after months of researching vendors, reviewing software, and comparing their problems to the functionality of the packages available.

Selecting the software was only the beginning, however. Hiring a consulting firm to assist in the transition from fragmented systems to an integrated system, structuring the BPS process for Electro Tech's needs, freeing up resources to take part in the BPS process, and carrying out the needed organizational changes was a very difficult task. The focus during this time seemed to be the SAP software, but at the heart of the project was a need to change.

The transition struggled at first because employees did not believe that change was necessary. They heard the words come out of upper management's mouths, but they still thought of the process as just another computer system. At first they kept trying to figure out how to make SAP do exactly what they had been doing before. The realization that their previous practices were outdated or misguided came hard to many employees. The structure of the BPS and ASAP methodologies that were employed helped push these truths home.

As SAP went live, many users complained that the system was hard to work with and demanding of time for data input. Much of this was due to the normal transition of using any new computer system. Many employees did not believe that a system could make their jobs easier. They carried an expectation of making phone calls and tracking down problems via printed reports from different systems. It took a while to see that an integrated system allowed them to track problems more easily, and that the system capabilities were only as good as the data input disciplines in place.

SAP's Approach

As the collective organization became comfortable with SAP and learned to trust the information within the system, things slowly began to improve. Customer service representatives like Bob Peters learned that all the information they needed was available to them online. It didn't matter if they called six times, including a call to Marge Houlihan, the Plant Manager. The production schedule was reflected accurately online. Bob and his fellow CSRs learned that no computer system keeps customer delays from happening but that, by providing sincere information up-front, customer respect grew and delays decreased.

Bryan Luther and his staff learned that scheduling the plant based on true MRP disciplines allowed a better schedule to be produced than knee-jerk reactions to phone calls. By working with Irving Mayer's plant maintenance group, equipment became more reliable and so did the production schedule.

Ted Goldfield's staff has been guided by the demand from the production schedule allowing for the reduction of unnecessary inventories. This has made Laurie Stewart happy. Warehouses are not overflowing one week and empty the next. The integration of the quality system into the management of purchasing and inventory activities has also helped.

Without a doubt, the best thing to come out of the implementation of SAP is the improved collection of information. J.J. Donaldson has been able to provide a much more accurate assessment of the state of the business. This wasn't a popular thing at first, but, as company metrics became standardized, understood, and reported consistently, the company and all of its parts began to flourish. Electro Tech could once again feel comfortable as a strong player in the electronics and production automation market.

The Assessment

Electro Tech realized an improvement through information. SAP is an amazing tool to help realize this objective. The transition from pre-SAP to post-SAP was not without pain. It would have been easy to understaff the BPS process or fall for the false sense of saving money by implementing only one or two modules. The problem with that approach is that integration comes from the linkage of all the modules.

This is not to say that Electro Tech installed every single SAP module. They chose not to use several modules and are planning a later application of Workflow to further improve the integrated communication the system can provide. What Electro Tech did do well was acknowledge a theory that the marketplace is a dynamically changing entity, and to stay competitive in it, it also had to change. Deep at the heart of any successful change is planning and direction. Electro Tech accomplished this and is better off because of it.

Electro Tech now has a higher understanding of its customer service performance, schedule performance, vendor performance, quality performance, and, most importantly, its costs and profitability. A company that understands these elements has a good chance of success. SAP R/3 helps provide this edge:

- The process of change is difficult but, if managed properly, can empower an organization to accomplish great things.
- An integrated system is a form of communication that allows for quick accessing of accurate, up-to-date information.
- Integration in the data collection systems makes information easier to obtain and analyze. SAP R/3 is a powerful tool to collect and analyze information needed to guide a business.

SAP Successes

This book has looked at what SAP can do for an organization. What is actually accomplished is dependent on how seriously the organization takes the change process often associated with SAP. Resources, time, and a willingness to reconsider and improve old business practices and institute new ones are all a part of implementing SAP or, for that matter, any integrated system.

Remember that the basic premise of SAP is creating a plan, executing the plan, evaluating the plan, and improving based on the results. This is true of the implementation approach or the use of the system in a live environment. True improvement does not come from a reactionary approach to problems; it comes from an informed, thought-out approach.

Understanding the Future of the SAP Market

SAP has been very effective in understanding the needs of the market and reacting to the specific needs of the industries in which it has clients. It has shown that the leadership of the organization can move into the dynamic market of the U.S. and still provide the service and responsiveness required for global operations of U.S.-based companies. SAP initially focused on the Fortune 500 companies and realized tremendous success with mainframe-driven operations.

SAP has also shown that it understands the needs of the market below the Fortune 1000 companies. It has proven that it is willing to change its pricing structures and implementation methods to allow smaller organizations the opportunity to realize the benefits of an enterprise focus and real-time, integrated processing. These companies are as complex in function processing as the Fortune 500 companies. You cannot reduce the cost of implementation by reducing the number of modules the company must purchase in the system. SAP has taken the steps to reduce the time and cost of implementing SAP and has made its entry into this market much smoother.

SAP Development

As enterprise business solutions continue to grow, both in breadth and depth, SAP will lead the industry. The amount of revenue that is invested back into research and development by SAP will keep SAP in a continuous leadership role.

SAP has broken the effort of maintaining its competitive advantage into both a horizontal and vertical attack. It is building additional functionality into the base configuration that will allow a complete enterprise focus on a business, and it has built industry business units to focus on specific industry requirements. This approach will continue to enhance the breadth and depth of the product. It will also allow for specific industry solutions that will not delay the release and im-provement of the software in general. With the establishment of the Public Sector division in the U.S., SAP even has shown its commitment to changing the internal operations to ensure its success and the success of its customers in specific industries.

At the same time, SAP has taken the steps to improve the implementation process of the software. It has built methodologies and tools to provide clients a true path to successful implementations. The ASAP methodology provides clients with a true understanding of how implementations. The ASAP methodology provides clients with a true understanding of how their projects should move forward. It also allows SAP the opportunity to evaluate and monitor individual projects and recognize issues before they hit a critical point and adversely affect the project. SAP has also built the Team SAP program to develop partner-implementation companies. This will improve the quality of consultants in the marketplace as well as reduce the cost of these resources. It will decrease the market's dependency on the large consulting houses for skilled resources, thus driving the cost of implementation down.

Cost of Consulting

To date the market has been heavily dependent on the large consulting organizations to provide SAP software knowledgeable resources. These firms have large overheads to cover and, with the shortage of resources, have been able to demand premium fees. With smaller consulting firms working as part of Team SAP, the quality of the resources will increase but the cost will be reduced. This reduction is due to lower overhead to cover and the fact that American-based consultants have now had time to build skills to match those of their European counterparts. With the establishment of local partners, there will be a greater likelihood of resource availability in the city where the implementing company is located and, therefore, reduction of travel costs for implementations.

Although it's expected that rates will be reduced, they will not fall back to the rate of system integrators a few years ago. This is not due to the software or any lack of skilled resources available. This is due to the change in skill sets now required to implement fully-integrated packaged software.

In the past, a system integrator was basically a programmer taking direction from a user to build a system that would affect a specific functional area of the organization. Once the system was built to support the requirements of the functional area, the programmer would then build the needed interfaces to the other systems of the company to pass the data, typically in batch mode. With the increased use of real-time, fully integrated systems, the system integrators must understand the business effects of each function of the organization on the next function. Basically, they must understand the process through the organization and how each transaction builds upon the next. Also, system integrators must have a very good knowledge of the SAP software—not just an understanding of a single module but an understanding of how each module interacts with the other. Integrators must possess strong business and technical skills to be effective integrating SAP. These changes in the skill set will justify much higher rates than have been supported prior to SAP or other enterprise software.

Understanding the Future of Enterprise Markets

As the SAP software and the individuals working with the product continue to change and improve so will the market place.

Internet capabilities are becoming more and more important to business success. Customers and suppliers themselves will be able to place orders directly into the client's system and determine ship dates and lead times for receipt. For this to happen, firewalls must become tamper

Part
VI

Ch
25

proof, and timely response to Internet requests will be required. SAP is on the forefront of Internet capability and development. Just as it has continued to improve the capabilities of the software, it has ensured that the software continues to progress with technological advances in the industry. It has made the move from mainframe to client/server platforms as this area of the market demanded and should continue to lead the industry as other opportunities arise.

SAP and enterprise software will also allow for other business enhancements. True paperless environments will be realized. The opportunity for such things as paperless audits, authorization procedures, and report generation will become available due to real-time processing. Video conferencing will become much more practical with the utilization of shareware, telecommunications improvement, and enterprise applications. Remote sites will utilize the same software, master data, and information, thus allowing for more efficiency in video conferencing.

Lessons Learned

The key to any successful journey is to have an educated, experienced guide to assist in the journey. CCAi, Inc. has experienced the SAP journey both from the perspective of the user and as the integrator, supporting other companies through the process of moving to a fully integrated, real-time, enterprise application.

This section will provide a high-level sketch of the lessons learned during multiple past experiences with the SAP R/3 product. This is not an exhaustive list but is intended to give the reader an idea of the issues that must be addressed as you move toward a decision to implement SAP R/3.

Project Sponsor

Support for the SAP R/3 implementation must come from the top levels of the organization. Without leadership and commitment from top management, the organization cannot establish scope, make decisions, solve issues, or allocate the needed resources to have a successful project. Because SAP R/3 is so integrated, it is critical that management truly understand the effects of real-time integration. This will likely be the first time many organizations have viewed themselves from a process perspective. Once the organization is viewed as a process, there will be many decisions and changes that will require input and support from top management.

If the CEO is not the project sponsor, it will require the support of CFO, CIO, COO, or the vice presidents of each functional area within the scope of the project. It is key to the success of the project that there be one single person within the company who maintains sponsorship of the project. Although he or she will have partners involved with the implementation, sponsorship should never be delegated to a partner. Only those who have a long-term interest in the success of the organization can truly ensure that tough decisions will be made in a timely manner to ensure the continued success of business operations while keeping the implementation of the new system on target.

Education

When preparing for an SAP implementation, start the education early, continue it throughout the project, and direct it as needed by the audience. Remember that many types of training may be needed. Basic computer education is almost always needed. Depending on the scope of your implementation, training on a new way of conducting your business may be necessary. Obviously, training on SAP itself will be needed and not just for the frontline user.

Executive-Level Training   There are several levels of education that will be needed for a successful project. The initial training is for executive management. Understanding the true cost and value of the software is very important. Executive management must take the time to understand the overall needs of the organization related to the SAP implementation and the specific areas that need change and improvement. The key to moving forward with the implementation will be return on investment. To effectively evaluate this, you will need to understand all elements of the implementation that will affect the total cost of going live with SAP.

Management at this level must also ensure that everyone fully understands the effects of an integrated, real-time, enterprise application. Throughout the implementation you will realize change in both the ways you do business and the resources required to operate the business. The fact that you are viewing the processes of the organization will threaten individual "kingdoms" that are inevitably established within organizations over time. It is important to realize these prior to the conflict that occurs when individual jobs are in jeopardy or, at minimum, will require a change in authority and organization influence.

Project Team Training   Although you will most likely require consulting support from a partner during the implementation, you will need to train the individuals selected from your organization to participate in the configuration of the software. This training should be fairly extensive to allow all project team members to understand the requirements of defining the functions they are responsible for and how to configure these requirements into the SAP R/3 software. They will also need to understand the integration points of the software and how areas for which they are responsible are affected by other areas of the software configuration. Since the individuals involved in the setup of the software will most likely be responsible for the long-term support of the software post-implementation, it is critical that these people be provided extensive training to be confident once the consulting support is no longer available.

User Training   This training is for the individuals who will be responsible for the day-to-day processing of transactions on the new system. These users do not need to understand how to configure the software. It is important, however, that they understand that the information they put into the system has a direct and immediate impact on other areas of the company. There will most likely be a change in job responsibilities at this level. As a result, there may be a need for additional training on tasks individuals have not performed in the past. These changes will be recognized as the processes are defined and the new organization structure evolves.

Project Team Setup

A successful SAP implementation takes proper support and guidance. Sponsorship by the highest levels of management, project direction based on an established company vision, and involvement by all levels of the organization lead to success.

Sponsors/Steering Committee   The Steering Committee is made up of the individuals who are ultimately responsible for the delivery of a functioning system. It is typically executive-level management. These individuals are charged with establishing the reasoning for selecting the new system and the assignment of partner consulting organizations and company associates to dedicate to the project. This committee will meet approximately once a month to evaluate the progress of the project and make changes or adjustments as needed. There should also be representatives from the SAP organization on this committee. The SAP representative will provide quality assurance and guidance to move the project forward and warn of any potential bottlenecks that may arise. There should be representation by the consulting organization chosen to assist in the implementation as well. This will allow an effective means of communication to all relevant individuals and partners involved in the delivery of a successful project.

Project Management   Project management is key to the day-to-day success and progress of the project. This person (or persons) will be responsible for handling and evaluating all issues that arise for quick resolution so the project doesn't slow down. If the organization has a skilled project manager who has successfully implemented an integrated system before, he or she should be assigned to lead the project. This individual will be involved with the Steering Committee, communicating information back to the project team and relaying any issues to the committee. The person selected for this position most likely will become responsible for post-implementation support. It is also recommended that a project manager from the selected consulting organization be included to manage the project. This should be an individual who has specifically implemented SAP in the past. This person will guide the company's project manager through project planning and delivery.

Consultants   When selecting a partner to assist in your implementation, there are several points to consider. Due to the lack of skilled resources and lack of knowledge by the company purchasing the software, there have been many individuals and consulting organizations who have been successful at selling their services with little ability to deliver a successful implementation. This has caused much negative publicity focused at SAP. In fact, many poor implementations are due to the lack of implementation skills by the integrator and not due to the software or the complexity of configuration.

When selecting a partner integrator, it is important to keep in mind that many individuals are being presented as employees of the organization. In many cases, organizations are truly only placement agents for contractors and have built a hierarchy billing structure that simply causes a higher cost of consultants for the implementing organization. It is important to clarify that the consultants who are presented are, in fact, employees and not contractors. Employees of an organization have more of an interest in the success of your project. Contractors are more likely to move on to a more lucrative opportunity should it arise prior to the completion of your project. This is not to imply that you should not allow for some contracting on your project. It is often necessary to fill a key skill with contractors at certain points of the project. However, the vast majority of the contractors should have a vested interest in your success and the success of the organization by which they are employed. Ask for the specific individuals who will work with you. Do not allow bait and switch. Perform individual interviews with each consultant recommended for your project. Be aware that many consulting organizations are looking to use you as the training ground for their consultants at your cost.

When selecting the partner consulting organization, you should look for successes it has had with prior implementations. It should provide references and details of successes. It is also important that the organization have a strong relationship with the SAP organization. SAP will provide you with a list of integrators who will provide quality services. Ask for knowledge of your specific industry. Individual industries will require specifications that are different from others, and it is important that your partner understand your business. You should also look for an integrator who can provide services other than just configuration support. Training capabilities are very important to the success of the project, and it is much more efficient to have a partner that can provide training as a part of his or her standard project delivery. Also, look for a consulting organization to support both your database and hardware requirements.

Functional Owners   The functional owners are the individuals from your organization who will work with the consulting organization day to day on the configuration of the software. These should be highly respected and capable individuals who are comfortable with decision making and who understand the details of the business activities of the company. For each functional area in the scope of the project, there should be at least one functional owner assigned to the project. Depending on the magnitude of the project, the number of sites involved, and the number of users supported, the number will go up.

The functional owners will lead their respective areas of expertise in the development of current process flows of transactions and work with the consultants to develop to-be process flows that will be supported by the software.

Users   Users are individuals who will eventually be processing on the new system. You will also rely on specific users to gather details of functional processing and to test the configuration of SAP as the project goes forward. These individuals will be utilized on an as-needed basis. It is very important to keep these team members up to date on the project and make sure they are available to assist the project. You must also be sensitive to the fact that these people are still performing their daily jobs and the project will be a significant drain on their time.

Retention   Retention of the resources you assign to your project is one of the biggest issues you will face. As these associates become trained and more skilled on the software, they will be heavily recruited into the consulting arena. Although consulting is a big change in lifestyle, the dollars that are available will more than pay for this change. There are steps you can take to minimize the possibility of a large exodus from your project.

You must establish and communicate to key project members how their individual career paths will be affected. If individuals will not be able to go back to the jobs they had prior to the project, give them an idea of where they will fit into the new organization. Your consulting partner should be able to assist in this task.

Establish retention bonuses for milestones of the project. Allow team members to share in any monetary benefits of bringing the project in on time and under budget. Also, these individuals are obviously knowledgeable of the new system, able to support the organization long-term,

Part VI

Ch

25

and now understand your organization in depth. Establish a salary structure that recognizes these skills. Most likely it will be outside the corporate norm. So begin the process early with your Human Resources department to establish a compensation program for these individuals.

Project Management

Managing the project can be a very tedious job. Depending on the scope of the project, the number of team members, the number of sites affected, and the number of users affected by the implementation, this task may take one or several individuals to perform. As stated earlier, the project management should be owned by the organization but may be shared with the selected consulting partner.

BPR   Business Process Re-engineering is often the reason for the large cost of implementation and the long times for implementation. Although you will be required to do some amount of re-engineering, it is possible to implement SAP R/3 with a minimal amount. Due to the lack of implementation skills by some consulting firms, business re-engineering has taken the forefront on many projects and, thus, has given a bad reputation to all SAP projects. You should evaluate just how much business change is required to improve your business and include this in your project. You can implement SAP R/3 with minimal organizational change, realize the benefits and the return on investment, and then choose to re-engineer post-implementation. This will allow you the opportunity to train your resources on the software. You then can reduce the amount of consulting support long-term.

Decision-Making Process   The most common bottleneck in integrated system implementations is the inability of the organization to make decisions in a timely manner. It is critical that the project sponsors establish a decision-making process prior to the kickoff of the project. Empower individuals to make the required decisions and define the process to quickly handle any issue that may delay the project.

Scope Creep   Knowing what areas of the organization will be affected by the new system is critical. What will often occur is that the software implementation will be sponsored by a specific area of the organization. Once other functional areas become aware of the project, they will want to become involved. The same issue arises if multiple sites become interested. It is very critical that the executive management establish what areas are to be implemented and move forward with minimal changes to the scope. Additional sites or functions can be implemented in other phases.

Technical Setup   Although it would seem to be a given, the technical areas are often the main holdups on projects. It is important to remember the hardware requirements to support the project team and the software.

Post-Implementation Support

As the hard work of business scenario discovery, planning, and configuration comes to a close, go-live arrives. Make no mistake about it, the work is not over. Success will be achieved, however, with proper support.

The First Month   The day a company goes live with SAP is a very nervous and happy one. Many companies worry about a total shutdown of their manufacturing facilities. Others welcome the change with open arms. Either way, the first few weeks after go-live require a lot of patience and hard work. Problems will occur. Solutions will, too, assuming that part of the planning and implementation process included providing go-live support.

If yours is a 24-hours-a-day, seven-days-a-week business, so must your support be for the first few weeks. Examine which areas of your business have the most risk associated with them. Have a mix of support personnel available. Consultants alone cannot support all go-live problems because the problem may be related to an unusual business situation. Likewise, plant personnel alone cannot be expected to know the options available to solve a problem within SAP.

It is often useful to establish a help center where anyone can call to get assistance in performing a transaction. If this approach is used, make certain that skilled personnel are available for all modules being implemented. Also make sure that calls will not be continually met with a busy signal.

On top of the establishment of a help center, floaters within the work areas are a good line of first defense. Take skilled employees (or "power users") and consultants and assign them to departments with high transactional needs. If this first line of defense cannot solve the problems, the help center can be utilized. By having support in the various departments, users feel more comfortable during the high-stress start-up period.

Remember that first impressions are hard to change. If proper support is not provided for the first month and big problems occur, the advantages the system provides will be forgotten. It takes time for the advantages of integration to be seen.

Six Months and Counting   By about the six month point, the system will be adequately tested so that the difference between a business practice that has not been adequately addressed and a system problem can be identified. Since most legacy systems are not as integrated as SAP, the data passed to SAP is often not clean. Determining what master data must be adjusted to realize the full advantages of SAP will take a few months. Determining how and when to make the adjustments will take a few more months. Cleansing of master data after go-live is not uncommon.

Like master data, changes to configuration may also be necessary. Many companies believe that by hiring teams of consultants and throwing large amounts of internal resources at an implementation, the configuration should be perfect on day one. This is not realistic. While changes to configuration should be limited, they will occur. This is most true when a phased approach to implementation is taken. For example, if the PP module is brought live in a Phase 1 implementation and the QM module is to be brought live in a Phase 2 implementation, PP configuration may need to be changed. The integration of these two modules means there is common configuration between them. The decisions made during the first phase may no longer fit with the decisions of the second phase.

Even if a phased implementation is not utilized, configuration changes will likely be needed. The ASAP and BPS processes discussed in this book are designed to provide for the maximum discovery of issues. It is still possible that issues that affect configuration will be missed. Likewise, new business practices may cause configuration changes. Constant changes to configuration or poorly organized changes should not be accepted, but don't expect a totally stagnant configuration, either.

One Year and Beyond   By this point, the advantages of SAP should be clear. Again, the effects of a multi-phase implementation may affect the benefits realized, but nonetheless, they should be evident by this point. This is sometimes difficult for employees to see. Since many of your employees helped design and build the previous legacy systems, these systems will always be near and dear to them. It is likely that the legacy performed exactly as they believed a job function should perform.

Since SAP is built on best business practices, not historical company practices, it will cause changes in the way business is conducted. The true measure of success for an SAP implementation is availability of information directed at improved profitability for the company. By understanding what the cost is of varying activities, problems can be recognized, prioritized, and addressed in due fashion. ●

Index